Sentiments of a British-American Woman

SENTIMENTS

of a

BRITISH-AMERICAN WOMAN

ESTHER DEBERDT REED *and the*

AMERICAN REVOLUTION

Owen S. Ireland

The Pennsylvania State University Press
University Park, Pennsylvania

Library of Congress Cataloging-in-Publication Data

Names: Ireland, Owen S., author.
Title: Sentiments of a British-American woman : Esther DeBerdt Reed and the American Revolution / Owen S. Ireland.
Description: University Park, Pennsylvania : The Pennsylvania State University Press, [2017] | Includes bibliographical references and index.
Summary: "Explores the life and work of political publicist and strategist Esther DeBerdt Reed, who, in a life highly structured by conflict, national identity, religion, and the overall importance of being a wife and mother, gave eloquent expression to the political aspirations of female patriots in Revolutionary America"—Provided by publisher.
Identifiers: LCCN 2017035006 | ISBN 9780271079288 (cloth : alk. paper)
Subjects: LCSH: Reed, Esther, 1747–1780. | Women political activists—United States- Biography. | Politicians' spouses—United States—Biography. | United States—History—Revolution, 1775–1783—Women—Biography. | United States—History—Revolution, 1775–1783. | United States—Politics and government—1775–1783.
Classification: LCC E302.6.R29 I74 2017 | DDC 973.3/1092 [B] —dc23
LC record available at https://lccn.loc.gov/2017035006

Copyright © 2017 Owen S. Ireland
All rights reserved
Printed in the United States of America
Published by The Pennsylvania State University Press,
University Park, PA 16802-1003

The Pennsylvania State University Press is a member of the Association of American University Presses.

It is the policy of The Pennsylvania State University Press to use acid-free paper. Publications on uncoated stock satisfy the minimum requirements of American National Standard for Information Sciences— Permanence of Paper for Printed Library Material, ANSI Z39.48–1992.

Additional credit: Charles Willson Peale, *Esther DeBerdt Reed*. Courtesy The Frick Collection.

For Susan

Contents

Acknowledgments | ix

Introduction | 1

1 Esther: Imprudent and Impatient Love | 5
2 Joseph: Love and Calculation | 19
3 A Willful Girl Matures | 35
4 Responsibilities and Schemes | 51
5 Politics: Old World Patronage | 68
6 Love Defeats Prudence | 83
7 Exiled Where Women "Stooped like Country Girls" | 98
8 A New Political Identity: "They" Becomes "We" | 116
9 "Unleash the Dogs of War" | 135
10 Politics: New World Democracy | 157
11 America's Female Politician | 178
12 Triumph and Tragedy | 198
Coda | 206

Notes | 215
Bibliographical Essay | 241
Index | 245

Acknowledgments

I would like to thank those who have encouraged, supported, and facilitated research on this project as well as those who have read and criticized earlier versions of it: Dr. Paul Yu (deceased), president, SUNY College at Brockport; Colleen Donaldson, grants development director, SUNY College at Brockport; The Research Foundation, SUNY; The Gilder Lehrman Institute of American History; Dr. Ursula Masson (deceased), West of England and South Wales Women's History Network, University of Glamorgan, Pontypridd, Wales, U.K.; Dr. Lee Ann Caldwell, Georgia College and State University; Dr. Susan Klepp, Temple University; Dr. Elsa Nystrom, Kennesaw State University; Dr. Jean Soderlund, Lehigh University; Dr. Patricia Veasey, curator, Museum of York County, Rock Hill, South Carolina; Dr. Susan Branson, Syracuse University; and my colleagues in the Rochester United States Historians [RUSH] working-paper group, headed by Dr. Alison Parker, SUNY Brockport, coordinator.

Dr. John Frantz, Penn State University (emeritus), has been a friend, counselor, and critic during much of my professional career, and in one way or another he prepared the way for this study of Esther DeBerdt Reed and politics in Revolutionary Pennsylvania. William Pencak, Penn State University (deceased), often in conjunction with John Frantz, provided me with opportunities to publish my research on Revolutionary Pennsylvania. The substance of chapter 8 in the current volume appeared in a somewhat different format in Pencak's edited volume *Pennsylvania's Revolution* (University Park: Penn State University Press, 2010).

Megan Webb-Morgan and Shannon Symonds found books, copied articles, prepared bibliographies, and did well all those things that research assistants do, and in addition Megan performed the herculean task of checking my citations. Lori DeLoe undertook research for me in London on Esther's family history and provided me with photographs of places in Esther's world that today might look as they did when Esther saw them. Jeffrey Macechak, education director of the Burlington [New Jersey] County Historical Society, helped my wife, Susan, and me to better understand the geography of Burlington. And never to be forgotten, the industrious, ingenious, and ever-patient staffs of the New-York Historical Society, the Historical Society of Pennsylvania, and the New York Public Library, where the Rose Main Reading Room provides a near-perfect place to read, think, and write.

I owe a special debt of gratitude to Dr. Tonio Andrade, professor of history at Emory University, who offered me encouragement, wisdom, and guidance at an important juncture in the evolution of this project.

The work of two historians did much to shape my thinking about Esther DeBerdt Reed and women in the late eighteenth-century English-speaking world when I began this study: Jean Soderlund and Wayne Bodle. Soderlund urged historians to see women as central to the Revolution, to go beyond the long-standing emphasis on New England, and, when we look at the mid-Atlantic region, to transcend the past emphasis on the female Quaker experience (Jean R. Soderlund, "Women in Eighteenth-Century Pennsylvania: Toward a Model of Diversity," *Pennsylvania Magazine of History and Biography* 115 [April 1991]: 163–83). Soderlund also cautioned against judging women in the past by anachronistic standards. I interpret that to mean that we should attempt to meet the women of the past on their own terms, to historicize, if you will, the lives of the women we study. Thus, to understand particular women in a particular context, the important question is whether they felt a sense of efficacy in shaping their own lives, and in influencing the lives of those people most important to them in those areas of greatest significance to them (Jean R. Soderlund, "Women's Authority in Pennsylvania and New Jersey Quaker Meetings, 1680–1760," *William and Mary Quarterly* 44 [October 1987]: 722–49. Wayne Bodle demonstrated that although the law generally denied a married woman the right to act politically or, on her own behalf, to buy, own, or sell property, to enter into legally binding contracts, or to sue or be sued, Jane Bartram, a contemporary of Esther's in Philadelphia, managed to do most of these things (Wayne Bodle, "Jane Bartram's 'Application': Her Struggle for Survival, Stability, and Self-Determination in Revolutionary Pennsylvania," *Pennsylvania Magazine of History and Biography* 115 [April 1991]: 184–200).

At the beginning, I also relied heavily on the work of Linda Kerber and Mary Beth Norton, both of whom had written useful short treatments on Esther, "The Sentiments," and the Ladies Association. As the manuscript approached conclusion, I was blessed with the criticism of Dr. Rosemarie Zagarri, who read the entire manuscript twice and offered detailed, and on occasion line-by-line, criticism. Finally, in preparing the manuscript for publication, I am deeply indebted to Kathryn Yahner at Penn State University Press. She has been kind, critical, persistent, and endlessly helpful. This will be a far better book as a result of her efforts. Thanks also to the extraordinary effort of the anonymous reader who twice provided a close reading of the text, much to my benefit.

I enjoyed the financial support of a fellowship from the Gilder Lehrman Institute of American History in support of my research at the New-York Historical Society.

A number of universities and historical associations offered me the opportunity to share my research on Esther DeBerdt Reed and to benefit from the comments of other historians: the history department, National University of Ireland, Maynooth; the history department, University of South Wales, Pontypridd, U.K.; Georgia Association of Historians Annual Meetings, April 1999 and April 2001; The Ninth Annual Conference on Women and Society, Marist College, Poughkeepsie, New York, June 1999; the Annual Meeting of the Pennsylvania Historical Association, Pittsburgh, Pennsylvania, November 1999; and the Sixth Southern Conference on Women's History, June 5–7, 2003, the University of Georgia, Athens, Georgia.

Finally, I want to thank my wife, Susan Ireland, who has lived with this project for almost twenty years, and who, after her retirement, played an indispensable part in bringing it to fruition. I have dedicated this book to her.

Introduction

On September 19, 1780, Virginia congressman James Madison reported from Philadelphia, "President Reed's Lady has been buried this morning."[1] Interred in the graveyard of the Arch Street Presbyterian Church, the thirty-three-year-old wife of the chief executive of Pennsylvania had died the day before, "taken off by the Dysentery."[2] Her death deprived the fledgling American nation of one of its most public, most effective, and most widely known political women.

In the three years before her death, Esther DeBerdt Reed had converted her husband from military to political leadership, participated with him in building a powerful political party, led the Philadelphia Ladies Association in a multistate fund-raising campaign in support of the Continental Army, and politely but firmly debated with General Washington about how to spend the money she and her Ladies had raised. In "The Sentiments of an American Woman," the political broadside she published in support of her fund-raising effort, she gave eloquent expression to the political aspirations of America's new female citizens, while her Ladies Association itself provided the model for public engagement that women in America would employ with increasing effectiveness over the next two centuries. Her active engagement in the political world, where by law and by custom only men were members of the state, only men played independent political roles, and only men exercised autonomous political will, makes her worthy of our attention. Her name deserves to be known. Her story deserves to be told.

Esther DeBerdt began life in London, England, in October 1746 as the indulged daughter of a well-to-do commercial family involved in the Atlantic trade with America. Her parents, evangelical Christians, were followers of the great sixteenth-century reformer John Calvin, and Esther grew up as a religious dissenter in a nation that was officially Anglican and in which religious and political identity were closely linked.

In the fall of 1763, at seventeen, Esther met and fell in love with Joseph Reed, an ambitious young American staying in London to complete his legal studies and to advance his family's interests. Esther's father objected to their marriage, and Joseph returned home to New Jersey. Then, over the next five years, the young lovers conducted a clandestine transatlantic courtship by mail while Esther (in London) and Joseph (in America) worked to change her father's mind and to use the patronage system of the British Empire to construct the economic foundation for their future family. In the spring of 1770, they married, and over the next ten years they negotiated a dynamic marriage distinguished by mutual affection, respect, and accommodation. Here, Esther challenged social norms and legal structures that emphasized parental power and pecuniary considerations in courtship and defined marriage as a hierarchical relationship between a dominant husband and a subordinate wife.

Esther and Joseph had intended to live their lives in London, but a family tragedy drove them into exile in America, where they struggled to reestablish their economic base. Her father had introduced her to the intricacies of oceangoing commerce while she was still in her teens. Now, living in Philadelphia (1770–74), she intruded into this traditionally male domain by collaborating in the construction of a complex and lucrative trading network that spanned much of the British Atlantic world.[3]

Esther's father had also introduced her to the complex world of patron/client politics in Georgian England, and she employed political means to advance her ends first in London in the late 1760s and then in Philadelphia. In the fall of 1775, she made a personal political decision to support the American struggle for independence and soon found herself plunged into the cauldron of war. After three harrowing years of disruption, disaster, isolation, and loss, she returned to Philadelphia and persuaded her husband to give up his military ambitions and accept political office. She then worked closely with him to advance themselves to the cusp of national political leadership. In 1780, acting in her own name, she launched a barrage of political initiatives that made her, at the time of her death, one of America's most sophisticated, poised, confident, admired, and efficacious public "female politicians."[4] Here, as throughout her short life, this bright, determined, self-confident, and skillful woman, slight of frame but strong of will and blessed with a way with words and with people, exercised a "suitable command of self" far greater than the law and the social norms her time and place seemed to permit.[5]

Throughout, however, she voiced little desire to end the existing gendered distinctions between female and male political action, or to assume male public responsibilities or obligations.[6] Rather, she understood politics as part of the process whereby she and Joseph collaborated to marshal the resources they needed to marry, to create and sustain a love-based, religiously informed family, to seek éclat in the broader world, and to establish the foundation for their own and their children's futures.[7]

Esther came of age at the beginning of the conflict between Great Britain and her North American colonies that produced the American Revolution. That world-altering conflict structured almost every phase of her life and bedeviled her at every stage of her evolution from a proud young English lady to a mature and ardent American wife, mother, patriot, political operative, and publicist. Esther's story thus illustrates and illuminates for us the contingencies and human costs of the complex process whereby the English-speaking residents of British North America became a separate people, a new nation.

After her death, Esther largely disappeared from our collective memory of the founding.[8] Today she is recalled, if at all, for her notable political activities in the summer of 1780. Even those who are aware of her extraordinary success in those few months, however, know little of the life that brought her to this prominence, of the political context that made her behavior so noteworthy, and of the character, personality, values, and lifetime accumulation of political skill and understanding that prepared her to become by September 1780 one of the foremost political female founders of the American republic.

Esther's story falls into four broad categories. Chapters 1 through 4 focus on her initiation and management of her courtship (1764–65). Chapters 5 and 6 explore how she and Joseph, living on opposite sides of the Atlantic Ocean, first sought to accumulate the political and economic capital that would allow them to marry and live in London, and then retreated into exile in provincial America (1766–70). Chapter 7 deals with her unhappiness in America, her ever-growing family, and the impressive financial success she and Joseph achieved in Philadelphia between 1770 and 1775. Chapters 8 through 10 probe the nature of her decision for American independence and describe her wartime suffering as well as the Reeds' rapid political ascent (1776–80). Chapters 11 and 12 detail her extraordinary political summer of 1780, her sudden death, the deterioration and death of Joseph, and the dispersion of their children. The coda offers a final appraisal of Esther DeBerdt Reed's place among the founders of the American republic.

A note to the reader: in quoting from correspondence, I have not tried to make eighteenth-century writers conform to modern prescriptions, but I have corrected a small number of obvious spelling errors.

CHAPTER 1

Esther
Imprudent and Impatient Love

On Saturday night, November 15, 1764, Esther DeBerdt stayed up late. Alone in her room on the third floor of her parents' fashionable London town house, she drafted and redrafted a letter on which, she believed, her future happiness depended. She was eighteen, in love, and perplexed. She wanted Joseph Reed, a young American, to love her. She wanted him to settle permanently in London and marry her. In addition, she wanted her father's approval of their courtship. She feared, however, that her father had driven Joseph away, that Joseph's ardor had cooled, that he would return to America, and that she would lose him forever. She wrote to test his sincerity and to encourage his "expectation of having me."[1] The obstacles she faced, however, were many and the risks high.

On the broadest level, powerful forces were structuring the context within which Esther was struggling. The British political nation was debating the management of the New World empire won from France a year earlier. At the same time, the economic depression that followed that war posed problems for her father's firm and threatened the future of Joseph's family business. On this November night, however, Esther thought very little about the relationship between her problems and those facing her father, Joseph's family, or the British ministry. Over time she would grow increasingly aware of how the public and the political interacted with the private and the personal, and she would become adept at using political means to advance her personal ends. For now, however, she saw her challenge as much more personal and close at hand. As she confided to Joseph, "I am doing what is contrary to my Father's will . . . and was he to know it, he could never forgive me."[2]

Dennys DeBerdt was not a man to be trifled with. He was rich, well connected, and powerful, one of those British import/export merchants who made (and on occasion lost) fortunes trading wholesale to foreign lands.[3] These "Citizens of the World" bought, sold, and rented oceangoing vessels, loaded them with varied and valuable cargoes, and hired skilled sea captains to carry those goods to trusted commercial men in remote places.[4] They provided the genius, the entrepreneurial energy, and the dynamism of the late eighteenth-century British trading world.

Business was life for these entrepreneurs. Daily, they dealt in London with a welter of other men engaged in similar or ancillary activities. They lived in leased town houses—usually three stories high, one room wide, and two rooms deep—and they used the two rooms on the ground floor for business: the front as a counting house and the rear as a work space. They clustered in or near the financial/commercial/shipping areas centered on the Thames River for easy contact with the men, services, and news that were vital to their business decisions.[5]

Politics was important to them. Political decisions often affected business, and powerful men in public office controlled patronage. A few of the richest of these commercial men aspired to sit in Parliament, but most eschewed both electoral and partisan politics. They cultivated public men as a means of advancing their business interests.[6]

They were, in general, among the most cosmopolitan men in London. They interacted regularly with ship captains and passengers arriving from exotic places, and they engaged in written communication with commercial men abroad. They also aspired to be gentlemen. For a few of them, that meant joining the landed gentry living on rents from tenants on large estates in England, Scotland, or Ireland. Most, however, settled for the external accruements of gentility: manners, dress, speech, household furnishings, horseback riding, expensive carriages, quality education, and advantageous marriages for their children. Many maintained a second home outside the city, close enough for easy travel to their counting houses and convenient enough for visits by business associates and acquaintances during the summer months. A few acquired large country estates farther afield.

DeBerdt enjoyed a middling rank among his peers. He leased a town house in Artillery Court, close to his church and a large parade grounds but a bit removed from the center of the financial commercial shipping along the river. He owned a country home in Enfield, about twelve miles from London, but it was far less elegant than the lavish country seats of his most successful peers. He had one business partner, but to the best of our knowledge he employed no male clerks in his business. His wife, Martha, probably served in that capacity, and his daughter assumed some of those responsibilities in her late teens. He owned a private carriage, employed a liveried servant, and kept a riding horse for his daughter. He loved his young wife, worried about his undisciplined son, and doted on his devoted daughter. But this night, his daughter's behavior would not have pleased him. A strong-willed young woman in a patriarchal world, Esther was evading her father's explicit command.[7]

A day earlier, she had erred. Joseph had come to her home to see her father on business. Excited that he had come and inclined to tease, she had asked him, in front of her father, "what brot you to our house?" Her intention, as she later explained, had been innocent enough. She had assumed that he had come to see her, and she wanted "to know what excuse [Joseph had used] . . . for coming." "I am sure," she wrote, "did you know the motive, it would have given you pleasure." However, her question had confused and embarrassed the young man. Uneasy rather than amused, and not sure what she had meant or how to answer, he left. Now, on Saturday night, or as she corrected herself, "rather Sunday morn," Esther needed to make amends, and she had a plan.[8]

Esther and her mother regularly mixed with the cluster of American men DeBerdt invited to dine with his family on Sundays. He collected useful people, and these young Americans could help him build and nurture his transatlantic networks. He traded principally with America, and in that distant and volatile market success depended on knowledge of current prices and reliable evaluations of the character of commercial correspondents. Personal contacts provided both, and DeBerdt invited into his home an almost endless succession of Americans visiting the metropolis. Joseph Reed, from Trenton, New Jersey, had been attending these gatherings for almost a year.[9]

Anticipating Joseph's presence in her home the next day, Esther wrote late into the night. With luck, in the eddy of bodies and conversation in the dining room, she might slip her letter to him, unobserved by her father or mother. But first, she had to draft it, which was no easy task. "This is the fourth time I have set down to write to you," she told Joseph, and "three times I went no further than to write my Letter half thru, once it was quite finished folded up and Directed" but not sent. Writing was not her problem. She was a wordsmith of no mean talent, as her correspondence reveals. Nor was indecision inhibiting her. She knew precisely what she wanted, but she was wading into deep and difficult waters.[10]

Her father's attitude posed the clearest problem. Two months earlier, he had rejected Joseph's courtship of his daughter, and then had forbidden Esther to communicate privately with him. In London society in the late eighteenth century, young ladies did not casually challenge the expressed will of the patriarch. Although English law and Christian teaching agreed that marriage rested on consent freely given, the law gave veto power to parents of underage children. In addition, custom, financial considerations, and the commandment to "honor thy father and mother" gave parents great influence over the marriage choices of their adult children. At the extremes, no coerced marriage was valid, and few parents could prevent two young lovers from pledging themselves to each other and consummating their union (eloping or "running off to Scotland," as the contemporary phrase would have it). Between these polar positions, the principals and their families tried to balance passion and property, or at least physical attraction with material possessions.[11]

Esther knew the rules. "Not only my parents," she wrote to Joseph, "but every prudent person would say I'm now acting a wrong part." "If at any time," she warned him, "you mention you still have an expectation of having me, he [her father] will immediately say that you would not entertain such expectations ... without some encouragement from me," parenthetically, a revealing comment for the light it sheds on the relative power in courtship. "It must never be known," she admonished Joseph, "that I ever gave you such encouragement, by writing a single line." Esther had the confidence to take the initiative, and she knew that her father understood that about her.[12]

She and Joseph had first met a year before, in the early winter of 1763. She had just turned seventeen, and he, twenty-two, had just arrived in London from the colonies. During the spring of 1764, they had seen each other often in the social swirl of London and at the family Sunday dinners. In the summer, she entertained him frequently at Enfield, the family's country home, and before fall came, Esther and Joseph had opened their hearts and pledged their love to each other.[13]

In September 1764, a month before Esther's eighteenth birthday, Joseph asked DeBerdt for Esther's hand in marriage. That ended the idyll. Until then, DeBerdt had regarded Joseph as one of a number of enjoyable and potentially useful young men who visited the DeBerdt home, ate at his table, and hovered about his charming, accomplished, and budding seventeen-year-old daughter. Now, this transient visitor from America had proposed marriage. DeBerdt responded abruptly. He banned further communication between the two.[14]

Her father's rejection of Joseph surprised Esther. She thought she had found the perfect partner. She loved him passionately, even recklessly, and she expected her family to approve. Joseph, educated at The College of New Jersey (later Princeton University) in New Jersey, had studied law with one of that colony's most eminent attorneys, Richard Stockton, and had won admission to the New Jersey bar in May 1763. That fall, he had come to London for two additional years of study at the Inns of Court, where an increasing number of American elite families sent their sons to mingle with the scions of the English landed gentry who were also there for legal training.[15] By December 1763, Joseph had paid his fees and taken up lodging.[16]

Joseph came well recommended. He had letters of introduction from men of weight, including the new royal governor of New Jersey, William Franklin. DeBerdt also knew Joseph's family. He had done business with his father, Andrew, and his brother-in-law, Charles Pettit, partners in the firm Reed and Pettit, operating out of Trenton and Philadelphia.[17]

As often happened in the eighteenth century, business and family intertwined. Joseph's father had instructed him to give his "affectionate regards to Mr. DeBerdt," and before Joseph had established his own residence in London, his family and his American friends addressed their correspondence to him in care of the DeBerdts. Mrs. Sam Tucker had "sent Jossie a box . . . care of Mr. Dennis DeBerdt, your father's worthy friend."[18]

Once Joseph had arrived in London, DeBerdt had looked after him. It was from DeBerdt himself, not Joseph, that the worried Andrew Reed learned of Joseph's safe arrival in London. Embarrassed and hurt, Andrew later chided his son for his negligence: "from a letter of Mr. DeBerdt," he wrote in pique, "I find that you arrived . . . 3 months ago."[19]

On a more practical level, a marriage connection between the DeBerdt and Reed families could advance the interests of both. Dennys DeBerdt in London and Andrew Reed in Trenton earned their living by buying, selling, and transporting goods across the Atlantic in complex financial transactions.

Family provided the surest and most reliable links. Marriage of DeBerdt's daughter to Andrew's son could cement a business connection.

Religion posed no problem. The DeBerdts, of Flemish ancestry, were religious nonconformists; that is, Protestant dissenters worshiping outside the official, national, tax-supported Church of England. Like most religious dissenters in England at the time, the DeBerdts drew their inspiration from the teachings of John Calvin. Hence, theologically they aligned with Presbyterians in England, Scotland, and Ireland, as well as with Puritans and Presbyterians in America. The Reeds, like the DeBerdts, also came from Calvinist backgrounds. Andrew, of Irish ancestry, had served as a trustee of the Presbyterian Church in Philadelphia in the late 1740s and had educated his son Joseph at a Presbyterian college.[20]

DeBerdt also had close ties with Presbyterians in America and thought well of Joseph's alma mater. In 1758, he had arranged the publication in London of a sermon by the Reverend Samuel Davies, a future president of the college. In 1766, he described Princeton as "the only College where vital [i.e., evangelical] religion is regarded." In the 1760s, DeBerdt had worked with William Smith of New York to obtain a British charter of incorporation for the Presbyterian Church in New York City. In much the same vein, DeBerdt helped Dartmouth College with its fund-raising efforts in England.[21] He also preferred to do business with Presbyterian/Congregationalist families in the Delaware River region and in New England. Shared religious values, while no guarantee of integrity, could strengthen confidence in distant trading partners.

DeBerdt also liked Joseph, or so Esther thought. As she explained to Joseph, "I have heard him say of you more than I have ever heard [him] say of any other gentleman from America, I love the man," and, she added, "I can assure you that's a great deal for him."[22] In Esther's mind, then, fortune, family, faith, and affection should have led her father to bless the engagement.

Esther's age may have played a part in DeBerdt's thinking. Many a father before and since had done what he could to prevent a young daughter from throwing her life away on a charming but insubstantial young man. And many a happily married woman has thanked her father for his intervention when she herself had been seventeen and foolishly attracted to a man unworthy of her.[23] In addition, few respectable women married before the age of twenty; most did not marry until their midtwenties, and marriage in their late twenties was not unusual. Engagements at seventeen, however, were not unheard of among the genteel. Esther understood she was making an extraordinary demand of her father. His reluctance might have been expected, but the intensity of his reaction surprised her. Engagement was not marriage. A commitment at seventeen need not be consummated immediately, and Esther was quite willing to wait.[24]

Esther also knew that her father loved her deeply, and she reciprocated his affection. She believed that should Joseph marry her and take her across the sea to the colonies, she and her father, then approaching seventy years of age, would say goodbye forever. That, Esther feared, would "bring down the gray hairs of my Dear and affectionate venerable parents with sorrow to the grave."[25] But Esther had an answer. She had no intention of going off to America with Joseph. Rather, she had a vague expectation that Joseph would finish his legal education in London, qualify to practice there, and then they would marry. Esther thought that she could eventually handle her father.

Others thought not. Charles Pettit, Joseph's brother-in-law back in America, saw the differences in the families' wealth as the major impediment. Writing to Joseph after the fact, he thought that, in light of Joseph's financial situation, a favorable decision by DeBerdt would demonstrate a "[g]enerosity not to be expected in a mere London Merchant."[26]

Stephen Sayre, Joseph's college friend, held the same opinion. In his letter of condolences to Joseph after DeBerdt's rejection, Sayre concluded that Joseph simply did not have enough money. In Sayre's view, Joseph was too socially peripheral, too financially insignificant for marriage into the DeBerdt family. However, Sayre offered Joseph some hope. Considering the age of Esther's father, it is possible, Sayre wrote, "the old codger must [be] off and leave his Fortune on this side [of] the Ferry." A patient Joseph might still have both the daughter and the money.[27]

Pettit and Sayre had a point. Disparities of wealth did separate the two families. Still, the Reeds brought much to the table: a commercial family with one foot in Trenton and the other in Philadelphia, and growing connections in New York City. The Reeds had a history of mutually beneficial economic endeavors with DeBerdt. They also enjoyed a strong reputation for integrity and shared DeBerdt's religious sensibilities.

Nor was Joseph himself without promise. His college education elevated him significantly above his family's commercial base and when combined with his legal training singled him out as one of a small group of young Americans with great promise. His current investment of time and money in advanced legal studies at the Middle Temple testified to his discipline and ambition, and would in time help to lay the foundation for future prosperity, prominence, and power in America: clearly not a run-of-the-mill provincial family nor a peripheral young man. From DeBerdt's perspective, the prospect of a marriage connection with a successful mercantile family living at the heart of America's most promising commercial region and the acquisition of a genial and talented son-in-law whose education and profession already elevated him to a social status above that of DeBerdt himself was worth serious consideration. Or so Esther thought, and so, she assumed, she could bring her father to see. For now, however, Dennys DeBerdt had no reason to regard his seventeen-year-old daughter's attachment as anything more than a passing infatuation, and he had even less reason to think that Joseph might someday be any more useful than dozens of richer and better-connected young men interested in his daughter, including some from America.

But if the father had rejected Joseph, the daughter had not. At first, Esther had appeared to acquiesce with her father's decision. In all of her correspondence, we find no harsh word toward her father, no hint of hostility, no disrespect for him and his position in the family, and no challenge to his right to act as he had acted. What she would not challenge, however, she would evade, and now, late on this November night, after two months of obedience, she was employing her considerable gifts to achieve her ends by circumvention rather than confrontation. Here and for most of the rest of her life, she employed this tactic to gain the time and space to employ her charm, her intelligence, her verbal dexterity, as well as her ability to assess the context within which she was acting and the character of those with whom she was contending. She did not challenge her father, but she did get her way more often than not.

Joseph himself presented a more vexing problem for Esther. In the summer, he had said that he loved her and wanted to marry her, but since their parting in September, he had largely ignored her. Far too easily, it seemed, he had accepted DeBerdt's decision, left the family's country home in Enfield, gone to London, and then departed for a tour of the countryside. Esther did not see or hear from him for weeks. She learned later that while traveling he had taken ill and returned to London, pale and worn out. Once recovered, he had rejoined the American cadre cultivated by Esther's father, but he had paid no particular attention to her. With others, he attended her eighteenth birthday celebration on October 22 and joined the family early in November when they saw "the Lord Mayor's show by water," probably a part of the annual anti-Catholic Guy Fawkes Day celebration on November 5. When he was in London," he rejoined the family's Sunday dinners but made no effort to communicate privately with Esther. Rather, he attended plays in the city with Esther's brother, Dennis, and pursued the pleasures of bachelorhood in what Esther called "the diversions at that end of the Town." Her brother did not share her family's disapproval of the London theater, nor did Joseph's New World Presbyterian training keep him away from this popular entertainment. Joseph had, it appeared, accepted DeBerdt's decision and was moving on.[28]

Esther's father interpreted the situation in this way, and often in the months after the failed proposal he assured Esther that Joseph was happy with the decision and remained friendly with the family. From DeBerdt's perspective, it had all worked out well. He had nipped the dangerous romance in the bud but kept Joseph as a useful American contact. The old man felt good about it. "Mr. Reed must see," he told his daughter, that "I have treated him with a great deal of tenderness, yet at the same time taken care of my daughter." Esther's mother, Martha, agreed.[29]

Esther's parents assumed that Joseph was an ambitious and prudent young man who had come to London to better himself and his family. He had met and liked Esther. He found her charming and attractive, and he knew that her father was rich and influential. He pursued her, charmed her, and proposed to her. Then DeBerdt had intervened. Joseph, disappointed but realistic, had sulked for a while but then accepted the decision and turned his attention elsewhere. London was full of interesting young women from well-to-do families.[30]

Joseph came from a world that saw courtship and marriage in that light. Joseph's friends in New Jersey speculated endlessly about marriage prospects, carefully balancing considerations of female temperament, beauty, and wealth. Their discussion of one local prospect illustrates the point. On March 22, 1764, Abraham Hunt wrote to describe her as a young lady of sense and fortune. In May, Isaac Allen saw her as a young woman "with a fortune of £1,500." A month later, Moore Furman went to the heart of the matter. She is, he wrote, "an agreeable young lady," "not quite so handsome" as some, but her "considerable fortune . . . makes her a desirable if not a Beautiful Creature."[31] Joseph's younger brother, Bowes, commenting on the marriage of Joseph's friend Jonathan Smith, encapsulated the prevailing ethos. Bowes thought of Smith as a young man of limited talent and prospects. When Smith married a woman reputed to be worth £10,000 pounds, Bowes was astonished. "Who would a thought!" he asked his brother in London.[32]

Joseph apparently wrote home in much the same way about Esther. Few of Joseph's letters from this period have survived, but one to him from John Cox, a relative in Philadelphia, suggests that Joseph had earlier hinted that he might bring Esther home to America as a prize. Cox responded that he understood Esther was "an agreeable girl," a "very pretty thing," and worth some £10,000 to £20,000, but he worried that Joseph might have given up the chase. "You don't mention a word of Miss DeBerdt" in your last letter, he commented, but Cox promised "if you have any thoughts of bringing her over to America, let me know and I will [illegible] for your reception."[33]

Courting a young woman of substance in London would certainly have been consistent with Joseph's motives for being there. His friends and family saw his sojourn in the metropolis as an investment, the "pursuit of what may be an advantage to you," and especially making the acquaintances of "considerable people there [who] may hereafter turn to your advantage."[34]

Marriage into a powerful mercantile family in London would represent a significant financial advance for Joseph and for the provincial trading family he represented. Even America's greatest merchants in its largest ports could not match the wealth of their counterparts in London, and Andrew Reed, while significant, did not rank among the greatest of the merchants in Philadelphia, Boston, or Charlestown.

But DeBerdt had ended that courtship. He may have seen Joseph as a promising business contact for the future. He may even have liked the young man, but he did not welcome his pursuit of his daughter, and he expected Joseph, as a prudent young man, to accept that decision without resentment or recriminations.

And Joseph was a prudent young man. He had not come to London to make enemies. His family had subsidized his trip expecting they would benefit from his success. Good London connections could facilitate provincial ambitions and compensate for parochial weakness. The metropolis controlled commercial credit and influenced political appointments in the colonies. William Franklin, the royal governor of New Jersey and the illegitimate son of Benjamin Franklin, illustrated the point. He had overcome the blemish of his birth through his father's ability to make effective use of the patronage system at the center of the empire. This reality the Reed family knew, and hoped to emulate. Dennys DeBerdt was a powerful man living at the center of the empire. No commercial family in the colonies would consciously offend him. Joseph understood the risks to himself and his family should he alienate DeBerdt.

Esther knew that ambitious provincials with slim resources and great expectations often came to London to court the daughters of the city's affluent families.[35] Indeed, she knew one such young American quite well. Stephen Sayre, Joseph's college friend, had preceded Joseph to London, and by the time Joseph arrived Sayre had ingratiated himself into the DeBerdt circle. Tall, lean, soft-spoken, good-humored, and with "astonishing comeliness," he freely admitted he had come to find a rich wife. He would have preferred a pleasant and attractive young woman with an independent income, but the larger her income the less important her age and beauty. Before DeBerdt hired Sayre to travel to the West Indies for the firm, Sayre had met, charmed, and reached an understanding with the young and wealthy Miss Charlotte Nelthorpe. When Sayre returned to London, however, a dispute over Charlotte's money ended their connection. Sayre, initially "a good deal unhinged" by his misfortune, soon renewed his quest for a wealthy wife and after a decade of effort married "one of the daughters and coheirs of the Honorable William Noel, Esq., deceased with an immense Fortune."[36]

Esther liked Sayre. She did not condemn his marriage aspirations. She sympathized with him when he failed to win Charlotte and worried when he later pursued a wealthy woman Esther thought far too old for him. "I can't help being a little afraid least he should be tempted to sacrifice too much for the sake of money . . . as his heart is rather grown callous to the [higher] feelings of love," she wrote.[37] She understood that Sayre was not unique, but she did not feel he reflected the best among Americans. "I don't take the coolness of Mr. Sayre's Love for the pattern of American Friendship," she told Joseph.[38] Nor did she take Sayre's model for her own. She aspired to something quite different.

She understood that coverture, that blend of law and custom that established the legal rights and duties of wives and husbands, defined marriage as a hierarchical relationship in which the wife obeyed while the husband exercised legal authority over their property, their children, and their domicile. Esther explicitly agreed with Joseph that a wife must be prepared to follow her husband to the ends of the earth should he so decide.[39]

But Esther did not want or expect to have a life together with Joseph based on his authority and her submission. She wanted and expected to have a passionate and fruitful partnership conceived and sustained in affection, friendship, and mutual esteem. She loved Joseph now; he said he loved her. What began in love would endure in love. Property, possessions, and prestige would play a subsidiary role. She understood that they would need resources in order to achieve the comfortable and independent status that she called "a competency." She expected a substantial dowry from her father, and she saw lawyers as men of stature and substance, but her dowry and Joseph's profession constituted the necessary preconditions for their marriage, not its purpose. She would not marry Joseph because he was a lawyer with prospects but because she loved him. She assumed that he would not marry her for her dowry but because he loved her.

Their love, as she understood it, was an "honorable a love," a "most unfeigned love," "a virtuous and mutual love," a deep and intense emotional attachment.[40] She saw herself as Joseph's "Affectionate Friend" whose "heart still glows with the warmest sentiment of esteem" and one whose eyes "speak the language of my Heart." She saw their present difficulties as "only the rough part of the road which leads to pleasure." She expected these feelings to persist and blend with the "tender emotions," the "tenderest passions" of married life.[41]

But that pleasure and that passion grew from their friendship and enhanced it. She hoped that esteem and friendship "may still continue to be the unshaken foundation of our Love." And that esteem and friendship allowed her to open her heart to him, her "only" friend, in the moments when "my heart is so full of anxiety." "'Tis yours to know every sentiment of my mind." And her love, her esteem, and her friendship would last forever. Commenting on female fickleness, she assured Joseph, "I am quite a stranger to such sort of Love as can [torn] change its object." She was and would remain committed to Joseph unequivocally, emotionally, possibly even rashly. "I don't expect it [happiness] in Grandeur or Riches. All I desire is a competency and then a companion who will make it his endeavor to be both friend and lover to me whom he chose for Life," and I in return may be able to have a "Religious well-regulated family." As she added in a later letter, a family that would "bring honor to God."[42]

She would have readily agreed that this kind of love-based marriage of friends united in mutual esteem was romantic, even naive. But she took her father and her mother as her model. DeBerdt's letters to her mother, Esther told Joseph, "would be [looked] on as love letters rather than of husband to wife," and Esther felt "that's the happiness I think the greatest that after twenty years living together, to find the same complaisance, the same warmth of affection as [at] first." Esther believed that she and Joseph now shared the same "warmth of affection" and the same "complaisance" as her father and mother, and that it would form the foundation of their marriage.

She understood that "this happens so seldom that it would really make me enter such a state with fear and trembling." But for Joseph, and with Joseph, she was willing to take the chance. "Do you want to hear that I still love," she asked, and then answered, "It is a truth which I am not ashamed to own."[43]

In September, when he had proposed, Esther assumed that Joseph felt the same way about her, that he was different from his American friends, and especially from the closest of them, Stephen Sayre. She believed that he shared her vision of their life together, that he loved her for herself and not for her money, that he respected and esteemed her and regarded her as his closest friend and confidant. She expected that in time they would marry not for money but for love, and that although they would divide their family responsibilities according to their reproductive responsibilities and the values of their society, they would live as companions in a mutually beneficial partnership based on affection, friendship, and mutual esteem.

Now, however, in mid-November, she was less sure. Her late-night letter and the difficulty she had in composing it suggest her concerns. Joseph's all-too-proper behavior in the long and silent weeks since early September troubled her and raised questions about his motives and feelings for her. Joseph's long absence and his aloofness on his return suggest that he, like his friend Stephen Sayre, might have been more interested in his own advancement and more attracted to a woman's wealth than to her person. He had met the charming Miss DeBerdt in the winter. She was rich and beautiful, and he enjoyed her company. She had encouraged his attention, the family seemed to approve, and he had proposed. When her father said no, Joseph moved on. He had tried one avenue of advancement and found it closed. He took time off to relax and prepare himself to search for other conquests. At the worst, his behavior over the past three months suggested that he had played fast and loose with the affections of a vulnerable young woman, more interested in her wealth and her connections than in herself. Thus, Esther wrote with a nagging fear that she might have erred in her judgment of this young man from New Jersey, and that he might have already abandoned her. If he had, she knew that social custom and family considerations would justify his behavior.

So, apprehensive but determined, working into the wee hours of the night, she wrote to renew Joseph's interest and to entice him to join her in evading her father's supervision while they worked to gain his approval. If she won this contest, she would have the man she loved in the city she loved with the blessings of the father she loved, but that outcome was far from

17

certain. Should she fail, she faced a devastating rejection by Joseph and the anger of her father.

Esther was bright and well educated. She was raised in a commercial family that, undoubtedly, shared with most other commercial families the desire to improve its status by imitating the landed gentry in the education of its children.[44] She had a sound grasp of written language. She had been trained in penmanship and disciplined to write and rewrite her sentences until they were clear and graceful. She could read French and probably could speak and write it as well, but we have no evidence that she knew Greek or Latin. As a child raised in a religious "vital" dissenting Christian home, she knew the Holy Scriptures, and she gives us hints that she had been trained in history. Her mother also ensured that she had acquired the cultural accouterments appropriate for her station. She owned a piano and rode her own horse regularly in London and Enfield. She painted, did needlework, and disdained women with poor deportment. Her grandson, writing with access to documents not available to us now, praised the "serious cast" of her reading, but the theater, he believed, had been "prohibited by the discipline of Artillery Court."[45]

She claimed that she wrote spontaneously and with candor, flouting the conventions of her time. "If you remember last night, it was remarked," she once wrote, "that young ladies when they wrote to Gentlemen, should study every word." She, herself, she said, ignores such advice. "Whatever the reason [for that counsel] it does not seem to suite me for I sit down and write what I think, and not what I should write." "I don't want a single sentiment of my heart . . . hid from you." But where she appears most forthcoming, she is often most artful. Here, in this first letter to Joseph, we catch a glimpse of the skill she usually conceals. She was blessed with a keen sense of the subtleties of social intercourse, and she had the discipline and the patience to craft her writing to serve her purposes. As she admitted in this, her first letter to Joseph, she drafted, redrafted, and then drafted again her most important letters, choosing her words carefully, bending them to her will and weaving them into persuasive prose, as she constructed an image of herself and shaped the thinking, and hopefully the choices, of others in ways largely invisible to them. Thus, this intelligent and strong-willed eighteen-year-old worked late into the night crafting the letter she believed would shape her future.[46]

CHAPTER 2

Joseph
Love and Calculation

The next day, Sunday, Joseph came to dinner, and much to Esther's delight, he brought with him a letter for her. This initial sign of his continued interest excited her, and for the next three weeks she was happier than she would be again for many years. Then, however, bad news from Joseph devastated her, and he soon departed for home, leaving their present status and their future unclear. The economic and political vagaries of the British Empire that would bedevil and frustrate them for the rest of their days had intruded into their lives. The Currency Act of 1764 had reduced the money supply in the colonies, and the Sugar Act of 1764 had disrupted the colonial sugar and rum trade. These parliamentary enactments exacerbated the economic depression that followed the end of the French and Indian War (1763) and threatened the financial base of the Reed family in America.[1] Joseph had to go home.

But, for the moment at least, Esther was happy. When Joseph tried to hand his letter to her, however, she refused it. She feared her mother would see. She "turns around so quickly sometimes," Esther later explained, "that there is no doing anything for her." Her mother's watchful eye also prevented Esther from delivering to Joseph the letter she had composed in the wee hours of the night.[2]

The failed exchange again upset Joseph. Esther saw his "uneasiness" but did not share it. In her mind, having his letter in hand mattered less than knowing that Joseph was taking the risk, that he wanted to renew their communication, possibly their courtship. Still, his confusion "vexed" her, and she tried to encourage him by her behavior. As she later wrote, she had done "nothing to curb [her] fine flow of spirits," hoping that he "would guess the reason" and know that she "could not unwillingly do anything that should give pain to a generous breast."[3] Esther's "fine flow of spirits" was part of her charm, one of the tools she used to get what she wanted. She could, and did, however, on occasion turn it off to express her displeasure or frustration, and, as Joseph learned, to be on the receiving end of that tactic could be a devastating experience.

The next morning, Monday, she added a lengthy postscript to her own still-undelivered letter of Saturday night. "Mamma being gone to market," she wrote, "gives me a quarter of an hour that I can call my own, which I devote to you."[4]

She apologized for refusing his letter, explained that she too had had one for him, and then further encouraged him. "I don't know whether I should have wrote so soon" (after her father's rejection of Joseph's suit), but, she explained, she had no one else to discuss it with. "I neither can speak nor can I hear anything that is quite to my mind," she said.[5] How Esther delivered this letter to Joseph is unclear, but we know that she succeeded, and that over the next two months she and Joseph continued to exchange notes, slipping them to each other at social events or passing them through friends.[6]

But, whatever the means, Esther and Joseph wrote often, and their secret correspondence added an exciting ingredient to Esther's daily life. Joseph wanted her. He paid her court. They had a secret. She felt confident enough to tease him: "I do believe you are in love," she wrote when he misdated one of his letters, writing "Tuesday instead of Monday evening."[7] And in this short statement, she illustrates for us the growing eighteenth-century debate about love and marriage. Esther herself regarded her parents' marriage as a love-based union, and thus her own model. Others, however, saw love as a dangerous emotion: fickle. It could go as easily as it came, and it could lead rational people to make irrational decisions. She certainly expresses her approval of Joseph's feelings about her, but at the same time she demonstrates how it could befuddle the thinking of even sophisticated lawyers.[8]

She reassured him that her parents had no marriage plans for her. "I don't think there is any scheme in their heads about me; if there is I am entirely unacquainted with it."[9] She understood that her parents had the right, possibly even the duty, to have marriage "schemes" for her, but she also knew that she would ultimately decide. Nor did Joseph have any rivals. She had only one suitor, a Mr. Wykoff. She wanted to be rid of him, but she had to wait for some overt act on his part before dismissing him. "I can assure you, my Cold Water is ready," she told Joseph, "but if he gives me no opportunity, I can't fling it."[10]

During these weeks in late November and into early December, Esther and Joseph saw each other frequently, but never alone. They dined in company with other Americans every Sunday at her father's table, and they met often during the week at social events, usually in the homes of friends.[11] The first week in December may have been typical. On Sunday, Joseph came to the DeBerdt home for dinner with the other Americans. On Monday, Esther and Joseph met by arrangement with others at the home of a friend. On Tuesday, Joseph failed to show up for tea at Esther's home, but they met again unexpectedly on Wednesday. Esther, writing later, explained to Joseph that the two-day separation had depressed her. "I had been vastly dull last Wednesday, before I came to Mr. Martin's," she told him, but discovering Joseph there, "I found my spirits rise."[12]

When Esther was not with Joseph, she found that others wanted to talk about him, sometimes to her discomfort. A conversation Esther had with one of Joseph's fellow Americans suggests that Joseph might have been more freely discussing Esther with his friends than Esther thought prudent. Chiding Joseph a bit, she reported, "Mr. Powell [Samuel Powel, future mayor of Philadelphia] drank tea here on Tuesday and he gave some very broad hints and jokes about you. . . . I can't think how he got a notion about it," she said, gently reprimanding Joseph for his apparent indiscretions. She also feared that she had responded unwisely to Powel's teasing: "I am almost afraid," she wrote, "my countenance betrayed what at present I wish to have hid."[13]

Meeting, of course, was not new. Even after her father had ended the courtship in September, Joseph and Esther had continued to see each other in social settings. Some of these meetings, such as the celebration of Esther's birthday in October, the outing to commemorate Guy Fawkes Day (November 5), or the regular Sunday dinners, were family events. Others were gatherings of young people structured and supervised by responsible adults seeking to bring eligible young women and men together.

For Esther, these social events now took on a special intensity as the two conspired to carry on a secret courtship before the very eyes of those who had forbidden it. Everything was exciting. Ordinary events took on special meaning. A polite word, a casual glance, an accidental touch, a dull posture, or a sudden show of spirits could speak volumes in a language only the lovers understood.

The secrecy enhanced the romance, and Esther seemed remarkably skilled at concealing her feelings from her parents. As she assured Joseph, "My parents have not the least suspicion of our correspondence." Esther did think it odd, however, that her father allowed Joseph free access to the family. "This [scheme] of letting you come to our House and imagining you will look on me with indifference," she allowed, "may not all together be consistent with every degree of Prudence."[14]

Esther's father saw it differently. Joseph might not be a suitable son-in-law, but he could soon become a man of influence in America. DeBerdt had built his fortune on his connections. Success in his world depended on knowing the right people, cultivating the correct friends, and building relationships with the most useful and trusted individuals. Joseph's college education, his admission to the bar, and his advanced study at the Inns of Court in London singled him out from his peers. He was a young man with ambition and promise who could well become a man of substance and significance in the Delaware River valley, the center of America's wheat production, milling, and export with Philadelphia, its largest city and an ever-expanding market for British exports. DeBerdt had every reason to cultivate Joseph's friendship, to make him a part of the DeBerdt family "interest." Both men recognized that they could work for mutual benefit. DeBerdt did not want Joseph to marry Esther, but Joseph's behavior since September posed no threat. The younger man seemed to have recognized the authority of the older man, and to have accepted his decision. In Esther's words, DeBerdt "seems very well satisfied that you [Joseph] have given it [marriage to Esther] up as a thing impossible."[15]

She was not sure about what her mother knew or how she felt. Martha DeBerdt, considerably younger than her husband, may have more easily empathized with Esther's emotional inclinations.[16] "Mamma is often saying," Esther reported to Joseph, "you have entirely forgot it, tho in her own mind I believe she does not think it, only she endeavors to hide it from me." Esther, in turn, teased and tested her mother, telling her, "I fancy otherwise," suggesting a more tolerant posture toward her daughter's feelings.[17]

Beneath the excitement of the secret correspondence, hidden glances, subtle body language, and the occasional touch slumbered what Esther had termed "the almost insurmountable problem" of going to America. From the beginning, she had made her position clear: she would not leave London. On this she was adamant. Her father would not permit it, and she could not defy his wishes. Nor could she bear to depart from her parents. Left unsaid, but possibly of equal importance, Esther could not imagine exchanging life in cosmopolitan and sophisticated London for life in parochial and primitive New Jersey. Esther's city was one of the great cultural and political centers of Western Europe and the capital of the greatest imperial power in her known world. The Treaty of Paris in 1763, which ended the war against France, made Great Britain the dominant power in eastern North America.

For eighteen years, this metropolis had structured her days, stimulated her mind, excited her senses, and defined her identity. For her, London meant music, painting, horseback riding, fireworks on the Thames, the artist studios at Covent Garden, the picture galleries in Pall Mall, and the river teeming with the world's commerce. It was the place to see and to be seen. It had more than 550 coffeehouses, 450 taverns, 200 inns, and great pleasure gardens such as Vauxhall, with its twelve acres of walks, shops, booths, gardens, and settings for outdoor concerts and fireworks displays. London was the place of never-ending shopping in the greatest emporium of the world, an overflowing cornucopia of goods offered in retail outlets whose numbers exceeded the total number of people living in Philadelphia in 1760: 21,000 stores in London, 20,000 people in Philadelphia.[18] Here, at home, Esther wore the latest London fashions; shopped in the best stores; attended fashionable teas; played the piano in polite company; rode her horse in the park; socialized with bright, informed young men and women; and interacted with people close to the centers of power. She could not imagine living anywhere else.

In contrast, Joseph's home in Trenton, New Jersey, was three thousand miles away across the Atlantic Ocean, a trip that in the best of times could take six to eight weeks in cramped quarters. And Trenton, with a few thousand people, was a rustic village where ladies wore out-of-date fashions, walked with bad posture, and enjoyed a pale and outdated reflection of the cultural life of London. "My spirits flag insensibly when I think about going to America," she candidly told Joseph.[19]

Her apparent intransigence agitated Joseph. He responded by pouting at one meeting, and then challenging her logic in his next letter, accusing her of being inconsistent. She had said she wanted to renew their courtship. She knew that, ultimately, he would have to return home, but she said that it was impossible for her to accompany him. In his best lawyerly fashion, he asked how she could express a wish for what she herself declared impossible. Esther responded tactfully, kindly, and even generously, but she refused to allow him to intimidate her. She first apologized for making him uncomfortable: "I am very sorry my Letter gave you uneasyness," she responded, "as I am sure I did not intend it should." She admitted that it would have been inconsistent of her "to wish for that which at the same time I say is impossible," but she reminded him that she had not taken a categorical position: "was there not an almost before the insurmountable in my last letter?"[20] She was correct. He had overreacted. She had trapped the lawyer in his own lawyerly games. "I intended there should be [i.e., the word almost] but if there was not, I am sure you will forgive me now I ask it." But she knew, as did he, that she had caught him, disciplined him, and taught him a lesson. The beautiful and charming young Miss DeBerdt was far too bright to be trifled with.[21]

Verbal victories, however satisfying, seldom advanced the cause of the heart, and Esther wanted the dialogue to continue. Joseph had, she reminded him, done her "so much honor to hint that my wishes will influence your Action." She had made her wishes clear. Now she reiterated them: she desired him to marry her and stay in London. She casually dismisses his economic concerns about finding suitable professional work in London: "I don't think it improbable you should live here genteely." She then offered her ultimatum: "If our happiness is connected with each other, that [i.e., living in England] is the only way we can be happy."[22]

Esther drafted these thoughts on a Saturday, but by the time she sent the letter on Tuesday, she had softened her position a bit. In a postscript, she offered a compromise, or at least a plan to get where she insisted they ultimately should be. "In the former part of this letter, where I mentioned you settling in England," she commented, "I don't mean immediately, for I am convinced of the necessity of you going to America."[23] In Esther's mind, the question was settled. And they had time. He had just completed the first of his two years of study at the Middle Temple. They had another year or more in which to work those things out. She was happy with the present and optimistic about the future.

Joseph appeared to have acquiesced, or at least he did not reject the idea of settling permanently in London. In his year there, he had learned to love what the magnificent city offered: the social activities, the endless teas, the witty exchanges, the serious conversations, the theater, the nightlife, and the excursions to the socially exclusive and exciting health resort and spa at Bath. He had given Esther reason to think he would stay if he could find a suitable means of supporting a family there and of meeting his obligations to those he left behind in America. Esther felt that she was managing things well. She had defined her position. She thought that Joseph had agreed.

Then, on Sunday, December 6, 1764, only three weeks after they had renewed their communication, Joseph shattered her illusions. He informed her that he needed to return immediately to America. He would go as soon as he could settle his affairs in London and book passage.[24]

Joseph's news inflicted on her, she said, "the most sensible pain" she had felt since her father had rejected Joseph's proposal in September. Although she "endeavored to hide" her feelings from the guests at the Sunday dinner, her behavior gave her away. Her mother "took notice of it," and Captain Macpherson, another American friend, seeing her agitation, "asked what was the matter."[25]

Two days later, as she wrote to Joseph, she struggled with her anger and her sense of betrayal. First, she attacked him. "My flattering hopes have raised me so high as to think you could find some way to make yourself happy staying in England," she wrote. "Indeed, you must try to find some other plan," she admonished him. She then charged him with deception: "Indeed, I always thought that you intended to stay here. Sure I did not raise my hopes without any foundation."[26]

In these painful few days, she considered sending him away permanently. Angered by his intention to leave her and dejected by the cruelties that threatened to "deprive us of the hopes of happiness," she had, she later admitted to Joseph, "almost taken a resolution to desire you would not come to our house anymore."[27] If he must go to America, they could remain friends, "though time shall force us to swear off our love." She prayed that "Providence will Point out some way to hinder the painful tasks of breaking the tye of friendship"; however, "if Providence has designed [me] for another, may it kindly follow you and constantly pour the greatest blessings it has to bestow on you."[28]

After her initial outbursts, however, she shifted the blame to herself, assumed responsibility for the misunderstanding, and asked for Joseph's forgiveness. She might have erred, she wrote, when she imagined his talk of returning home "was only what you should like, not what you intended." She was seeing only what she wanted to see, she admitted, "but maybe," she wrote, "had it not been in my wishing it so ardently in some measure blinded me, I should have taken more notice of those distant hints you sometimes dropped. I am afraid you will blame me in this respect and I hope you will impute it to the true cause, and then rather pity me."[29]

The news Joseph shared with her on December 6, however, was not news to him, not something that he had just learned. Rather, a financial crisis that had been looming for months had finally overcome him. Back in America, his family teetered on the edge of ruin. The firm of Reed and Pettit, having difficulty paying its bills, faced default on its debts to its English creditors, including its large financial obligations to the DeBerdt firm.

Dennys DeBerdt had been shipping goods to the firm of Reed and Pettit on credit. That was standard practice. American merchants imported goods from English merchants with promises to pay when the goods were sold retail. After selling what they had imported, they paid their debts to their English creditors, and then imported more goods, again on credit. When an American firm had trouble paying for last year's imports, London firms faced a dilemma. If they insisted on immediate payment, that could drive the American firm into bankruptcy, and both the Americans and their London creditors would lose. But if the London firm allowed the American firm to import more goods on extended credit, the London firm increased its vulnerability. Therefore, in the early fall of 1764, the difficulties faced by the firm of Reed and Pettit in Trenton, New Jersey, posed a threat to the DeBerdt firm in London.[30]

As early as December 1763, the month Joseph first arrived in London, letters from Trenton and Philadelphia reported to him the deepening postwar depression, Andrew Reed's business concerns, and his increasingly irascible behavior.[31] Throughout the spring and early summer of 1764, Joseph's correspondents noted the scarcity of money, the multiplicity of bankruptcies, the negative impact of British limits on American trade, and parliamentary decisions that, out of ignorance or maliciousness, favored the West Indies' interests over those of the mainland colonies and threatened a "staggering burden" of new taxes.[32]

The news, however, was mixed. Andrew Reed's "helter-skelter management" of the family firm upset old business friends, but when Andrew wrote to Joseph, he focused on castigating his son for failing to write home in a timely fashion. The tone of the letter as well as the comments of others suggest that the older man retained his vigor and his authority. Charles Pettit, Andrew's partner and Joseph's brother-in-law, complained about the way in which DeBerdt had handled the legal and financial difficulties of a ship they owned, the *Britannia*, and noted the overall economic decline in the Delaware River valley but seemed cautiously optimistic about the prospects of the family's new distillery in Philadelphia and about the possibilities of profits in land speculation. Abraham Hunt and Richard Stockton also noted the accumulating difficulties but focused principally on social and political news. Moore Furman, the most pessimistic of Joseph's correspondents, raised questions about Andrew Reed's personal and business behavior, and urged Joseph to return home, but then softened his message by promising financial help should Joseph decide to stay in London. Dan Cox envied Joseph's good fortune, expected him to remain in London for the full two years, and speculated about joining him in the metropolis. John Craven, clerk to the firm of Reed and Pettit, wrote to tell Joseph that trade was dull, that bankruptcies multiplied, and that he, disgruntled, had "left Mr. Pettit." However, Craven felt that the distillery offered good prospects of success and that Joseph's father remained vigorous. Pettit also complained about the hard times and the defaults of debtors to the firm but, like Craven, seemed optimistic about the distillery as well as opportunities to profit from land speculation in Pennsylvania.[33]

In his early June 1764 letter to Pettit, Joseph acknowledged their mounting difficulties but was not yet alarmed. He noted tensions between the Reed and Pettit firm and that of DeBerdt and reported that DeBerdt had concerns about Pettit's business practices. Joseph, however, defended DeBerdt's integrity, if not the quality of the decisions that emerged from the DeBerdt firm, and noted that he, himself, was pleased with the "Old Gent's approbation, as he has shown me much civility."[34] Thus, in Joseph's mind, in the early summer of 1764, his financial foundation seemed shaky but far from collapsing, and he continued to feel good about DeBerdt.

Then, at summer's end, at about the time Joseph and Esther were planning his proposal to her father, a cascade of letters brought unequivocally bad news. Abraham Hunt predicted they were all "like to have prodigious hard times." Bowes, Joseph's brother, and his father continued to fight, and the "great scarcity of money among us" frustrated real estate transactions. Moore Furman lamented, "O Commerce, where art thou fled" and hinted that recent actions by Joseph's father threatened Joseph's inheritance. John Cox, who was older, more experienced, and better connected in Philadelphia than most of Joseph's friends, enumerated the accumulating financial problems at home, castigated Parliament for its insensitivity, and predicted "Rebellion." He reported that America never was "so effectively aroused." Bowes Reed virtually pleaded with Joseph to come home, and Abraham Hunt made it more specific. He expected Joseph home that fall. Pettit, long sick and still struggling, seemed incapable of restoring order to the family finances and now revealed that he had not yet found the money to reimburse DeBerdt for the advances on which Joseph continued to depend. Sympathetic to Joseph's vulnerability, he promised to send money to cover Joseph's costs should DeBerdt "grow cold" and refuse further loans.[35] Thus, by September, Joseph was well aware that he might have to leave London before he finished his full two years of study, and sometime in the middle of the month he began to suggest to friends that he might be back in America early in the New Year.

Esther knew nothing of all of this, but her father undoubtedly did, and that knowledge probably contributed to his response to Joseph's proposal. By the nature of things in the Atlantic trading world, the news of the difficulties of Reed and Pettit must have reached him. DeBerdt had good connections in America, and few secrets were kept for long among the men in the transatlantic trade. Although the firm of Reed and Pettit had not yet collapsed, rumors were rife and must have reached DeBerdt. After all, that was the principal purpose of his Sunday dinners. Joseph's economic base showed unmistakable signs of imminent collapse.

Thus, at the time of his proposal, Joseph knew that his family's finances were in disarray, that his father and his brother were squandering time and energy on acerbic internecine warfare, that his friends were predicting financial disaster, and that because of the family's financial setbacks, he, Joseph, would continue to depend on money borrowed from the man who had rejected his marriage proposal.

When Esther and Joseph had renewed their courtship in November, she had interpreted his willingness to communicate with her as evidence of his noble and unselfish love. However, while she exulted in the revival of their romance, Joseph had chosen not to reveal the precarious state of his finances or his worries about an early return to America. Seen from a distance, Joseph's silence on this crucial question raises questions about his motives. He was acting less like an anxious lover than an ambitious young man of slender means who had come to London to advance his own and his family's interests and was concealing his financial liabilities from the well-to-do woman he hoped to marry. In this light, he looked like his friend Stephen Sayre: more interested in his own advancement than in romance and more attracted to the woman's wealth than to her person.

A letter from Charles Pettit to Joseph in December 1764, however, suggests a more generous interpretation of Joseph's feelings and motives. Pettit, responding to letters from Joseph after his rejection by DeBerdt, understood that DeBerdt's September decision had stunned Joseph and precipitated an emotional reaction of epic proportions on his part.[36] Until that point, Joseph had felt confident. With Esther's encouragement, he had spent much time with her under the family's supervision and had, he assumed, won their confidence. Joseph's father had reported that DeBerdt, in "two very kind letters," had expressed "his high opinion of you."[37] His father's news had complemented Joseph's own impressions.

DeBerdt's rejection had both surprised and angered Joseph. He felt that he had acted honorably. Her family had, it seemed to him, encouraged him, and then, without reason, rejected him. He, like Esther, was hurt and frustrated and confused by DeBerdt's apparent sudden change of heart, and in a private meeting with DeBerdt, Joseph challenged that decision.

DeBerdt had, in turn, softened the tone of his rejection. He stood by his decision but did not preclude some later reconsideration, presumably when his daughter was older, when Joseph's family finances were more in order, and when Joseph himself had demonstrated he was capable of fulfilling the potential promised by his obvious educational attainments.

DeBerdt had offered something. Not much, and nothing specific, and certainly not enough to assuage Joseph's own hurt and anger at the abrupt termination of his courtship with Esther, but enough to give him hope.

During the next two months, Joseph's separation from Esther tormented him, and he poured out his heart to Pettit. Pettit's response testifies to the intensity of Joseph's feelings. Joseph loved Esther: completely and unequivocally. Indeed, so deep was his emotional involvement that he, a man of the world, felt embarrassed to reveal to Pettit the intensity of his emotional engagement and the depth of his distress. He worried that other men would make sport of his vulnerability.

Pettit reassured Joseph that he, Pettit, did not see Joseph's feelings for Esther as an imprudent and irrational "youthful whimsy." He told Joseph that he would never consider treating "so exalted a subject and [one] so near to your Heart" with "unbecoming Levity." He assured the emotional younger man that he, Pettit, did not "think you do more than Justice to the Charms" of your young woman and that he respected "Joseph's real love" for his "Angel."[38]

In November, Joseph had received Esther's first secret letter with mixed feelings. He welcomed her initiative. She had indicated that she still loved him. Her willingness to risk her father's displeasure enthused him, but she did not know the risk she was asking him to take. Joseph had religiously abided by DeBerdt's strictures, not from indifference, as Esther had feared, but from the frail hope that his respectful behavior would in some remote future win concessions from her father. Esther, unaware of this, did not appreciate the magnitude of the problem her initiative could cause. Should her father find out, he would be angry with her, but that would pass. What would not pass would be DeBerdt's renewed determination to preclude any future connection between his daughter and this obviously untrustworthy American.

Equally important in understanding Joseph's state of mind and his motives is the timing of his decision to leave London for America. If Joseph had made his decision to return home before Esther's first letter on November 15, then his initial response to her as well as his behavior over the succeeding three weeks would indicate a serious degree of dissimulation. But that seems not to have been the case. When Joseph received Esther's November 15 letter, he was still struggling with the question of his own immediate future. Although in September he had hinted to his friends that he would be home in America soon, Pettit had continued to assume that Joseph would remain in London for a second full year of study. He assigned tasks to Joseph that could not have been undertaken before early spring. He also had encouraged Joseph to be optimistic in his expectations about Esther since he would have considerable time in London to continue to impress her father and thus to advance his own cause. In the same vein, as late as December 20, in the last letter Joseph received from Pettit before departing for home, Pettit gave no hint that he thought Joseph would or should return home immediately.

Joseph probably made the decision to return to America shortly before he told Esther about it. The key to this timing was his upcoming bill at the temple. Twelve months earlier, in December 1763, he had paid for his first year of study. Now, early in December 1764, he had to pay for his second and final year, but he did not have the money. Pettit's funds had not arrived. Joseph either had to seek more financial assistance from DeBerdt, to whom he was already in debt in excess of £100, or go home.[39] He chose to go home and within days informed Esther.

His letter writing reinforces this conclusion. On November 29, he sent a flurry of letters to his American correspondents, answering both recent letters and some as much as six months old. He seems to have been tidying up things in light of an early arrival in Trenton.

The crisis in his family finances, building for almost a year, had finally caught up with him. His continued silence on these matters in his interactions with Esther had intensified the problem, but he had waited not to deceive her but, rather, to devise a strategy that could modulate her expected response and produce an outcome that both of them could tolerate. His love for her, and his fear of losing her, had silenced him. But now, he could no longer find a way to postpone the inevitable. In the midst of some of his most joyous moments with Esther, Joseph had to tell her.

She reacted with an explosion of emotion, accusations, and self-flagellation, but she remained adamant on the basic point. "I am sure," she restated emphatically, "that it is not for me to go to America." An additional phrase, however, suggests a degree of uncertainty in her mind: "I don't think you expect it." But the thought of a permanent separation overwhelmed her, and she poured out her feelings to Joseph: "My heart is so full of anxiety that it must vent itself somewhere, and to whom can I do it better than into a bosom that entertains so honorable a love."[40]

Now, Esther and Joseph had plans to make and little time. Their inability to meet privately and to speak intimately complicated that task. "I should be very glad of half an hour's conversation with you," she wrote to Joseph, "but [I] am entirely at a loss to contrive it."[41]

Esther was seldom alone, even at home. Esther's mother, her companion and guardian, took her responsibilities seriously. Affluent women of London understood the social significance of a young woman's reputation—and how easily it could be tainted. And Martha's eighteen-year-old daughter, on the cusp of full womanhood, had never been more vulnerable.

The ever presence of her watchful family deprived Esther and Joseph of private moments. They met often but always in company. They conversed extensively but always in public. In desperation, they resorted to subtle body language to convey their emotions to each other. Sometimes, Esther feared that she had revealed too much in this way. More often, she used her deportment to show Joseph her displeasure. "Your surmise of my looking dull last Monday night," she later wrote to him, "was founded on truth." He, in turn, could do the same, conveying his displeasure and thereby sending her into paroxysms of self-blame. "I am uneasy what made you so dull [last Sunday]," she wrote. "There seems as if there was something that I did with particular wait [weight] on your spirits."[42]

Their lack of private, frequent, and casual conversations prevented them from sharing those intimate trivia that help to weave together the lives of those in love. Long after Joseph had returned home, Esther still did not know the important details of his life: his birthday, whether he owned a house of his own, who might care for him when he was sick, or how many siblings, in-laws, nieces, and nephews might depend on him for support.[43]

When Esther first learned that Joseph soon intended to leave her, she had expressed a strong desire to be alone with him but lamented that she could see no easy way to do so.[44] By early February, however, she had contrived to escape her parents' scrutiny. On Monday evening, February 5, shortly before Joseph's scheduled departure, the young lovers spent an evening alone together. For the first, and last, time in their six-year courtship, they found themselves in each other's arms.[45]

How they arranged the meeting, where they went, and how long they were alone together, Esther does not choose to tell us. We do know that this extraordinarily rare event must have taken long and complex planning. It required her to deceive both her family and her friends. It frightened and excited her. We can retrieve some sense of her exhilaration from her brief note to Joseph on the morning after. The experience had exhausted her and its intensity had left her feeling ill. "I have been a good deal unwell," she wrote to Joseph. "I knew I should [be] after being so uneasy. I always feel the effects of such things afterwards." But, she reassured Joseph, they had so far escaped detection. "As there is so little chance of my having the Opportunity to tell you how I got over my difficulties last night," she said, "and as I know [you] will be anxious to know the consequences. I take this [moment] to inform you. Everything was right at home. They did not think me late."[46]

One loose end, however, bothered Esther. Her married friends, Mr. and Mrs. Wood, had unwittingly assisted in the deception, and Mrs. Wood was a "little affronted" when she discovered the role she and her husband had played. The Woods had, it appears, expected to meet Esther, and possibly Joseph, at "the Greyhound." When Esther and Joseph failed to appear, the Woods, correctly, "imagined we served them a trick" and worried that they, the Woods, might be blamed for a breach of social etiquette. The Woods assumed the worst: "They thought we was gone to Scotland [i.e., eloped]," Esther told Joseph, "but they comforted themselves they had had no hand in it."[47] After Esther parted from Joseph, she had paid a quick visit to Mrs. Wood to construct an alibi for her absence from home and to assure Mrs. Wood that she and Joseph had not run off together. Esther's visit partially relieved Mrs. Wood by ending her responsibility for an elopement, but she remained angry with Esther for placing her in an untenable position. Mrs. Wood needed further explanation, a more robust apology, and many soothing words, but Esther could not get back to her until Thursday, two days afterward. In the meantime, Esther felt "uneasy till I do [see her]."[48]

Esther ultimately resolved this problem by involving Mrs. Woods in the conspiracy. In time, Mrs. Woods became one of the principal vehicles through which Esther and Joseph continued their secret correspondence. Here, again, we catch a glimpse of Esther's charm and her skill in managing people.[49]

Then, within days, Joseph was gone and Esther collapsed. Her health deteriorated and her emotions overcame her. On the day they parted, she wept openly before her family and friends. Her behavior both troubled and moved her family. Her brother said "he did not think it [i.e., the romance] was gone so far," and her father "was a good deal affected." Apparently, the intensity of the parting alerted him to the strength of his daughter's continuing attachment to this young American. Certainly, for the first time, he expressed some sensitivity to her feelings.[50] He attempted to defend himself while he sought to console her. "He said," she later reported to Joseph, "that a private meeting would only make us both worse [and] that had he thought it would be any [use] to us, he would have done it."[51] Esther, in a rare expression of disapproval, later criticized her father to Joseph. She could not help thinking that he might have allowed them a few minutes together before Joseph parted, but almost immediately she recanted her harshness and apologized for her father. "However hard it seemed," she told Joseph, "he, I am sure . . . did it for our good." Esther remained the dutiful and affectionate but conflicted daughter.[52]

More importantly, Esther and Joseph had worked out the rudiments of a secret transatlantic correspondence to keep alive what she now began to call their "connexion." Joseph wanted to return to Esther and to London. She now fully expected him to come back, marry her, and settle there. In their final weeks together, she may also have hinted that she might come to him in America, if he called for her. "I don't think you expect it," she had written to him, suggesting a willingness to consider such a possibility. But in February 1765, he had not asked it of her nor had she volunteered.

It would be five long years before the lovers saw each other again, and by then much would have changed. The crisis of the British Empire would continue to accelerate. The colonial economy, led by the commercial sector, would continue to decline. The Stamp Act (1765) and the Townshend Acts (1767) would precipitate a debate between English-speaking people in London and English-speaking people in America about the nature of the constitutional relationship between Parliament and the legislative bodies in the thirteen colonies. These British initiatives and the colonial reactions disrupted trade and complicated the economic lives of both of the families of the two young lovers. None of this augured well for their future, but for now they had agreed to write regularly, to wait patiently, to conspire together to win her father's approval, and to acquire the economic and political capital that would enable Joseph to return to marry her and live with her in London.

CHAPTER 3

A Willful Girl Matures

Esther began her separation from Joseph absorbed in her own suffering. She was angry with him for leaving her, overwhelmed with the pain of her loss, struggling to gain control of her life, and only vaguely aware of the crisis he faced. Only much later did she come to acknowledge his difficulties, recognize and praise his dedication to his family, and begin to think about how she might help them both. Equally important, over time she had become increasingly aware of how the British Atlantic trading world was shaping her life and how knowledge of that world could advance her ends.

When Joseph said goodbye to Esther in mid-February, he felt the pain of parting, the excitement of going, and great apprehension about what he faced upon arrival in America. He knew that he would miss Esther, and he seemed to enjoy anticipating his sadness. Two days after sailing, he wrote, "This little absence has only served to endear you to me more, and if possible, I love you more than ever." Exaggerating their time apart, he lamented, "We seldom know the Value of those we love till we leave them a little while." Calling her "my Charmer," he confessed that, although it brought him pain, he thought of her often: "I do not try to wean my Attention from you," he wrote.[1]

But Joseph was young and excited about his trip. The Atlantic in winter was unpredictable, and Joseph played up the risk by treating it casually, working to convert the pedestrian into the perilous: "I go into a little danger," he told Esther.[2]

If Joseph faced vague and uncertain dangers in his winter crossing on the *Britannia*, he knew that he was sailing into an unequivocal financial catastrophe at home. The firm of Reed and Pettit was in financial free fall, and Joseph, at twenty-three, had become the new patriarch of his family, its effective head, responsible into the indefinite future for his own welfare and for that of his family's three living generations: his elderly father, his under-age siblings, the Pettit family with its small children, and, at least to some degree, for one of his aunts, a penurious sister of his mother.

A year earlier, Andrew Reed, senior partner at Reed and Pettit, had led a prosperous, dynamic, and expanding firm that generated more than enough profit to support in style an expanded family of nine or ten in America and a dependent law student living well in London. By mid-1764, however, after a major physical injury and a series of business setbacks, the frustrated old man had retreated from Philadelphia to Trenton and largely abandoned the firm's day-to-day management to Charles Pettit. By December 1764, Pettit himself had lost control. "Our affairs [are] at present so wide," he admitted to Joseph, "that I cannot satisfy myself with a proper estimate of them." Moreover, he saw no "prospect... that affords the least ray of comfort."[3] The firm owed its creditors and could not collect from its debtors.

In the prosperity of the war years, the firm had extended these credit/debt networks backward to Britain and forward to American middlemen and consumers. Local firms owed increasing amounts of money to Reed and Pettit, who in turn owed increasing amounts of money to their London suppliers. As long as American consumers bought and paid, American firms could meet their obligations to Reed and Pettit, and they in turn could meet their obligations to London while reaping substantial profits. By 1763, Reed and Pettit had built their credit/debt structure to dizzying heights, and profits had soared. This edifice, however, rested on a fragile foundation of trust and regular payment that in turn depended on continued economic expansion in the Atlantic economy. But when the French and Indian War ended in 1763, spending declined, consumption slowed, debtors delayed payments, and the entire structure teetered.

The problem for Reed and Pettit began with the failure of other firms that owed them money. In the summer of 1764, the bankruptcy of one of its debtors cost the firm £700 (about $70,000 in twenty-first-century U.S. dollars). The failure of a second debtor in the fall cost them far more, in part because this firm owed them far larger sums and in part because of the way Pettit handled the settlement. The sheriff had seized the assets of the failed firm and ordered them to be sold at public auction. Reed and Pettit had first claim on the returns from this auction as partial payment for the credit that they had earlier extended to the failed firm. Pettit, fearing that the assets would sell at "trifling" prices, attended the auction to bid up the sale price in order to increase his own returns. Unfortunately, he outbid all others and in the end committed his firm to pay £2,500 for assets against which he already had a legal claim.[4] Pettit thus paid himself.

These two blows constituted only part of the firm's accelerating problems. Pettit had also invested £600 (approximately $60,000) in a land speculation scheme in Pennsylvania. He expected the value of the land to double in a year, but that did not happen. He blamed the British limitations on colonial trade for depressing the market price for crops, and thus the demand for land. The land's value would, in all probability, grow in the long run. Reed and Pettit, however, needed cash now, but if forced to sell assets at current depressed prices, they would suffer further devastating losses.[5]

The firm had also expanded into manufacturing. In Philadelphia, Pettit was managing two distilleries. Running at full capacity from April to October 1764, they had converted more than seventy thousand gallons of West Indies molasses into rum. However, the Sugar Act (1764) now threatened the firm's source of supply, and the seasonal decline in demand reduced its market. Reed and Pettit would soon be out of the business of making rum.[6]

The firm's investments in shipping and its potential losses in this area are less clear but also of awe-inspiring magnitude. During the late war period, Reed and Pettit had joined with other entrepreneurs in funding privateers: private ships authorized by the government to raid the shipping of the enemy. By late 1764, however, legal tangles in London over these ventures, especially involving the *Britannia*, combined with disputes among the investors, tied the whole scheme in knots. Costs accumulated and profits remained elusive. They had already lost the firm £800, and now the courts had seized the ship. Legal disputes over two other ships threatened to cost Reed and Pettit another £1,000, and the firm of R. W. Shippen was suing Reed and Pettit for £1,400 for failing to make good on an earlier pledge. In these maritime ventures, Reed and Pettit thus faced immediate losses, probably well in excess of £3,000, with little or no hope of income from any of them.[7]

As this fragmentary account makes clear, in addition to the always-risky import/export business, Reed and Pettit had invested large sums of money (the equivalent of hundreds of thousands of twenty-first-century U.S. dollars) into a wide array of ventures. Now, few, if any, of these investments were returning a profit or maintaining their value, while debt accumulated and deadlines loomed. Pettit saw only two ways out of this crisis: bail out now or gamble on a miracle. The first would require them to admit failure and do what they could to limit the damage. The firm still had some assets, including real estate in Philadelphia and Trenton, speculative agriculture land in Pennsylvania, two idle distilleries, and significant quantities of debt owed to it by other firms. Reed and Pettit could liquidate everything and make an honest effort to pay their creditors. This option would end the firm, but it might save something for each partner. More importantly, it would preserve their individual reputations, and thus their personal credit, and therefore their prospects for another start. Pettit told Joseph that he, Pettit, had consulted his wife, his "best friend" and Joseph's older half sister, and they had agreed. Option one was the best.[8]

However, Pettit worried about "aged and infirm" Andrew Reed, "whose fortune had been sunk by my [Pettit's] means." He also fretted about Andrew's children. Bowes, near manhood and about to finish his indenture with Moore Furman, was still immature, volatile, and rebellious. Polly [Mary], in her teens, was living in Philadelphia with the Pettit family and studying "dancing, writing, and needle work." Then there was Joseph, who also would be immediately cast adrift. Pettit had sent him two bills of credit for £50 each in the fall and promised one final sum sufficient to pay Joseph's personal debt to DeBerdt. That, however, he wrote, "would be the last good office in this way that I shall have it in my power to do you."[9]

As for himself, his wife, and their small children, Pettit did not know. Possibly, they could retire to the country, or maybe he could borrow money and go to sea with a cargo, or if all went well with the dissolution of the firm, its creditors might hire him to collect some of the old debts still owed to the firm. His health, however, made everything uncertain. He felt better but still had relapses. In the past, he had found "a tour in the country" or a visit to the "salt shore" helpful. In any case, he had little confidence in his ability to hold on much longer, and he wanted the pain, the worry, the confusion, and the responsibility to end.[10]

Or, they could gamble: hold out as long as possible, conceal losses, avoid creditors, hound debtors, and hope for an infusion of cash sufficient to tide them over until times improved. If that strategy failed, it would destroy not only the firm of Reed and Pettit but would also threaten the personal resources of the individual partners, blacken their reputations, end their chances for future credit, and largely preclude an eventual recovery.

The miracle they needed for this scheme to work, Pettit explained to Joseph, was "remittances from abroad," especially some part of the huge sums now tangled up in legal battles in London over the firm's maritime adventures. Here, Joseph could play the crucial part. He was a lawyer, he was in London, and he had good connections through DeBerdt. If he could untangle the legal knots, settle the claims, keep other creditors at bay, raise some cash, and devise a way to put one or more of the idle ships to work, he might save them all.[11]

With this final suggestion, Pettit shifted family responsibility, and thus family authority, to Joseph. As Andrew Reed had earlier abdicated to Pettit, Pettit now abdicated to Andrew's son, and in February 1765 young Joseph Reed found himself with awesome new obligations, few resources, and slim prospects of success. However, he was returning to America on the *Britannia*. That implied that he had freed it from its London confinement and had successfully taken the first step, but, as he soon learned, that was not sufficient. Before he landed in Philadelphia, the firm of Reed and Pettit had collapsed.

If Joseph left London with mixed emotions, Esther's feelings were unequivocal. When he departed, she thought little of the chaos of his family's finances or of his new responsibilities for his father, his siblings, and the Pettit family. Although she had some sense of the crisis that drew Joseph home, she felt that he could and should have solved these problems from London.[12]

She concentrated her attention on her own loss and on punishing Joseph. His decision to go had angered her. His actual departure had devastated her. Then his tardy goodbye letter hurt and agitated her. Joseph's friends had seen him off. Mr. Wright Burkitt, Dennys DeBerdt's younger business partner, and Samuel Powel, a fellow American, journeyed with them from London to the actual point of debarkation. The send off lasted longer than Esther thought appropriate. When Burkitt returned to the city with Joseph's letter for her, she responded a bit tartly: "Mr. Burkitt has come home but last night. I thought it long, as I expected to hear of you, Tho' I doubt whether among the hurry of so much company you could be able to find an opportunity to let me hear from you. I knew you would if you could."[13]

Her emotional collapse at the parting persisted long after the event. For days, she remained overwrought, inconsolable, and prone to persistent but vague maladies. Nothing mitigated the pain. She had not wanted him to go. She was not convinced that he had to leave. She hoped he would return quickly, but she feared he might not. She tried to console herself with the thought that his trip was merely a protracted visit, a sojourn to tend to important but transient family matters.

Joseph encouraged her to think that way. Writing from the *Britannia* as it waited out a storm, he speculated, "Perhaps *it may not be very long* [emphasis added] before I may have it in my power to contribute to [your happiness by returning to England]."[14] Once in America, he made that point more explicitly: "I look upon myself as a traveler here and wait impatiently for that happy time when you will be restored to my Arms."[15]

Possibly, Joseph believed that he would soon return to London, but he chose his words carefully. He hinted at a stay in America of indefinite length; he anticipated, he wrote, "an Absence whose length is a *little uncertain* [emphasis added]," and he suggested that circumstances might compel him to stay longer than either of them had expected. He desired her, he wrote, and he longed for the time when it would be beyond the "reach of [fortune] or accident to keep her from his arms," implying that fortune or accident might well keep her from his arms for some time, maybe forever.[16]

Esther understood. She read and reread Joseph's letters, studying his meaning. She too appreciated the role fortune (or, as she more often called it, Providence) played in human affairs. She also understood, possibly more than did he, the tendency of time, distance, and distractions to erode the most intense attachments and weaken the most fervent pledges. At some deep level, Esther feared that she was losing Joseph, and she could do little about that except through a secret, circuitous, and uncertain correspondence across the three thousand miles of ocean that now separated Joseph from her.

Esther's general knowledge of the Atlantic shipping patterns and her familiarity with some of the ship's captains (e.g., Captain Macpherson) made a secret correspondence possible but difficult. Over time, conniving to circumvent her father's scrutiny in the arena in which he himself was most engaged and informed had an indirect benefit. It piqued her interest, deepened her knowledge, and expanded her contacts in the oceangoing commercial world on which her family's current fortune depended and in which she would herself someday play a part. But the immediate problem was how to correspond with Joseph.

In order to avoid detection by her father, Joseph's letters had to come to Esther indirectly through a number of precarious routes. Mr. Burkitt, her father's partner, had hand-delivered Joseph's first letter but said he was uneasy with his part in the transaction. He encouraged Esther to look elsewhere for help. He feared he was too close to her family to avoid detection. Esther had intended to have Joseph write to her in care of the Woods, but she told Joseph, "I forgot to mention it to him when I saw him last and have not had time to go to ask him."[17]

She also came to rely on her friend, Miss Edmunds, but that too involved difficulties. The plan called for Joseph to send his letters to Esther in envelopes addressed to Miss Edmunds, who in turn would pass the enclosed letter to Esther without knowing the identity of the sender. Joseph followed Esther's instructions, but, much to her chagrin, he inadvertently revealed his identity through the wax seal he used on the letter. As Esther later explained to him, with a hint of exasperation, one of the letters that "you sent to Miss Edmunds was sealed with a Great Seal and a large JR on it and she having seen one of your letters to Mr. Sayre said immediately who it came from."[18]

Esther also found it difficult to send her letters to Joseph. Her family connections both helped and hindered. Living in London gave her unusual access to Atlantic shipping, and her father's business connections provided her with detailed information about ships, their captains, and their schedules. Devising means to utilize this information without arousing the suspicions of her father, however, tested her ingenuity. When Esther anticipated spending some time with her mother at Bath, she thought that would ease her problem. The health resort, southwest of London, was closer to the port of Bristol. Once at Bath, she told Joseph, she should "have opportunities of writing by way of Bristol and they at London [i.e., her father and her brother] know nothing of it."[19]

The vagaries of transatlantic travel further complicated Esther's difficulties. Most ships sailing between Great Britain and America would carry mail for a fee. Packet ships left on a fixed schedule: usually once a month. Other ships departed whenever they were ready. However, both kinds of ships arrived at their destinations whenever the weather, human skill, and chance determined. Six months could easily elapse between the time Esther wrote and the time she received Joseph's response. Equally frustrating, letters did not always arrive in the same sequence in which they were sent. The time lag between letters and the irregularity of the sequence of their arrival made it difficult for Esther to ask and answer specific questions, to assess Joseph's state of mind, and to keep track of the details of his daily life: his family, his work, his health, and his social interactions.[20]

In addition, Joseph sometimes seemed to neglect her. Esther constantly hoped but was often disappointed. She tracked arriving vessels from

America, expecting to hear from Joseph with each new ship. She noted his correspondence with others in London, and once she made Joseph aware of her displeasure when he neglected her. She commented that the packet ship had arrived from New York with letters from Joseph to her father but "not a line for me." "You can't think how I felt at first," she told Joseph, "but when I found [from her father] what hurry you was in I was satisfied." However, when two more ships arrived without "the letters I expected and have so long waited for," she was tempted for a brief moment to question Joseph's commitment. It was, she told him, too painful to think "you forgot me." She then reminded him that, even if he neglected her, she remained true to him: "If I judge of your heart by my own, it still cherished the same warmth of Esteem and Friendship as when we parted."[21]

One major development made the entire enterprise more workable. Soon after Joseph's departure, Esther's mother joined the conspiracy. Not only did this make the deception easier, but it also gave Esther someone to talk to, and she now found her mother to be, "more than ever, . . . [her] sincerest friend." The two often discussed Joseph, and almost every one of Esther's letters included her mother's "sincerest love" for him. By the fall of 1765, Esther told Joseph that her mother did not "know which she loves best, you, or her own children."[22]

Esther does not tell us when and how her mother learned of her continued attachment to Joseph, or when the mother joined the daughter in furthering it, but Martha DeBerdt was participating by February 22. Esther's letter to Joseph on that date conveyed to him a brief message from the new conspirator. How long Mrs. DeBerdt had known is unclear. It seems unlikely, however, that she knew on February 5, when Esther met secretly and alone with Joseph. Had she known of Esther's continued liaison with Joseph, she would have taken special pains to prevent such inappropriate behavior. But Esther's collapse at Joseph's departure certainly made her aware that she had a problem and possibly contributed to her willingness to help. Indeed, that may well have been one of Esther's half-thought-out intentions in allowing herself such a display. On occasion, later in life, she employed such tactics effectively to achieve her ends.

Why Martha would join her daughter in behavior explicitly forbidden by her husband is more difficult to explain. Martha's relative youth (she was probably in her early forties while her husband was in his sixties) may have predisposed her to empathize with her daughter's emotional turmoil. But that alone would not have led her to violate her husband's explicit wishes.

Possibly, she sensed a subtle shift in DeBerdt's attitude after Esther's breakdown. His confused response to that disturbing event suggests at least a momentary softening of his rigid opposition. Moreover, DeBerdt could afford to worry far less about his daughter's attachment to a young man living on the far side of the Atlantic Ocean. He could wink at a connection he continued to formally oppose.

Such a shift in attitude would also be consistent with DeBerdt's interests and with his character. He liked Joseph, and he understood that Joseph's learned profession, the law, could someday make Joseph an important man. Tacitly allowing a secret correspondence between Esther and Joseph in direct contradiction to his own stated opposition could give him the best of both worlds. It would keep Joseph linked to the family, while it left DeBerdt himself free of any obligations or commitments. DeBerdt could wait and watch with little danger or cost to himself or to his daughter. If, in time, Joseph did become an American of substance, then DeBerdt could change his mind and welcome him into the family. If not, nothing lost. Nonetheless, DeBerdt continued throughout 1765 and into 1766 to proscribe any correspondence between the two, and he policed Esther's correspondence with other Americans seeking to ensure that she was not violating his orders.[23]

Despite her mother's cooperation and the hints of her father's softening, Esther found Joseph's absence intolerable. She was eighteen, passionately in love, and determined that Joseph would have her. Now, Joseph had gone to America with no more than vague promises to return someday, somehow, to make her his. Under the strain, her spirits wilted, her fears multiplied, her health deteriorated, and sporadic headaches debilitated her. Esther had lost control, and for the better part of the next year, she suffered intensely. And, deliberately or not, she also ensured that others shared her pain. Both her suffering and the ways in which she shared it reflect her age: just eighteen, both a woman and a child, mixing adult passions and commitments with the self-absorption of the young. At the same time, it also suggests her determination to mold her world to advance her ends.

The charming and beautiful Miss DeBerdt expected to get her way with gentlemen, especially young ones. The shock of Joseph's news had first provoked her anger and disbelief. She had collapsed, physically and emotionally. On the day he left, she later told him, her emotions had overwhelmed her and she suffered as "those only who love can form the least idea of." Once he was gone, she could not think calmly about "the several circumstances which

43

attended our parting," and she told Joseph "while [she could] . . . remember anything," she would never forget the pain that separation caused. And these feelings persisted. In September, she wrote that the seven months since his departure had been the longest in her life. In February 1766, a year after they had separated, she reported that thinking about it still brought back the pain. "It is more a twelvemonth since I was happy seeing you," she wrote. "The tender, painful scene of our parting was before my eyes, and brought to my Recollection that affecting sentiment of which nothing will ever make me forget."[24]

Esther's emotional agitation and the apparent deterioration of her health concerned her mother. Martha first tried to distract and amuse the distraught young woman, but with little success. "Indeed," Esther wrote, "I have everything done to make me easy, and I am [made easy] so much as it is possible for me to be."[25]

Esther tried to be brave, or at least that is what she said. She reminded Joseph and herself, "We have so often been favored with the most unexpected and pleasing circumstances that it would be . . . the most aggravated fault to complain." But she could not resist indulging in what she called "such pleasing, painful ideas which naturally arise in the mind."[26] Nothing worked, however, and her mother, increasingly concerned, consulted the family physician. He recommended a visit to Bath, a health resort noted for its mineral waters and for its social distractions, and it seems probable that this medical prescription eased whatever guilt the DeBerdts, committed to their "vital" religion, might have felt at such an indulgence. Joseph, also concerned for Esther's health, encouraged her to go: "reap every Benefit that the Doctor intended when he prescribed it," he wrote to her from aboard the *Britannia*. And, indeed, Esther and her mother soon departed for Bath, where they stayed through March and most of April.[27]

Bath was a center of genteel and aristocratic social life in late eighteenth-century England. A thousand years earlier, the Romans had discovered its mineral waters, and over the centuries wealthy and leisured English families had gradually converted "taking the waters at Bath" into a major social event. By Esther's time, the English elite incorporated extended stays into their annual social calendar.

Esther and her mother lived in this world for two months or more in the late winter and early spring of 1765.[28] We need to understand the context of Bath in order to appreciate Esther's letter-writing strategy while there, and a contemporary male participant has conveniently left us a description of his typical day at the resort. He began with "prayers" and drinking the water in the pump room. He then listened to the music, walked, talked, breakfasted, and dressed for the day. He played at "Shuttle Cock with the Ladies," read the papers in the book shop, dined "in company with about twenty Ladies and Gentlemen who in general are very sociable and agreeable," and then in the evening joined the happy throng in the "song room or the Play House which takes up the evening till late Supper and by the time that is done and drank our absent friends, it is One [a.m.] when we think it is time to go to rest." The principal problem at Bath, he wrote, is "the days are too short and the nights not long enough."[29]

Esther was now living at the center of an intense social enterprise of the first magnitude, where taking the waters constituted at best only a small portion of the day's activities. It was a place for the well-to-do, and especially for those with children of marriageable age, to see and to be seen. And it is probably not too far-fetched to assume that Martha DeBerdt had brought her daughter here for just that kind of distraction. Once there, Esther could not have avoided that social swirl if she had wanted to, nor would her mother have countenanced her efforts to cloister herself had she tried. And we have no evidence that she tried.

But in her frequent letters to Joseph, Esther chooses to focus almost entirely on other aspects of her life. They contained little gossip, less description, and almost no anecdotes about noteworthy events or people and few comments about other women. In part, this may have reflected what she called her disdain for "everybody seeing which can be admired most."[30] But there was more to it than that.

Esther's letters focused first on her pain, her suffering, and her health. Shortly after her arrival, she wrote that she had improved little. "I have not drank the water before today," she reported to Joseph, "for I have had a very bad cold and cough which has kept me at home." But she was optimistic. "I go tonight into the bath for the first time, and [my] next letter will, I hope, tell you that I am quite well."[31] But her progress was slow. By the middle of April, a month of bad weather had given way to spring, and Esther could begin to allow herself to think about that terrible day in February when they had separated, or as she called it "our parting." She tried to look forward to the time when "we shall be happy at last." Despite this small progress, she still had to struggle against "giving way to thoughts of" loss and sorrow.[32]

But health was not her only subject. Possibly by accident, more likely by design, her letters repeatedly affirmed her affection for Joseph while they

45

shared with him news about the young men she encountered, especially their American friend Samuel Powel.

Powel, far richer than Reed and far better connected in the Delaware River region, had been fluttering about Esther and her household for some time. Back in December, Esther had reported having tea with him. Powel had made her blush, teasing her about her possible suitors. On the eve of Joseph's departure, Powel had dined at the DeBerdts' and behaved, as Esther described it, "with mistaken complaisance but nothing more."[33]

When Esther and her mother traveled to Bath, Powel made the two-day journey in the carriage with them. Once arrived, he was at Esther's beck and call. He entertained her, escorted her about, helped her evade her father's scrutiny by carrying her letters to the ships at Bristol, and, as she described it for Joseph, he "does my humble servant." Esther felt she had to tell Joseph about Powel because "maybe you will hear that in America, as things do get about strangely."[34]

Esther herself, however, was also becoming concerned about Powel's attentions. Obviously flattered by his attentions but fearing that he might become a serious problem, she decided to give him indirect but convincing evidence of her attachment to Joseph. She allowed Powel to know that she was secretly writing to Joseph. "He saw the direction of one of your letters" was how she described it to Joseph.[35]

Powel understood and immediately drafted a letter to Joseph, assuring his countryman of his honorable intentions and his respect for Joseph's interests. Powel showed his letter to Esther before posting it. She thought it was "very generous of him" and felt "really obliged to him," both for writing and for doing so with so much candor.[36]

But Powel did not go away, and Esther could not leave the subject alone. "He is constantly with us every day," she told Joseph, and he talked much of love.[37] "He told us [i.e., Esther and her mother] of a lady in London who he likes very much," she reported to Joseph, "but . . . he sees a lady here which he seems to like very well too." Esther's mother thought that this second lady was Esther herself, and that Powel "regrets being late in that affair [i.e., in pursuing Esther]." Esther herself could not "help being quite of another opinion." Still, she felt it worthwhile to tell Joseph about it, and then to proclaim her fidelity. She knew that men thought of women as fickle, she told Joseph, but she was different. "I should be [unhappy] if I thought you entertained the opinion of me which I own [has] been [too] true of many of the Sex, that they are as changeable as the wind." Other women might indeed be that way, but she was not. Her behavior would prove her fidelity. Trust me, she said. "Many have promised fair but I rather leave mine for time to show." She assured Joseph that he "needs not be afraid of [Powel], which I dare say you was not before. I give you no reason," she insisted, and then penned one of those marvelous lines that occur throughout the correspondence of this articulate young woman: "A heart once given is not easily called back," she told her distant companion.[38]

There can be no question about her feelings about Joseph. She had committed herself: unquestionably, intensely, and even imprudently. But, without doubting her commitment, it is also clear that she carefully crafted her letters to focus Joseph's attention where she wanted it focused: on her suffering and on Joseph's potential competition for her affections.

Over time, as her pain subsided, and as her health improved, her references to other young men declined and her general disposition slowly improved. She also began to think more sympathetically about Joseph and his situation. She wrote that she hoped "you will find everything better than we had reason to fear." She looked forward to hearing better than expected news from America but admitted that she had braced herself for the worst. Then for the first time since December she expressed her concerns for him, recognizing, "you will have so much care on your head . . . for everything lies on you." She feared, "it will be almost too much for you." Forgive me, she continued, "if I think too much of that," but she worried that "fatigue of the mind" could wear out his body and destroy his health.[39]

Summer at the family country estate in Enfield cheered her. As she wrote on May 11, "the morning . . . the most Beautiful I have ever saw . . . has made me rise something earlier than usual to write to you." "The birds are busier for building their nests while to amuse themselves they are singing . . . a cheerful song. . . . Everything else is quiet, the trees are in the height of their bloom, but I acknowledge in the midst of this delightful scene there wants something to enliven it." She meant news of Joseph's safe arrival, but whether intentional or not, she was also using words and phrases often associated in her world with budding female fecundity. She was enjoying better health and asked Joseph to "join me . . . in praising and adoring the merciful giver."[40]

For the first time in months, she felt lighthearted enough to tease Joseph. But even here, the teasing contained a barb: "I suppose you must have heard," she wrote, "of my intended marriage with Mr. Wykoff and from good authority, too." It was, she said, "given out" by Mr. Symonds, who heard her father "jokingly" say, "Mr. Wykoff is an admirer of my daughter."[41]

Although she felt well and was inclined to tease, she now worried about him, "surrounded with difficulties which need a good heart and a good head." She feared that his obligations might weaken his health, and now, almost six months after Joseph told her of his family's need for him, she pressed him to do "what is right and what will bring most glory to [God's] name." The "disagreeable news" about his family crisis concerned her, but she reported, "Several of my Father's letters from different people mentioned your vast success in Business," and her father had reassured her of "his continuing regard" for Joseph, and especially Joseph's concern for his "family, and especially your good Father, stripped of his fortune."[42]

By summer, she had made some progress with her father. He himself was undoubtedly preoccupied with the Stamp Act and its impact on business between London and America. Esther seemed largely unaware of the great potential for mischief posed for her family and for Joseph by this infamous piece of parliamentary legislation, but by early summer her father was sharing with her at least a portion of his American correspondence. Hence, she knew an increasing amount about trade, commerce, ships, and shipping, and how they tied together London and America, as well as the DeBerdt and Reed families.

By August, Esther's health was still mixed. "I am much better than when you left me," she told Joseph, "but cannot say I am quite well. My old complaint of the headache sometimes troubles me."[43] Throughout the fall, her spirits rose and fell, and her mental state fluctuated. In September, she rather wistfully lamented, "If God spares us to see each other again, I hope and believe it will be the happiest day of our lives." Her teeth also bothered her. She later reported having had three drawn since summer.[44]

She found November to be particularly difficult. She had not seen Joseph in nine months. Her health had improved, and she told him, playfully, "I have grown fat." However, the family had returned to Artillery Court for the winter, and everything Esther saw there brought "remembrances of scenes of pleasure which I cannot taste." "This day last year saw me much happier," she told Joseph. "Don't you remember seeing Lord Mayor's shew by Water?" she asked.[45] Sundays she found particularly trying. "I still seem to expect you to dinner," she told him, and "I have not been able to keep up my spirits as well as usual on that day."[46]

As the weather turned cold, and the days grew short, Esther occasionally approached despair. In her more realistic moments, she knew that they might never again see each other. On November 9, she wrote, emphasizing the contingent nature of their future together: "If," she said, "we shall be so favored as to spend our lives together."[47]

Despite what she called these "chilling Frosts of Adversity," she reassured him, and possibly herself, that her "Esteem is not at all abated." She continued to hope, she said, "for it is very true that Love can hope where reason would despair." By December, she had grown more reconciled to her situation. "I am not so happy in some respects now as I was then [a year ago], tho very far from being unhappy, as I enjoy many mercies that I do not deserve and for which I ought to be more thankful."[48]

By then, she had forgiven Joseph for abandoning her. His reports of the problems he faced at home and the information she gleaned from her father's correspondence had softened her heart. Joseph's father had gone bankrupt; his brother-in-law had no source of income and had sent his wife (Joseph's half sister) and their children to live with Joseph.[49]

As she became more sensitive to the "great difficulties and perplexities" he faced, she admitted that his return to America might have been necessary. She told him that her own father's praise of Joseph's efforts on behalf of his father, Andrew, gave her "the greatest pleasure." Family was family. She approved. And in December, she praised Joseph for sacrificing his own pleasure (and implicitly hers) to return to America to care for his family. In a backhanded apology for her earlier attitude, she wrote, "I should be sorry, if anybody had the least reason to think your attachments in England hindered you from doing what was right."[50]

By December, she had also matured in other ways. She had grown in her confidence in Joseph. She was far better informed about the economy of the British Atlantic world and its personal relevance to her. She learned much from her mother at Bath. DeBerdt wrote regularly to his wife about their American trade, Joseph's success in America, and the accumulating economic difficulties facing both Joseph and the DeBerdts. Martha shared these letters with Esther, and soon Esther's letters to Joseph began to reflect the broadening of her world. By the time she left Bath, she had begun to discuss with him business and political news: the economic implications of the Stamp Act, rumors that Lord Dartmouth was ready to take steps to undo "what the late Ministry have done," the political significance of the death of the Duke of Cumberland, her own concerns that her father was losing "a great deal of money this year in America," rumors that Mr. Burkett was thinking of leaving his partnership with DeBerdt and withdrawing his money, and the conversation of the Boston Men at DeBerdt's Sunday dinner, who were "hot about these new regulations."[51] At the same time, in her eagerness to correspond secretly with Joseph, she had developed a rather amazing understanding of the details of transatlantic shipping: a familiarity with the captains who conducted it, the ways to anticipate their erratic arrivals and departures, and how to communicate discreetly with them.

In addition, she was more comfortable with herself, with Joseph, and with their secret "connexion," and she had resigned herself to a long wait. She was now thinking of their separation in terms of years, not months. She had hinted at this shift in her thinking as early as September. Remembering their times together at Enfield, she had written, "Perhaps it will not be many winters before I shall be allowed this satisfaction again."[52]

She had also eased the pressure on Joseph. In an interesting reversal of roles, she now urged upon him the patience and forbearance she herself had acquired in a year of pain and growth. She instructed him not to think about coming to London for just a short time. "I had rather not see you, than know you came only for a visit." Rather, she said, "keep in America till you can come [and stay]."[53]

Their "connexion" had survived their first year apart. It would, she believed, endure. Esther thought of herself as pledged to Joseph. For now, it was a private and personal commitment, but she expected it would lead to a public engagement and a permanent union. She often prayed that God would shower great blessings on Joseph, but she saw the future as uncertain. She had committed herself to Joseph, but the fulfillment of that commitment now seemed to depend on events beyond her control. Or at least beyond her ability to control with the tactics she had so far principally employed. She was growing in wisdom and in maturity, in knowledge, understanding, and patience. In the end, she remained hopeful, even confident. "We both are young enough to wait some years yet."[54] And she was increasingly willing to play an active part in moving that future forward.

CHAPTER 4

Responsibilities and Schemes

During their first year apart (1765), political events in the British Empire had complicated their lives. The Stamp Act, passed by Parliament in the spring of 1765, had provoked a vigorous and violent colonial reaction. That, in turn, had disrupted trade in the Atlantic world, and both families had suffered economic reverses. In the spring of 1766, Parliament repealed the Stamp Act, trade revived, and prosperity began to return, but ironically, that good news complicated Esther's efforts to help solve the problems that kept her and Joseph apart. For the first time, she faced an array of practical challenges that would test her resolve and her skill: How could she and Joseph marry? How could they support themselves? How could they achieve the éclat to which they both aspired? How could they manage the levers of political power to achieve these ends?

Before Joseph left for America, Esther had delegated to him responsibility for solving their "difficulties." "[Y]ou must," she had informed him, "think of another plan." By late summer of 1765, however, she had begun to take charge, and in the succeeding eighteen months, as she struggled with disappointment and despair, she evolved from a lovesick girl into a young woman with a plan and the determination to make it work. She was, if you will, discovering her own agency.[1]

Joseph had inadvertently contributed to this outcome. When he had sailed from London in February 1765, he had accepted Esther's assignment, and by the time he reached New Jersey, he had developed a proposal. Possibly Esther's injunction had spurred him on. Possibly the long, dull journey home had given him time to think. Possibly the family crisis that met him in New Jersey had stimulated his creative powers. Maybe living in New Jersey reminded him of how much he had given up in leaving London and Esther.

Whatever the cause, Joseph had a plan, and by midsummer Esther knew what it was. Unfortunately, she did not like it. In her response, we see her beginning to take some personal responsibility for their life together. First, she narrowed the limits within which Joseph must work, and then she suggested alternatives. Finally, she took increasing control of devising a plan for achieving the goals they had worked out between them.

Joseph's plan was simple. As he explained to Esther in the summer of 1765, he would return to London as soon as possible and ask her father to take him into the family business. He knew that DeBerdt was looking for a younger partner, and he thought that DeBerdt would accept him. Esther had often told him that her father liked him, and Joseph knew that he could bring much to the partnership, including his legal training and his important American connections.[2]

Joseph's proposal should have pleased Esther. He would return soon and become a merchant like her beloved father. Now, however, when Joseph made his offer she discovered that she wanted more. But how to convey that discovery to Joseph?

Esther began on a positive note. She was, she wrote, "agreeably surprised" at Joseph's idea about "coming into trade." Her mother was very pleased, and she herself saw "nothing that should make it disagreeable to any part of our family." Certainly, Joseph's participation in the family business would help her brother, increasingly burdened as their father's interests expanded and shifted.[3]

Having praised Joseph's initiative, she then suggested impediments. She reminded him that the Stamp Act controversy was stifling the London export/import business, and that "trade is so perplexed and so hazardous a situation I imagine you have given over all thoughts of it at present." She then threw him a few crumbs: "If trade returns ... you may perhaps think again of your scheme." But clearly, she did not favor such a future, and the reason emerges slowly as the letter progresses.[4]

"What I fear," she wrote, possibly with less than full candor, "is you would still be hankering after your own profession, and that would make you unhappy." His unhappiness in turn would make her miserable. She feared, "the tender friendship and love which you entertain for me ... should extinguish [your] . . . nobler flame of ambition." And to her, Joseph's nobler flame of ambition was important. Preserving and protecting it was the crux of the matter.[5]

She saw the profession of law as socially superior to that of a merchant, and she would prefer to marry a lawyer. She explained it in terms of Joseph's ambition, but she shared that ambition. In this preference, she reflected the norms of her society. Although her father was in trade, and trade had provided her with far more than a competency, the profession of law conferred far higher status. In case Joseph had missed the point, she cited her brother. "His [Dennis's] esteem increases every day for you," she reports. "He often wishes you were a merchant, tho he says he would not spoil a good Lord Chancellor [the head of the judiciary]." Esther shared her brother's estimate of the relative social worth of the two occupations. Merchants make money. Lawyers, professional men with formal education and status, aspire to the highest levels of public service. To obtain such a prize was worth waiting a few years. She might accept Joseph in London and in trade. She hinted at that when she wrote, "If no other better way offers." But for now, she was not ready to settle for that less exalted conclusion to their romance.[6]

Something else also made it easier for her to wait. Joseph's offer to come into trade with her father removed the doubts she had about him and his intentions. Knowing that Joseph would abandon his family, his native land, and his professional career for her "makes me easy," she explained, "when otherwise I have a thousand uneasy thoughts." Her sense of security and her confidence in the future made her more patient.[7]

Her doubts about Joseph's scheme led her into a search for other ways to bring him back to her. She was generally familiar with her family's business. Her participation in the DeBerdt Sunday dinners, where she regularly interacted with ambitious young men from America, would have assured her some understanding of the broader world. Still, in August 1765, when she first began to think about this new challenge, she was only eighteen and far from the experienced participant in the complex worlds of commerce and politics that she would later become.

Indeed, this was a decisive moment in Esther's maturation, not only in her growth from a child into a mature adult responsible for managing her own life but also in her understanding of the complexities of the world in which she lived. From this point on, Esther's interest in how her family made its living (international trade, commerce, finance, interest and commission rates, ships, shipping, and ships' captains), interests that had at least in part been already stirred by her need to conduct her secret transatlantic correspondence with Joseph, grew apace. In the same vein, so too did her understanding of how her father's cultivation of a patron/client relationship with the powerful Lord Dartmouth opened doors and protected interests, and how her family's religion as dissidents in England's Anglican world played a vital role in DeBerdt's business and political connections with the Calvinists in America: the Congregationalists (old Puritans) in New England and the Presbyterians in the middle colonies, especially those Presbyterians who DeBerdt saw as exemplars of "vital" religion.

How much of this Esther had sensed before Joseph's plan provoked her into action remains unclear, but there can be no doubt that from this point on considerations of transatlantic commerce, political patronage, and religious identity played increasingly powerful parts in her campaign to have Joseph, to have him in London, and to have him with her father's full approval.

But right now, she needed information, and for that she needed access to powerful people. To whom could she turn? Certainly not her father. In September 1764, he had forbidden her to communicate with Joseph. Since then, he had given her no hint that he had changed his mind, although he may have known more than she suspected.

Her mother, Martha, supported her. She and Esther talked often and at length about Joseph, about Esther's future with him and about politics and business. Martha might have done more to help. Not only were she and her husband close, but he trusted her business acumen sufficiently to appoint her as one of the executors of his estate. However, DeBerdt's limits on Esther also constrained Martha. Within the family, she needed to honor at least the form of the rules he had imposed. Beyond the family, she could do little without advertising her daughter's defiance of her father.

Esther's brother, Dennis, did not seem very likely to help either. He was more cosmopolitan and more experienced in the ways of the world than she was, but neither his circumstances nor his attitude inclined him to assist her in this endeavor. He was at an early stage in his mercantile tutelage under his father, who tended to view him as an irresponsible young man unwilling to take business, or even his own life, seriously. Dennis needed to cultivate, not annoy, his father.

Nor did Dennis share Esther's feelings about Joseph. He seemed to resent the competition of another young man for his sister's time and affection. Esther herself in the past had contributed to the friction between the two young men. In late fall of 1764, angry with Joseph for leaving her and suspecting that he was enjoying himself in the seamy side of London while she suffered alone, she castigated him for his earlier carousing with Dennis. "You'll do much better not to go with him to Plays," she wrote, and added that Dennis "ought to obey his Papa," and, by implication, so should Joseph. Her words seem unlikely to have enhanced Joseph's respect for Dennis, or Dennis's affection for Joseph, but they do suggest the degree to which she had internalized her family's religious disapproval of the theater.[8] Thus, in the fall and early winter of 1765 those most able to help Esther could not or would not. Then, to compound her difficulties, Joseph's letter of late December 1765 or early January 1766 disturbed her deeply. It reopened the question of settling in America.[9]

Esther had, she thought, defined the parameters within which she and Joseph would work out the details of their future: Joseph would practice his profession, he would do it in London, and they would marry and spend their lives together in her "native land," her home, the center of the world. Joseph's letter challenged these assumptions.

In recounting a recent conversation with Captain Macpherson in Philadelphia, Joseph told Esther that the captain did not think highly of their plan to settle in London. Esther understood that the captain wanted her to marry Joseph and settle in America. She also understood the captain's motives. Although often in London, he lived in Philadelphia, and his swashbuckling days were over. He had, during Britain's recent wars, lost an arm and had made a fortune as a privateer. Now, he sailed the North Atlantic not as a pirate but as a man of commerce, and he and his wife were building Mt. Pleasant, a magnificent mansion on the banks of the Schuylkill River just west of Philadelphia. The captain was making America his home, and he wanted his two favorite young people to join him there.[10]

The captain's motives did not particularly disturb Esther, nor did she fear that he would have undue influence over Joseph. What mattered was what Joseph's comments about the captain told her about Joseph's thinking. Neither she nor Joseph cluttered their letters with casual comments, idle gossip, or unimportant news. Joseph reported the captain's comment with a purpose. He wanted Esther to think about joining him in New Jersey.

This unpleasant and unexpected news agitated her. She failed to write to Joseph by the January 1766 packet ship, and when he later asked her about her omissions she brushed it off with a casual remark: "It is so long ago I have forgot the reasons of my not writing."[11] It seems more likely that she needed time to think through a response to this upsetting challenge.

By early February 1766, she was ready. In two long letters, the first in February and the second in March, she clarified her position. She began by attacking the captain. "I don't at all wonder at the Captain's being against the plan . . . especially as he entertains the Romantic notion of my going to America." But the captain lacked sensitivity. "He does not know what the strongest attachments are to the best and most affectionate parents." She also expressed doubts about his character. The captain had, she reminded Joseph, adopted a "pernicious set of principles [while] in England" (he had become an Anglican) and therefore could no longer be relied upon. Having dismissed the captain, she admonished Joseph: "I hope . . . you will never suffer [the captain] to have influence with you." "You know my sentiments."[12]

Joseph did know her sentiments. She had made them clear at the beginning of their renewed courtship late in 1764. As she had written then, "I am sure it is not for me to go to America. . . . It cannot be."[13]

While he had been in London, and even during his first few months in Trenton, Joseph had agreed. He, like Esther, loved London. Moreover, he loved Esther and wanted to marry her, and the thought of living with her in London had seemed far better than living in Trenton, with or without her. But now, a year or more later, he was in New Jersey, a remote outpost of the empire, and he was there without her. He could see nothing in the near future that would bring him back to her and to London. In these new circumstances, having Esther in New Jersey was far better than not having her at all. "I can be happy anywhere with you. Without you, no where," he wrote.[14]

She, however, felt differently. She reminded Joseph that her departure from London would "give pain to my dear and honorable parents." She assured him that she accepted the principle he had earlier articulated when he said that he "would not marry an Empress unless she was willing to go to the part of the world where [his] honor and esteem called." But, she continued, he did not have to stay in America. "If you could live genteelly in England, there would be no difficulty in your supporting your Father as comfortably as while you are there." It was cruel, she said, of your family "not to lend you an assisting hand."[15]

Until this point in her argument, she had said nothing Joseph had not heard before, but now she revealed a new and uncompromising reality. "You must not ever think of seeing me in America." Parents or no parents, Joseph or no Joseph, Esther would never leave London, never live in America. Joseph had asked her to think about it. She had refused. Their future now rested on his response, and she did not know what he would do.[16]

Her outburst against the captain at the beginning of her letter suggests the enormity of her gamble, the depth of her emotional investment, and the intensity of her fear and apprehension. She had brutally attacked an old and favored friend who had long abetted their secret courtship. In the past, she had often mentioned her affection for him and was pleased thinking how he was "enjoying himself with his wife and family at Mount Pleasant" in Philadelphia. As recently as December 1765, she had sent him her "affectionate regards," but in her February and March 1766 letters to Joseph she launched an ad hominem attack on his person, his character, and his new "pernicious [religious] principles." "An error in Religion is a fatal one," she declared.[17]

But she understood that the captain was not the principal source of her concern. She turned her fury on her old friend, but she understood that it was Joseph who threatened her world, and she had thrown down the gauntlet before him. Esther knew, on one level at least, that Joseph would sympathize with her desire to stay in London. He too loved the city. She knew on a deeper level, however, that Joseph's love for London would not alone determine his response, and for five months she anxiously waited.

In her letters during those months, she concealed her concern behind a pose of casual confidence. She teased him about his impatience and reported that she and Stephen Sayre had passed many "pleasant hours" talking about plans for Joseph's future in London, but none of them were "yet well grounded enough to tell you." She continued to assume only one outcome, encouraging Joseph to be happy for a while on that side of the water until "in time you will come where we can add to each other's Happiness on this side [of the water]." She discussed Joseph's land speculation plans with Lord Dartmouth and reported that she and her mother had visited the House of Commons. Both women avidly followed public and political life in the newspapers, but this was a special occasion. They had "been most agreeably entertained by hearing Mr. Pitt speak." Undoubtedly, they had been there to hear the debates on the repeal of the Stamp Act, completed in March 1766, a decision with significant economic implications for the DeBerdt family and for the future of Esther and Joseph. After the repeal, both Esther and her father rushed the good news to Joseph, each separately. Here, and with increasing frequency, Esther shows us her interest in public affairs, and especially in those political questions that impinged most immediately on her own life. She also sent Joseph rare bits of social news. Mrs. Wood, for example, had a new baby boy, and she named him after Joseph. Esther also sent Joseph a picture of her father that she had drawn and a new set of ruffles she had been making for him for more than a year. She even included special washing instructions.[18]

She only occasionally hinted at her underlying concern. In April, she wrote, "I long to hear an Answer to some of my last letters," and she asked about his affairs, "which by your last letter seem to be at present discouraging to your return here." In a rare burst of candor, she also admitted the complexity of their present problem and the dim prospects for the future autonomy of the family they hoped to create together. Were Joseph to come to London and marry Esther without adequate resources and an independent income, they would remain dependent on her father. "I really have as much pride as you, for it would be as [torn] to me to live on an absolute dependence after I am Mrs. Reed . . . as would to yourself. I am sure we could not be so happy [torn] stances. Indeed it would be disagreeable to everybody concerned."[19]

She also continued to work to structure the conditions under which Joseph would return, and in this effort she and he were working at cross-purposes. She wanted him to come to London as a lawyer, not as a merchant—as a professional man, not a man of commercial business. Joseph, however, continued to pursue his original plan. He came from a commercial family. He knew and understood the intricacies of the transatlantic trade. He might be a lawyer, but he did not see that as incompatible with trade and commerce. Almost from the moment of his departure from London, in February 1765, he and DeBerdt had conducted regular business correspondence, largely beyond our view because it was largely beyond the view of Esther, our principal historical source. Fragments of the Dennys DeBerdt–Joseph Reed exchange, however, suggest that Joseph may have written more frequently to DeBerdt than to Esther in his first year away.[20]

Joseph provided DeBerdt with useful information on the status of the American markets and about the political climate in the colonies. DeBerdt used this information for business decisions and for his own political purposes, sharing Joseph's "sensible accounts of American affairs" with DeBerdt's principal patron, Lord Dartmouth.[21]

Joseph also worked to resolve the lingering dispute over the ship *Britannia* and to collect debts owed to the DeBerdt firm by Americans, including the now-defunct firm of Reed and Pettit. DeBerdt was grateful. The Stamp Act crisis of 1765–66 had put DeBerdt in a precarious position. Like most London mercantile houses, he traded with America on long-term credit. Americans protested the Stamp Act by cutting imports and slowing or suspending their payments for past debts. The same credit/debt crisis that had destroyed the firm of Reed and Pettit now threatened the DeBerdt firm.[22]

Throughout 1765 and 1766, Joseph had also worked with DeBerdt and the Philadelphia merchants to petition their London counterparts for support in their efforts to repeal the Stamp Act. He assisted DeBerdt in conveying to England the petitions of the American Stamp Act Congress. In March 1766, DeBerdt sent a special vessel to America with news of repeal.[23]

In this year of interaction, DeBerdt's estimation of Joseph continued to grow, and on occasion he discussed Joseph's future with him. In February 1766, for instance, he recommended that Joseph seek to become an agent for one or more of the colonies. These agents, chosen by individual colonies, usually lived in London, kept their American clients informed, and lobbied to advance their clients' interests. The next month, DeBerdt wrote that he wished he had enough influence in America to help Joseph procure an agency.[24]

Meanwhile, Esther worked to close off the chance that Joseph would return to London as a merchant in business with her father. Without actually saying so, she conveyed to Joseph, again and again, that it was a bad idea. In February, she worried that he "would not be happy [in London] unless you had a preference in your business [i.e., practicing law] here ... as you have in America." In March, she reported that her father agreed with her. He was not himself displeased with the thought of having Joseph in the family business but was "apprehensive that it would not be agreeable to your disposition."[25]

In the end, deeds, not words, settled that question. It was with some satisfaction, one presumes, that Esther could report that her father had added a new man to his firm: none other than Joseph's old friend Stephen Sayre. She had hinted of this possibility earlier, and now she could tell Joseph that, for all intents and purposes, it had been accomplished. Bringing Sayre in was "as far decided on as the situation of affairs will admit." It still depended on the situation in America. Her father hesitated to explore this possibility with his current partner, Burkitt, but once affairs between England and America were settled, "which cannot be long now," it would undoubtedly go forward. As a major step in that direction, DeBerdt arranged to send Sayre to America as his agent to collect debts, and Sayre departed on May 10, 1766. While Sayre had not yet actually joined the family firm, he stood next in line. Esther was happy, and she, possibly tongue in cheek, assumed that Joseph would share her joy at Sayre's success. Whether or not Joseph shared her feelings was irrelevant. That door was closed. DeBerdt would not take two new young Americans into his firm at the same time.[26]

Also, while she waited, Esther began for the first time to talk to her father about Joseph and about ways to bring him back to London. This startling development began in February 1766, when Stephen Sayre revealed to DeBerdt that Esther and Joseph had been writing to each other. Initially, nothing seemed to change. DeBerdt expressed no surprise or anger. He continued to correspond with Joseph and, to the best of our knowledge, never acknowledged to Joseph that he knew about the young man's connection to his daughter.[27]

Nor did DeBerdt's knowledge of Esther's correspondence with Joseph produce any sudden or conspicuous changes in Esther's relationship with her father. Her letters from that point on, however, suggest his increasing willingness to discuss with her both his business in America and Joseph's involvement in that business and in the DeBerdt family. She explored with Joseph the possibility of his returning to his study at the Inns of Court. She speculated that he must stay a year "before you can practice regularly."[28] Then he could be a lawyer in England, and they could marry and depend on his profession, not on her father, for their income.

But a colonial agency, Esther reported, seemed most promising, repeating advice that DeBerdt had conveyed to Joseph a month earlier. Rumor had it that many colonies were unhappy with the work their agents had done for them during the Stamp Act crisis. "Poppy" (a familiar name she had not before used in her correspondence), she reported, said he thought that Joseph might pick up one of these and had already mentioned Joseph's name to a prominent lawyer in New York. She and Sayre had also speculated that her father himself might become the regular agent for Massachusetts. DeBerdt had been useful to that province during the Stamp Act controversy on an ad hoc basis, and now Massachusetts was very dissatisfied with its present agent, Jackson, who earned £1,000 a year. If Massachusetts appointed DeBerdt as its agent, he might then appoint Joseph as his deputy and share that income with him. Esther estimated that they could marry and live well in London on £200–£300 a year. But, as Esther admitted later, this was mostly speculation on her part. She cautioned Joseph that it was a scheme that she and Sayre had concocted, but "I never drop the least hint that he would do so, and besides it is uncertain if they make him Agent, his present appointment being only for the purpose of delivering the Petition [against the Stamp Act to Parliament]." The next month, acting on her own, she urged

Joseph to get to know Mr. Kelley of New York, a man who, she thought, carried much weight there.[29]

Throughout the spring and summer of 1766, Esther continued to think of schemes, and she continued to worry about Joseph's long-awaited response to her February ultimatum: "You must not ever think of seeing me in America."[30] Meanwhile, she revealed to us her growing familiarity not only with trade but also with the complexities of the political context within which trade operated.

Joseph's answer, which she received in July, drew from her a torrent of gratitude and a flood of correspondence and advice. "I most sincerely thank you for the generous Sentiments you express that you are willing to Indulge my darling wish of staying in [my] Native country," she wrote. She promised to reward him by dedicating her life to "endeavouring to make you happy," and she followed this letter with a barrage of others, averaging one every two weeks over the next two and a half months, an extraordinary outburst far exceeding that of any other period in her five-year transatlantic exchange with Joseph.[31]

Joseph, however, while accepting her wish that they settle permanently in London, raised some additional questions and, in a very real way, shifted an increased proportion of responsibility for their future to her. His began with a lawyerly point to defend himself against accusations of inconsistency or dishonesty. "I never entertained a thought of you coming to America while it gives your parents pain," he wrote, but by clear implication he was now telling her that he thought of her coming to America when it would no longer give her parents pain. He had seen her commitment to London as contingent, not absolute, as dependent on the situation and the feelings of her parents. He had hoped, possibly, that with time circumstances could change and she would then be more amenable to living with him in provincial New Jersey. Esther had corrected his understanding. Her position was not contingent. It was absolute. She was not going to live in America.[32]

Joseph now knew and accepted that reality. He had no principled objection to settling permanently in that magnificent city with Esther. In addition, he recognized that she was correct. A successful Joseph in London could probably provide for the material needs of his father and his other American dependents.

But he wanted her to understand his situation and its implications for their future life together. He would readily return "if Providence points any tolerable way or prospects." But for now, Providence was not offering any tolerable way for him to settle in England. He was doing well in New Jersey, and he had no present hope of doing well in London. He was ambitious and proud. He wanted to be somebody, and he assumed that she too wanted him to be somebody. He did not want to "languish in obscurity." The choice they faced, he said, was "an honorable distinction and affluent fortune . . . in America" or to "live unregarded with scanty income in England." She had once told him that she did not expect to find happiness in "grandeur or riches." But she had already compromised that ideal when she had decided she preferred him as a lawyer rather than a merchant. Now, as his prospects grew in America, he was reminding her of their real alternatives. If he returned to England, he might do so at the cost of his income, his status, his autonomy, and his self-respect. He had said that he could be happy anywhere with her and nowhere without her. That remained true, but he and she both wanted more. He saw no prospect of that in London. She could have him in London without money and status or she could have him in Trenton, New Jersey, with good money and relatively high status. Or, clearly implied but not spoken, she could do something to help them transcend this cruel choice.[33]

Esther understood, agreed, and, by implication, accepted growing responsibility for finding a way to bring Joseph to her. "Thank you most sincerely for the frankness with which you expressed your sentiments. It is far from being impolitick. Indeed, it answers [a or the] better end for it makes me repose a confidence in you . . . which nothing can move." Three weeks later, she reiterated her understanding and supported his conditions for returning to London. "I should be unworthy [of your love] if I wished you to live here in an unhappy situation which must be if you were unknown and unregarded."[34]

Now, once again they agreed, but their new agreement rested on a more candid and more realistic foundation. Joseph would return to London to finish his studies, and they would marry, live in London, and Joseph would pursue his profession. Both would work to ensure the independence and éclat they desired, and Esther would play a major part in bringing all of this to fruition. She also knew that time was her enemy. The longer Joseph stayed in New Jersey and prospered, the greater the difficulty in matching that status in London.

Joseph's response initially energized her. In the next few months, she badgered him with suggestions and plans that again illustrate for us her growth in political and commercial sophistication. She encouraged him to tell her father: "You depend on him to watch for an opportunity to introduce you in England." She lamented that Lord Dartmouth's resignation from office deprived her family of one of its principal patrons. She cautioned Joseph about a man from New York whom she had previously praised. She admitted that her family could do little to help Joseph in his pursuit of a patronage position in New Jersey. She briefly discussed the colonial agencies in New Jersey and in the Three Lower Counties (later the state of Delaware), but she talked far more about the one in Massachusetts, which was becoming the focus of her father's own interest and hope.[35]

The situation in Boston was complex. The royal governor and the popularly elected legislature disagreed on who should represent the colony in London. The governor continued to support Jackson, the current agent who had lost much popular support because of his failure to anticipate and then help solve the Stamp Act crisis. The Massachusetts legislature had then turned to DeBerdt for help and employed him as an ad hoc agent for conveying its concerns to London. Now that the crisis was over, DeBerdt hoped that the legislature would put him into Jackson's place. Esther, with Sayre's encouragement, had come to hope that that would happen, and that her father would call Joseph to London and appoint him his deputy. In September, she reported that the Massachusetts legislature continued to send business to her father as need arose, and she speculated on whether DeBerdt could expect a "stated salary."[36]

Meanwhile, a visitor from America complicated Esther's efforts. Richard Stockton of Princeton, New Jersey, charmed her, and then distracted, annoyed, and possibly deceived her. At the same time, however, he added to her growing political sophistication by reminding her that most Americans came to London looking for something, that many of her American visitors saw her and her family as a portal into the corridors of power in the metropolis, that the most charming and ingratiating Americans were not always candid, and that at least some of them had come to London to compete for the very opportunities that might facilitate Joseph's return to her.

Despite her discomfort and anger, or possibly because of it, she had emerged from her brief encounter with this charming and talented man from Joseph's area of America a politically wiser young woman. By December, she noted that Stockton was still around, "very much taken up at the other end of town" and visiting the DeBerdts only when he suspected that they had news from America.[37]

But through the fall of 1766, Esther found her overall situation had deteriorated, and before the end of their second year of separation her enthusiasm and her initial confidence had begun to wane. She and her mother continued to talk about "many schemes," but little had come of any of them. Back in July, at the height of her excitement, she had chided Joseph for his impatience and reminded him that they "were young enough to wait." Two months later, she thought differently. The approach of her birthday (in October) brought back fond memories of their previous times together at Enfield and in London. It also reminded her of the passage of time. In a few weeks, she would turn twenty, and she reminded Joseph, "It is now above three years since our Intimate Friendship first began." She again realized that she and her family had not yet done much to move things ahead, and on her worst days she reverted to her earlier passive position, shifting responsibility back to Joseph. Expecting Sayre to visit Philadelphia soon, she wrote, "I wish between you [Joseph and Sayre], you could contrive some scheme which could be executed either here or in America" to bring Joseph back to London.[38]

By early November, she reported, "our dear friend" Stephen Sayre predicted that Massachusetts will appoint DeBerdt as its new agent and that DeBerdt will need "some active person to assist him," but she remained skeptical. At the same time, Joseph's activities in New Jersey continued to remind her that time worked against her. Joseph had sought to "get a place in America about the Paper Currency" (a paid New Jersey patronage appointment), and that heightened her fears. The more entangled and attached he became there, the more difficult his return to her would be. Now, despairing that they would never have their wish, she sadly wrote, "I must still hope that we shall one day meet again."[39]

Esther's health also deteriorated. She had suffered periodical medical difficulties in the two years since Joseph left. She had been sick throughout her months at Bath in the spring of 1765. The following summer, the sunshine, flowers, trees, and riding at Enfield had revived her. In August of that year, she had reported, "I enjoy it [good health] much better than when you left me, but . . . my old complaint of the headache sometimes trouble[s] me." Dr. Morgan's prescriptions helped get her through the winter of 1765–66, and then the yearly cycle began again. She had gained weight in the summer of 1766 and reported, "It's now about three weeks since I have [had] any serious fit of the headache," but by November she reported, "My health is as usual" (i.e., not very good).[40]

In this already troubled situation, a new crisis overwhelmed her. In mid-November, her father developed a serious illness, and the doctor and the family feared for his life. His death would devastate Esther on a personal level, but it would also destroy her hopes for a future with Joseph in London. Equally important, even if DeBerdt survived, news of his illness could erode his influence in London, make his own creditors anxious about their funds, and destroy his prospects for the Massachusetts agency. In desperation, Esther wrote to Joseph, "Now you must be my Father as well as my Friend."[41]

A number of undated notes Esther wrote to herself at the time provide us with a glimpse into her inner turmoil, and especially her religious sensibilities. Although the notes reveal no order and contain much redundancy, taken together they show us her perception of her afflictions, her catalog of the sins for which, she believed, she had incurred God's displeasure, and her prayers for help.[42]

Clearly, God was heaping coals on her head. Her father's illness had brought him "near to the borders of the grave," and his "worldly affairs in Trade" have suffered catastrophic reverses that threaten to "destroy his respect and his credit." Joseph remained separated from her "by 3,000 miles" of ocean, and God seemed to have "shut up every way" for him to return to her. She feared that they might never meet again in this life but prayed that they would be happy together in heaven.[43]

She blamed herself for God's displeasure. She worried that she would have "forfeited... my soul and must perish forever" were it not for the "meritorious life and atoning death" of Jesus Christ, and she castigated herself for her failure to appreciate fully her own sinfulness: "Oh, that my sins were more my burthen," she lamented. She chastised herself for the sin of pride: pride in her "supposed accomplishments," pride in her undue "confidence in creatures" rather than in the God who made them, pride in forgetting "the changing nature of all earthly enjoyments," pride in allowing her attachment to Joseph to "draw away my Love and affection for... God," pride for raising too high "expectations of some future period of my life in this world," and the pride that led her to refuse what God had planned for her. "I did not ask counsel of God in the beginning of this important transaction." She had not controlled the "impatient flame" that had "taken possession of my Heart," and "before I was afflicted in this respect [i.e., before Joseph departed] I indeed went astray and was grown carnal and secure."[44]

She prayed that "I may have an humble heart," "that I may know how frail I am," and that she might understand God's chastisements as his "kind hand" teaching her that there is to be no ultimate happiness in this world. She prayed also that Joseph "may have a Heart to know and serve" God, that he may "seek first the Kingdom of Heaven and the Righteousness [thereof]," that he "may have an interest in Jesus," and that he may be "brought back to this country with comfortable circumstances." Finally, she begged God to help her in the "important affair lying before me which my dear and absent friend has committed to my determination," a task on which her "future settlement" in life depended.[45]

It was December 1766, the second anniversary of their renewed courtship and the third year of her passion for Joseph. She was twenty years old. Her family teetered on the brink of disaster, and Joseph's return to her seemed less and less likely. This accumulation of obstacles to a future life with the man she loved had again pushed her close to despair. But despair did not conquer her. The same accumulation of impediments in time drove her to action.

During the late stages of her father's illness, Esther and her mother took the initiative to protect his reputation, to advance the family's interests, and to bring Joseph to London as a lawyer and as Esther's husband. The two of them narrowed their focus to winning the appointment of DeBerdt as the regular agent for Massachusetts with the full salary and with Joseph as his legal assistant.

While the goal was straightforward, the means to achieve it were complicated and serpentine. Esther explained it all to Joseph in her letter of December 12. They wanted Joseph to become a "little more known in Boston," and they wanted him to ask Sayre "to tell his friends [in Boston] that Mr. DeBerdt intends to have a young gentleman of the law . . . to assist him in his agency." She admitted that neither she nor her mother had shared any of this with DeBerdt, and they wanted Joseph to have Sayre "mention it [the plan] to my Pappa to have his approbation before he says anything in public" and to ask "whether it would not be best to add that he [the young and energetic lawyer] was to be his son-in-law."[46]

To put it another way, Esther and her mother wanted Joseph first to build up his own image in Boston, then to ask Sayre to propose to DeBerdt that Sayre let it be known in Boston that DeBerdt was enhancing his own competitive position in the contest for the agency by appointing as his deputy a young and energetic American lawyer who was also to be his daughter's husband.

The plan was both ambitions and audacious. At its heart, this was a political plan dependent on the shrewd assessment and careful manipulation of influence and connections in three widely separated and markedly different parts of the British Atlantic empire: London, Boston, and Trenton. In addition, the uncertainties of the empire itself and the accelerating conflicts between London and America added complexities and uncertainties. The colonies and the mother country had settled their dispute over the Stamp Act, but the Townshend duties would soon reignite the issue of taxation with incalculable consequences for Esther, her family in London, and Joseph in America. But, still, they had a plan: something concrete to work with.

Its advantages were clear. Esther and her mother were for the first time actively collaborating to push forward a scheme that could go far to solve DeBerdt's financial problems and bring Joseph to London as Esther's husband. The expected £1,000 annual salary would rebuild the family's finances while making them less dependent on the vagaries of the Atlantic trade during these times of political disruption. Joseph would come to London as a lawyer. And DeBerdt would give his official endorsement to Esther's marriage to Joseph.

The plan's success, however, depended on linking a long succession of contingencies, each of which was necessary, each of which was problematic, and some of which would, at least on the surface, run counter to the current intentions and predispositions of one or more of the key players. Still, it was a plan, and Esther was determined to pursue it. After one year of passivity and self-indulgent suffering, and a second year of experimentation, frustration, and disappointment, she had moved beyond working to evade her father's authority. Her efforts to communicate with Joseph had enhanced her knowledge of the commercial shipping patterns within the British Atlantic world and of the men who commanded Great Britain's oceangoing vessels. Still, she had made little progress in bringing Joseph back to her in London. Now, at age twenty, this determined and clever young woman, working under the tutelage of her mother, was coming to see how she might manipulate the patron/client politics of Georgian England to advance her own ends. The next step was to put that new political understanding to work.

CHAPTER 5

Politics
Old World Patronage

Esther's success depended on her ability to manage the complex interactions of three men: her "friend" Stephen Sayre, whose attentions seemed to hurt more than they helped; her love, Joseph, whose success in America impeded his return to her; and her father, Dennys DeBerdt, whose preference for Sayre over Joseph combined with his own mounting financial difficulties made him a reluctant and ineffectual supporter of his daughter's wishes. The political and economic volatility of the empire, on both the local and the imperial level, exacerbated the situation. The Townshend Acts (1767) again led Americans to boycott British goods and to hold back payment on debts to British merchants. This economic pressure had produced political results. In 1770, Parliament repealed the Townshend Acts (all but the tax on tea). But, in the meantime, the colonial economic-political war on London merchants had driven the DeBerdt firm to the brink of bankruptcy, greatly complicating Esther's life as she stepped forward to solve her problem and to recalibrate her aspirations.

Stephen Sayre told Esther over and over that he intended to help, but whether by accident or by intent his efforts seemed best suited to advance his cause at her expense. He proclaimed himself a friend, first to Joseph, and then to Esther, and, within his limits, he probably told the truth. Esther seems to have taken him at his word. But Sayre was all artifice: an "active gallant," "a remarkably attractive charmer," soft-spoken, good-humored, and sympathetic—in his own words, a "rascal."[1]

Born into a modest tanner's family in rustic Long Island in 1736, Sayre propelled himself from obscurity to the margins of wealth, respectability, and power at the center of the empire: London. He began his odyssey at the College of New Jersey (later Princeton University) in 1756 and graduated the next year with Joseph, possibly his cousin. In rapid succession, he captained a New York militia company on the Niagara frontier, embroiled himself in dispute with his men over pay, returned to college for a master's degree in 1760, and then worked with two or three different merchants in New York City. In 1762, one of them, William Alexander, sent him to London to argue his cause before the Board of Trade. Once in London, Sayre quickly established himself as a merchant in Tokenhouse Gate near the Bank of London, claimed an annual worth of £600–700 a year, joined the DeBerdt Sunday circle, won the heart of the rich Miss Charlotte Nelthorpe (worth £3,000 a year), and then hurried off to the West Indies to solicit business and collect debts for the firm of DeBerdt and Burkitt. In Saint Croix, he kept in touch with events in London, consoled Joseph when DeBerdt rejected his proposal of marriage to Esther, entertained a rich young woman with a dying husband, failed to entice his fiancée to invest in a sugar plantation, and returned to London in late 1765.[2]

Once back in England, Sayre expected to use Miss Nelthorpe's fortune to buy a partnership in DeBerdt's firm. DeBerdt was eager and Charlotte was willing, but those who controlled her money said no. DeBerdt generously responded by hiring Sayre to go to America to solicit new business and collect old debts.[3]

During his months in London, Sayre also cultivated Miss DeBerdt. She saw him as an old family friend ten years her senior and available for long talks on dreary winter days: the first worldly and experienced adult male with whom she could discuss Joseph and plan strategies for bringing him back.

How Sayre saw Esther is more difficult to say. When he had left London for the West Indies, she had been a girl. Now, she had matured into a beautiful and refined young woman, well read, articulate, informed on public matters, and engaging. She liked him, enjoyed his company, and welcomed him into her confidence. Maybe that was enough for Sayre.

More likely, he also saw Esther as another avenue of access to her father and possibly as an alternative to Miss Nelthorpe, should that young lady fail to meet his financial needs. He wanted to stay in London and prosper there. "I can't bear the thought of living in America or starving in England," he had confessed. He also wanted a "refined Love" with a "girl who may possess my whole heart." He preferred Miss Nelthorpe. Her fortune was larger. But the beautiful young Miss DeBerdt also promised to bring a respectable if somewhat less weighty dowry to the marriage bed. If necessary, Sayre could fall in love with Esther.

In any competition with Joseph for Esther's hand, Sayre had formidable advantages. Joseph was far away in America with little chance of an early return. Equally important, Esther's father loved Sayre. He saw him as a future business partner, a moral guide for young Dennis, and a reliable friend to Esther.[4]

Sayre spent a year and a half in America working for DeBerdt. He returned to London with no money and with little new business. He had wasted the family's already diminished resources, but they greeted him with enthusiastic praise and killed the fatted calf to celebrate his return. He seemed to have mesmerized them all.[5]

Now back in London, Sayre's own situation had changed. He had lost Miss Nelthorpe. She had grown suspicious, inquired more closely into his finances, discovered that he had been deceiving her, and then broke off their engagement. Sayre, now free to seek another marriage partner, told Joseph that, for the benefit of the DeBerdt family, he was considering marrying an old duchess worth £3,000 a year in order to save them all.[6]

Three aspects of his statement deserve close attention. First, Sayre absolved himself of all responsibility for the family's current difficulties, while in reality his fruitless trip to America had exacerbated their problems. Second, he depicted himself as making great personal sacrifices for the benefit of the family, a sacrifice largely at odds with his past patterns. Third, he was once again active in the marriage market.

Throughout 1768 and 1769, Sayre's behavior in London continued to raise doubts about his motives. Repeatedly, he urged Joseph to sail for London to claim his loved one, but he frequently couched his appeal in ways that hinted at Esther's wavering commitment while deprecating her monetary value.[7]

In October 1768, he again urged Joseph to hurry but cautioned him to expect no financial help from DeBerdt. The old gentleman had no money and faced "becoming bankrupt." He emphasized the continued deterioration of the family finances, pushed Joseph to come, and exhorted him, "You must not . . . think of breaking your engagement here tho every impossibility may stare you in the face." How did he expect Joseph to interpret this exhortation? Joseph had never suggested deserting Esther.[8]

In all of this, Sayre remains an enigma. Throughout, Esther continued to trust him, at least in her correspondence with Joseph. At best, however, he did nothing to help. At worst, he acted to advance himself while complicating Esther's life and frustrating her ambitions. In either case, at the end of the day, she was no closer to her goal. How much her trust was misplaced we cannot tell. It is also possible that here she was using Sayre much like she had earlier used the male attention at Bath: to continue to test Joseph's commitment. It seems a bit odd that she did not at some point think about why he spent so much time with her. She understood the marriage mores of her society and Sayre's obsession with marrying for money. Conversely, given her commitment to Joseph, and her experience with Richard Stockton from New Jersey, she may well have understood his motives and turned them to her own advantage in ways not obvious to us.

Meanwhile, Joseph had clawed his way back from the precipice in New Jersey. Ironically, the greater his success there, the greater his difficulty in returning to London. Joseph arrived home in April 1765 not quite twenty-four years old and without resources or support. The economic foundation of his family, the firm of Reed and Pettit, had collapsed. Its creditors had seized its remaining assets. The London firm of DeBerdt and Burkitt pressured Reed and Pettit to settle their accounts, including the losses associated with the ship *Britannia* as well as the money Joseph had borrowed from DeBerdt to finance his year at the Inns of Court.[9]

Neither Joseph's father nor his brother-in-law seemed able or willing to confront the crisis. Andrew Reed, angry, irascible, mercurial, but impotent, had retreated into grumbling isolation in rural Amwell, New Jersey, north of Trenton. Pettit, whom Joseph blamed for the fiasco, flailed about, wringing his hands, castigating himself, and dithering before dashing off on a quixotic quest to recover his losses through land speculation in Nova Scotia, an area of the world that even DeBerdt in London knew as a "bleak, barren country."[10]

Joseph's assessment of Pettit's responsibility for the collapse of Reed and Pettit may have been unfair. The firm had expanded both the range and the magnitude of its affairs during the boom years of the war, but Andrew Reed, the senior partner, had acquiesced in its expansion. Also, in its collapse, Reed and Pettit was far from alone. The postwar contraction had driven a number of American firms into bankruptcy, and some of these failures had themselves contributed to the travails of Reed and Pettit. Thus, in a very real sense, this economic disruption was another in a series of crises in the British Empire that would continue to disrupt Joseph and Esther's life over the next decade.[11]

Whatever the causes of the family's financial disaster, Joseph now found himself the sole provider for ten people in three separate households. In addition to himself, he was also responsible for Pettit, who continued to maintain a residence in Philadelphia; his father in Amwell; his brothers, Bowes and John; his teenaged sister, Mary (Polly); and his older half sister, Sally Pettit, and her three small children, who now lived with him in a large, two-story brick house on King Street in Trenton. In addition, Joseph's aunt, Mary Sayre, his dead mother's sister, occasionally importuned him for support.[12]

Sally Pettit's presence in Joseph's household was a mixed blessing. A few weeks after her arrival in August 1765, she gave birth to another child. She had an additional child shortly before she moved out three years later. Joseph had taken her into his house "much against my inclination," and he continued to hope that her husband would soon take full responsibility for his own wife and children. Pettit visited but showed little promise of taking Sally and her children off Joseph's hands.[13]

Conversely, Sally certainly enriched Joseph's life. In late eighteenth-century America, husbands and wives created reciprocal, mutually beneficial family economies in which each contributed essential support in ways consistent with reproductive responsibility and prescribed gender roles. Sally, Joseph's older half sister and the well-experienced head of her own household, undoubtedly managed Joseph's household well, and along with Joseph's teenage sister, Polly, contributed far more than their share. Joseph's frustration after Sally's departure suggests the degree to which he had come to depend on her. He asked her to stay for a few months after her husband had made ready their new home in Burlington in the spring of 1768 and pestered her for help months after she left.[14]

To cope with his new responsibilities and to amass the resources necessary to return to Esther in London, Joseph had considerable, if largely intangible, assets. Trenton was his hometown. He had been born and raised there. He, like his father, was closely linked with the Presbyterians, one of the major denominations in the area. His father, widely known in the mercantile community of the Delaware River valley, had managed his bankruptcy in an orderly fashion. Reed and Pettit had negotiated with its creditors, who now had a vested interest in supporting the efficient liquidation of the firm's debts, and the reputation of the two former partners escaped intact. Andrew himself still held some assets in his own name.[15]

Joseph's mother's family also carried weight in the Trenton area. Theodosia Bowes Reed had married Andrew shortly after the death of Andrew's first wife. Her father, Francis Bowes, had been prominent in business and in iron manufacturing in Hunterdon County, just north of Trenton, and through the Bowes family Joseph had a connection to the local Anglican community. He also maintained contact with his mother's two sisters. Theodosia Bowes Reed named her second son Bowes, suggesting the importance, at least in her mind, of her family connection.[16]

Joseph's profession elevated him far above the run-of-the-mill young men in his region. His study with Richard Stockton had linked him with one of the more prominent families in New Jersey, and his education at the College of New Jersey (Princeton) differentiated him from most of his fellow lawyers in the province. His year at the Inns of Court added a credential and an image that few in New Jersey could match. While in London, he had corresponded with some of New Jersey's more notable businessmen and public officials, including Sheriff Samuel Tucker of Trenton and William Franklin, royal governor of New Jersey.[17]

Immediately after his return to America, Joseph put these assets to work. Pettit had assumed that the younger and less experienced man would welcome his counsel. He tried to advise Joseph on business matters, and he sought to mediate the explosive exchanges between Joseph and Andrew Reed. Joseph, like his father and his own younger brother, Bowes, did not take easily to subordination or condescension. Soon, he and Pettit had reversed roles. Joseph decided the course, and Pettit did his best to carry out Joseph's decisions.[18]

Under Joseph's direction, his family gained a sense of order. By midsummer 1765, he reported to Esther that he was doing well, and over the course of the next year others reported much the same to her. As a silver lining, the economic difficulties that had subverted his family's commercial business, and ruined many others as well, also generated business conflicts that provided work for lawyers.[19]

In early winter, imperial affairs again set him back. The Stamp Act, passed in March 1765, went into effect in November. New Jersey's stamp distributor, however, had resigned, and New Jersey's legal community ceased "to do business in Court" until after news of repeal in March 1766. The courts closed, and Joseph's business stagnated. He reported in January 1766 that he could have easily met his extended family's needs but for this politically based economic disruption.[20]

Better times soon came, and his ascent continued. According to one source, by 1767 Joseph "stood . . . with the most eminent men in the Province." Old friends now saw him as a threat. Richard Stockton had been Joseph's mentor and friend, one of a small number of those in New Jersey who addressed him in letters as "Josie." Less than a year after Joseph's return from London, Stockton had come to regard Joseph as a serious rival. In London in the summer of 1766, he did what he could to undermine Joseph's reputation with the DeBerdts, and when he returned to America in 1767 his relationship with Joseph continued to deteriorate. The young Joseph Reed had become a force to be reckoned with in New Jersey.[21]

Joseph estimated his legal income in April 1767 at £1,000 per year, an extraordinary sum in a world in which the typical working family in Philadelphia lived on about £25 a year or a well-to-do family in London could employ a full-time servant for about the same amount. In 1759, the royal governor of New Jersey, Francis Bernard, earned £800 annually and the next year £1,000 when he became royal governor of Massachusetts. Joseph's expenditures also suggest his growing affluence. He had acquired horses, a carriage, and at least one slave.[22] He purchased an additional horse for Pettit and invested some £6,000 in land in New York, Pennsylvania, and New Jersey. His law office brought him more work than he could handle alone. He employed his brothers, Bowes and John, and at least one other full-time clerk.[23]

Joseph paid a price for this success. He worked long hours, and on occasion well past midnight. Like most of his legal colleagues, he also followed the migration of the circuit court from county to county in New Jersey and Pennsylvania. Typically, he would spend a week, more or less, in each of a number of different local courts collecting clients, pleading cases, eating on the run, and sleeping in strange beds before returning home to a house full of dependents. He reported little of his social life to Esther and complained to her that "the fatigue of business impairs his constitution." He had fallen sick in the summer of 1765 and again in the fall of 1766. This latter bout of the "Ague," while less severe, lingered on for months. Well into the spring of 1767, he continued to take "The Bark." Esther worried about who took care of him during his illness, and Sally's presence pleased her.[24]

Joseph quickly acquired a reputation as a brilliant and successful litigator enjoying significant status in New Jersey and in the Philadelphia area. That income and that reputation, however, were geographically rooted and not easily transported to London. He needed a means to transcend that limitation, and early in 1766 he began to construct a package of enterprises beyond his legal practice that would allow him to continue to support his family in America and also settle permanently in London with Esther.

Joseph took the first step in that direction when he won the post of deputy secretary for the province of New Jersey in 1767. The secretary served as clerk of the Governor's Council, clerk of the provincial Supreme Court, clerk of the provincial Surrogates Court, and keeper of the registrations and records. The crown appointed the secretary, who usually remained in England and hired a deputy in the provinces to do the actual work. By April 1767, Joseph had successfully negotiated with the current secretary, Maurice Morgann, to serve as his deputy.[25]

The details of that negotiation remain obscure, but in broad strokes Joseph had competed vigorously for the position, and in time both the New Jersey Provincial Council and the royal governor, William Franklin, had cooperated. The DeBerdt family played a supportive but minor part. When Joseph had first mentioned it to Esther in mid-1766, she reported that her father knew nothing about the office but would help as he could. Lord Dartmouth's resignation in August, however, deprived DeBerdt of his principal patron, and from November until early the next year, DeBerdt's protracted poor health immobilized him. During the intervening months, Esther reported to Joseph what little she could learn. In the spring, DeBerdt signed the final agreement for Joseph and posted the necessary performance bonds, but throughout he had done little to win the prize for Joseph.[26]

The appointment illustrated Joseph's rising prominence in New Jersey and further enhanced his access to power. More importantly, it freed him from most of his responsibilities for his extended family and provided him with a regular income he could take to London. Joseph performed some of the deputy's duties himself for £30 a year, while Charles Pettit oversaw the office in Burlington and a nonfamily member handled things in Perth Amboy. By the summer of 1767, Pettit had established a home in Burlington, and Sally and the children had joined him. Bowes and John worked there for Pettit. Joseph's immediate responsibilities now included only his sister, Polly, and his father. Equally important, Joseph calculated that after paying Pettit and his two brothers, and taking his own £30 salary, he would still have an additional profit of £100 a year, a profit that could serve as the first piece in the package he needed to support himself and a family in London.[27]

By the end of 1767, Joseph had performed a near miracle. In two and a half years, he had brought his family back from the edge of the abyss. Joseph had also won DeBerdt's grudging acceptance of his interest in Esther as well as the family's tacit recognition that it would lead to marriage at some undefined point in the future. Although not a formal engagement, Esther's mother and brother used that or similar phrases when they spoke of Esther's relation to Joseph. Even DeBerdt himself on rare occasions spoke of his daughter's engagement to Joseph.[28]

Most men would have been well pleased with themselves, but Joseph's extraordinary success had not yet provided him with sufficient means to rejoin Esther. He needed a way to earn an appropriate and independent income in London, and by now both he and Esther had come to believe that her father and his political connections in Boston and London held the key to that end.

DeBerdt's intentions remained obscure and his behavior inconsistent. In the end, his efforts on their behalf bore little fruit. As Joseph prospered and Esther's attachment persisted, DeBerdt's attitude had softened. He hinted, implied, and encouraged but made no promises and produced nothing tangible. At times, he seemed more interested in using Joseph for his own purposes, especially to collect money from his American debtors, including the defunct firm of Reed and Pettit.[29]

On a personal level, DeBerdt still preferred Sayre. He had known Sayre first. He had incorporated Sayre into his family business and saw Sayre as a pillar of strength and virtue to whom he could entrust the future of his family. In 1766, he wrote, "He is a man after my own Heart who will take my Son by the Hand and animate Him to fill up my Place in the Church and the World when I shall be no more." Two years later, Esther wrote to tell Joseph that her father believed that Sayre "would prove as Father to his Son when he was [gone]." In sharp contrast, DeBerdt expressed no such feelings about Joseph. Rather, he appeared to hope that Joseph would prosper alone in America as an energetic lawyer advancing the legal claims of the DeBerdt family while Stephen Sayre in London assumed responsibility for managing the DeBerdt family finances, molding the moral character and the business acumen of the young Dennis, and caring for Esther, quite possibly marrying her.[30] Esther, however, continued to think about how to use the imperial patronage system to bring Joseph back to her. From early on, she had focused principally on obtaining a colonial agency for Joseph as the most attractive option.[31]

From December 1766, the Massachusetts agency had attracted the bulk of her father's attention and remained the center of Esther's hopes. The legislature of the province favored him, but opposition from the royal governor and the governor's council prevented the legislature from converting DeBerdt's special or partial appointment into a regular one with a fixed and substantial salary. By 1768, Esther's father and the province of Massachusetts seemed to offer slim hopes for Esther's plan.[32]

Meanwhile, imperial politics compounded Esther's problems by threatening to destroy her family's financial base. The Stamp Act crisis in 1765–66 and the controversy over the Townshend duties between 1767 and 1770 disrupted trade and distressed the finances of many English merchants trading to America. DeBerdt, a prominent member of this exclusive and once prosperous group, suffered severely. The crux of the problem was the colonial response to the stamp tax and the Townshend duties. Many colonists boycotted imports and refused to pay their debts to the London merchants. Even in the years between the two disputes, some American firms could not pay. They, like Reed and Pettit, had gone to the wall. Other firms chose not to pay, withholding money not from necessity or principle but to evade their legitimate responsibilities.

But, whether American mercantile houses failed to pay their debts for political or pecuniary reasons, DeBerdt suffered. Esther reported to Joseph that throughout 1767 the family was under great financial distress "for want of ... remittances" from America. Trade looked up a bit late in 1767, and the arrival late in the year of £1,000 that Charles Pettit and Joseph had collected from DeBerdt's debtors helped considerably, but 1768 offered DeBerdt little real recovery, and by 1769 the firm teetered on the brink of bankruptcy.[33]

Esther and Joseph wanted to marry, to live comfortably, and to enjoy a modest degree of recognition. In America, Joseph's extraordinary success had freed him from much of his financial responsibility for his extended family, and the post of deputy secretary provided an important step to bringing him back to Esther, but by itself it could not support them in London. Despite Esther's best efforts, her collaboration with her mother to manipulate DeBerdt and to use the byzantine world of the patron-client politics of Georgian England failed to augment that first step, nor did any realistic assessment of the financial status of her family promise success in the immediate future. The chances for an early and happy union of these two young people seemed remote until Esther, in the summer of 1768, took control.

Until mid-1767, she had been willing to wait: somewhat dissatisfied but not impatient. She had written endlessly about her love for Joseph and her anticipation of their future together, but she had not actually pressed him to return quickly and marry her. Indeed, when in early 1767 Joseph had told her, "Say but the word, my Charmer, and I shall be with you," she had demurred, urging patience.[34]

But as she moved toward her twenty-first birthday in October 1767, her letters suggest a subtle shift in attitude. She began to write more specifically about marriage. In June 1767, she mentioned that her mother, Martha, wanted Joseph to repay Martha's long devotion to their cause by "making me a husband." In October, she asked, "How long will it be before I can let them [friends and family] know whom I have distinguished . . . as the companion of my future life?" In February 1768, she declared she was ready to "resign my Liberty into your hands." Six weeks later, she looked forward to the time when her dear friend "will take me by the hand and assist me to perform every duty which lays in my way."[35]

In these same months, Esther assured Joseph again and again that he had no rivals. Do not "entertain any suspicion of my constancy. It would be inconsistent with honor." She reminded him that all their difficulties had "never made me entertain a wish that it [their connection] should terminate but with our lives." Her love had "stood the trial of absence" and led her to reject "many solicitations." He had nothing to fear from rivals who "tho in some circumstances suitable are very far from having the least share in my Love." Some of these comforting statements came in response to Joseph's expressed concern, but some of his expressed concerns came from her reminders that she had waited a long time and that many other suitors waited in the wings.[36]

Whatever her intention, Joseph came to see her reassurances as hints that she had changed her mind. He responded gallantly, if a bit melodramatically. He assured her that if her love had ceased, he would rather hear it from her than from strangers, and that if she had changed, she should say so and "not let honor bind what love has unloosed."[37]

Joseph's words, in turn, surprised and disturbed her. At first, she worried that he, rather than she, had found another. She wrote to tell him that if that were the case, he should tell her. But before Joseph could respond to her doubts, probably before her letter had reached him, she confronted the issue head on, and in that way largely determined the course of their future together.[38]

In her letter of July 4, 1768, she momentarily considered ending the connection. She declared her eternal love and fidelity but wrote, "If this obstacle [folded over] to our happiness do appear insurmountable to you, my will shall be yours, and we must leave the hand of time to erase the traces characters of our mutual friendship." Then she abruptly pulled back, "But oh my dear Friend how does my heart recoil [folded over] . . . no. It must be otherwise. . . . Providence will sure smile on us and give us the opportunity of joining our hands since it has united our hearts."[39]

Then, after resigning their fate to Providence, she again took over and defined what in later letters she called her "scheme." Joseph must not stay in America until everything "is quite right." That will never happen. Joseph must come now. She saw no reason to wait, even for a year. Boston, she recognized, remained uncertain, but it looked as if her father's temporary appointment may continue to the end of his life at £300 a year. He would not now make a promise to Joseph about sharing that money, but Esther expected he was actually counting on Joseph's help. Joseph's share of the Boston money, as Esther called it, combined with his income from the job as deputy secretary would give him a base in London. If all else failed, he must bring enough money to support himself for a year at the temple. They would postpone their marriage until he had completed his studies and established his law practice in London. Soon, she was lining up future legal work in London for Joseph.[40]

She admitted that this all sounded rather "romantic" and suspected that her father would disapprove, but that did not daunt her. She instructed Joseph to tell her father that he was simply coming to England for a visit in order to negotiate the details of a land speculation scheme. Once there, something would work out. She knew she was asking Joseph to "run some chance," and she appreciated that he was giving up a secure and successful situation in return for "uncertainty," but she wanted him to do it immediately and to do it for her. "An advocate within my Breast as well as your repeated assurances convince me that you will make some sacrifice of applause and éclat in the world to her whose faithfulness and affection [in] some sort demands."[41]

Esther's age undoubtedly played a part in this dramatic shift. Now, no longer a teenaged girl but a mature woman, she wanted a household of her own and the privileges of the married state. "We, in the bloom of Life most capable to taste the joys of a refined and delicate friendship, yet separated," she wrote.[42]

Her father's health also urged haste. She loved her father. His loss would devastate her. On a more practical level, it would dramatically increase her vulnerability. Like her father, she had little confidence in her brother's ability to head the family. Joseph alone could care for her. But Joseph needed to come before her father died. He "could introduce you with ease into the World, and such an introduction we cannot reasonably hope from any other quarter."[43]

Another factor may have also been in play in her thinking. Joseph was emerging as one of the most eligible bachelors in the province of New Jersey, indeed in the Delaware River valley. He gave her no hint that he ever thought about other women or that other women thought about him. Still, she would not have been human had she herself not thought about possible competitors in America. That may help explain something she wrote in the spring of 1768: "Jealousy that . . . canker worm which would make absence [insupportable] has never once entered my breast." But, if so, why bring it up?[44]

Joseph responded positively to her "scheme" in October 1768. She had asked. He had agreed. He would risk all for her.[45] There could have been no doubt in his mind about the risks. Success depended on the happy conjunction of a number of improbable events. DeBerdt had promised, or at least had appeared to promise, £100 a year, but only his continued health and the viability of his firm would make that possible. Joseph's income as the deputy secretary depended on his ability to renegotiate the contract and to shift the title temporarily to Pettit without a loss of income. A year of study at the temple would not guarantee him clients in London. If everything worked out well, Esther and Joseph could marry and establish an independent family in London. But failure and disaster would never be far away.

Then, to add to further uncertainty, Esther informed Joseph that they could expect no dowry, at least not until trade and her family's finances improved. Esther's news was worse than Sayre had earlier anticipated in his cautions to Joseph. Referring to her dowry as "a fortune," Esther told Joseph that it "is not possible for my dear Father to give at present." This news heightened Joseph's awareness of DeBerdt's financial difficulties and his own. And to the degree that the marriage mores of his culture guided his thinking, this news would have significantly reduced the value of the prize for which he now planned to gamble his hard-won success in New Jersey.[46]

By then, Joseph had decided. He had said yes. Soon they would be together. It took more than a year for them to work out the details. Some questions were mundane: important but not decisive. Would he bring Polly? Would he bring his slave?[47] Would he sell or rent out his Trenton house? How soon would they marry? Other issues were of more significance. Was the New Jersey agency still an option? And what about the Massachusetts agency? And, possibly a deal breaker, could Joseph renegotiate his contract with Morgann to permit Pettit to replace Joseph as the official deputy while Joseph made a "visit" to London?[48]

On a different plane, Esther continued to remind Joseph about the importance of collecting DeBerdt's American debts, adding new urgency. Joseph's success in this endeavor, she wrote in January 1769, "will conduce more to our ease and happiness than you can imagine." She apologized for laying this "burden" on him, and she recognized its "disagreeable" nature, "especially as it [the debts] lie chiefly among your acquaintances," but the DeBerdts needed the money and they relied on Joseph, their lawyer, to collect it. Esther had little sympathy for these American debtors, especially now that their recalcitrance threatened her future with Joseph. "I am sure they do not exert themselves as they might," she commented in March.[49]

While Esther and Joseph negotiated these and other details of their immediate future, Esther lowered her levels of aspiration and nudged Joseph toward the same end. They principally sought a happy union. All other things took second place. She had taken a hesitant step in this direction in September 1767 in her discussion of how much money they needed to maintain an independent household in London. "Our expectations and hopes of Happiness are far from being founded on grandeur and riches," she wrote. She and Joseph needed only a "competency," she thought, but she shifted the decision to him. "Can you taste happiness under these circumstances?" she asked.[50]

Six months later, she took on the question of distinction and reputation. "Happiness does not accompany those who spend their time and talents in pursuit of ambition or a desire of making an éclat in the world," she declared. Not so long ago, she and Joseph had been far from indifferent to "making an éclat in the world." Now, determined to marry and to spend their "future . . . together . . . enjoying the sweet pleasures of domestic happiness," she would forgo the "many ingredients" that the "superficial thotless world may suppose we want" and "make our Religion our Virtue" and "smile with indifference on that they falsely call happiness." Then, in her most important and significant concession, she hinted that, all else failing, she might reconsider her position on going to America.[51]

And here, in September 1769, as she was approaching her twenty-third birthday, Esther articulated for Joseph, and thereby for us, her priorities and her understanding of the context within which she was working while illustrating again the knowledge and skills she brought to the task. She was now ready and determined to marry the young man she had chosen for herself at age seventeen and, if necessary, to forgo "grandeur and riches," "world éclat," and even London itself in order to unite with him in the full "bloom of life," to "taste [with him] the joys of refined and delicate friendship," and to spend her life with him enjoying "the sweet pleasures of domestic happiness" that depended on the virtue prescribed by her religious beliefs and nurtured by the love of the God she worshipped.

To this lifework she brought a detailed knowledge of her father's transatlantic import/export business and a sophisticated understanding of the British patron/client political system. She had a way with words and with people, as well as a growing skepticism about the motives of those men who sought her company. Finally, she had determined to take charge of her life and, in union with Joseph, to build a God-centered family to which she would sacrifice all but virtue and, if absolutely necessary, to do all of that in America.

But Joseph had made coming to America unnecessary. By midsummer 1769, he had his affairs in order. He spent two months in Boston while the Massachusetts General Court reappointed DeBerdt as its agent over his two strong rivals, and then he returned to Philadelphia. He was ready to leave for England. His father's health delayed him, and then on the eve of his father's death he announced his own imminent departure. He left behind "the company of friends . . . connections of nature . . . my native country and whatever is thought dearest in life—to return and give you this last and greatest proof of my affection." But contrary to Joseph's expectation, his love for Esther soon placed far greater demands on him.[52]

CHAPTER 6

Love Defeats Prudence

Joseph's odyssey from Philadelphia to his love in London began poorly—and then spiraled into disaster. The weather on this winter crossing, the low quality of his traveling companions, bad luck, and possibly the incompetence of the mariners account for much of his early distress. More importantly, Joseph's recent political activities in opposition to British policies had contributed to the disaster that awaited him in London. The boycott of British imports that he had championed had played a part in the collapse of the DeBerdt firm. Meanwhile, Esther, apparently safe and secure in London, had eagerly anticipated his arrival and their life together in London. Instead, by the time he arrived, Esther and her family had been reduced to penury, her resources gone and her prospects for the future bleak. Coping with that tragedy tested both of them: their love, their resolve, and their ingenuity.

In America, Joseph spent "two very disagreeable days on the Pilot [boat]" waiting for a fair wind. Once on board his ship, he found his accommodations "very indifferent"; the company was not much better. He felt confined in his small quarters, and the rough seas made him sick for much of the trip. Mercifully, the crossing was quick: twenty-eight days from land to land. But the land on which he landed was not the land he sought. The ship, headed for Liverpool, ran aground off the Irish coast, twenty miles from Newry.[1]

When the ship finally made port, it needed repairs. Joseph fumed and fussed. Irritable and fatigued from his rough crossing, he found the Irish country and the Irish people annoying. He had not, he wrote home to Pettit, "experienced the slightest mark of that hospitality for which the Irish have been remarkable." "Even if I had no particular inducement to hasten ... away," he continued, "I would make my stay short."[2] "Unsure when the vessel would sail" and "very impatient to be up to London," Joseph went on ahead to Dublin. With luck, he would return to the ship and "go with my baggage" to Liverpool. If not, he would take a packet boat across the Irish Sea to Holyhead and then hurry overland to London, leaving his baggage to follow.[3]

In Dublin, Joseph's disposition improved. Rested and again on the move, he found the Irish more likeable and the future more promising. And there was great news: the British government had repealed the Townshend taxes, all save that on tea. That pleased Joseph. The British had again backed down in the face of the vigorous colonial resistance, resistance that Joseph had supported. More pleasing, Joseph found, "the people of this country are fully on our side," and they "consider us fellow sufferers." Most pleasing yet, he expected to be in London in three or four days. Although "a horrible storm in the Channel" kept him in Dublin for the day, he planned to "go over to [illegible] tomorrow and so up to London by way of Chester."[4]

Then, catastrophe struck. The London papers reported that Esther's father, Dennys DeBerdt, had died. Joseph's future disappeared. He tried to share this unbelievable news with Pettit but found his mind "so agitated I scarcely know what to write." He had counted on DeBerdt for his immediate source of income in London and for his long-term hope of patronage and prosperity. Without DeBerdt, Joseph could not stay in London. "God knows what effect this melancholy event will have on my life," he told Pettit, "but I think it not unlikely you will soon see me in America."[5]

Anxious about Esther, about her family, and about his own prospects, he left Dublin the next day, crossed the Irish Sea, and then rode night and day through Wales and the English West Country to London. There, he found the situation worse than he had imagined. "Everything in confusion," he told Pettit.[6] Esther, his "dear girl, was almost worn out with sorrow and fatigue."

In the weeks between her father's death and Joseph's arrival, Esther and her mother had struggled with grief, with funeral arrangements, and with the business crisis that DeBerdt's death had precipitated. Mrs. DeBerdt, one of the executors of DeBerdt's will, remained fairly optimistic about the family's financial future, but soon they were meeting with the creditors of the firm and trouble began to loom. Esther's brother, Dennis, appears to have played a minor role at best, and DeBerdt's partners, Sayre and Burkitt, distanced themselves from the negotiations.

From Joseph's correspondence home, it appears that when he arrived, Martha and Esther initially shared with him responsibility for working out the legal details of settling the estate, and then the two women left for Enfield, a village about twelve miles from London where the DeBerdts had summered for the past twenty years. Now, they were in large part retreating from the embarrassment of their declining situation. Joseph himself also spent much of his time there, planning their strategy with Esther and her mother, and traveling back and forth to the city to negotiate the details of the settlement.[7] He needed their knowledge of the firm and its relationship with its creditors, and they relied on his legal training.

The business affairs of Dennys DeBerdt's firm, now DeBerdt, Burkitt, and Sayre, appalled Joseph. "It is impossible to describe to you," he wrote to Pettit, "the wretched management of this counting house [i.e., the business office]." "No kind of attention whatever to business." The senior partner, DeBerdt, "quite exhausted and worn out" with age, "has given little attention to business for some time." The other two partners, Burkitt and Sayre, were "encumbrances on the firm." "Mr. Burkitt," the elder partner, "is a man of very narrow defective abilities." Stephen Sayre, DeBerdt's young partner, had failed to revive the flagging enterprise. "Taken into the partnership purely on this account," Joseph wrote, Sayre had turned out to be "quite a man of pleasure and unacquainted with business." Sayre's long and expensive journey to America had generated more debts than profits, Joseph concluded. It would have further agitated Joseph had he known that even now in Philadelphia, lawyers "had attached [the] accounts of DeBerdt, Burkitt and Sayre for £1600," part of the debt Sayre had incurred on his earlier trip to the colonies.[8]

Despite the incompetence of Burkitt and the intemperance of Sayre, however, the principal responsibility for the present debacle, Joseph concluded, lay with the elder DeBerdt. He had failed because of "his trust in the integrity of his American correspondents." "The books of this House [i.e., the firm of DeBerdt, Burkitt, and Sayre]," Joseph lamented, "show a very handsome fortune acquired and I fear lost again by credulity on the part of Mr. DeBerdt and dishonesty on the part of our countrymen [i.e., Americans]."[9]

DeBerdt had been, Joseph wrote, "particularly unhappy in his Philadelphia correspondence, even our own particular friends." Thousands of pounds had been "lost by negligence and ignorance," but "the greatest part had been lost by trusting people unacquainted with business and recommended by religious people." DeBerdt had allowed his religious sympathies to dictate his business decisions; now his entire family would suffer for his naivety.[10]

Joseph did not explore the role played in the DeBerdt collapse by the imperial disruptions of the previous five years or his own role in those disputes. In the Stamp Act crisis of 1765–66 and the Townshend crisis of 1767–70, American merchants had boycotted British imports and withheld payments from British creditors in hopes of pressuring them to lobby Parliament for changes in its colonial tax policies. Joseph and his brother-in-law, Pettit, had supported that tactic and had castigated those they viewed as too ready to resume trade without full repeal of all the Townshend taxes. Thus, American political agitation against Great Britain had compounded, if it had not created, the financial difficulties of the firm of DeBerdt, Burkitt, and Sayre. And the failure of that firm now lay at the heart of Joseph's personal crisis. But if Joseph saw the connection between his political agitation in New Jersey and his financial crisis in London, he did not share that insight in his letters home to Pettit.[11]

At first, Joseph, like Esther, had expected that a small surplus might remain when the books were closed. "There appears," he wrote shortly after his arrival in London, to be "an overplus of some thousands." Although the firm owed more than £34,000 (sterling), others, particularly in America, owed it more. "America's remittances," he estimated, could save the firm.[12]

Soon, however, Joseph changed his mind. More careful analysis of the accounts and more realistic assessment of the prospects of payments from America demonstrated that "Mr. DeBerdt's estate will not pay the debts." "The creditors will, with the best of management, receive no more than 12/6 in the Pound [i.e., about sixty-two cents on the dollar]." The company was bankrupt and the family destitute. There will be "not a shilling" for Mrs. Martha DeBerdt and her children. They must throw themselves on the mercy of strangers. "We have," he concluded, now including himself in the equation, "no prospect but the Honour and Generosity of the Creditors."[13]

Equally disturbing, the family had also lost its political capital, those personal connections that opened doors to lucrative public appointments. DeBerdt was dead. Morgann, who had helped the family in the past, now "has not interest [i.e., influence] enough to make a constable." "All the remaining interests [connections] of this family lay with the [political] opposition," and those in office distrusted DeBerdt. Lord Halifax, a leading member of the current administration, "hates his [DeBerdt's] very name." Not an unreasonable position for the British statesman in light of DeBerdt's close association with the Boston Men and their leadership in opposition to the evolving British colonial policy—but still rather disconcerting for Joseph, who again missed the irony in his situation. American resistance to the British over the past five years, led by men in Massachusetts and abetted by Dennys DeBerdt in London, had undermined the political connections on which Joseph had hoped to build his new life with Esther.[14]

Joseph and the family faced a grim situation. The DeBerdts had lost money and influence. The firm owed far more than it could pay. If the creditors demanded their full rights, they could legally seize and sell the personal possessions of Martha, Esther, and Dennis. Moreover, the family had few human resources on which it could rely. Esther's brother was a liability: more likeable than useful. As Joseph described him, he was "the gay, volatile and lively" young man who had been "brought up in the expectation of a handsome fortune." He was, Joseph admitted, "far from wanting in sense, but it was not the sense of a man of the world." Dennis had, Joseph said, the "kind of understanding which makes him agreeable rather than useful." Since "he has never been made master of business," Joseph concluded, "he is as much at a loss as you can suppose any person to be entering into life with a disappointed mind, a turn for company, and ignorance of business." He "would accept some office," Joseph thought, "if he could get it," but given the attitude of the current administration, that was a vain hope. "Rather too gay and lively to act ploddingly in a counting house," some (probably Joseph himself) thought that the best solution was to send the young man off to India to make his fortune in the far reaches of the empire.[15]

Mrs. DeBerdt, like her son, compounded rather than eased the family's difficulties. Her plight illustrates the terrible vulnerability of eighteenth-century widows, especially those of commercial men without land. For a quarter of a century or so, Martha DeBerdt had lived as the wife of a respected London merchant. Her husband's wealth had provided well for her and her two children. She lived in a well-furnished three-story row house on a fashionable street in the cosmopolitan center of the British Empire. She had a horse-drawn coach for her use in town, a riding horse, and a piano for her daughter. In the winter, she stayed in the city, where she shopped, entertained, went to teas, supervised her children, organized dinners for her husband's commercial friends, and discussed business with dinner guests. In the summer, she moved her family and her functions to her country home in Enfield, and at least on one occasion she had visited Bath, the exclusive health spa for families of London's most successful entrepreneurs. She had enjoyed autonomy in her home, standing in her community, and purpose in life. Then, suddenly, she found herself without funds and dependent upon others.

Her initial reaction was denial. On one level, she must have understood the magnitude of the crisis she faced. She had a fair understanding of her husband's business affairs. He had had sufficient confidence in her knowledge and judgment to appoint her one of the three executors of his estate. She, as one of the executors, had already begun to negotiate with the creditors before Joseph arrived.[16] But on a different level, she continued to act as if she were still financially independent. She said that she was unwilling "to live as it were pensioners upon the bounty of others." In reality, that was precisely what she had to do, yet she continued to live as she had lived for years: shopping, spending, coming, going, seeing, and being seen while the creditors threatened to invade her home and seize her furniture. Martha DeBerdt needed to face reality, and in time it would be Joseph's responsibility to help her understand, but he hesitated. She "still flatters herself there will be some surplus," Joseph wrote to Pettit, "and it is almost a pity to remove the delusion, but it will be necessary to regulate her conduct."[17]

Esther, in contrast to her brother and mother, better understood the nature and the extent of the calamity. With them, she had lost her beloved father. With them, she had also lost much of the material base of her daily life. These things she had come to grips with early on. Although Joseph thought it was "necessary for health that she should ride," she sold her horse.[18] But, in addition, and of far greater consequence for her and for them, she had also lost her bargaining power in the marriage market. John Cox had once estimated that Esther was "an agreeable girl," a "very pretty thing," and "worth some £10,000 to £20,000." A dowry of that magnitude would make Esther a very desirable young woman.[19] But she had lost that dowry. How would Joseph handle that now?

Until the death of her father, Esther had expected that her life of comfort, love, and security would continue. She would marry Joseph. They would live in London. They would be happy. Indeed, as Joseph described it, Esther, like her mother, had lived in "comfort and love," and he might well have also added "security." But now, the money was gone. She brought no economic resources to the table, and Joseph had no future in London. What would he do?[20]

Esther knew that ambitious young men in her social world would hesitate to marry a penniless woman. She also knew that if Joseph chose to abandon her, everyone in her world, young and old, male and female, would approve of his decision. They would expect a prudent young man to act in that way, and they would harbor grave doubts about his judgment and maturity if he persisted in such an unwise connection—if he allowed romantic love to blind him to practical realities.

Then again, marrying Joseph under these changed circumstances could also cost her much. She would have to move to America; she would lose, as Joseph put it, "the connections of her youth, her native country, and those objects she has been familiar with." She would leave all of this for an uncertain welcome in America. And this too she knew. She would come to join Joseph's American family as a burden, not a boon.[21]

Joseph's American relatives had expected Esther to enhance their situation: to bring them, through Joseph, a handsome fortune, powerful political connections, and significant social statue. Now, she brought no money, no connections, and no status. Worse yet, in her total dependence on Joseph, she would deplete rather than augment the family's resources and compete with them for the time, attention, and care that Joseph had previously bestowed upon them.

Five years earlier, when Joseph had returned from London to New Jersey, he found his family destitute. At age twenty-two, Joseph had assumed responsibility for all of them: they were family. He had no choice. Now, he had left them to go to London in 1770, not to abandon them but rather to expand the geographic and occupational scope of the family's enterprises. His marriage into a well-to-do and well-connected mercantile family, and his permanent residence in London had promised to further enhance the family's welfare and expand its opportunities. In that context, Joseph's American family would have joyfully welcomed his new bride.

But now, Joseph would return empty-handed. He had squandered scarce resources, and his family would suffer. Any new obligations Joseph assumed would compete with his commitment to them and thus intensify their suffering. The claims of his new wife would trump theirs.

Esther had good reason to worry. Joseph, were he wise, would not marry her. But if he did, she would have to go to New Jersey, a fate she had resisted for five years. And if she went to America, she could expect a cool reception from those who rightly saw her as a competitor for Joseph's support.[22]

Joseph, like Esther, understood the magnitude of the disaster they faced, and almost daily his appreciation of his responsibilities grew. That burden sometimes overwhelmed him. He had spent lavishly in anticipation of his new life. "You know what expectations I had," he remarked to

Pettit. He had had solid reason to believe that he would marry Esther, join her father as agent for the province of Massachusetts, complete his legal studies at the Middle Temple, and ultimately practice law in London. Now, none of that would happen.[23] More immediately, the longer he remained in London, the more his difficulties multiplied. Daily expenses eroded his funds. He had no current source of income, and the DeBerdt family could not help. Indeed, he may have had to assume some responsibility for their daily sustenance. He thus continued to spend ever-increasing amounts of money to finance himself on an expedition to London that no longer had a purpose. He had stepped into quicksand, and every day he sank deeper. He had reason to feel oppressed as his world collapsed. In the past five years, his efforts and sacrifices had dragged him and his family back to respectability. Now, it all seemed to be slipping away. Five years of industry, five years of frugality, five years without the woman he loved now teetered on the brink of oblivion. "I am again embarked on a Sea of Disappointments" and difficulties, he lamented to Pettit, "and seem ever destined to this school of affliction."[24]

Joseph wrote those discouraging words in early May, after his first assessment of the situation. Six weeks later, he felt much the same way. He apologized for the "gloomy" tone of his previous letter but saw no improvement in their circumstances. "Very unhappily," he wrote, "the causes remain, and if I am more at ease now it is from the familiarity of the subject." Things were bad and getting worse. "It would be difficult," he declared to Pettit, "to convey any adequate idea of my situation." He had faced disaster before and overcome it, but in his mind not a disaster of this magnitude. "I can assure you," he wrote to Pettit, "my former difficulties, and you know I have had my share, appear as trifles in comparison of the present." He complained, "I am sure, my worst enemy would pity me if he knew."[25]

DeBerdt's death and the condition of the family shattered Joseph's dreams, frustrated his expectations, clouded his future, and threatened his financial security. But underlying all of these particular problems, at the heart of his personal crisis, intensifying and multiplying and amplifying all else, was embarrassment. His failure could reshape his image in the eyes of his American peers. He had risked much and lost. The provincial boy from New Jersey had left his parochial friends at home and had gone to seek his fortune in the metropolis. He had failed. Now he must slink home in disgrace, mocked by lesser men without the courage to try. "I dare not allow myself to think," he wrote to Pettit after being in London for three months, "for if I do, I shall be completely miserable. For which way [ever] I turn myself, embarrassments and difficulties arise."[26]

This dimension of the problem also influenced Joseph's thinking about marrying Esther. Embarrassment in front of his peers could have powerful, if incalculable, implications. His current difficulties would raise questions about his judgment and tarnish his reputation. Eighteenth-century entrepreneurs placed great weight on character. They lived in a volatile and insecure world. They conducted complex financial transactions across long distances and in slow time. Charlatans and incompetents competed against each other to drag down the honest and industrious. Legitimate traders had few judicial remedies with which to protect themselves. The weak, the foolish, the naive, the imprudent, and the improvident failed and disappeared, unmourned.[27]

In such a world, trust was essential, and trust depended on character: an image of integrity, a habit of honesty, a pattern of prudence, a reputation for caution, a succession of successes. Thus did a man build a reputation. Thus did a man project confidence, demonstrate competence, and construct a persona for his peers.

But images were fragile, and opinions fickle. Failure hurt, and failure attributed to imprudence, to overreaching, to undue striving, to overconfidence, to hubris—that kind of failure could shatter an image, destroy a character. Who would trust such a man to pay debts, to manage money, to try cases, to negotiate agreements?

Joseph appreciated his vulnerability. Ironically, he had charged the firm of DeBerdt, Burkitt, and Sayre with these very failings. He saw the old man and his younger partners as careless, inattentive, negligent, extravagant, credulous, and naive. Now, he had opened himself to similar charges. When his peers in America learned of the depth of his disaster, of his extravagance, of his naïveté—his reputation could suffer irreparable damage.

He needed to conceal his failures and put the best face he could on a bad situation. Again and again, throughout the spring and summer, Joseph warned Pettit to tell as little as possible and conceal as much as he could. In June, he told Pettit, "I have wrote this letter informing you of my situation in full confidence for however poor we may be there is no necessity of making it known to the world where there will be more to rejoice in our disappointments than to sympathize with or assist [us] under them."[28]

At times, Joseph tried to reassure himself, to justify his actions, to convince himself that he had acted prudently, that he was simply the unfortunate victim of circumstances. "You know," he reminded Pettit, and possibly himself, "what expectations I had . . . and from such authority."[29] The truth was, he had acted unwisely, and he admitted it. "My prospects have led me astray," he wrote, and he castigated himself: "Oh, those ideal expectations how have they diverted me from the plain path of industry and certainty into experiences beyond my ability." He had danced. Now he had to pay the piper. His failure in London would weaken his reputation in America. Returning home with a penniless wife would further erode the confidence of his peers, who tended to judge a man's character by the size of the fortune he married. "I confess," he told Pettit, "I see so many difficulties on my return to America that nothing seems left."[30]

But Joseph, young, talented, and ambitious, had pulled himself and his family up once before, and he could do it again. And, at bottom, he seemed to know this. His self-flagellation and his recriminations, honestly felt and candidly expressed, were also cathartic, a means of venting and thus relieving the psychic pain of failure. Later, he admitted as much. As he said to Pettit, "a communication of grief sometimes eases the mind. . . . I find it so and therefore have indulged myself to a length nothing but friendship can excuse."[31]

Already, he had a plan to salvage what he could from what he had come to call "this wreck." But first and foremost, he needed to deal with Esther, and here we see Joseph at his finest. The most momentous decision he had to make in the midst of all of these confusions he made quickly, decisively, and firmly, and then spent much of the following months justifying it.

From the beginning, Joseph had known what he would do. Within days of his arrival in London, he had told Pettit, "I expect in about three weeks of this time my dear girl will make me happy." And so she did. Late in May, Esther and Joseph married in a simple ceremony at St. Luke's, a small chapel near the DeBerdt residence in Artillery Court. She was twenty-three, and he was twenty-eight. Their five-year separation had ended. Esther had married the man she had chosen for herself at age seventeen. Henceforward, they would face the future together.[32]

He informed his family, and then, anticipating their criticism ("the event . . . will condemn me"), he began his defense. "I dare say [the] selfish world may censure me and laugh at my romantic virtue as they may know it," he wrote. He admitted the strength of the wisdom of the worldly. "I see and feel as much as anyone can the impropriety and imprudence of marrying without a fortune on either side," he said. He also admitted his own hesitancy: "The conflict in my mind is easier conceived than described." But, as he explained, his hesitancy, his uncertainty, and his awareness of the economic difficulties involved had, at least in part, prompted him to act quickly. "I pressed my dear girl to give me her hand[s] lest time and the difficulties we met with might prove too strong for my love and the noble passion be born down by Interest." Under different circumstances, he might have waited. "Could I have stayed here, or were we in America, I should have deferred it [the wedding] for some time," but "I thought it my duty to prevent any rising fears and doubts and ensure my virtue." In short, he married her to stop the arguments in his head, to prevent his more calculating self from overwhelming his emotional attachment.[33]

Joseph loved Esther. That caused his problem. Without that, he could have made noble gestures toward her and her family, and then returned home, alone. True, in addition to his love, he also felt a sense of duty. He hurried Esther into an early wedding so that his awareness of the difficulties, his sense of his "interests," as he phrased it, would not overwhelm his love and his sense of duty.

He knew the arguments against what he had done. He understood the principles on which contemporary marriages were based, and he knew that he had violated them. But, he argued, their situation was unique, "so circumscribed that no general rule could govern it." Esther had waited five years. She had "refused many advantageous offers." When, five years ago, his family had lost everything and his own prospects looked dim, she had stayed with him. She had, he said, given "me the highest proof of her disinterested regard [i.e., love without expectation of return]." When circumstances had reversed their positions and her prospects looked as bad now as his had then, he felt that he could not abandon her. "I could not," he explained, "have acted otherwise without being stigmatized as a villain," at least in his own mind. "I could not have left her to struggle with an unfeeling world tho I have had little besides poverty and embarrassment for her to share." Once again, an old patriarch had died and Joseph, the new patriarch, would step forward to assume responsibility for another family.[34]

Marrying Esther thus allowed him to do what he wanted to do and what he felt his duty required. It earned for him, as he put it, both "the approbation of my own mind and the possession of the girl I love."[35]

Joseph made it clear that he expected his family to respect his decision and to cooperate with him to make the best of a bad situation. Esther, he told them, has "apprehensions that our settling in America will affect your interests [i.e., your financial situation]." Indeed, they all knew that. But Joseph intended to hold them to a higher standard. "I believe these misfortunes will not affect your sentiments towards her," and she will not be "lessened in our affection by these changes and disappointments," he cautioned them. He reminded them, "had her fortune been quite to her expectations, I know that she would have shared it with me and mine, and rejoiced in the opportunity." He expected no less of them. "Providence has ordered it otherwise and tho we cannot see why—yet doubtless for wise and good purposes."[36]

Joseph, in effect, offered his American family a rebuke, an apology, and a promise. He reminded Pettit of his past dependence on Joseph: "Your prospects have been in some measure founded upon mine," he wrote. He accepted full responsibility for their current predicament: "My prospects have led me astray and involved you in my embarrassment." But he pledged his full efforts to save them all. "You may depend upon my taking every step that I can with any consistency or prudence to show how much I have you and my dear sister's comfort and happiness at heart." "I shall save what I can out of the wreck of this estate," he promised, but he cautioned Pettit that they must work together and not against each other: "We must endeavour to trust each other," he said. He hinted that he might have to impose a major sacrifice on Pettit: "I may perhaps be obliged to ask you some assistance to extract myself from the difficulties into which my disappointed scheme may plunge me." He meant that necessity might compel him to take back from Pettit the patronage appointment he had first won for himself and then delegated to Pettit. He hoped that it would not come to that. "Nothing would give me more pleasure than to have continued the same proofs of affection and regard, but I assure you, I feel great apprehension and am in every respect of fortune a very unhappy man." We can only imagine Pettit's agitation at this news. He depended on that position, and if Joseph took it back Pettit would have no employment.[37]

But, as Joseph said, it all depended on the negotiations with those who had claims against the firm. The executors of the estate had met with "five of the principal [creditors] and the best friends of the House [i.e., the firm]," who would act as trustees for the whole. These trustees in turn had drawn up a set of proposals that "discharged Burkitt and Sayre of the debt . . . of the House," allowed Mrs. DeBerdt to keep her personal belongings, including her furniture, and left open the prospects of additional provisions for the DeBerdt family. Joseph worked for the better part of June to convince the remainder of the creditors to agree to these proposals. Many, especially the smaller ones, were reluctant, but in the end all but two or three agreed, and Joseph expected them to sign the final deed of trust soon.

Joseph pushed the trustees to agree to provide some kind of support for Esther and her mother, and worried much about the consequences should that not happen. "I look forward with no small apprehension to the difficulties I may be under should the trustees refuse to make allowances" for the DeBerdts.[38]

Joseph also wanted the trustees to authorize him to collect the debts owed to the firm by Joseph's countrymen. Although he did not specify why he favored that tactic, it seems likely that he would earn a portion of the money he collected as compensation. He did not need to explain that part of it to Pettit. Those in the eighteenth-century commercial world expected it. Moreover, Joseph thought that he could profit from collecting these debts when he told Pettit that, if the trustees did not agree to his proposal, he would charge them a sizeable amount for his previous legal work in America on behalf of the firm.[39]

To facilitate these negotiations, Joseph and Esther kept their marriage a secret. The goal, as Joseph explained it, sounds rather Machiavellian: to provide the DeBerdts and Joseph himself with the maximum opportunity to play on the sympathy of the creditors and to "influence their friendship as much as possible." As soon as the trustees decided, Joseph and his new family would "take our passage on the first ship." He wanted to arrive, if at all possible, before "the fall courts" opened. To that end, he asked Pettit to help him raise the money necessary to set up a household for his new family in Trenton. "I shall be exceedingly distressed for money when I return," he explained, and requested Pettit to arrange to sell some land Joseph owned in York, Pennsylvania, to raise cash.[40]

Joseph hoped to sail as early as July, but the negotiations dragged on, and they could not depart until August. By that time, Joseph had made significant progress toward minimizing the damage and establishing a foundation for future recovery. Although he did not spell out those arrangements, three things seem clear. First, Joseph did, indeed, win the right to collect the debts owed to the firm by its American correspondents, and at a reasonable profit for himself. He began these collections soon after his arrival home and continued to harass American debtors until the eve of the final break with Great Britain. His commissions on these collections formed one element in his own financial recovery. In that way, Dennys DeBerdt's estate did contribute significantly to the future success of Joseph and his expanded American family.

Joseph also negotiated an agreement with the trustees whereby young Dennis, Esther's brother, performed the same task for the trustees in England

and on the European continent. Dennis, like Joseph, worked diligently at this responsibility, and the income he derived from these activities provided for his maintenance in London, where he stayed when the rest of his family went to America. This benefited Joseph in two ways. It relieved him of financial responsibility for the young man, and more importantly, it allowed Dennis to remain in London, and there he served as a listening and negotiating post for a complex transatlantic trading nexus, focusing on Esther and Joseph and linking key commercial nodes in London, Dublin, Trenton, Philadelphia, Boston, and the West Indies. Within months of his return to America, Joseph, working with Esther and through Dennis in London, had begun the shipment of iron and potash from America to the mother country, the arrangement of major purchases in London for his American friends, and the complex negotiations with Londoners for speculation in American land schemes and investment in London companies.

The third key element in this negotiated settlement allowed Mrs. Martha DeBerdt to keep much of her furniture, and probably provided some ongoing support for her from the money collected by Joseph in America and by Dennis in London. We know from Esther's correspondence that she had kept her piano. We can infer from the extraordinarily high value of the household furnishings listed by Joseph in his 1774 inventory that Martha had brought most of her household furnishings with her. We also know that shortly after their arrival in America, Joseph and Esther had sufficient money for luxury expenditures. They almost immediately moved from Trenton to Philadelphia, and then commissioned Dennis to buy a carriage in London for them, a luxury in Philadelphia that later governments singled out for special taxation.

While Joseph negotiated the details of the settlement of the DeBerdt estate, he also took time to build his London network and to solicit legal work he could do in America for Londoners with interests there.

When Joseph and Esther sailed from London, Joseph had salvaged enough to offer some reasonable hope for a prosperous future in America and wanted to return and get to work. Esther, we can assume, felt differently. Doubtful about her reception in America, reluctant to leave home, and only partially consoled by Joseph's promise of an early return to London, she accompanied her new husband into what she saw as an exile, and an exile that she fervently hoped would be short. Joseph, on the eve of their departure, wrote that, despite her fear, "her most complying temper and her wishes to see my friends become hers, all lessen her anxieties." One suspects that Esther might well have put the best face possible on an overall situation she found depressing. After five years of planning, manipulating, and sacrificing, this sophisticated, cosmopolitan, talented young woman, raised in the cultural and political capital of the British Empire and increasingly well versed in the commercial and political world of London, was headed for a fate against which she had directed all of her many talents for several years: a life in New Jersey. We can seriously doubt the accuracy of Joseph's assessment of her mental state as she set out for America.[41]

But they had survived a great tragedy with their love, like gold, tested by the fire of catastrophe and found to be pure and true. No matter what happened next, they had each other. They were a family. An extended family that included not only Joseph's dependents in America but also Esther's brother now alone in London and her mother living with them in Philadelphia. They would face far more deadly crises in the future, and their love would be tested again in powerful ways, but they had finally achieved what Esther had said she had always wanted: to be to Joseph "the companion who would make it his endeavor to be both friend and lover to me."[42] Joseph was certainly to be her friend and lover for life, as she was to him, and they did indeed create a family in which and thorough which they strove to do the will of their creator, and they did succeed economically and politically in a remarkable way before the Providence that had brought them together and guided and tested them called them home at very young ages.

CHAPTER 7

Exiled Where Women "Stooped like Country Girls"

Esther arrived in Philadelphia on October 26, 1770. By then, things were looking up in the British Empire. Parliament had repealed all of the Townshend taxes, save the one on tea. The colonial boycotts ended, trade resumed, tempers cooled, political distractions declined, and for the next three years peace and prosperity reigned. In time, the Reeds would benefit greatly from these developments, but in Esther's mind, things were moving from bad to worse. She was twenty-four years old, five months married, two months pregnant, ill, and unhappy. Seasickness and morning sickness had plagued her throughout the eight-week crossing, and she arrived "worn almost to a skeleton by constant sickness" and in "very low spirits." But her journey was not over. She, her new husband, and her mother continued on to the Pettits' home in Burlington: twenty-two miles on a stagecoach over rough roads and across two rivers.[1]

In Burlington, Esther regained her health but not her good spirits. For the past six years, she had struggled to win for herself the man she loved and to live with him in London. Now, married at last, she found herself where she had insisted that she would never be: in rustic New Jersey. Economic necessity had uprooted her from her cosmopolitan life in the center of the world's most powerful empire and propelled her across three thousand miles of ocean into exile among welcoming but dull provincials. But it was, she and Joseph agreed, a temporary exile. They had retreated to America in order to accumulate the resources, both financial and political, that they needed to return to London. Over the next few years, they learned to cooperate with Dennis in London and Charles Pettit in New Jersey in developing and exploiting commercial opportunities in the Atlantic trading world. Esther also began to adjust to the different ways of the colonies. America, however, was not home. In her own mind, she did not become an American. She remained an English woman, a Londoner, living in a strange and inferior land and scheming to return home.

Esther did not adapt easily or happily to her new life in the provinces, but she and Joseph prospered, and that gave her hope that they could soon return to London. She, Joseph, and her brother, Dennis, constructed a lucrative transatlantic trading network. Esther's assistance with Joseph's legal correspondence and Joseph's London legal training, his natural talent, and his extraordinary discipline produced a flourishing law practice that quickly propelled him to the top of the profession. The Reeds invested their surplus income in land, and Esther managed their household accounts efficiently. She also delivered three babies in five years. Throughout, she continued to look for ways to return home, and it seems probable that she and Joseph would have ultimately achieved that goal had the American Revolution not intervened.

The Reeds spent almost two weeks in Burlington, but despite the attentions of the royal governor and the best efforts of Esther's new family, she found herself bored to distraction. "America," she wrote to Dennis, cannot "compare to England in any way." Burlington was "remarkable for nothing." "Governor [William] Franklin tells me," she continued, "that a person may sleep there for a month, without danger of being disturbed." An American imitation of a British foxhunt both amused and depressed her. Only the promise of an early return to "dear England" made life bearable in this primitive land.[2] Her discontent in Burlington led Joseph to radically alter his plans, and soon they were on their way to Philadelphia: a significant change of venue with both risks and opportunities.

The move to Philadelphia changed little. The capital of Pennsylvania dwarfed Burlington but shrank into parochial insignificance in comparison to London. The city did not, she wrote to Dennis, "answer my expectations. ... [T]he houses are low, and in general, paltry."[3]

The elite of the city welcomed Esther with enthusiasm, but she did not reciprocate. Within days of their arrival in Philadelphia, Mrs. Foxcraft invited the Reeds to join her at the Philadelphia Dancing Assembly. This prestigious social event offered an exclusive evening of formal dancing, refined conversation, card playing, and female competition in grace, beauty, and cultivation. A colonial imitation of similar institutions in London and Bath, it was Philadelphia's preeminent social venue for the display of gentility and wealth, and would most certainly attract families like that of her old "friend" from Bath, Samuel Powel, and his new wife, the daughter of the great merchant Thomas Willing.[4]

Esther found the event disappointing. She saw some "American belles," which she considered pretty, but no real beauties. American women, she wrote, "stoop like country girls." She also scorned their pettiness. "My ladyship opened the ball," she wrote, "much to the satisfaction of the company, as something new to criticize."[5]

The incessant gossip drove her to distraction. "We meet with much civility," she reported, "but I can't say the place suits me very well. The people either talk of their neighbors, of whom they know every particular . . . or else of marketing, two subjects I am very little acquainted with." She did not see herself as a gossiper or a shopper, at least not a gossiper or shopper in Philadelphia. Equally important, one suspects, Esther felt uncomfortable in this company. She took her religious beliefs and affiliations seriously. She was a religious dissenter, a member of a "vital" (evangelical) denomination, as her father had described it. She and her mother would soon join the Second or the Arch Street Presbyterian Church in Philadelphia, and in time Esther drew her friends mostly from that congregation. At the Assembly, however, she found herself mixing socially with few who shared her religious sensibilities or identification. She expressed her general dissatisfaction quite candidly to Dennis. She cautioned him, however, to keep her comments to himself, "for we hardly dare tell one another our thoughts, lest it should spread and be told again all over the town."[6]

Even the weather displeased her. When she had arrived in the fall, she had commented that the sky in Philadelphia might be clearer, but the country "will not bear the most distant comparison" to home. Later, after a summer in Philadelphia, she complained, "There is so much clear burning sunshine in these three summer months, that I do not wish for any more all the year."[7]

Esther's initial living circumstances exacerbated her difficulties. After a short and hectic stay in the crowded Pettit household, she and Joseph moved to Philadelphia, but for most of the next two months they had no fixed abode. Joseph, racing across Pennsylvania and New Jersey to revive his legal practice, often left her for days at a time. Not until mid-December could Esther inform Joseph that they had leased the Tilghman house and that Captain Moore had arrived from London with their possessions. Pettit then sent Joseph's papers and some household furnishings from Burlington, but the kitchen furniture and Joseph's desk from Trenton had to wait. Not until late January or early February 1771 did Esther become mistress in her own functioning household, and by then she was well into the sixth month of her pregnancy.[8]

In June 1771, after nearly eight months in America, Esther again assured her distant brother that America and England "are two different places," with the differences not to America's advantage. However, she concluded, "for the present we must be content." Esther's "presuppositions," as her old friend Arthur Lee had called them, undoubtedly influenced her reaction to this new, raw country. She herself later admitted, albeit indirectly, that she, and "almost every" Englishman on his arrival, "falls" into many errors "very much to their prejudice."[9]

Simple nostalgia played a part. Joseph anticipated this problem. "[I]t is natural to my dear Hetty to feel some reluctance at leaving the connections of her youth, her native country," he explained to Pettit, using much the same words he had earlier used to describe his own feelings about leaving home in December 1769. But Joseph failed to grasp, or at least to articulate, the magnitude of the difference between his departure from Trenton for London and Esther's travel from London to Philadelphia.[10] Joseph had given up a familiar and desirable world for an exciting and exotic one. Esther, in contrast, had given up much to live in a different and, by almost any objective standard, lesser world. She had left London, the largest, the most diverse, and the most prosperous city in Great Britain for Philadelphia.[11]

Esther's new city was compact, quiet, and peopled by provincials. Visitors described the city as clean and neat with straight lines, square angles, broad streets, brick houses, wide sidewalks, artificial light supplied by oil lamps, and shops on or near Market Street, the city's principal east-west axis. Its flourishing public market, "near 1200 foot long," ran down the middle of the city's widest street, "as wide as Broad Street or way in New York City." Silas Deane of Connecticut, attending as a delegate to the First Continental Congress in the fall of 1774, described the city as "simple and pure," but he added a caveat: "I mean simple and pure only comparatively, for here are Debauchees and Whores and Rogues as well as in other places, but not so numerous." Clean streets, brick walks, artificial lighting, the best mutton in the world, and a low density of "Debauchees and Whores and Rogues." What more could one say?[12]

Esther found it difficult to know and maintain metropolitan standards in Philadelphia. At home, she had learned what was fashionable by wandering the elite shopping streets, browsing in the Strand, or strolling in Vauxhall Gardens. Her peers confirmed or refined her judgment. In Philadelphia, she had no easy way to keep current and no informed peers on whom to rely.[13]

Frustrated, she turned to Dennis, still in London, and fired off a steady barrage of requests:

> "A fine damask table-cloth"[14]
> "A very neat fan"[15]
> "A cap for a boy . . . something genteel, like a gentleman's child, not a butcher's"[16]
> "A half-dressed handkerchief . . . whatever is fashionable"[17]
> "A handsome spring silk, fit for summer, and new fashion . . . and send it to Long's warehouse to be made up and trimmed or not as the present taste requires"[18]

The key words here are *fine, neat, genteel, fashionable,* and *the present taste.*

London defined these terms, and Londoners learned them from one another. Esther expected to live a fashionable life. She wanted to dress and act like a fashionable woman in London, but she knew that here in Philadelphia, she, like the city, would remain a pale reflection of the metropolis. Exasperated, she one day declared, "I would give something to be in . . . Mr. Anybody's shop in London, even in Thames Street." Arthur Lee, writing to Joseph in February 1773, commented, "I dare say the ladies hardly think of poor old London any longer." He could not have been more mistaken.[19]

The birth of her daughter, Martha (called Patty), in May 1771 intensified Esther's discontent. Earlier in the month, she had written to Dennis that her baby was due soon, but, as it turned out, she still had three weeks to wait. When the time arrived, it threw the household, or at least Joseph, into a panic. He was at home but unprepared. On Monday, May 20, he had told Pettit to expect him in New Jersey on Wednesday, "nothing happening in the mean time," but "in the mean time" something happened. In the early evening on Tuesday, Joseph hurried Jack (one of Joseph's slaves) off to Burlington with a letter for Pettit. Written "in hurry and distraction," it told his brother-in-law that Esther had "taken ill about three o'clock," and it asked Pettit to cover Joseph's cases in Trenton on Wednesday.[20]

Esther's travail was severe and protracted. By the time she delivered her little girl, whatever enthusiasm the new mother might have had for her new role had atrophied. "I believe," Esther wrote to her brother, "I shall make a good nurse, and I think I shall like my little girl very well someday."[21] The baby was baptized by the Reverend James Sproat in the Arch Street Presbyterian Church. Esther's father would have been pleased. James Sproat was among the most evangelical of Presbyterian ministers in the city, and old Dennys DeBerdt had long championed "vital religion."[22]

But happy or not with her new responsibilities, Esther remained committed to an early return to England. The birth of Martha simply added another justification to go home. "If she lives," the new mother wrote, "it will make me more anxious than ever to return . . . as the education of girls is very indifferent indeed here."[23]

If Esther was ambivalent about her new daughter, Esther's mother, Martha, delighted in her new namesake and immediately took charge of the care of the frail creature. Despite her best efforts, however, the baby failed to flourish. The child worsened when Esther weaned her at nine months, and Esther later blamed herself on this account, but she had had little choice. By then, February 1772, she was well into the second trimester of her new pregnancy.[24]

In the winter of 1772, Joseph's aunt and Esther's new American friend, Mrs. Esther Cox, lost her little boy, a few months older than Patty, and Joseph and Esther feared that they might lose their firstborn. In desperation, Esther returned the girl to the breast, but nothing reversed Patty's decline. Through the spring and early summer, as her second birthday came and went, she continued to decline, and by midsummer, despite some signs of improvement, Joseph saw her future as "yet very doubtful." Then, for no obvious reason, the pattern changed and Joseph reported, "our little girl seems rather to mend." However, she remained, a "prodigy of leanness." The next spring, Esther reported, "My little girl has grown strong and will soon call on me for instruction." Although the worst was over, Patty remained "of so delicate a constitution that she often droops and alarms me," Esther wrote in October 1775. As late as the summer of 1776, Patty's inclination to be "droopy" continued to make Esther anxious.[25]

Meanwhile, by the summer of 1774, Esther had borne two additional babies. In mid-July 1772, after a relatively short labor, she delivered a boy and named him Joseph. Joseph reported that Esther "was taken 5 minutes after I set out," and when he returned between eight and nine o'clock that evening, she "presented me with a baby boy." Dennis wrote from London that he hoped this new arrival might make his mother, Martha DeBerdt, more content in America and draw "off her thoughts of England and of me." Be that as it may, the arrival of young Joseph had no such effect on Esther. As she wrote in October, three months after Joseph's birth, she was in good health with "nothing . . . wanting but cleared prospects of returning to dear England."[26]

Nor did the energetic new baby boy encourage Esther to want more children. Young Joseph had arrived fourteen months after his sister. In twenty-six months of marriage, she had produced a daughter and a son. "I wish I could stop with that," she wrote in the fall.[27]

Twenty-four months later, however, she delivered another baby, a girl she named Esther and called Hetty. The delivery was apparently uncomplicated, although, according to Joseph, Esther had complained excessively in the final weeks. Moreover, young Hetty, born in the summer of 1774 on the eve of the arrival of the representatives for the First Continental Congress, was only the third of the six children Esther would ultimately bear between 1771 and 1780, an average of one new baby every eighteen to nineteen months, well ahead of typical eighteenth-century women, who averaged a new baby every twenty-four to thirty months.[28]

Esther, never strong, now enjoyed excellent health. In October 1772, she had told Dennis, "I think I never enjoyed a greater share of health and spirits." After the birth of Hetty in the summer of 1774, Esther informed Dennis that she was particularly busy. She was nursing a newborn, tending to the needs of a rambunctious two-year-old boy, and teaching her delicate three-year-old to read, a task she took seriously in a world she saw as indifferent to the education of girls. "I assure you, my hands are pretty full of business," she wrote, but with no hint of her previous concern to limit future conception. It was living in America, not having babies, that depressed her.[29]

The presence of Esther's mother in Philadelphia reinforced Esther's desire to return to London. Martha DeBerdt enjoyed good health, her snuff, and the latest news from London. She advised Esther and Joseph on childcare, sewed clothes from London patterns, joined the family at the Presbyterian church on Sundays, took the children on trips, enjoyed the summers with Esther and the children in the countryside, and complained about the local editors who printed condensed versions of news from London, "which destroys one half of the entertainment."[30]

But Mrs. DeBerdt, like her daughter, was in America under protest, out of sheer necessity, the direct consequence of her sudden and radical change of status. One moment, she had been the happy and respected wife of one of London's more successful merchant traders, head of her own household, and part of a busy social circle with a home in London and a place in the country. Then, abruptly, her husband's death transformed her into a dependent widow. She reluctantly agreed to migrate to America and, implicitly, to accept a subordinate place in her daughter's new home.[31]

Once in America, Martha DeBerdt made her discontent known to her lonely son in London, and in time he responded, as a dutiful son might, by proposing that she return to London and live with him. Esther rejected this suggestion. For Dennis to take their mother from Esther's home in Philadelphia to his home in London conflicted directly with his own best interests, she argued. Having a dependent mother in his household would impede his search for an appropriate wife. Unstated but implied, Esther argued that her need for their mother exceeded his. She was a young woman with small children living in a remote part of the empire. He was a bachelor enjoying himself in the metropolis. Her moral claims trumped his. At bottom, however, beyond the questions of his interest and her need, Esther simply could not imagine her mother returning home while she remained in exile. Dennis read between the lines and gave up the contest. Esther and her mother were staying in America until they could go to London together.[32]

Throughout their first half decade in America, Esther and Joseph continued to look for opportunities to make that happen. In January 1771, Esther reported to Dennis that Joseph wanted to become agent for Massachusetts, a position that her father had held in one fashion or another until his death and one that would require them to live in London. The post went to Benjamin Franklin.[33]

In 1772, they learned that Lord Dartmouth would replace Lord Hillsborough as colonial secretary. Joseph and Esther understood the importance of friends and connections. Great men built their interests by cultivating, using, and rewarding talented young men. Dartmouth's reemergence offered a new opportunity to cultivate an "advantageous acquaintance." "I wish," Esther wrote to Dennis, "some use could be made of him to advance that foremost wish of our [herself, Dennis, and, by implication, Joseph] hearts to spend the remainder of our lives together [in London]." In the meantime, she pleaded with Dennis to come to America for a visit or to settle. "Then England would have less charm for me, less attraction in it, and

I shall enjoy as much happiness as I have reason to expect in this world." She assured him, "once used to it you would find your life happy here."[34]

Dennis never came, and Esther continued to hope while she and Joseph worked to build the financial resources necessary to survive in America and then return to London. Joseph focused on reviving his legal practice, and Esther concentrated on Dennis and the potential for profitable trade between London and Philadelphia. She understood better than her brother the world of transatlantic commerce into which he was now venturing. She had worked closely with her father while Dennis had enjoyed himself in the fleshpots of London. Within weeks of her arrival, and well before she had settled into her own home, she reported to him that the American market was glutted with "common articles of wear" and "articles for gentlemen's use" but urged Dennis to export "little and unusual things." "Mrs. Pearson," Esther pointed out, "is making a fortune by going to England and bringing back new fashions" for women.[35]

Esther also advised Dennis on how to succeed in mercantile London. He was handsome and gregarious but untrained and undisciplined. Esther instructed him that he must develop "a knowledge of merchant's accounts" and a "perfect and accurate knowledge of . . . exchange." He must focus his attention on detail, on the cultivation of clients, and on the hard work of negotiating contracts and building his reputation. He must add to his charm the discipline, the focus, the technical skills, and the specialized knowledge of the world of trade that she had achieved between 1765 and 1770. When he became a "perfect master of merchant's accounts," Joseph would help, but Joseph must first be "convinced that you are more capable of transacting business."[36]

Convincing Joseph would take some effort. He had initially liked Dennis and enjoyed his company during his early months in London. He found him to be gay, volatile, and lively but also a young man with a near total "ignorance of business."[37]

Dennis struggled alone in London. For a while, the trustees employed him in collecting debts owed to the old firm of DeBerdt, Burkitt, and Sayre while he studied "my old Merchant account books" and thought about finding a trading partner in Boston or Philadelphia. He made progress, at least in his own mind. "I wish to decline public amusements," he told Esther, but admitted that he had "spent Sunday evening with Mr. Bodington and his lady." Arthur Lee reported that Dennis was reforming himself, becoming "diligent and prudent," but at the end of the year Dennis had not yet devised a way to support himself, and he felt depressed and discouraged as he saw "my little [income] grow less."[38]

In 1772, with Esther's counsel and Joseph's support, Dennis began to prosper, and by early 1773 he had active trading accounts with merchants in both England and America. He had also rented his "own counting house near the London Tavern for £15 a year," begun to pursue some of the old debtors to his father's house, and "danced attendance at [the home of] Lord Dartmouth" with good results. Dartmouth had agreed that Massachusetts should pay its £1,600 debt to the trustees for Dennys DeBerdt's service as its agent in the late 1760s. The trustees, in turn, promised Dennis an ample reward.[39]

Esther praised Dennis for his accomplishments but castigated him for doing business with Cox for "less than five percent," because now he could never charge more. She cautioned him against taking into his counting house a young man of dubious reputation "so young a master [as you] could not have had sufficient influence over him and he could be of no service to you." She also pushed him to pursue Dr. Rustin, who, she thought, needed a reminder of "his debt to the old house."[40]

Esther heard "good accounts" of her brother's private affairs, and his ability to save £1,000 and put it at interest impressed her. That certainly was "more than I expected," she wrote. In time, Joseph acquired for Dennis an appointment as the New Jersey agent at an annual salary of £60. Both Esther and Joseph congratulated Dennis on his plans for "marrying a clever girl with a handsome fortune."[41]

By 1775, Dennis, Esther, and Joseph had built a mutually beneficial commercial relationship. Each brought much to the enterprise, and between them they constituted a powerful and successful mercantile trio. Joseph, although concentrating most of his time on his legal practice, knew the law of the seas as well as the men and the trading companies in the Delaware River valley. He also had access to, if he did not actually own, a number of oceangoing vessels, and with Esther, they also knew, on a personal basis, the men who might captain such ventures, one of the central keys to success.

Dennis was young, naive, undisciplined, and untrained in the mysteries of the Atlantic trade. Alternatively, he was charming and now desperate for an income sufficient for him to live as he had while his father supported him. He benefited from his father's strong if a bit tarnished reputation and the business-like way the family had handled its bankruptcy. He also knew some of the men in the mercantile trades, and he had inherited his father's connection with Lord Dartmouth, a connection whose value was beyond calculation. In short, Dennis had great potential. The key question was how he would develop. And that was in large part up to Esther.

Esther brought together her husband and her brother, and thus the trading worlds of Philadelphia, London, and the West Indies. Moreover, she was far better trained than Dennis in the modes and mores of the international trade. At the time of her father's death, she had been working closely with him for three years in what one may assume approached the status of an apprentice merchant. She knew who owed back debts to the now-defunct DeBerdt firm, who could be trusted, and how to negotiate the fine print on a contract as indicated by her criticism of Dennis for his overgenerous contract with one of the traders in Philadelphia. She also understood the subtleties and unwritten rules of the game, the mores of the profession, and the importance of honesty, integrity, and reputation in the complex exchanges of goods worth hundreds of thousands of pounds among men spread out across the empire, from London to the West Indies and North America. Her contributions thus included guiding, educating, disciplining, and on occasion praising and encouraging her brother while she cooperated with her husband in keeping the accounts, maintaining the correspondence, and analyzing opportunities for profit.

We need to stop a moment here to put Esther's weighty contribution in perspective. In Esther's commercial engagement, she was far from unique among colonial American women, especially in its urban areas. More and more historians are coming to appreciate the degree to which women living in intact families contributed to the family's economic base. We are also increasingly aware of the degree to which married women separated from their husbands, widows, and single women found ways to support themselves in commerce. Even Abigail Adams, the epitome of New England Puritan rectitude, loaned money in speculative investments without her husband's knowledge and collaborated with him in marketing in America the goods he deceptively shipped to her from his foreign posts. In some cases, such as that of Elizabeth Murray of Boston, the wife's commercial activities far outstripped those of her husband. Our growing realization of women's economic contributions to the family's welfare helps us to put Esther's contribution in perspective without diminishing it. She was certainly unusual, but not unique.[42]

With the help of Esther and Joseph, Dennis was becoming one of the three lynchpins in an expansive and lucrative transatlantic trade network. He imported iron from Cox (Joseph's uncle, married to his mother's sister,

Esther Cox) and potash from John Rhea in Philadelphia, an old acquaintance of Esther's who supported Joseph's interests in exporting lumber. Dennis was also making commercial trips to Amsterdam with "young Mr. Morris," brother of Robert Morris of the powerful Philadelphia firm of Willing and Morris and an occasional partner in business ventures with the Reeds, regularly shipping significant quantities of consumer goods to Esther's friend, Mr. Cary, in Boston, and financing and marketing a fishing enterprise in the Bay de Chaleur. Dennis had become one anchor of the emerging Reed family-based Atlantic enterprise.[43]

Joseph worked at a frenetic pace to reestablish his legal business, and here too Esther played a crucial if somewhat less conspicuous part. From his base in Philadelphia, Joseph ranged across eastern Pennsylvania, and then north and east across New Jersey to Perth Amboy and New York City, and south and east to New Castle, Delaware. Always impatient, Joseph usually traveled alone, and by the end of March 1771 he was making the four-day, 140-mile round-trip to Perth Amboy with little baggage and a "mail pillion" strapped behind his saddle to carry his legal papers. Joseph rode hard, and Pettit later admitted that he feared to "venture . . . a journey on horseback" with him.[44]

The Reeds lived a block or so from the courthouse, and by the spring of 1772 Esther had become an active participant in the business. In her seventh month of a new pregnancy, and worrying about her sickly baby, she informed Dennis, "I am now private secretary" to Joseph. She handled much of his legal correspondence and undoubtedly kept most of the office records.[45]

Joseph rapidly moved to the top ranks of the legal profession. "Providence has remarkably favored our settling in this place," Esther wrote in the fall of 1772. Three of the top four lawyers in the city had retired. Joseph Galloway, old and rich, practiced little. John Dickenson had "married a wife worth £20,000 and is improving and building on his estate." Nicholas Waln, a Quaker who had been at the temple with Joseph, had turned preacher and given up a legal business worth £2,000 a year. The younger men in the profession posed no threat to the more experienced and London-trained Joseph. "Joseph's situation here is pretty certain with respect to income, and it rather increases than otherwise," Esther reported. "He has in this last week," she continued, "tried two causes that gained him considerable applause. . . . In short, there is but one person [Mr. Chew] who can make much figure against him." In the fall of 1773, Joseph was busy beyond belief. During the month of October, he tried a case in Philadelphia courts every day but Sundays, and then rushed off to the circuit courts to the outlying counties.[46]

By 1775, Joseph's legal work extended from James Wilson in Carlisle in western Pennsylvania to clients with interests in Ireland, the West Indies, and London. This legal practice constituted the core of a family-based enterprise that radiated out from Philadelphia across the British Empire. It is difficult now to tease out all the individual threads in the transatlantic tapestry, but one of the most important was the position of deputy secretary to the province of New Jersey, a patronage post demanding continual political attention. It supported the families of Charles Pettit and Bowes Reed, as well as two or three others who worked with or for them. It also served as a magnet in attracting law business for the Pettits and the Reeds. Pettit technically held the contract, but Joseph and Esther, working with Dennis in London, renegotiated and protected it against formidable competitors.[47]

Joseph also continued to collect commissions on the collection of debts owed to the old firm of DeBerdt, Burkitt, and Sayre by American houses in Philadelphia, New Jersey, and New York. No easy task, as Joseph himself testified when he lashed out at these commercial debtors. "It is a prevailing evil among the merchants of this country to trade upon the money which should be employed in payment of their debts," he declared. They were leveraging any cash they might accumulate into new debt rather than using it to pay down past obligations.[48]

Throughout, the Reeds continued to invest in land. In time, they acquired at least six hundred acres in Bucks County, Pennsylvania, as well as additional tracts in Orange County, New York, and in the swamp area of Philadelphia County, northwest of the city. They also owned shares worth £1,300 in a London syndicate that held legal title to vast acres of land in New Jersey. Joseph superintended the syndicate's affairs in America and defended its interests in the New Jersey courts. Through Dennis, he also explored additional land-speculating possibilities with Lord Dartmouth, the DeBerdt family's old London patron. The Reeds' obsession with land occasionally made them short of cash. "I have been paying away so much money for land that I am quite poor," Joseph wrote to Pettit. "I wish you may squeeze some out of the Sheriff for me." The family also managed the sailing of the ship *Nancy*.[49]

Esther and Joseph cultivated their New England connections. Esther knew many of these "Boston Men" from her father's Sunday dinners, at which Joseph himself had been a regular while in London. In the late 1760s, Joseph had visited Massachusetts, and in the 1770s, "Boston Men" had made contact with the Reeds. Josiah Quincy from Massachusetts spent a pleasant and potentially momentous time visiting them. Quincy had come to Philadelphia as an unofficial ambassador of goodwill representing the more radical leadership of his own province. His job was to create new links as well as to nurture and sustain old ones that had been forged in earlier crises surrounding the Stamp Act and the Townshend Acts but had eroded in a period of relative quiet. His visit went well, and he and the Reeds became close friends. Joseph also corresponded with Mr. Richard Cary, another Boston Man, on business matters, and Joseph and Esther planned for a visit to Philadelphia by Cary's daughter, Nancy, thus further extending and strengthening their political, economic, and personal network.[50]

The Reeds' success seemed almost miraculous. By 1775, they coordinated and directed a complex mix of family-based enterprises that included a thriving legal practice, oceangoing commerce, debt collection, land speculation, property management, and shrewd manipulation of the imperial patronage system. Based in Philadelphia, it radiated out through New Jersey into New York and Massachusetts, and across the Atlantic to London and into the islands of the West Indies. It made them rich.

In 1774, Joseph estimated their total worth at £7,335, with a law library worth £150, house furniture worth £300, a wine cellar worth £70, their nonlegal library worth £40, two enslaved African Americans worth £150, a lot on Chestnut Street valued at £300, as well as shares in the West Jersey Society and land in at least three locations worth £1,000.[51]

To help put that in perspective, a successful and industrious craftsman working in Philadelphia in the early 1770s could expect to earn about five shillings a day. If he worked six days a week for fifty weeks, a rare occurrence, he would have earned about £70, the value of the Reeds' wine cellar. If he worked a more interrupted and truncated schedule, as was typical, an average craftsman might earn £35–40 a year. At that rate of pay, he would have needed to use his entire income for ten years to pay for the furniture in the Reed home.[52]

Status mattered to Esther, and possessions played a key role in defining status. She had sold her horse and left her piano in London, but once in America she imported "candlesticks" and "very genteel" rugs for her new home, and in time "ivory letters" for the children. She dressed herself, her children, and her husband carefully. Joseph used "the best razors" and did not worry about the price. He wore "light and genteel but not [gaudy]" summer suits, "white silk stockings," and "a neat white hat suitable for our hot climate," and he had four or five "summer waistcoats."[53]

Their carriage, the apex of conspicuous consumption in Philadelphia, was their most visible extravagance. Philadelphia was a walking city. Its approximately twenty thousand to thirty thousand people lived within a relatively circumscribed geographical area. Almost everything one needed or wanted was within a few minutes' walk, and that was particularly true as one moved up the socioeconomic scale. The rich lived downtown. They often conducted their business out of their homes. The men strolled to the City Tavern for coffee and news. Craftsmen and craftswomen displayed their wares in shops on the ground floor or the front room of their residence. Women walked to the "High Street Market," which stretched up the middle of Market Street, west from Front Street. The church was a few blocks away. Doctors made house calls. The rich, like the poor, got sick and died at home. The cemetery was just around the corner, next to the church. Livery stables hired out horses and wagons for hauling heavy loads. Thus, private carriages in late eighteenth-century Philadelphia served less a transportation than a psychic need. They took longer and cost more than any alternative mode of traveling short distances within the city. But that, after all, was the point. Carriages also allowed the well-to-do to maintain summer homes for the family in the country while the head of the household commuted to the city.[54]

Esther and Joseph played this game hard and well. They had acquired their "post-chariot" directly from London. Dennis had purchased an "elegant" one for them. Esther had supervised the purchase and insisted that "the harness should be neat, as we shall want something to set off the horses." When it arrived, they added the necessary accouterments. The horses themselves must be just right. Joseph asked Dennis to find them a pair of chestnuts, about three years old and fifteen hands high. Dennis had difficulty filling the order. He estimated that each horse would cost £22–25, and then an additional £10 for shipping to America. It was "difficult to get any color but black," and the orders needed to be placed well in advance. Frustrated, the Reeds then shifted their attention to the local supply. By the winter of 1774, they had one, a beautiful animal, sixteen hands high that carried himself with quiet dignity. Now, the Reeds wanted a second to match the first.[55]

To care for their animals and equipment, they had already spent £90 for a new slave, Cyrus. Cyrus turned out to have rheumatism, a fact that Joseph used in his postpurchase negotiations to reduce the price to £60. Whether Cyrus's seller agreed or not, we do not know, but within a few months Joseph reported that Cyrus "behaved very well" and he used him to carry legal papers between Philadelphia and Burlington.[56]

The final touch in the construction of this symbol was livery. The Reeds ordered a "strong, well made velvet jockey cap for a man to ride postilion," and then "two livery hats for Servants, one pretty large, and other middling." They wanted those who handled the horses and the carriage to be dressed properly.[57]

The Reeds lived well by 1775, but their overall affluence was relatively modest in the context of Philadelphia's wealth structures. We cannot know precisely how much income the Reeds enjoyed from their various enterprises, but whatever its actual amount, it would have paled in light of the income from the £92,000 estate that Samuel Sansom left at his death in 1774.[58]

Nor did the Reeds match the lifestyle of Esther's old friend Samuel Powel. The Reeds leased a home on Market Street. Powel, an alderman in the city, married Elizabeth Willing in 1769 and built her an elegant mansion just around the corner on Third Street for £3,000. John Adams, in the city in the fall of 1774 for the First Continental Congress, compared Powel's house favorably with the mansion of John Cadwalader, "a gentleman of large fortune, a grand elegant House and furniture."[59]

Adams's testimony on his social experiences in Philadelphia also helps to make this point in a different way. He dined with a number of prominent families in the city. His description of the Powel event emphasized the almost unbelievable richness and variety of the fare: "a most sinful Feast again! Everything which could delight the Eye or allure the taste . . . curds and creams, 20 sorts of tarts, . . . Trifles, Parmesan cheese, Punchy wine, porter beer etc." The day before, Adams had found an equally sumptuous table at the home of Quaker Myers Fisher. Three days later, he enjoyed much the same splendid feast at the table of Mr. Thomas Willing, Powel's father-in-law, and still later at the home of Chief Justice Chew. In sharp contrast, when Adams dined at the Reeds, he recorded the names of those at the table, and then quoted Joseph at length on the political efficacy of nonimportation. He did not mention the food. John Adams, the prominent but far from wealthy Puritan lawyer from Braintree, Massachusetts, was awestruck by the "costly," "splendid," and "sinful" opulence of Philadelphia's wealthy Anglican and Quaker elite. He was more impressed with the political leanings of the professionally prominent and economically respectable Presbyterian Reeds. Esther and Joseph enjoyed a level of affluence not available to the vast majority of the people of Philadelphia, but the Reeds could not match the financial power of the truly wealthy in the city.[60]

Equally significant, the Reeds' prosperity depended on how much their various enterprises earned in a given year. "Everything, *while his life and abilities last* [emphasis added], is promising here," Esther observed. In February 1776, Joseph made the same point in quite different circumstances. He told Dennis that he was considering public employment as an option now because the accelerating conflict between America and Great Britain had disrupted his business, and he was living on "my little capital." The Reeds lived well, but they did not enjoy the financial independence that characterized many of the city's richest families.[61]

Another aspect of the Reeds' success in the city was certainly more troubling to Esther. For most of these years, Esther understood their efforts and their success in Philadelphia as building the base for their return to London. Joseph agreed, at least initially, but by the mid-1770s he had come to see the irony in their success. They had sunk their economic roots into this particular place. The more they prospered in Philadelphia, the less likely they were to return to London. In her own mind, however, Esther remained a visitor in the provinces, a stranger in a strange land, a Londoner in her thinking and in her expectations—an exile living in America as a prelude to going home, but their success made this increasingly problematic.

Joseph's professional reputation and his web of connections tied them to Philadelphia. Although Joseph and his office might do legal work for clients in London, Ireland, the West Indies, and a number of North American colonies, the bulk of his business, and thus his income and the center of his reputation, came from his work in the local courts within a fifty-to-seventy-five-mile radius of Philadelphia. Possibly in time his legal practice and their economic and political connections could have grown sufficiently to allow the family to relocate to London. Or, possibly their investments, especially in land, could provide them an independent income sufficient to sustain a pleasant life in London.

In 1775, this economic reality frustrated Esther's desire to go home, but we have no evidence that it diminished her desire to return to London. Still, she continued to hope, and that hope persisted as the hostilities between Great Britain and her North American colonies erupted into violence in the spring of 1775. Two months after the battle of Lexington and Concord, she wrote that given Joseph's "civil and military" roles, his "return [and thus hers] to England at present [is] totally improper." The tone of her comment suggests near despair, but the phrase "at present" suggests a glimmer of hope.[62]

Joseph's thinking is less clear. Initially, he had shared Esther's view of their retreat into exile in America as a necessary but temporary tactic. He had gone to London in 1770 to stay. By 1774, however, Joseph's position in

America, and possibly his thinking, had evolved. Before their wedding, he had told Esther he could be happy anywhere with her. On the eve of his departure from Trenton to marry her and settle permanently in London, he had reminded her: I "leave all of these, my native country and whatever is thought dearest in life to return and give you this last greatest proof of my affection." Now, he had both Esther and his native country. Early on, commenting on Joseph's initial success in America, Dennis warned Esther that Joseph "may come to love [America] too well" and reminded her that Joseph had once said that he would "rather be the first man in a [village] than the second in the city." A year later, Dennis, elated by Joseph's continued success, speculated, "He may sooner accumulate a comfortable independence and return to his and your favorite country," but then asked, "Does he still talk of it with pleasure or is he more and more reconciling himself to America?" By 1775, the Reeds' success could lead them in either direction: to a growing attachment to life at the peak of social prominence in the provinces or to the accumulation of the fortune necessary to live more modestly in the center of the empire. The Tea Act of 1773 and the accelerating constitutional struggle between Great Britain and her North American colonies through 1774 and 1775 posed that question in increasingly stark terms and compelled both Esther and Joseph to choose.[63]

CHAPTER 8

A New Political Identity
"They" Becomes "We"

The Tea Act, passed by Parliament in 1773, reignited the constitutional conflict between Great Britain and her North American colonies. The Boston Tea Party in December provoked the British to enact the harsh Coercive or Intolerable Acts the next spring. The First Continental Congress assembled in Philadelphia in the fall of 1774, and war broke out between the mother country and her North American colonies in April 1775. This escalation of the conflict complicated Esther's life, and, at least for a time, she and Joseph moved in different directions.

Joseph joined the small cadre of business and professional men who initiated opposition to the Tea Act in Philadelphia during the fall of 1773. He also supported the Reeds' friends in suffering Boston, renewed old friendships, and made new contacts when Congress met in his hometown in the fall of 1774. In the winter of 1774–75, he led Philadelphia's preparation for war, and then went off to join Washington at camp in Cambridge, Massachusetts, in June 1775.

Through this escalating conflict, Joseph continued to act, in his biographer's phrase, as a "Patriot who would be Peacemaker."[1] He appreciated the economic benefits he and many Americans derived from their British connection. He looked to England for his cultural standards and his political principles. He had for years hoped to make his home and his reputation in London. He thought of himself as one with the English people, the English nation. But, as he explained to Charles Pettit, "the right of taxation was incompatible with my idea of our rights derived under the British Constitution."[2]

From the fall of 1773 through the winter of 1777–78, Joseph supported American resistance and worked, negotiated, and fought bravely and heroically to preserve both American rights and America's connection to Great Britain. He wanted the English political nation to see that their political choices were driving reasonable, loyal, and respectable people toward desperate ends. The British were threatening the property, interests, rights, and historic internal self-government of each of the colonies, and compounding the problem by suggesting that colonials were somehow inferior people.

Esther remained a sympathetic but apprehensive observer who initially saw this dispute as another impediment to going home. Only late in the fall of 1775, after two years of disappointment, frustration, and rising disillusionment with the English people, did she, like Abigail Adams, make her personal decision to actively support resistance and commit what in her mind was treason.[3]

Esther understood the conflict as a political problem amenable to a political solution. The ministry in London now in power pursued policies that upset a growing number of colonials. The answer was to change the ministry or its policies. In her experience, ministries came and went, and policies changed accordingly. She hoped and expected that interests in America would come together with sympathetic interests at home to overcome the ignorance, the myopia, and the arrogance of men in power in London at that time and compel them to change. That, she thought, was how the political world worked. In the end, however, as first one and then another powerful voice at home turned against the colonies, and against her, she came to valorize American resistance and committed herself to support what she called this "glorious cause." Here, in the political, as in the domestic realm, she saw herself as an adult freely making choices and assuming responsibility for her decisions.

During the buildup to Philadelphia's confrontation with the tea ship in December 1773, Esther said little. Parliament had passed the Tea Act in May, keeping that hated tax on tea and authorizing the East India Company to market its tea in America through consignees with virtual monopoly privileges. The *Pennsylvania Gazette* reported the news on September 19,

117

and the city's merchants, including Joseph, met on October 18 to plan their resistance. Esther, in her October 28 letter to Dennis, ignored both the issue and Joseph's first foray into public political action. She did, however, hint at her feelings and her realization of how all this would impact her life. She reiterated her desire to return to London and her belief that Joseph agreed with her. For now, she wrote, she chose to "not press him to form any intention concerning it." If he "had a handsome fortune," she wrote, he would be "willing to enjoy it in England." But lacking that, they had to stay where they were for now.[4]

Parliament responded to the Boston Tea Party in the spring of 1774. It punished Boston by closing its harbor, and then imposing a cluster of changes intended to strengthen central control over local government in the province. Esther sympathized with the people of Boston but did not identify with them. "News of . . . [the closing of the port of Boston] distresses every thinking person," she wrote in May 1774, and reported, "The Provinces are determined to . . . make a common cause." Here, as throughout her correspondence for the next year and a half, her choice of words suggests much that she does not explicitly say. She wrote, "Every thinking person" and not "I," and "the provinces," not "we." Esther knew that Joseph felt sufficiently upset by these questions to neglect his law business and to redirect his talents and energy into a leadership position in the political agitation. She also would have understood the threat to the family's secondary source of economic success (commerce) posed by the East India Company's virtual monopoly on the American tea market. She may not, however, have appreciated fully the constitutional question at the heart of the evolving dispute between America and the mother country. She had been raised and acculturated in a world in which the sovereignty of the king in Parliament had been the dominant mode of constitutional thought since long before her birth. Nor had she yet developed the American sensitivity to the condescension reflected in the British assumption of colonial subordination and therefore of colonial inferiority. Indeed, she had started with such feelings about the colonies. For the next seventeen months (from May 1774 to October 1775), she did not share Joseph's political perspective. As with Jane Bartram, her contemporary in Philadelphia, Esther maintained her internal political autonomy, her private political subjectivity, and her separate political consciousness.[5]

The First Continental Congress met in Philadelphia in the fall of 1774, and Esther joined Joseph in greeting, entertaining, and interrogating the delegates, especially those from New England. For a month, she provided room, board, and conversation for her old family friend Richard Cary, down from Massachusetts to observe the Congress. After he left, she commented, "I never entertained any person more affectionately or with greater pleasure."[6]

Esther also organized dinners in her home for delegates, and she participated in these typically all-male occasions in much the same way that she had mixed freely with the male guests at her father's regular Sunday dinners in London during the 1760s.[7] John Adams and Silas Deane attest to her presence and participation. Adams usually recorded the details of the setting and the servings at the dinners he attended, but he seldom mentioned the presence of women. When he dined at the Reeds', however, he explicitly noted that Esther and her mother dined with the men.[8]

Silas Deane, a delegate from Connecticut, seldom mentioned women at all in his letters to his wife, but after dining with Esther and Joseph he described for her not only her physical appearance but also his impression of her political beliefs. She is, he wrote, "small . . . [with] a most elegant figure and countenance. She is a Daughter of Liberty zealously affected in a good cause."[9] Here, as in most cases, Esther's social skills allowed her to move easily in a variety of complex political contexts. She may well have appeared to Deane as a zealous "Daughter of Liberty" while the First Continental Congress met in September 1774, and especially in meetings with New England men, but she did not make her own personal commitment for another year or more. In the fall of 1774, her primary concern was for the safety of her family.

The visiting New Englanders, and especially Esther's "Boston Men," encouraged her to see the conflict through their eyes, but once they departed, her enthusiasm waned. She understood that a hostile response by the British could precipitate violence. People in Pennsylvania, she reported, remained optimistic about a peaceful settlement, but "the people of New England have no such expectations." They are ready, she said, to die for liberty. "These dreadful events," as she described them, made her "wish for a safe retreat in Old England." Still, she admitted, "I hardly know in which country the safest retreat could be found."[10]

In December 1774, Joseph won election to the Philadelphia committee charged with enforcing the Congressional Non-Importation Agreement, and in January 1775, he presided over a province-wide convention that added military preparedness to the economic boycott. By February 1775, Esther reported that Joseph's "engagements in business are so numerous and extensive that his head is almost overcharged . . . his late attention to politics has engrossed him more than common."[11]

Esther remained conflicted, as her comments on the Quakers and on Benjamin Franklin reveal. The "Quakers," she wrote, "are endeavouring to steer a middle course and make perhaps a merit of it to Government at home. How far their conduct will answer, I don't know, but it is despised here." Two features of her word choice stand out. First, for Esther, "home" is still England ("the Government at home"). Second, she writes in the passive voice (the Quakers' behavior "is despised"), allowing herself to describe without taking sides.[12]

In contrast, she explicitly criticized Franklin for his equivocation and his motives. "[T]ell us ... whether he has the openness to declare his sentiments before he sees which way affairs will terminate," she wrote to Dennis. She herself, she admitted, had "a share in both countries and am interested in the welfare of both more than the common run of the people here."[13] She worried that her feelings differed from those of her neighbors. "I love to think of England and of old times," she wrote. "[P]erhaps I may see it again. It is surely a noble country, but such wishes and hopes I must keep concealed." Here, shortly before the outbreak of war, she reveals a conscious effort to restructure her thinking. "[P]erhaps," she continued, "they [such thoughts and hopes] had better not arise at all."[14]

Between the adjournment of Congress in late October 1774 and the outbreak of war in April 1775, Esther badgered her brother for political news from London. She wanted to know about the evolution of public opinion in the capital, and especially about the political activities of the merchants who, she expected, would support America's interests. She wanted to know about the divisions in Parliament itself. "[W]rite us every piece of intelligence concerning American affairs . . . especially what is said in the House and who is on *our* side [emphasis added] and who is against," a significant but temporary shift in pronouns.[15]

In turn, she analyzed for Dennis the political developments in America. She believed that in New England no "power on earth could take . . . liberty . . . from them but with their lives." However, she denied British accusations that America sought independence. "This country," she wrote, "wishes for nothing so much as dependency on the Mother State on proper terms, [and] to be secure in their liberties," a view that would have resonated well with the thinking of many of those most actively engaged in the resistance.[16]

News of the bloodshed at Lexington and Concord arrived in Philadelphia on April 24, 1775. Within days, Joseph rushed off a letter of support for the people of Massachusetts, and then devoted most of his time to mobilizing military and financial support for the eastern provinces. When Congress reassembled in Philadelphia, Esther and Joseph entertained George Washington and a small number of men from New England, Philadelphia, and Virginia. The group, including Esther and her mother, stayed up past midnight discussing "the most feasible and prudent method of stopping up the channel of the Delaware River to prevent the coming up of any large ships to the city." One of the New England visitors, an admiralty court judge from Salem, Massachusetts, on his way to becoming a loyalist, noted, "I could not perceive the least disposition to accommodate matters."[17]

In June 1775, Congress appointed George Washington commander in chief, and before he left to take up his new responsibilities near Boston, Washington dined with the Reeds. Before the dinner ended, he had persuaded the young lawyer to ride with him as far as New York on his way to Cambridge. On the way, the forty-three-year-old planter from Virginia convinced the thirty-three-year old lawyer from Philadelphia to accompany him to Cambridge to serve as his secretary.

Joseph's departure with Washington disrupted Esther's daily life, intensified her fears, and compelled her to think about the future in very specific terms. Throughout these years of accelerating crisis, Esther had been serving as "private secretary to Mr. Reed," as she had earlier to her father. She therefore knew much of Joseph's thinking. Her brother understood that she had access to Joseph's personal and business correspondence. In late May 1775, he wrote directly to Esther about business he had undertaken in London for the Reeds. Joseph, diverted by his political activities, had failed to respond to letters from Dennis, and Dennis turned to Esther, knowing that she had both the information and the understanding to guide him.[18]

Esther not only knew about Joseph's political activities, but she also believed that she could influence his decisions. That had been the case between 1765 and 1770, when he had relied on her counsel and her London connections as he struggled in New Jersey and when she determined that if they were to marry, they must live in England. It also seems to have been the case in their abrupt departure from Burlington for Philadelphia shortly after their arrival in America. Esther hated that tiny and remote village, and they had soon decided to live in Philadelphia, a move Joseph had not planned before their arrival in America and one that involved increased financial risks.[19]

In 1775, Esther expressed much the same sense of efficacy. For some months, they had discussed returning to England. Esther, Dennis, and Joseph had each mentioned it at one point or another in their correspondence, and Dennis expected it to happen. For Dennis, only the timing remained uncertain. In the end, Esther and Joseph chose to stay, but Esther felt that she had been part of that decision. In June 1775, she wrote, "For much as I wish him free of danger yet I could not ask him to act so cowardly a part as to fly when his country so eminently needs his assistance." She had not asked him, but she felt that she could have asked, and she also felt that such a request on her part would not have been unreasonable, inappropriate, or futile. She believed that Joseph would respond to her needs, should she express them strongly, but she had not yet decided.[20]

Meanwhile, Esther found Joseph's absence difficult. His decision could not have surprised her. Washington had, for some time, been pressing Joseph to join his "family," and she had been part of the conversation at the dinner in her home. Undoubtedly, she and Joseph had discussed it. Washington had accepted the position of commander in chief on June 16 and spent the dinner hour of June 19 with the Reeds. This was his second visit to their home since his arrival from Virginia on May 9. Indeed, he spent his first evening in Philadelphia with the Reeds. Moreover, this was a highly coveted position actively sought by a number of other young men with far better political connections. It placed Joseph close to power and close to the action, and it involved no great sacrifice since Congress intended to pay a respectable salary while Joseph's income in Philadelphia promised to suffer as hostilities intensified. Esther's words in June and Joseph's in August suggest they had discussed it before he left the city. But if the move did not surprise her, the difficulties of living without him tested her. She had become the head of her growing family with a household to manage and increased responsibilities for overseeing the law office. As Joseph wrote, "You will hear and know what is to be done on the law business of which I beg you to give me the earliest intimations." "I confess it is a trial I never thought I should have experienced," she told her brother, "and am the less prepared to bear it."[21]

Esther missed Joseph. Since their long-delayed marriage, they had seldom been apart for more than a few days. As Dennis later wrote, undoubtedly expressing feelings Esther had conveyed to him, "Alas, my dear Hetty, what dreadful times. . . . War in the country where you reside. Your dearest friend taking an active part [and] . . . friendship's sweet channel stopped up."[22]

The war frightened her. Young (twenty-eight), the mother of three small children, with the youngest still at the breast, and living among a people she still saw as "the other," as "them," as "they" fighting for "their liberties," she needed comfort, support, and familiar faces. In her straits, she implored

Dennis to come to America to "protect and take care of us if my dear Mr. Reed should be called to act in defense of his country."[23]

Family and friends, in their concern for her, added to her burdens. Her brother-in-law, Charles Pettit, pressed her to come live with his family in Perth Amboy, New Jersey, but the tone of his letter implied some hesitation. He would come to get her, he said, but he was "tied up here for a few days" and suggested that he and his wife might not easily accommodate all of Esther's family. John Cox, long one of Joseph's friends and the husband of one of Esther's closest American friends, urged Esther to send some of her family to live with Joseph's married younger brother, Bowes Reed, in Burlington, New Jersey, and take the rest to live with Mrs. Cox at their summer place by the river.[24] Given Esther's independent spirit, having others plan her life undoubtedly discomforted her. Moreover, no adult woman, mistress in her own home, happily accepted the implicit subordination involved in living in another woman's household. For most of July, Esther tried to solve this problem. She and Joseph usually took a place outside the city for the summer, especially for the benefit of their eldest daughter, Patty, whose health seemed better away from the city in the hot months. Joseph encouraged Esther to do the same again in his absence, but she could find nothing that suited her purposes, either near Philadelphia or in New Jersey. Finally, late in July or early in August, she gave in and divided her family between Burlington and Perth Amboy.[25]

By the time she returned to the city in late October 1775, she had made America's cause her own. She understood the risks. She anticipated that supporting the American cause would brand her a traitor. She continued to hope that the king would consider the American petitions and thereby "lay the foundations for negotiations" so "we may again be reconciled," but she anticipated that the British would remain intransigent. The temporary stranger in this strange land now identified with her new countrymen and joined a small but growing cadre ready to declare "our" independence and defend "ourselves" to the utmost against what had been, not long ago, "Dear England."[26]

An intelligent, articulate, charming, ambitious, cosmopolitan, strong-willed, well-educated, and politically aware young woman, Esther DeBerdt Reed cared about public affairs, took pains to inform herself, engaged prominent men in serious discussions of weighty public matters, and felt capable of influencing her family's political choices. In the summer of 1775, she understood the implications of the decisions that she and Joseph faced. Late that fall, she chose America over England and took a conspicuous stand on the matter. Why remains to be explored. Family considerations pushed her both ways. Her brother was in London and her mother was with her in America, but mostly she worried about the safety of her children. Friends also played some role. Over time, Esther's letters mention her English friends less and her American friends more. The New England men who first visited her home in the fall of 1774, and intermittently thereafter, also had an effect. Esther had known some of them in London, where they had congregated at her father's house, and she had regularly mingled with them at her father's Sunday dinners. Esther had undoubtedly also corresponded with many of them when she served as secretary to her father. Mr. Cary, from Massachusetts, who had worked with great diligence in support of DeBerdt's appointment as colonial agency for Massachusetts, had a warm place in Esther's heart.[27]

Esther's religious beliefs and affiliation contributed. Remember: her father's people had migrated to England from Flanders "for the sake of religion." In London, Esther's parents, Calvinists living in an Anglican nation, had identified with religious dissenters, and their religious affiliation had helped cement the commercial links with the Presbyterian Reeds in the Delaware River area and with the Boston Men in Congregational Massachusetts. Her father had maintained close and financially supportive relations with at least two of America's Presbyterian colleges.[28] Joseph later criticized Dennys DeBerdt for allowing his religious identity with Presbyterians in America to override his business sense and believed that DeBerdt's religion-influenced business decisions had contributed significantly to the collapse of the DeBerdt firm in 1770.

Esther, like her father and mother, took her religion seriously. A fragment of Esther's youthful diary suggests a rather intense and introspective spirituality.[29] Esther's Calvinist background linked her to the Congregationalists from New England, and her father's religion had played a part in the decision by Massachusetts to choose him as their agent in London. When she and Joseph had moved to Philadelphia, they joined the Second Presbyterian Church on Arch Street, and she and her mother attended regularly. Her Calvinist theology made it possible for her to see resistance to establish authority as morally acceptable, and her regular participation with the Presbyterians in the Arch Street Presbyterian Church under the leadership of Reverend Sproat surrounded her with a people who strengthened and reinforced her transformation. A visitor to the Arch Street Presbyterian Church reported that Esther's minister, Mr. Sproat, had "entertained them . . . with a truly American patriotic sermon."[30]

In contrast, Joseph was far more casual in his formal religious beliefs and observance. He was a child of a mixed marriage. His Presbyterian father had married Joseph's Anglican mother. Although she had died when he was young, as an adult he maintained close contacts with at least two of his mother's sisters. Joseph also felt that differences in religion posed no difficulties for young people in love. In response to a question from Dennis DeBerdt about his courtship of a woman who did not share his religious attachments, Joseph assured Dennis that he should not hesitate to marry her on those grounds. His own Presbyterian father, Reed pointed out, had married "three Episcopal [Anglican] wives," and "such matters are so frequent here and no fatal misunderstanding arises from them." Thus, if "in all other respects she will make you happy . . . the difference among Protestants is not so essential as that a man do violence to his inclination on that account."[31]

The family's financial success also exerted pressure on Esther's political decision. The Reeds had prospered in Philadelphia. Joseph, in Esther's estimation, headed the city's legal hierarchy. They lived well in Philadelphia, spent summers in the country, and asserted their rising status by dressing the slaves who drove them in livered uniforms.[32] If they fled to England, they would take little of their wealth or status with them. Conversely, by the summer of 1775 the Reeds' financial situation in America had grown less secure. Disruption of the courts restricted Joseph's legal income. The trade boycotts had already reduced the family's commercial profits, and the British effort to close American ports would further erode those profits. Then, early in June, Joseph learned that he had lost his major patronage appointment in New Jersey, a post that constituted the principal support of his brother-in-law's family.[33]

Indeed, the Reeds might have had better prospects in London. Although their wealth and status would not travel well, Joseph and Esther would bring with them their industry, their skill, and the rudiments of some important connections. With an additional year of training at the Inns of Court, Joseph could practice his profession in England, and he had already done legal work in America for both English and Irish clients. Joseph himself had started over in 1765 when he had returned home from London to care for a family suddenly plunged into financial crisis. Esther and Joseph together had made a near miraculous economic recovery between 1770 and 1775 after their hasty retreat from London. Esther's brother had developed important connections in London. Joseph had worked closely with him between 1770 and 1775 to help the inexperienced young man enter the business of international trade, and by 1775 Dennis had regained some of the income and stature his father had enjoyed at the time of his death in 1770. In 1775, Joseph used his connections in New Jersey to obtain Dennis's appointment as London agent for that province.[34] In the same vein, until 1775, Joseph had corresponded regularly with Lord Dartmouth, and as late as the summer of 1775, Dartmouth had continued to express his interest in hearing from Joseph. Had the Reeds chosen England over America, they would have faced another financial crisis, but given their past accomplishments, their London connections, and the possibility of support from the ministry as well as Esther's London family, they could have had reasonable expectations of a third recovery. The cost of returning to England would have been high, but not impossibly so, while the costs of remaining in America, already high in 1775, promised to grow.

Other factors, difficult to calculate precisely, also shaped their thinking. The war itself changed things. Beneath the city's apparent calm during the late winter and early spring of 1775, its people had waited with growing apprehension. Then, in April, news of bloodshed in Massachusetts broke the emotional logjam, and the city exploded with martial spirit. Until then, the city had been calm, almost boring. Four days before news of Lexington and Concord reached the city, Dr. Robert Honyman had toured Philadelphia and seen no signs of martial spirit. Staying at the Indian Queen, walking the streets, shopping, and eating in public places, he reported no military preparations: no drilling, no marching, and no uniforms.[35] By the first week of May, Honyman would not have recognized the city. News of war disrupted normal activities, and emotions intensified almost daily. Friday, May 5, for example, saw "drums beating, colors flying, and detachments of newly raised militia parading the streets." Saturday, May 6, brought "the ringing of bells to the great joy of the city" and announced Franklin's return home. The same day, the city "turned out over 4,000 men, 300 of whom are Quakers," in what one observer described as "The Rage Militaire." By Monday, May 8, "almost every man that can produce a firelock [was] . . . learning the military discipline." The New England delegation to Congress arrived on Tuesday, May 9, in a magnificent "cavalcade" escorted through the city by "two or three hundred gentlemen on horseback, preceded . . . by the newly chosen city militia officers, two by two, with drawn swords . . . [while] the rear was brought up by a hundred carriages, the streets crowded with people of all ages, sexes and ranks, . . . [and] all the bells set to ringing and chiming." That night, Esther and Joseph stayed up past midnight debating military tactics with newly arrived congressmen. In the heat of such public frenzy, both Esther and Joseph might, understandably, have made decisions without a careful assessment of the costs.[36]

The Virginians added a new ingredient to the mix. Esther knew Philadelphia men, and she had close personal ties with New England men, but Virginians were different. Men of authority with stature, grace, and power, masters of thousands of acres and hundreds of lives, and showmen of the first order, they cut a fine figure among the rather dowdy Philadelphians and the plain New Englanders. In Esther's experience, these Virginia planters came as close as anyone in America to replicating the English landed gentry to whom even wealthy merchants and successful lawyers in England paid deference. As Joseph wrote in September 1774, "there are some fine fellows come from Virginia. . . . The Bostonians are mere Milksops to them. They are the capital men of the colony both in fortune and understanding." In May 1775, Esther entertained at least three of them in her home: the solemn, forceful, and flammable Richard Henry Lee; the six-foot-four Benjamin Harrison, grandson of Robert "King" Carter and now speaker of the Virginia House of Burgesses; and the most charismatic of them all, George Washington: well over six feet tall, a horseman, a dancer, an eloquent "presence" with an "animal vitality" and "an air of power reined in."[37]

Washington's impact on people would be hard to exaggerate. "There is not a king in Europe," one man noted, "but would look like a valet de chambre by his side." Women responded with similar hyperbole. Abigail Adams, in a letter to John shortly after she met the new general, first multiplied her own flattering images: "modesty," "dignity," "ease," "complacence," "the gentleman and soldier . . . agreeably blend in him." Then she turned to the poet Dryden for help: "Mark his majestic fabric; he's a temple / Sacred by birth and built by hands divine."[38]

Esther has left us no description of Washington, but she understood and shared Joseph's attraction to this handsome, imposing, charming man of military bearing and vitality who played court to the Reeds. He dined at Esther's table, where they discussed political and military matters. He invited Joseph to ride with him to New York, and on the way he persuaded Joseph to risk his life and the security and prosperity of his family by taking up arms against his sovereign.[39]

Esther had long been sensitive to subtle social distinctions. She had informed Joseph, early in their courtship, that she wanted him to be a lawyer, not a merchant. When she and Joseph arrived in America, they had tarried only a short time in New Jersey. In Philadelphia, she took pride in their growing wealth and increased status as Joseph moved quickly to the top ranks of the legal community. But, at least in Esther's traditional English scale of values, landed gentry such as the Virginia planters trumped professional men. Close association with such men would have been a new and enticing experience for her. By the summer of 1775, she may well have understood that in marching with Virginia rebels, she and Joseph stood shoulder to shoulder with men who overshadowed anyone in Philadelphia, including her spurned suitor Samuel Powel.

None of this would have made much difference, however, had the British intransigence and condescension not driven both Esther and Joseph away. Both had started with a predilection in favor of reconciliation. They assumed that the problem lay with a group of myopic and arrogant British officials who had initiated and then perpetuated the conflict, possibly on the advice of malicious appointees in the colonies. Over time, however, the Reeds grew increasingly impatient with the entire English nation. Joseph's letters throughout 1774–75 suggest his concern about British ministers who "despise the good will of this country," about "the scandalous treatment of Dr. Franklin," about a "spirit of domination in the Mother Country," and about English "contempt" for America's petitions against the "absolute uncontrolled power of Parliament." His letters also reflect the erosion of his affection for "Great Britain, a country wherein I have spent many happy hours," as he saw her begin "to play the tyrant over America."[40]

Esther, too, had come to appreciate, and possibly to share, the colonial resentment of the arrogance and insensitivity of her visiting English countrymen. Charles Pettit, Esther's brother-in-law and Joseph's close business associate, expressed these resentments in a letter to Joseph in January 1774, when he complained about Englishmen who "come . . . intoxicated with the absurd Prejudice . . . that they are of an order of Beings superior to the rest of their species." The young and cosmopolitan Esther had herself exhibited much of those same feelings toward provincial Americans when she had first arrived, and she later conceded that her attitude might have made her own transition to this new country difficult. Relying on her personal experience, in the fall of 1774 she cautioned Dennis that if he came to America, he would need to take care not to fall "into the many errors, which almost every Englishman does on his arrival here." Now she too was coming to share the colonial resentment of this British condescension.[41]

During the winter and early spring of 1774–75, Esther and Joseph saw America's efforts at economic coercion and military preparations as political vehicles to mobilize powerful forces in England, especially merchants and manufacturers, in support of changing the policy or the ministry. From late December 1774 through early 1775, letters arriving from their British correspondents encouraged them to think this might be happening. Late in January, Joseph reported to Pettit that the "tide is certainly turning towards America," and "on the whole we have more reason to hope than to fear." In mid-February, Joseph, writing to Dennis but aware that his message would probably reach Dartmouth, said, "all parties are not so far from reconciliation as may be imagined." "The proceedings of Congress," he conceded, "have been pitched in too high a key for some of these middle provinces." He insisted that all Americans, with the possible exception of officeholders under the crown, remained united on the question of the tax, but he outlined plans to defuse this immediate crisis and build toward structural changes that would prevent future conflicts. Esther, as late as March 14, told Dennis, "If the popular and mercantile voices [in England] are in our favour, I think there is great reason for our hopes."

Esther and Joseph believed that there was, indeed, a middle ground. Joseph himself had proposed at least two ways "to prevent apprehended extremities." One was for the mother country to "temporize" with respect to "the acts lately passed, leave the question of rights undiscussed," and have the colonies pay for the tea in deference to the "dignity of the Mother Country." A second approach, one that Joseph preferred, would be to suspend the present acts, and then call together representatives of the assemblies to negotiate a new constitution for America that would provide for "those restraints necessary for the interests of the whole."[42]

Letters arriving in the late winter and early spring of 1775, however, suggested that the ministry intended to take a hard line, and that the expected support from key economic interests in England had failed to materialize. The Reeds had had hints of ministerial intransigency late in 1774 in an unsigned letter from London, presumably from Lord Dartmouth. Although the author remained cordial to the Reeds, he took a decided stance against Americans who "totally forget the nature of that connexion by which they are held to the Mother Country. . . . The Supreme Legislature of the whole British Empire has laid a Duty." If Americans refuse to submit, they say "in effect that they will no longer be a part of the British Empire." If, in fact, Dartmouth had written this letter, then the Reeds had reason to worry. They had long thought of Dartmouth as a family ally, and as one of the more moderate members of the current ministry.[43]

Dennis heightened the Reeds' concerns. He felt that "the inflamed zeal of a few [in America] will destroy the mild measures of the Congress," and he reported British preparations for war. He explained that the London merchants trading to America, while concerned for their business, had not united in support of America's position or its principles, and he expected the ministry to prevent the meeting of Congress scheduled for May 10.[44]

Josiah Quincy, visiting London, confirmed DeBerdt's analysis. Quincy found the commercial world in London "ill-disposed" and predicted that neither the economic consequences nor the "religion of the British ministers will . . . restrain them." He asserted that the "threat of arms in our hands" would do more than petitions from the British merchants to advance the American cause, and asked, "Hath not blood and treasure in all ages been the price of civil liberty?" Soon, the London merchants trading to Americans disintegrated as an effective lobbying force. By March, they had divided among themselves over whether to focus their efforts on protecting their "interests" or to expand their concerns to the broad questions of liberty and the constitution. Even Dennis seemed to be wobbling. In February 1775, Joseph had cautioned him, and then chided him a bit: "I suspect you . . . have fallen off a bit from the old principles of your family with respect to this country."[45]

Then, on April 19, much to Esther's frustration, the British resort to arms at Lexington and Concord in Massachusetts placed new and powerful obstacles in the path to reconciliation, postponing, if not actually precluding, a compromise. Joseph had stated that any effort by the British to use force would unite the colonies, "change those now questioning Congress," and lead to widespread bloodshed. Esther expressed much the same understanding: "Whatever our fellow subjects may think, the people here are determined to die free," she wrote in June. By the time Joseph left her to ride with Washington, Esther had begun in earnest to do what she had hinted at some months earlier: to suppress her feelings of attachments to England and refashion her commitment to "this glorious cause."[46] Before he returned, she had decided.

In complex questions like these, probably no particular moment can be singled out in which fundamental change occurred. One's thoughts move first one way and then another. External circumstances of the moment, as well as the accumulation of experiences over time, shape and reshape feelings. One is never sure, seldom absolutely convinced, and rarely so transformed as to resist looking back. Nonetheless, there can be little doubt that the four months between June and October were decisive for Esther.

Four letters she wrote to Dennis in these months show her moving, in fits and starts, toward new loyalties and a new political identity. She began in fear; progressed through anger, frustration, and increasing idealization of the American cause; and ended in disillusionment with her people at home and to the understanding that the British were driving Americans, including herself, toward the unthinkable: separation from Great Britain and the creation of a new people.

On the day after Joseph's departure, Esther expressed her anxieties to Dennis. She did not know precisely what Joseph would do, but she understood that they were stepping into murky and treacherous waters. "What melancholy scenes we have lived to be engaged in; civil war, with all its horrors, stains this land," she wrote. She worried about Joseph's health. He had been "very unwell this summer with an intermitting fever." She also knew that "the part which my dear Mr. Reed has taken in the civil and military affairs of his country" now prevented them from returning home. She may have indirectly criticized Joseph's recent behavior in her description of the intensity of popular feelings in the city: "The people here are determined to die or be free. They are now raised to a pitch it was thought they never could arrive at; but so it is, and they shrink not at anything that appears before them."[47]

But if the emotions of the American people frightened her, she accepted the legitimacy of their position, and she prayed that "a kind Providence will interpose yet in our favour and find out some way for our relief." She tried to be brave but felt increasingly vulnerable.[48]

A month later, she wrote again. By now, she knew that Joseph would not return soon. Patty's poor health concerned her, she could not find accommodations in the country, and she faced a division of her family and a protracted stay in another woman's home. In a rare instance of complaint, she asserted that Joseph's unexpected absence had left her poorly prepared to deal with the consequences. Then, however, she exhibited her growing determination to valorize the cause. She still hoped for the sympathy and understanding of the British people. "What do you think—what do the people in general think of our distresses and conduct?" she asked. For the first time, she explicitly praised the American position. "Certainly, my dear brother," she wrote, "it is a glorious ... [cause].... Virtue, honour, unanimity, bravery,—all conspire to carry it on." And then, half hoping and half asserting, she concluded, "And sure it [the cause] has at least a chance to be victorious. I believe it will, at last, whatever difficulties and discouragements it may meet with at first."[49]

Early in September, about ten weeks after Joseph's departure, she again wrote to Dennis, suggesting the difficulties she faced in putting a good face on things. She was living in the Pettits' home in Perth Amboy, where she had taken her eldest daughter. Her mother was with the other two children in Burlington. Joseph's law business in Philadelphia had languished, despite the effort of his clerks, and Joseph remained vague about the time of his return. Those who reported on Esther's condition emphasized both the strain under which she suffered and her courage in bearing it. "The good Mrs. Reed," John Cox told Joseph, "bears your absence with a degree of heroism that does her inexpressible credit yet the good soul at times cannot help showing an anxiety for your return which sensibly affects us, her friends." He assured Joseph that he himself had tried to "keep up the good Mrs. Reed's spirits during your long absence," but despite his best efforts, "she begins now to be rather uneasy."[50]

In contrast, Esther paints a rather more sanguine picture of her immediate living circumstances. She informed Dennis that their mother had recovered from a mild illness, and that Esther herself and Patty were in Perth Amboy, where the air and the food had agreed with the child, and Esther herself was enjoying her visit.[51]

The broader political situation, however, bedeviled her. She worried about Joseph at camp "amidst all the confusion and horrors of war." She admitted that the continued disruption "sometimes shakes my firmness and resolution," but she also acknowledged that one can get used to almost anything. Moreover, she now knew that Joseph was relatively safe, serving in the councils rather than in the field, and she would therefore more "cheerfully give up his profits . . . and . . . acquiesce without repining at his being so long absent from me."[52]

She continued to praise "the cause in which he is engaged, so just, so glorious," but she backed off a bit from her July judgment. "I hope," she wrote, instead of the earlier "I believe," it "will be so victorious."[53] By "victorious," she meant that the American effort would produce political change in England. She thought that the American demonstration of military prowess might convince the ministry of America's determination, and she asked Dennis "what effect the Battle of Bunker Hill [June 1775] has both on our friends and our enemies." At the same time, she felt betrayed by those at home as well as disillusioned. She asked, "Where sleep all our friends in England? . . . Where sleep the virtue and justice of the English nation? Will nothing rouse them, or are they so few in number, and small in consequence, that though awake, their voice cannot be heard in the multitude of our enemies?"[54] For Esther, politics on one plane was a question of virtue and justice, but on another it was also a question of friends and enemies. And transcending both of these was her understanding of herself as a member of a nation, a people, a community, and a family.

She allowed herself a few minutes of regret. "Could we have foreseen it, when we [Esther and Dennis] parted in England, it would probably have prevented that separation," she wrote, but then corrected herself and reasserted her will. "[But] I believe it is right we should not, for though our private happiness might have been promoted, yet our country would not have been benefited." She ended her letter on a revealing note: "I hope it is no treason to say I wish well to the Cause of America." Here, as earlier, she maintained a distance between herself and "the Cause of America." Although she wished it well, it remained their cause, not hers. She had had an interest in both countries. Their divergence compelled her toward a choice, and while she saw the justice of the one, she continued to feel an identity with the other. More significantly, she revealed that she thought of herself as close to committing treason. She assumed that government officials opened and read her letters. She thought of herself as a member of the English nation supporting rebellion against it. Equally important, Esther here assumed that she was a free agent capable of making an independent, and therefore punishable, political decision.[55]

Late in October, Esther again wrote to Dennis. She had recently returned to Philadelphia and expected Joseph to join her there within the week. She sent this letter by private hands, not via the postal system, and thus felt freer of "any prying intruder." She worried a bit about her earlier indiscretions but then reaffirmed her position: "If I have committed treason, it must remain," she declared. She had acted and now must follow it through.[56]

In this October 28 letter, Esther defined the issue as "the cause of liberty and virtue," but, as Joseph himself wrote at about the same time, she still saw the struggle as one for change of policy or change of ministry, to "return to the old ground of 1763." She hoped that the recent petitions from Congress might modify British policy and thus "lay the foundation for negotiations ... [so that] we may be again reconciled." She asserted, however, that should that fail, "WE SHALL DECLARE FOR INDEPENDENCE, and exert our utmost to defend ourselves." Now, "if the ministry and the Nation will drive us to it, we must do it, rather than submit," she concluded. Americans had become "WE" and "ourselves" and "us."[57]

Esther, like many of her neighbors, would have preferred to remain English, but her countrymen had driven her away: first the ministry, then Dartmouth, the king, the merchants, the manufacturers, possibly Dennis, and finally "all our friends in England" and "the virtue and justice of the English nation."[58]

CHAPTER 9

"Unleash the Dogs of War"

Joseph returned to Esther in Philadelphia in November 1775, but the fighting and its disruptions followed him home, and for the next two and a half years Esther and Joseph lived in the cockpit of the war of the American Revolution. In the spring of 1776, the British evacuated Boston, and then, before the end of that year, defeated the Continental Army in Brooklyn, chasing Washington the length of Manhattan and across New Jersey to the Delaware River within sight of Philadelphia. When the next campaign began in 1777, they attacked Pennsylvania from the south, defeated Washington at Brandywine Creek and at Germantown, and then occupied Philadelphia for the winter of 1777–78.

These were the two worst years of Esther's life. She endured physical disruption, emotional turmoil, transient living, protracted separation from her husband, and the death of her daughter and the birth of her son, both in a remote area of New Jersey. Her persistent dispute with Joseph over how he should serve his country intensified her suffering. Not until the fall of 1778, three months after the British evacuation of Philadelphia, did she again feel safe with her children and secure and united in purpose with her husband. In these crucial years, few, if any, patriot women of Esther's status paid a higher price for their commitment to the American cause.

But that was still in the future, and for now she was content. Joseph had returned to her, and she once again presided over her own household.

Martha Washington's visit added some excitement. Traveling from Virginia to join her husband at camp with the Continental Army at Cambridge, Massachusetts, Mrs. Washington stopped in Philadelphia for a protracted stay with Esther, who welcomed her into her home.[1] This visit may well have been part of the general's campaign to bring Joseph back to him in Cambridge, a social occasion with a political agenda, a practice Esther knew well. Indeed, at a dinner in the Reed home in June 1775, Washington had persuaded Joseph to ride with him as far as New York City when the general left to take command of the fledgling Continental Army assembling in Cambridge, Massachusetts. Equally significant for Esther's future, Martha's visit also established a personal friendship between the two women that was brought to full flower when Martha again spent time in Esther's household in June 1780.

In midwinter, rumors of a British peace offensive offered hope of an end to the troubles, but Dennis reported from London that the ministry was preparing for a "bloody campaign" and that America could expect little support from the people of Great Britain. Those at home who paid attention to public affairs, he wrote, generally supported the government, while the rest were "immersed in business or sunk in sensuality." Much to America's disadvantage, the ministry had persuaded the English landed interest that Americans were rebelling in order to avoid any taxes and that subduing America would reduce the land tax in Britain. The ministry also depicted Americans as a wretched people "murdering the king's good subjects, scalping and abusing all those unhappy men that fall into [their] hands."[2]

Joseph and Esther each responded to Dennis in late February 1776, Joseph first and then Esther the next day. Here, as in the past, they coordinated their efforts, and here, as in the recent past, they assumed that they wrote not only to Dennis but also through him to the ministry. Both argued for reconciliation between Great Britain and her North American colonies on the basis of peace, prosperity, mutual respect, and a return to the harmony of the years before 1764. Each, however, adopted a different strategy.

Joseph wrote aggressively. He declared that the barbarism of the British was driving America toward the independence America had not intended. Only prompt concessions by the British could prevent that outcome. He condemned the British for seizing American ships, burning its towns, and killing its people. He praised America's unity, its military might, and its determination to fight to "preserve our country from tyranny and bondage." He threatened retaliation against British property in America if the

British seized American property in England. He asserted that reconciliation depended on far more than pardons and suggested a face-saving strategy for the British: blame the trouble on the rascally royal governors who had deceived the ministry with their "falsehood and misrepresentation of the American behavior and motive." "It would have been happy for both countries if we had hung them all years ago," he wrote.[3]

Esther postured less, asserted less, and accused less. Like Joseph, she identified with America: "our country," she wrote. On occasion, however, she still referred to Americans in the third person: not we, but they. She explained her mother's great desire to return "home," and at least by implication she suggested that she shared some of this feeling. She admitted that Americans might have misunderstood British actions in the past, but, right or wrong, they think "they merit the applause of every friend of liberty and mankind . . . [and] it is hard they should be stigmatized with the name of rebels." "Even supposing their liberties not in the danger they imagined," she continued, "they surely have reason to be alarmed." Esther, like Joseph, depicted Americans as principled people driven into the hard "necessity of defending themselves at the hazard of their lives." She, like Joseph, emphasized misunderstanding and the need for meaningful concessions by the British.[4]

But while Joseph concentrated on the costs of military escalation, Esther focused on the felicitous consequences of peace. Joseph accused, blamed, and threatened. Esther soothed and enticed. And in their chosen approaches, each reflected recent experience. Joseph had spent the better part of five months at camp near Cambridge, Massachusetts, among military men led by the charismatic General George Washington. He admired and respected the Virginian who in turn trusted and depended on him. These were exciting times for Joseph. His friends had at first questioned his decision to accompany Washington, and then to stay with him for a protracted period. Soon they came to envy him.

Esther, in sharp contrast, had no good memories of those five months of separation, confusion, and dislocation. She had lived in other women's homes, without Joseph, without her mother, and without most of her children. No one had envied her. Now, in February 1776, she anticipated, possibly better than Joseph, what full-throated war would bring. She wanted admission of error on both sides, reconciliation, and peace.

The difference in tone between the two letters also reflected a difference in political instinct. Joseph, an aggressive lawyer and businessman impatient with ambiguity and intolerant of what he saw as incompetence, relied on threats with weighty consequences that, he assumed, would impress men of weight in London. Esther, in contrast, looked to negotiations, compromise, and face-saving tactics that would achieve the same end with less conflict. Here, we can see a demonstration of her political skills that in time would contribute much to her family's success in 1778 and 1779, and to her own rise to national political prominence in 1780.

But despite their different strategies, both knew they had to prepare for war. They agreed that Philadelphia, easily accessible up the Delaware River from the Atlantic, would soon become dangerous. Joseph noted that "most families of any ability have provided themselves with retreats into the country." Those who could not or would not leave early suffered later when the British came. In December 1776, for example, when the British troops approached Philadelphia across New Jersey, a young woman reported seeing "one family of ten . . . one of which was a young woman and her child six weeks old with their household goods in two open wagons" fleeing through the snow over frozen ground.[5]

Through February and March 1776, Esther and Joseph negotiated where best to seek a secure refuge. Joseph proposed Perth Amboy, New Jersey. The Pettits lived there, and Esther knew the area. Esther refused. Perth Amboy was just across the river from New York City and therefore was just as dangerous as Philadelphia.

They finally agreed to look in central New Jersey. Joseph shopped around and, in a stroke heavy with irony, rented the former residence in Burlington of the royal governor of the province, His Excellency William Franklin, one of the first great homes in America Esther had visited on her arrival more than five years ago. The rent was very attractive: £40 a year, half their rent in Philadelphia, and they could keep a lease on their Philadelphia home at least through December.[6]

Burlington offered much. It was about a day's ride north of Philadelphia on the east side of the Delaware River, just across from Bristol, Pennsylvania, and well beyond the practical reach of British warships. It was quiet and pleasant. It had served as one of the two official capitals of the province of New Jersey for most of its history, and it had treelined streets, houses with attached gardens, a courthouse in the middle of High Street, and two public markets. The governor's house fronted on the river, a bit south of High Street, and had a sixty-foot-wide "river walk" lined with butternut trees and a fine view of Bristol.[7]

Esther had begun her American sojourn in Burlington with the Pettits and had returned there for a number of summers with her children. Her friend, Mrs. Esther Cox, also spent summers there, and Bowes Reed and his wife and children lived nearby. The Pettits, now in Perth Amboy, expected to relocate to Burlington soon, especially if the British attacked New York City. Joseph, commenting on the size of the house, suggested that possibly the Pettits could join the Reeds there and divide the cost. Esther made no response to this suggestion, nor did she act on it.[8]

At the end of March, Joseph expected to "move there as soon as I can," but his business and public responsibilities kept him in the city at least until May. Esther and the children probably went up to Burlington a bit earlier, about the time gunfire on the lower Delaware River announced the presence of British warships.[9]

Deciding on a refuge for the family had been relatively easy. The thorny question was Joseph's public role: Would he serve in a civilian or a military post, with Esther or with Washington? If Joseph should return to the army, Esther would again face loneliness, new burdens, and the possible loss of her independence. She also anticipated a far more frightening possibility. At camp with Washington in 1775, Joseph had been relatively safe. As Esther had commented, if he had to serve in the military, far better that he be at the counsel table than in the battlefield. But the next time could be different. The British intended to shed blood until they had restored their sovereignty over the colonies, and Americans intended to shed blood in resistance. This time, Joseph might well put his life at risk.

That thought terrified Esther. She loved Joseph. She needed him. She had devoted six years of her young life to winning him and six years to building a life together with him. War, and especially Joseph's role in combat, threatened all of that. Esther could not envision living without this man who had given focus and purpose and meaning to her life since her seventeenth year.

And how would she and her babies survive without him? The Reeds had lived well in Philadelphia on their income from law, trade, and land. Esther had collaborated with Joseph in building and maintaining their very successful family economy. But she could not practice law nor could she earn money as an officer in the army to compensate for the wartime decline in the legal business. Their land investments promised more for the future than they could now deliver, and the war had largely constricted, if not destroyed, the area in which Esther would have had the skills and the contacts for success: the import/export trade.[10] But, most importantly, the loss of one partner would hobble the other, and Esther, at this point with three small children and another on the way, was most vulnerable.

Joseph expected that in the event of his death his family would care for Esther and the children as he himself had cared for them in the past. However, the Pettits had long been dependent on Joseph, and Joseph's brother, Bowes, was at best unpredictable. Esther's own brother offered no better prospects. After six years of struggle, and with the help of Esther and Joseph, he had established himself in the London commercial community and was about to marry. But he was far away, as yet untested on his own and soon to have his own wife and children to care for.[11]

In time, Esther would manage to help Joseph recognize the strength of her argument. War and military combat were not for married men with young families and no independent source of income. He later noted that most of the men in the army were single, and those who were married, especially among the officers, had independent resources and few young children.[12]

But that admission was still far in the future, and Joseph was now searching for something useful to do. Esther worried about how he would resolve the tensions that bedeviled him. When he had arrived home from Cambridge in late 1775, he confided to Pettit that he had "given up all thought of returning to camp" and admitted that he thought he had not much "military talent." But if not the military, then what? Public life offered him a legitimate and honorable alternative to service in the army, but politics frustrated him. He continued to serve as an elected member of the Philadelphia Committee of Observation and Inspection, and in January 1776 the city also elected him to the provincial legislature. He worked hard at both jobs but grew impatient with what he saw as the endless factional bickering that delayed decisions, divided the people, and weakened the war effort.

Nor did he want to resume his legal business. His absence had estranged his client base. More importantly, his interest in the practice of law had declined.[13]

By the end of March 1776, Joseph "never felt so much puzzled to know how to act," as he wrote to Pettit. His business was sinking, his expenses were increasing, and public affairs absorbed his time but provided no income. He leaned toward a return to military life, where he felt he could "at least bear my own weight."[14]

Washington wanted Joseph back. He filled Joseph's position with a succession of temporary replacements and negotiated a significant salary increase to entice him. "I am so pressed to return," Joseph wrote to Pettit, "that I hardly know what to say."[15]

In the spring, Washington finally appointed a permanent replacement but obtained from Congress the power to appoint Joseph as adjutant general of the army with responsibility for recruiting the troops, keeping military records, managing the camp, distributing orders, and maintaining discipline. Washington's offer solved Joseph's problem. It produced a near-instant "resolution in my Prospects and Views," he said, and within a day he accepted.

But if Washington's offer solved Joseph's problem, it only exacerbated Esther's. Joseph, aware of this problem, wrote immediately to reiterate his arguments for her. He was sick and tired of partisan politics. He could make no money in business. He had lost his appetite for the law. In addition, the new job would pay £700 a year, and that amount would "help support us till these calamitous times are at an end." The post was honorable and its administrative responsibilities would not place him in harm's way. And, if the "issue is favorable to America," it would put him "on a respectable scale."[16]

He then got to the crux of the matter. "The life I live here [Philadelphia] is Irksome beyond measure. It is a most disagreeable circumstance to think of continuing it." The "state of uncertainty" and "the confusions which prevail" contrasted with his life at camp, where "the succession of business and company" would support his spirits in contrast to his present circumstances, where "with all my endeavors . . . it is otherwise."[17]

Esther knew all of this. She knew that her husband was a man of energy, most happy when vigorously pursuing clear goals, a professional and a businessman who succeeded through discipline and focus. She knew he made things happen: he did them himself or he directed and disciplined others to do them for him. She also knew that he was restless, frustrated, eager for action, and angry with himself for his indecision. She knew that he needed something new, something different, but his choice of the army both frightened and angered her. And, at bottom, her agitation grew not primarily from concerns about her own or her babies' security but from her love for him and her need for him. And, in this world of coverture and the legal subordination of wives, she shared this with other women who loved their husbands, resisted protracted separation, and worried about death. Mary Silliman in Connecticut, for instance, writing in April 1776 to her husband, lost control of her pen and smeared her letter when she learned that he had been called to battle. "What can I say, What can I do but commit my dearest husband . . . to the care of that God that directs the lightning . . . and can preserve you safe, tho instruments of death fly thick around you." In the same vein, Mercy Otis Warren deeply felt her husband's absence from her during the long stretches of time he spent attending to his political responsibilities, and her feelings may well have contributed to his withdrawal from public service.[18] All three of these women loved their husbands, wanted them near, and resented their absence. Some women who lived in a more providential world learned to console themselves for this loss by thinking that their suffering, like the political or military activities of their loved ones, "weighed as heavily in the scale of contributions to the war effort as the exertions of the men in the army or at the helm of government."[19] Esther, however, seemed never to have sought this consolation. She simply held Joseph responsible.

Nor did she hide her feelings when Joseph arrived at Burlington. She lost control of her emotions, or at least that was how it looked to Joseph. How much her behavior reflected actual loss of control or emerged from a deliberate strategy is, of course, difficult to know, but either way she managed to inflict much pain on him. After a few tense days, Joseph, also upset, left to join Washington in New York. On the road, the dust, the heat, his emotional turmoil, and "the condition I left you in" made for a "very unpleasant ride."[20]

From his perspective, he had done the best thing. The position of adjutant general would provide a good income in a time of professional and financial uncertainty. It would give order and focus to his days. It would free him from political squabbles in Philadelphia, and it would reunite him with the general, a reunion both men wanted. Moreover, he had provided well for his family. Esther lived in the former governor's elegant mansion. Her children could play on the grounds or walk with her a few blocks along the Green Bank to High Street with its public market and private shops. In the afternoons, she could socialize. Mrs. Esther Cox and Mrs. Bowes Reed were there, at least for the summer, and Joseph expected the Pettits to join them soon. When her baby came in October, she would have her mother, Polly, and her friends with her, and Joseph himself would be less than a day's ride away. Joseph, in his mind, had done his duty to his family and was now off to do his duty to his country.[21]

Esther disagreed. Joseph was missing the main point. He was her husband, her lover, and the father of her children, her companion, her confidant, and her comfort. He was depriving her of his person, his support, and his intimacy. He was putting himself in harm's way. He could return maimed, deranged, crippled, or he might not return at all. In that light, all of his arguments faded into insignificance. She could not imagine how she and her babies could survive alone. More importantly, she simply could not imagine life without him.

Joseph heard her words. He understood her concerns. But he did not feel them, and, at least for now, he did not share them. He had made a good decision. She must make the best of it. On that ground, they parted: the new soldier hurrying off to camp and the young pregnant wife left alone with her small children.

What began poorly spiraled downward over the summer. Through June, July, and early August, the army anticipated the British attack on New York City. In these months of preparation for battle, Joseph, writing from camp, repeatedly assured Esther that his "post will not call me into the same danger" and promised that he would not take unnecessary risks. He teased her a bit while mocking the public bravery of several visiting Philadelphians at camp. Surely, he pointed out, the presence of these timid creatures visiting the camp demonstrated that "danger is very much out of the question."[22]

Esther knew better. War was all about killing and dying. On one level, Joseph also understood this reality. Like a good lawyer and a responsible husband and father, he drew up a new will on the eve of his departure. This document, he acknowledged, was made necessary "by the dangers to which in the course of Providence, I am called into the Defense of the Liberties and Interests of my country." The will named Esther one of three executors, but the details of the document itself epitomized for Esther the horror she imagined. In case of his death, it read, Joseph hoped his "wife and fatherless children will find some such Friends as my own family has found in me in the days of their distress." But what were family and friends in comparison to a husband and a friend and a lover? And how much could and would these family and friends help? In the past, as Joseph's words imply, his extended family had more often than not depended on him for discipline and direction. More importantly, they remained her friends and her family and not her husband, and regardless of their good intentions, they would, by the very nature of things, make her dependent and subordinate.[23]

From camp, Joseph repeatedly assured her that he was well, but his reports did nothing to settle her mind. He wrote, "Small pox had done us infinite Mischief," and "bilious and putrid fever with the dysentery" had "taken down great numbers of our men."[24]

Then the fighting began. The British landed on Long Island on August 22, and for the next month Joseph's descriptions of his experiences in battle drove Esther to the edge of despair. His frequent letters detailed for her the things that she had anticipated. As the British pushed the Americans west from Long Island across the river into Manhattan, and then north through

Harlem and into Westchester, the fighting was sporadic but fierce, and Joseph was usually at the heart of the action. He began many letters with the terrifying statement "I am alive." Certainly good news, but not necessarily reassuring about the prospects for tomorrow when the best news for today is that he had survived.[25]

But in time it grew worse. During these months, Joseph reported accelerating bad news. "[E]very night we lie down in the most anxious fear," he wrote, and as conditions worsened, he came to accept the probability of his own death. "If my life would render essential service to my country," he wrote to the frightened Esther, "I would cheerfully lay it down": noble sentiments, nobly uttered by one of the few men of his standing and status daily facing death on the battlefield, but cold comfort for Esther.[26]

Indeed, he now seemed to be courting danger, and he shared the details with her. He plunged into the action, narrowly escaping death, and found it exhilarating. "I do not find my spirits sink under difficulties but rather rise," he told her. Usually mounted, always dashing, he encouraged, ordered, and disciplined the green troops, who sometimes fought heroically against the greatest military force in the Atlantic world and sometimes cut and ran. He lost two horses, both shot out from under him in combat. Companions died by his side, officers and men. And at least once he escaped death at the hands of a deserting American soldier. Joseph challenged the man who raised and fired his gun at him from a rod away. The gun misfired. Joseph's gun then misfired, and he subdued the man with his sword.[27]

Night after night, Joseph shared these exploits with Esther. He admitted that many people might well think him rash and imprudent, but, he argued, dispirited troops "would not go into danger unless their officers led them." One suspects there was more to it than that. Joseph had never been more engaged, more excited, more exhilarated. He had become a warrior on horseback, leading men in mortal combat for a noble cause, and he found it profoundly satisfying.[28] Esther was living a nightmare.

But if Joseph had come to love war, he knew almost from his first days in camp that he hated the job of adjutant general. He initially hoped that things would improve, but if they did not, he told Esther, "I shall turn my thoughts most seriously to getting out of the army." "I do not know that I should be happy at home, amidst the confusions which prevail . . . but I am far from being so here," he wrote a week later. The day-to-day responsibilities of the adjutant general were "entirely out of my line." He lacked the special skills and training needed to manage such a large-scale human enterprise. Moreover, this collection of citizen soldiers had its own particular problems. Troops came and went as new recruits replaced those headed home. All too often the replacements arrived late or not at all. Those who showed up felt free to wander off, and those who remained exhibited little discipline and less inclination to acquire it. He found that a troubling propensity for "democracy" prevailed, at least among New England troops who exhibited so "great an equality and . . . a leveling spirit." He was appalled to come upon a Connecticut captain shaving one of his men. The captain had been the village barber at home.[29]

From the beginning, Joseph did not "relish" his situation, and early in August, on the eve of battle, he restated his intention to "quit this service at the close of this campaign." In mid-October, when he thought the campaign was near its end, he felt "every succeeding circumstance has confirmed this sentiment."[30]

But he felt quite differently about actual combat, and in this Esther and he had never been at greater odds. From the beginning of the Battle of Long Island, through the terrible days of early November, Joseph performed brilliantly. A superb and fearless horseman, he rode fast and hard, organizing, encouraging, intimidating, and commanding troops. He concluded that he was far better suited for leading troops into battle, and especially troops on horseback, than for the administrative tasks of the adjutant general. Washington agreed. Esther, emphatically, did not. In January 1777, the general reluctantly accepted Joseph's resignation and immediately nominated him to Congress for appointment to the rank of brigadier general in command of the Continental Cavalry.[31] Esther's nightmare intensified.

Throughout the fall 1776 campaign, Esther had lived in constant dread. Joseph's initial response had been to urge her to be brave and to trust in providence. That soon gave way to admonitions to be strong in order to help him. He begged her to "tell me your spirits are recovered" because "my comfort depends so much on yours." He needed her love and her reassurances so that he could do his duty.[32] She needed him at home with her and her babies.

She could not conquer her loneliness, her sadness, and her fears. Throughout the summer, she repeatedly urged him to visit her. He refused on grounds that it would be far too painful for both of them. "A second parting under the prospects we now have would be very distressing to us both and would renew those gloomy sensations which I have not been able wholly to conquer." Rather, he proposed a "happy meeting in the fall which would be infinitely better than a painful interview of a few hours now."[33]

Nor would he countenance a visit by her to the military camp in New York. Esther knew that other wives came to see their husbands. Martha Washington had been on her way to camp when she visited Esther later in the fall of 1775. Mrs. Catherine Greene visited her husband, Nathanael, periodically, and Esther's friend Mrs. Esther Cox was even now, in mid-August, at camp with her husband. Esther suggested that she too might come, but Joseph discouraged her. He admitted that it had become fashionable and that he felt some pressure to "give up my opinion" on this subject, but her "situation will not admit it." If she had been "unencumbered [i.e., not in her eighth month]," he might have invited her.[34]

He was trying to shift the blame to her, and she pushed back. That, in turn, prompted a more annoying response from him. "Women of delicacy and respectability with a family at home," he wrote, "would not find much satisfaction after the novelty was over." She, in turn, asked if he included her friend Esther Cox among those who exhibited their indelicacy by visiting. Joseph, caught, retracted his statement. He did not mean his comments to apply to "our Friend whose delicacy is unquestionable." Esther had had the best of the argument. But Joseph did not capitulate.[35]

The truth of the matter was that he did not want her at camp for the same reason that he did not visit her. He did not trust his own emotions. On August 7, he noted, "Calamities abroad seem to enhance the value of domestic comforts and draw the cords of love closer and tighter." A few days later, he reported that an early morning dream of her had been shattered by a painful awakening. Two days into battle, he declared, "It was the delightful duty of my life to share it [his life] with you," and by early September he found the pain of missing her and the children so great that he could "almost wish" I could "forget you and them." He might appear brusque, even insensitive at times, but his behavior reflected not indifference or callousness but quite the opposite. Joseph loved Esther. He had loved her forever. His attachment to her and to the children with which their love had blessed them was powerful and deep, and it had never been more intense than now. Esther undoubtedly knew that, but that knowledge did not solve her problem: she wanted him home with her, and she wanted him there on a permanent basis. To achieve that had become her simple resolve, and she pursued that end with the same determination with which she had initially pursued Joseph in London and during their five-year transatlantic courtship.[36]

Esther gave birth to her new baby, Theodosia, on October 2 while Joseph was "exposed to all the dangers and fatigues of a campaign," as she later described it to her brother. She expected him to be with her. He had promised. But as her time grew near, he equivocated: "What shall I say to your request of my coming to you on an expected event?" In the end, he could not abandon his post, and Esther delivered without him. That bothered him, and soon after that event he made his most fulsome declaration of love for her and his dependence on her. "All my hopes of comfort and happiness in this world would be extinguished," he wrote, should she not have survived the delivery. And, in some powerful and disturbing way, this declaration foreshadowed the end of their life together in the not too distant future.[37]

Undoubtedly, the new mother welcomed this declaration of love and this assertion of her importance to him, but, had she been inclined to argue, she could have pointed out that his decisions, made against her best counsel, had kept him from her and now threatened to destroy what they had built together. His need for her and his love for her did little to assuage her anxieties, and his emphasis, even now in her most vulnerable moment, had been on his loss, not hers.

Then again, if she read Joseph's words carefully, and she had long been a master of that skill, she understood that his thinking was shifting. His emerging perspective became increasingly prominent after the birth of Theodosia, but he had given hints of it as early as August. On the seventeenth of that month, on the eve of battle, he acknowledged her difficulties with the heat and "her particular situation." Granted, this expression of sympathy was, at least in part, a strategy to forestall her visit to camp, but it did acknowledge her pregnancy, now in its eighth month, and the limits that imposed on her. He also acknowledged the "terrible trial" that his absence had become for her.[38]

While in this retrospective and empathetic mood, he tentatively raised a sensitive question: Esther's frequent pregnancies. She had conceived four babies in the six years of their married life: Martha, Joseph, Esther, and the soon-to-be Theodosia. He began his comments with a bit of philosophy. "Love," he wrote, "like all other blessings, has its alloy": its costs. Their love had "too great a portion" of that alloy. The intimacy they shared, the pleasure they exchanged brought them joy. It united them and strengthened their ties. It also brought new life and the blessings of children. However, he feared that too frequent "trials" could shatter her frail constitution and thereby threaten the very physical basis of their love. He broached the issue cautiously and obliquely, and then backed away. They had had this conversation before. They did not agree. "This is a painful subject," he admitted. "I will not dwell on it." But possibly we should dwell on it a bit longer, for we have here an early reference to a momentous change: the deliberate separation of making love from making babies. When Joseph wrote, few married women placed limits on their natural fecundity, and completed families averaged eight or more children. But sometime in late eighteenth-century America, a few married women began to limit their total family size. Over the following two centuries, that became the new norm on a worldwide basis. Historian Susan Klepp has explored this question in some detail, highlighting the degree to which eighteenth-century Americans, especially women, valorized and privileged female fertility, and then demonstrating the beginnings of the shift toward limits on this uniquely female function.[39]

In the midst of battle, Joseph also began to appreciate the impact that his death would have on Esther and their children. Early in October, while Esther was lying-in after the birth of Theodosia, Joseph declared he had "never meant to make arms a profession." His devotion to Esther and their children came first. He had done what he had to do, but he had no desire to "sacrifice you and them to fame."[40]

Joseph undoubtedly believed what he wrote in October, but since late August he performed brilliantly, fearlessly, and effectively in his military role. Throughout these exhilarating days, he had often spoken of his own death, but now, approaching the end of the campaign, he began to understand, if not fully admit, the dangers his choices had threatened for his wife and family. He began to see, and for the first time to feel, the position Esther had first articulated in those emotional hours before they had parted in mid-June.

His new mode of thinking, his new sensitivity to his obligations to his family did not change his situation or modify his behavior or alter his current commitment. What changed was his realization of the fundamental threat this posed to those he loved and for whom he was responsible. Now he saw Esther's point. He was a married man with four young children, and the family had no fixed income. Most men in these circumstances acted with greater prudence. Writing in early November, he summed it up: "When I look around me, I see none but single or childless persons and most of them of such fortune that their loss could only be lamented as [dissolving] the ties of blood and friendship but all the real wants of life would be supplied."[41]

He reassured her that he would take great care, but he had assured her of that before. This time, however, he saw, "You and the dear pledges of our love form a powerful restraint when I should otherwise be led to expose myself." He apologized for preaching resignation to her in the past. "It is a lesson more easily given than practiced," he admitted. He understood and felt in an intense way how vulnerable his recklessness had made her. Because of her peculiar, almost unique position, his death would deprive her of any way to supply the "real wants of life" for herself and her children. He acknowledged that the "torrent of calamity" had swept them back into the vale of adversity from which they had just begun to emerge. All of that, the loss of material possessions and the discomfort of living, he would regard as insignificant if "Providence spares us for each other."[42]

Now, in November, for the first time in five months, Esther and Joseph agreed, but before she could begin to relax and enjoy her victory, a new threat endangered her and the children. By mid-November, the British had chased the Americans across the Hudson into New Jersey. At first, Joseph worried that the enemy intended to strike straight through Burlington toward Philadelphia. Soon, however, he changed his mind and assumed that the British were preparing to go into winter camp. Washington sent Joseph to Burlington, then the working capital of New Jersey, to beg for troops. While there, he visited his family and held his new baby daughter in his arms for the first time. He also wrote to resign his post as adjutant general, fulfilling his long-standing promise to Esther, and to himself, that he would leave the army at the end of the campaign.[43]

But Joseph had erred. The British did not go into winter camp. Instead, they turned toward Philadelphia, driving Washington before them. Joseph immediately retracted his resignation and for the next two months spent most of his time on horseback, first in support of Washington's retreat, and then as part of the successful American counterattack at Trenton and Princeton.

For that month, Esther was largely on her own. On December 10, the day before Hessian cavalry swept through Burlington, Esther, aided by Jack (one of their two slaves) and accompanied by her mother, Polly, three small children, and her eight-week-old baby, loaded their possessions in a wagon and headed for Evesham, about twenty miles south on the edge of the Jersey Pine Barrens, a five-to-six-hour trip if the roads were good and the weather held. The highway was frozen and the temperature in the high thirties when they left; it had fallen below freezing when they arrived. Once there, they found themselves "surrounded by woods and inhabitants of the common class of country people." Esther described her flight for Dennis: "You cannot have any adequate idea of the scenes we have passed," she wrote. "One day's escape from an army of foreigners" and for "several weeks [living] within a few hours march of them."[44]

As the new year 1777 began, Esther and her children were safe but isolated and living in a province largely under the control of the British, or, in Joseph's more dramatic phraseology, "a wife and four children in the enemies' hands." Her isolation protected her and her babies, but Joseph was farther away and largely beyond contact for more than two months. What Esther could not know, she imagined.[45]

The American success at Trenton (December 1776) and Princeton (January 1777) ended the 1776 campaign. The British evacuated most of New Jersey, and that eased Esther's concerns about Joseph's safety and her fears of raids on her family. Joseph, usually near, visited often during the first two months of the New Year. Although he had resigned his post as adjutant general in early January, he devoted much of the remainder of the month to settling the troops in winter quarters, scouting British troop movements, and harassing British foraging parties.

During February, Joseph also moved back and forth between Philadelphia and Evesham, and Esther reported that they were "now enjoying a few weeks together in peace and safety." She thanked God for delivering "us from the hand of oppression," claimed that she could "look back without regret on our past distresses," and anticipated a bright future under the guidance of that "great arbiter and Ruler of nations who alone can give success to our arms and peace to our land."[46]

There were brave words about the past and hopeful words about the future, but they masked the major question that would continue to trouble her relationship with Joseph for another year and a half: his future role in the defense of his country. The military campaign of 1776 was over. The new campaign would soon begin. Washington wanted Joseph to command the Continental Cavalry. Joseph had all but promised Esther that he would return to civilian life, but still he was tempted. Through the late winter and into the spring, the issue festered, unresolved.

Joseph's friends in the new state government, in particular George Bryan, a fellow Presbyterian congregant in the Philadelphia Arch Street Church and now vice president of the Supreme Executive Council, offered him a timely solution. Late in March, Joseph learned that he had been named the new chief justice of the state on an annual salary of £1,000. Esther was enthusiastic, and once again the Reeds packed up and headed for the city. While Esther and the family stayed at the home of the Coxes on Arch Street, Joseph headed west of the city to find the family a permanent refuge from the expected British attack on Philadelphia in the spring. Within a week, he had rented a farm, or at least a farmhouse with some land, near Norristown, Pennsylvania, about seventeen miles up the Schuylkill River northwest of Philadelphia. On April 9, he appeared before the Supreme Executive Council to indicate his interest in the appointment and to ask for time to settle his family.[47]

In the next few months, Esther became a farm wife. By June, she was buying seed, renting land, planting flax, and negotiating the purchase of a cow with a two-week-old calf for £15. She and her five-year-old son, Joseph, helped bring in the hay. Jack probably helped with the heavy work, and Joseph, sometimes in person and sometimes from a distance, offered advice.[48]

Esther took to her tasks with some pleasure and a great deal of satisfaction. "We go on pretty well in our country life," she reported, but admitted that it was all new to her. "I am not famous for making bargains for things out of my sphere." She also found Norristown a pleasant place. In contrast to the remote Evesham, Esther now lived on the main road west from Philadelphia. People and news traveled easily between her town and the city, and a number of other Philadelphia families had taken places nearby. The Reeds' friends John and Margaret Bayard and some of their family visited Esther early in June and soon became neighbors.[49]

But the question of the chief justice versus the cavalry remained unresolved. Esther favored the judicial appointment. The salary was good and the status high. In some ways, accepting the post would fulfill Dennis's earlier prediction that Joseph would someday become lord chancellor, albeit in a somewhat less exalted context. In addition, it offered a legitimate and honorable alternative through which Joseph could serve his country.

Joseph argued against it. He claimed that becoming the chief justice would embroil him in the raging party politics that was engulfing the state. The crux of the matter, however, was elsewhere. Joseph's performance in combat during the previous campaign marked him: a firm disciplinarian, an inspiring leader, a fearless risk-taker, and a superb horseman. God seemed to have destined him to lead cavalry charges in the field. Washington, recognizing this, pushed hard to bring him back to camp before the 1777 campaign began.[50]

Joseph wanted the appointment. He had had a taste for leading men into battle, and he wanted more of it. His blood was up, and he was seething at the British behavior: the inhumanity with which the British nation had made war against America, "[t]he ravages in which age and sex have indiscriminately suffered," and "the havoc which avarice and lust and wantonness have made [of] this fine country." The British had left no choice for a "man of honor" "bound to transmit to his posterity the blessings of liberty unimpaired." He must fight to serve and to save his country.[51]

Congress, however, had delayed his appointment to lead the cavalry and twice slighted him. In February, it appointed ten new brigadier generals but omitted Joseph's name. Then, when Washington pushed, Congress made Reed a brigadier but failed to name him to lead the cavalry. Between these two congressional rebuffs, Joseph drafted a letter to a member of Congress to advance his own cause.[52]

Esther, however, was appalled. The responsibilities of the job would take him far from home for long periods of time and put him, almost daily, in harm's way. It would be another version of the 1776 nightmare but at a more intense level. She would not support Joseph's desire to lead the cavalry.

And Esther had considerable bargaining power. She believed that Joseph could not and would not go without her approval. Just such an assumption of wifely authority underlay a comment she made at a later date to her friend Mrs. Cox, whose influence, Esther thought, kept Mr. Cox from joining the military. "I hope you will give your consent to give him up ... I must say, I hope you will have courage to resign him, especially as his office does not expose him to danger of person."[53] In this, Esther was giving expression to a widespread assumption among patriot women that they did indeed have the power to withhold from public and military service the men in their lives, especially their husbands and sons. In Kingston, New York, for example, women upset by the lack of tea told the county committee, "Unless the committee gives them tea, 'their husbands and sons shall fight no more.'" Both the women making the threat and the committeemen hearing it saw this as credible.[54]

Moreover, Joseph had already conceded her main point. Late in the fall 1776 campaign, he had recognized the moral weight of her argument. Active military engagement in the field by married men with young children and few fixed resources put wives and children at great risk. But now, he wanted to go.[55]

By early June, they had reached an impasse. Again, as a year earlier, they argued. Esther, in "very low spirits" again, precipitated an emotional confrontation. Joseph again left, and then refused to return to face her fury. Congress, however, stepped in to solve their problem, or at least to provide Joseph the cover he needed to back down. Congress would not appoint Joseph to command the cavalry. Washington then asked if Congress would allow him to make the appointment himself. Congress replied, in effect, that Washington might do as he felt he had to, but that Congress would not take the initiative.[56]

Joseph chose to see this new congressional sleight as an attack on his person. He rejected the earlier congressional appointment as brigadier general and informed Washington that he would not serve in the army.[57]

Esther, ecstatic with the news, now offered concessions. She apologized for her "want of resolution" and for the "distress I occasioned you when I ought to make your duty light as possible." She promised she would make amends with her "cheerful . . . and usual spirits." She assured him of her "endeavor to conquer a weakness I know gives you pain." She had recovered herself, she said, and concluded, "I wish I could find words sufficient to express how much I approve and admire your conduct, in which the tenderest regard for my happiness mingles with your disinterested exertion for your Country's Service." She hoped to see him soon.[58]

The Reeds had reached a compromise. In the upcoming campaign, Joseph would live at home and serve in the state militia as the need arose. Esther would control her emotions and support his service. In late July, Joseph turned down the appointment as chief justice, and then, almost as if to seal the bargain, early in August Esther conceived a new child, ten months after the birth of Theodosia.

Joseph spent most of July with the Pennsylvania militia or at camp with Washington in New Jersey. In August, he returned to Esther at Norristown. Then, the 1777 campaign began, and during the next nine months Esther's life again descended into chaos, disruption, and horror.[59]

Later in August, the British landed some fifty miles south of Philadelphia at the top of the Chesapeake Bay and began their march toward the city. Joseph again joined in America's defense. He could not stay off his horse, could not avoid danger. Esther could not overcome her declining spirits, control her emotions, or conceal her mounting terror.[60]

The British quickly defeated the American forces at the Battle of Brandywine on September 11, occupied Philadelphia by September 26, and repulsed an American counterattack on October 4. From then until late in December, the two armies skirmished in the fifteen-to-twenty-mile middle ground between Philadelphia and Norristown. Esther lived again in daily fear as Joseph fought sometimes in the militia, sometimes under Washington, and sometimes virtually alone as circumstances determined. Throughout, his visits home ranged from a few days to a week.[61]

Again, as in the past, Joseph invited risk. At least three times that fall he narrowly escaped capture or death. In September, and again in November, he missed marauding patrols by minutes. On December 6, as the British ventured out to try the American forces, Joseph's horse was shot, he fell to the ground, and British soldiers with bayonets advanced on him. Only the rapid response by his companions saved his life.[62]

Early in December, as the season wound down, Joseph continued to push against the limits of his compromise with Esther. He pressed Washington to conclude the campaign with an audacious strike at New York City. They would move rapidly across New Jersey in small contingents, converge on New York, and surprise the lightly defended city. Whatever the final outcome, the strike would "raise the spirits of the army and the country," "prop up the sinking credit of our money," allow us to replenish our supplies from the British stores, and demonstrate to America and to Europe that "the enemy cannot retain their conquests."[63] In the same spirit of reckless adventure, Joseph urged the president of Pennsylvania to establish a state cavalry to roam the disputed lands during the winter to protect civilians from raiders and renegades. He volunteered to lead the new mounted troops.[64]

Throughout the fall 1777 campaign, Esther lived in the no-man's-land between the two contending forces. The end of the campaign in December 1777 reduced her anxiety, but the pause passed far too quickly. In late February 1778, she lamented, "Returning spring will, I fear, bring a return of bloodshed and destruction." But, she added, it had already become unsafe for Joseph to visit her. "Indeed," she wrote, "I am easier when he is from home, as he being here brings danger with it." Those "disaffected to the cause . . . lie in wait for those who are active in it."[65]

Also, irregular troops and private marauders in no-man's-land harassed and abused the civilian population, seizing animals and stores, and on occasion posing threats to the lives of the civilian population. Isolated, fearful about the approaching birth of her baby, living "entirely in the hands of strangers," and again obsessed with the thought of Joseph's death, Esther could not regain her spirits or overcome her "discontent." Faced with challenges she could not handle and prospects she could not tolerate, she often simply refused to think about it. "I confess" she wrote, "I find the greatest relief in chasing away all thoughts of what is before me."[66]

Joseph, aware of Esther's growing vulnerability, had asked Pettit, now living in Trenton, to help find a safe place for her and possibly for the Pettit family. In April, as Esther was entering her ninth month of pregnancy, they moved to Flemington, a village northeast of Trenton and about sixty miles from Norristown over the circuitous route they had to follow to avoid the British. This was the fourth time in two years that Esther and her children had moved, and the second time she had packed her dwindling possessions in an open wagon in severe weather seeking safety. In Flemington, she delivered her fifth child, Dennis, on May 12. The next day, her nineteen-month-old daughter Theodosia died of smallpox.[67]

The death of Theodosia nearly destroyed Esther. The little girl had been born in September 1776 amid the violence and turmoil of that campaign, and then, at eight weeks of age, hurried out onto a cold December highway in a wagon headed from Burlington to Evesham. Weaned in Norristown and then engulfed with her mother in the dangers and uncertainties of the 1777 campaign, the toddler, just learning to navigate her limited but transient world, had died in an isolated hamlet in the far reaches of rural New Jersey, as much a victim of the war as if a stray musket ball had struck her. Joseph, who had not attended her birth, was there for her burial.

Esther was inconsolable. The loss, she wrote, "sits very heavy on me." She struggled to regain her composure but then found that "it overcomes me and strikes to the very bottom of my heart." She blamed herself, her "neglect of my dear lost child. . . . I did not take the necessary precautions [i.e., inoculation against smallpox] to prevent this fatal disorder." She struggled to resign herself to God's will, but with difficulty, and begged her friend Mrs. Cox to continue to send her "consoling advise" and to help "to make me more perfectly acquiesce in the Divine pleasure." And she pleaded with her friend to come to visit. "How earnestly do I wish that I could see you," she wrote in June and again in July. "O I have great hopes of seeing you." "I have very few here to hold conversations with," and even the mail was difficult. She sometimes waited three or more weeks for an opportunity to send or receive letters. But her friend could not visit, and Esther remained alone with her sorrow, her fears, her self-incrimination, and her struggle with her God.

Esther's brief comments in her letters give us, at best, an incomplete understanding of the immediate devastation and the prolonged suffering the death of Theodosia caused her, but the experience of one of her contemporaries may help us more fully appreciate how devastating the loss of a child could be. Mary Silliman, a young mother in Connecticut, lost her four-year-old daughter in the spring of 1770. The child's death after a ten-day illness plunged the mother into a depression so deep that for months afterward her family feared for her life. Even after she had regained some of her physical strength, Silliman remained spiritually dead. A year after her loss, she wrote, "I mourn that I have no more connection with God. . . . Oh, the dreadful deadness of heart!" Esther DeBerdt Reed had paid a terrible price for her choice of America over Britain.[68]

CHAPTER 10

Politics
New World Democracy

In June 1778, the British evacuated Philadelphia. The patriots quickly resumed control of the city, and then disagreed among themselves over how to treat those in Philadelphia who appeared to have collaborated with the enemy. This question was not new in Pennsylvania. The state had struggled with the question of loyalty since independence, but now the presence in Philadelphia of a significant number of suspected Tories, traitors, and trimmers gave it a new and immediate political salience: What was to be done, here and now, with these people? Strong feelings on this issue led to violence in the streets, an increasingly acerbic debate among patriots, the emergence of two surprisingly modern political parties, and the political engagement of Esther and Joseph, which propelled them to political prominence in Pennsylvania and to the cusp of power on the national level.[1]

After the birth of their son and the death of their daughter, Joseph stayed with Esther for a few weeks, and then returned to his congressional responsibilities. From May until September, the couple lived apart, partly due to the circumstances of their lives but mostly because of their inability to agree on two unsettled and unsettling questions: how to deal with the death of Theodosia and how to define Joseph's future public role, and, by implication, Esther's. Joseph wrote often but did not discuss the death of his daughter, nor did he offer Esther his comfort or consolation while she continued to pray for the strength to cope with her loss and to understand and accept the will of her all-wise and all-powerful God. Isolated in rural New Jersey, she pleaded with her family friend to visit and struggled on a daily basis to do what was necessary while worrying about what Joseph would do.

At first glance, Joseph's reaction to Theodosia's death appears insensitive. He urged Esther to be brave, to be resigned, and to be cheerful. "I will not have you a dull, moping, dejected wife," he wrote.[2] In the same vein, although he mentioned the toddler in a May letter to Dennis DeBerdt, he largely avoided the subject in his correspondence. In the past, he had often expressed his affection for his children. Moreover, he lived in a world where a man who married assumed responsibility for protecting those fragile creatures that he and his wife created through their love. The war that Joseph fought to protect his country, his liberty, and his posterity had contributed to the death of his youngest and most vulnerable daughter. Still, he expressed no sorrow, no grief, no remorse, and little explicit sympathy for his suffering wife.[3]

However, Joseph's reaction reflected neither his indifference to the death of his child nor his insensitivity to Esther's pain. Rather, his behavior reflected his lifetime effort to discipline his emotions and to control those strong feelings that, on occasion, threatened to overwhelm and disable him. In the past, he had not dealt well with Esther's outbursts. Again and again, he had pleaded with her to control and constrain herself, for her own sake and for his. When she did not, he had left her.

Joseph handled the death of Theodosia in a similar manner. He did not argue. He did not discuss. He did not commiserate. He neither gave nor sought comfort. He would not and could not allow himself to break. Rather, he fused his grief over the loss of his baby girl with his anger at the British for the suffering they were imposing on America. This combination of grief and anger provoked in him a rage that completed his alienation from the people he had long admired and had striven to join in London. It made him a bitter enemy of those in Philadelphia and its surroundings who had collaborated with the British occupiers, and in time it made him a political enemy of those among his fellow Whigs whom he saw as too quick to forgive that collaboration.

Esther expressed no anger at England or its people, but in time she also admitted that the experiences of the past year had ended any expectation she might have of ever returning home. Home was now America. In a long and sad letter to her brother, Dennis, she expressed no hostility. She told him that she loved him and longed to see him, and that she hoped someday to meet his new wife and their baby daughter. She knew that her mother wanted to return to England, but she herself no longer desired or expected that. Rather, she tried to entice him to come to America. "I know your turn of mind so well," she wrote, "that I do not imagine you would be pleased with it [America] at first, but I think after a little time and when some of the pleasures and refinements of London wear off, you will find yourself and family extremely happy here." "The country," she continued, "must soon be desirable. If peace did but spread her olive [illegible] on our shores, we might via with any part of the world."[4] Esther knew that she would not return to England, that London was no longer her home, and that America, without London's "pleasures and refinements," was her country, and she, like Joseph, was proud of that fact.

While Joseph expiated his pain by attacking the British, the collaborators, and the frivolous Whigs, Esther turned her grief on herself. "I cannot help reflect on my neglect of my dear lost child. Too thoughtful and attentive to my own situation, I did not take the necessary precautions. . . . Surely, my dear friend," she wrote to Mrs. Cox, "I ought to blame myself." And, just as surely, one hopes, Mrs. Cox would tell her that the child's death derived not from its mother's weakness or neglect but rather from the war and the family's exile. Esther's constant movement and the disruption of normal life had deprived her child of the medical assistance and the settled and protected environment necessary for the inoculation procedure.[5]

Esther's circumstances also focused her attention on the immediate and the practical. She lived in a remote and primitive village where she operated under the pressure of daily necessity. She nursed Dennis, her newborn son, and struggled to educate Patty (seven), Joseph (six), and Esther (four) and to learn to be the working head of a farm family with responsibility for buying and selling cows, training horses, and making clothes.[6]

Within this framework of self-flagellation and domestic toil, Esther had little time to think or at least express her thoughts about public affairs or about the future course of the conflict. She had developed, however, a healthy dislike for the foreign mercenaries and the roving bands that had twice driven her and her babies onto the public roads in bad weather. She also heard the stories of British extravagance in Philadelphia, and the cooperation of many Philadelphia belles in the military celebrations and social events. Although tempted to pity them now that their protectors had departed, she confessed, "I cannot feel much for them."[7]

One bit of news from Joseph may have given her some satisfaction. Samuel Powel, Esther's old "friend" from London and Bath, and his wife had remained in the city when the British came—at best, neutrals, at worst Tories and traitors. In the final days of the British occupation, the head of the British peace commission had chosen to live with the Powels. He took possession of "all the best apartments" in their magnificent home on Third Street, placed sentries at the doors, and made liberal use of Powel's possessions, including his wife's expensive serving dishes. In addition, as Joseph noted, the lord had brought "his Girl [his kept woman] with him, much to Mrs. Powel's mortification."[8]

By the time Joseph left Esther at Flemington, he too had abandoned all desire for reconciliation with Great Britain. Until recently, he had continued to hope for a settlement. In the summer of 1776, while preparing for battle, he had explained his thinking to Esther: peace and reconciliation would come when the British exempted America from parliamentary taxation and respected the "regulation of our internal government."[9]

Joseph reemphasized that point in February 1777. In a letter to Dennis DeBerdt about the abortive peace efforts of Howe in the previous summer, he wrote that if Howe had had power to offer terms that "would give my country any security against the unlimited power . . . to deprive us of our property," he would have vigorously promoted an accommodation. Thus, seven months after the vote on the Declaration of Independence, and long after he himself had been bloodied in battle, he could still imagine some form of reconciliation. The campaign of 1776 had hurt him, but it had not alienated him. He complained about the havoc, the insults, and the inhuman ravages of the British and their "foreign" mercenaries. He declared that "no reconciliation can ever efface the inhumanity with which it [the war] has been conducted." He believed that, faced with British demands for "unlimited submission," a man of honor had no choice but to fight if he intended to "transmit to his posterity the blessings of liberty unimpaired." But he also criticized those Americans who heaped "illiberal abuse" on the king and his ministers. The British political leaders were not evil men, he argued, but rather their "mistaken ideas of the true interests of the nation" had led them astray. By clear implication, should the British political nation come to its senses, see the true nature of its interests, rescind its demands for "unlimited submission," and give men of honor a legitimate means to "transmit the blessings of liberty unimpaired to their posterity," then some accommodation might still be possible. That was Joseph's position in 1777.[10]

But now, in the late spring of 1778, riding away from his daughter's grave, he no longer felt that way. Another year of war combined with the suffering of his wife and the death of Theodosia had ended any desire for reconciliation. His letters that summer testify to his final break from the mother country and his unequivocal commitment to his new country, his new nation, and his new people.

In his letter to Dennis DeBerdt, Joseph wrote with scarcely suppressed rage. He expressed his warm family feelings for Dennis, and then, supposing that Dennis would be "impatient to know how friends as near and dear to you have fared . . . living in the very seat of war," he catalogued their suffering, concluding with a stark and piercing sentence: "We lost a fine little girl near two years old about a fortnight ago." Near the end of the letter, Joseph half-apologized for losing his discipline: "I forbear least my resentment should get the better of my prudence."[11]

A month later, in the draft of a letter to one of the new British peace commissioners, he declared, "The day of Reconciliation and Dependence is past, and the Sovereignty of Britain over this country is gone forever."[12] This personal declaration of independence takes on greater significance in light of the commission's instructions. The king had empowered its members to grant to the Americans precisely the concessions that Joseph had earlier defined as the basis for peace and reconciliation, terms that Joseph would have fought to accept had the British offered them in the summer of 1776. Now, he saw these terms as irrelevant. He had joined the war to seek redress of grievances within the British Empire. Now, he fought for the creation of a new and glorious nation. In his July 1778 letter to Dennis DeBerdt, Joseph reinforced this point and offered his bold new vision of America's future. "Nothing short of Omnipotence can now check the Rising Glory of this Western World."[13]

Once the British had evacuated Philadelphia, Joseph turned his anger against those residents of the city who had collaborated with the enemy, and then against those patriots who, in Joseph's mind, were far too eager to forgive and forget the betrayal of the collaborators. When the British occupied the city in the fall of 1777, a sizeable portion of its population had remained in place. Some had nowhere to go. Some maintained a principled neutrality. Some welcomed the forces of the king, to whom they had remained loyal. Some acted from expediency, and others joined with the British in a "frivolous life style."[14]

Prominent families dined at the home of Sir William Howe, where they enjoyed lavish entertainment: music, concerts, and dancing. Additional numbers regularly attended one or more of the thirteen theatrical performances at the Southwark Theatre between January and May 1778, spreading out after the last curtain for social life at taverns, dancing at private balls, and an occasional fireworks display.[15]

In the late winter of 1778, while those in the city played and profited, Esther, in her last month of pregnancy, had fled her home and traveled some sixty miles or more with her children in an open wagon across the Delaware River to a refuge in Flemington, New Jersey. Then, in May, while she held her dying baby daughter in her arms, the British and their political collaborators in Philadelphia prepared a celebration they called the Meschianza to commemorate the return home of General Sir William Howe.[16]

This British-Tory-trimmer entertainment began in midafternoon on May 18, five days after Theodosia's death, and ran through the night. It started with a parade and fireworks, went on to a faux medieval tournament and a dinner for more than four hundred guests, and concluded with dancing till dawn. Elizabeth Drinker, one of the principled neutrals in the city, was appalled: "This day may be remembered by many, for the Scenes of Folly and Vanity."[17] Esther and Joseph were among those who remembered it that way.

After the British evacuation of Philadelphia, Joseph demanded strict punishment for those who had helped the British, and he could not understand the inclination of some of his fellow Whigs to favor an easy integration of collaborators into polite society. Equally galling to him after the occupation was the frivolity and indulgence that emerged among the Whigs and those who had again trimmed their sails to the prevailing winds. The Southwark Theatre, that symbol of extravagance, remained open until Congress compelled its closing in October.[18]

Respectable Whigs now socialized with Tories, loyalists, neutrals, and those who had exploited the British occupation for personal gain. It agitated Joseph that "treason, disaffection to the interest of America, even assistance to the British interest is called openly an error of judgment" by his fellow patriots, who insisted it should be overlooked and "laid aside under a perfect oblivion for past offences." Joseph singled out General Benedict Arnold for particular criticism. Arnold held a public event at which "common Tory ladies and wives and daughters of persons proscribed by the State and now with the enemy at New York, formed a very considerable number." Joseph feared a "settled fixed system to subvert the Whig interest."[19]

The behavior of many Philadelphia Whigs, had she known of it, would certainly have appalled Esther. Sarah Bache, daughter of Benjamin Franklin, described the general tone of social life in the city after the British had left. "There never was so much dressing and pleasure going on," she wrote, and she described her own exciting evening at the Powel home. "We danced at Mrs. Powel's on your birthday," she told her father, but Franklin, in France desperately seeking funds to keep the American effort afloat, wrote that he considered this kind of behavior unseemly. Esther would have agreed.[20]

The question of Joseph's future overshadowed most other concerns. Esther knew he was angry, but she did not know how he would direct that anger. A year earlier, they had worked out a compromise. Joseph would not accept leadership of the Continental Cavalry, and Esther would try to be brave and tolerate his participation in the state militia. During the campaign of 1777, Joseph had stretched the boundaries of that agreement but had not broken it. He understood her concerns and, at least in his own mind, had sought to alleviate them. As he told Dennis, "Your sister is so much affected at the risk of my military life that last fall I accepted a seat in Congress."[21]

From Esther's perspective, Joseph's blend of congressional responsibility and military service during the campaign of the fall and winter of 1777–78 had kept the family poised on the brink of disruption and disaster. In the end, it had precipitated their grueling exodus to Flemington. Now, in June 1778, Joseph's behavior again threatened his family's welfare.

Shortly after he left Flemington, Joseph joined Washington and the American forces in attacking the British as they retreated from Philadelphia toward New York. At the Battle of Monmouth, on June 28, Joseph plunged into the fray and again lost his horse in battle. Esther, in reporting this news to Mrs. Cox, put the best gloss she could on it, but it unsettled her. Joseph's quick response to the call of battle and his disregard for his safety demonstrated the porous nature of the terms of their agreement. The possibility that Joseph, angry, restless, and impatient, might find it impossible to resist a full return to military life again frightened her. What she feared, Joseph had earlier admitted to Dennis: "I am very strongly urged to take command of the cavalry. I do not know but that I may take the field again this summer."[22]

Three aspects of Joseph and Esther's relationship during the summer of 1778 suggest the unresolved nature of this issue. Neither he nor she mentioned it in their letters to each other, a silence that spoke louder than words. In addition, Joseph seldom, if ever, visited Esther in Flemington, and Esther resisted Joseph's efforts to have her meet him near Trenton.

Joseph could have gone to Esther at any point during the summer. It was a long ride (forty miles), but under normal circumstances he would have seen that as a challenge, not a barrier. Nor was he particularly busy after the British left. He fulfilled his obligations to Congress, but most delegates came and went with a high degree of flexibility. Joseph admitted that he spent much of his time waiting for others to show up. The flimsy excuses he offered Esther for failing to visit conveyed the real message. He did not want to confront her. He knew where she stood. He needed to decide what he would do. Until then, there was no point in meeting.

Esther's apparent contentment at Flemington reflected, in part, her habit of taking the children to the country for the summer. She also felt safe. She had learned in the past two years that living close to Philadelphia, even in the countryside, placed her family in danger. Flemington was small, rural, isolated, and boring, but secure. In addition, she was not alone. She had her mother, Joseph's sister, and probably Mrs. Sally Pettit and a portion of Sally's family living with her. She had recovered more slowly than usual from the birth of her most recent baby, but now she delighted in him. She reported that he "grows so fast" and "has as few complaints as any child of his age I ever saw." She had found a school of sorts for the other three. She had the newspapers from Philadelphia. And, one can surmise, she was in no hurry to leave the still-fresh grave of her youngest daughter. At bottom, however, she waited for Joseph to decide, using her absence and her silence as powerful arguments.[23]

Joseph again faced a difficult choice: civilian or military leadership in the struggle against Great Britain. In midsummer, he hinted at a third option. In a letter to Dennis, he suggested he might return to private life and work to restore the family's financial base. But had Esther heard of that, she would have easily dismissed it. The Reeds felt no such pressure. Despite the vicissitudes of war, they were financially secure. The details remain unclear, but the overall pattern was evident. The war had not destroyed their financial base. Most of the time, Joseph earned a military or a civilian salary, and he had invested money in at least one successful privateer. More dramatically, he had advanced the interest of his extended family. In the winter of 1777–78, he had served as a representative of Congress in restructuring the army's procurement system, bringing it into line with best business practices. General Nathanael Greene headed the new quartermaster's office with Charles Pettit and John Cox as his deputies collecting commissions on all purchases. In addition, should Joseph choose to practice law again, he remained one of the best lawyers in Philadelphia. Soon, he invited young Jared Ingersoll to revive the office. Ingersoll, an earlier student of Joseph's, had just returned from

Europe. He accepted Joseph's offer, and the office soon flourished. Ingersoll also joined the family when he later married a daughter of Charles and Sally Pettit.[24]

The Reeds also continued to hold income-producing property, and they retained a major interest in the West Jersey Society with its vast land holdings in New Jersey and Pennsylvania. Joseph hoped in time to buy out the remaining English investors at favorable prices, expecting they would sell cheaply because they feared that they would lose their entire investment should the Americans win. If the Reeds gained control of the West Jersey Society, the family would possess a land-based fortune comparable, possibly superior, to that ultimately developed by Henry Knox in Maine and William Cooper in the Susquehanna Valley of New York.[25]

More importantly, regardless of the family's financial situation, Esther knew that one way or another Joseph would play an active part in leading America's fight for liberty as well as in the crusade against those who had insulted his manhood, threatened his family, and contributed significantly to the death of Theodosia. Esther knew this and she supported it. The question was: Would he direct his energy, anger, and animosity into civilian or military channels?

Esther much preferred the political to the military role, and opportunities abounded for Joseph in that arena. He now sat in Congress. He had won election to the Pennsylvania Supreme Executive Council but turned it down because of compelling responsibilities in Congress and at camp. Friends were urging him to seek the presidency of the state.[26]

In the past, Joseph had shied away from what he saw as the endless bickering of politics. Early in August, he told Esther that the political controversies then raging in the state "lessen my attachment to public life and enhance the pleasure of domestic [life]."[27] Like most Americans then and now, Joseph hated what he saw as political factions: those agglomerations of narrow, self-interested individuals conspiring to use public resources and authority to advance personal and private ends at the expense of the common good. He, again like many Americans then and now, assumed that government, those who exercised public authority, should act to advance the public good, the common cause, the common welfare, and the commonweal, the commonwealth.

In private business, Joseph had vigorously but honestly pursued his family's interests. He competed and, more often than not, won, and the goal he pursued was private and personal: the advancement of his family. But in the military, he had lived by a different code and exemplified a different set of principles. Great military officers led by example. They risked all for the noble cause. They expected to ride at the head of their men. They expected to have their horses shot from beneath them. They expected to confront, face-to-face, one-on-one those weaker men whose courage failed them. One suspects that Joseph's admiration for Washington derived at least in part from Washington's ability to exemplify these values and this mode of conduct. In the same vein, one suspects that Joseph's dissatisfaction with the routine administrative work of adjutant general and his heroic abandonment during battle reflected the warrior's impatience with the mundane and his exhilaration in combat.

Esther felt differently about all of this. Few husbands ever died in political conflict, and none that she knew had ever returned home from a political campaign maimed and condemned to lifelong dependence on the wife and children for whom they had once been responsible. Moreover, she seemed to have a more intuitive feeling for how politics worked in the culturally heterogeneous Pennsylvania, and a better and more pragmatic understanding of how politics might work to her family's benefit. For now, however, Joseph's hint that he might return to "the pleasures of domestic life" disturbed her. She knew he would be active somewhere, but she feared his criticism of public life suggested he was moving toward the cavalry. And his recent adventures in the Battle of Monmouth offered her vivid proof of the power of that option to attract him.[28]

A week or so later, however, he sent her a different message. Writing from camp, where he was finishing his congressional responsibilities, he said that he was about to return to Philadelphia, "where my interests evidently call me." He did not spell out the details, but if he was at camp and saw his future in Philadelphia, then he was leaning toward the civilian rather than the military option. At that very moment, Vice President George Bryan and the Supreme Executive Council were preparing to ask him to serve as a special legal assistant to the state's attorney general for the prosecution of the "important trials of treason [that] will occupy the court during the next winter."[29]

Few offers could have been better suited to tempt him away from the war. He wanted harsh penalties for actual traitors and equally harsh treatment for those who had collaborated with the British. He accepted the offer and immediately wrote to Esther: "I believe [it] will please you."[30]

Indeed, it did. Joseph and Esther now agreed. He had come to see the wisdom of her argument. Esther was relieved and pleased. As she later wrote to Dennis, "Mr. Reed is as much engaged as ever, though in a different and *more important* status" [emphasis added]. She was entitled to brag a bit. She had won an important victory, not only for herself and her family but also for Joseph and his country. That victory, in turn, would soon bring them to national prominence.

Shortly after his letter to Esther, Joseph visited her at Flemington, and by the end of the month she returned to her household in Philadelphia. Then, in rapid succession, Joseph resigned from Congress, prosecuted traitors in Pennsylvania, won election to the Supreme Executive Council, and by December had been chosen as its president and therefore the chief executive of the state of Pennsylvania. Thus, by the end of 1778 three key families in Philadelphia had come together to shape the political agenda of the state. Joseph led the executive branch; Speaker John Bayard led the legislature; and Vice President George Bryan, still in the executive branch but soon to join the judiciary, continued the part he had assumed in the spring of 1777: the untiring political operative marshaling support for the state constitution of 1776 and recruiting men to serve under it.[31]

Esther knew and was known by each of these families and had interacted regularly with Margaret Bayard and Elizabeth Bryan. All three women lived in the center of Philadelphia and frequented the city's public market and its local shops. All were in the same age cohort: Esther, the youngest, was in her early thirties; Margaret Bayard was in her midthirties; and Elizabeth Bryan was in her early forties. Each managed a large family. Esther had started a decade or so behind the others but was catching up quickly. By December 1778, she had given birth to five babies. Margaret had at least six children, and Elizabeth had ended her childbearing at ten. Each also knew the world of international trade and commerce. Elizabeth Smith had married George Bryan, at the time one of the most successful Philadelphia merchants and a man with close commercial and family ties in Dublin, the place of his birth. Esther and Margaret came from commercial families and married men with an interest in the Atlantic trade. In addition, all three women were married to men who had played public political roles in opposing British measures.[32] Thus, for Esther DeBerdt Reed, Margaret Hodge Bayard, and Elizabeth Smith Bryan, almost every aspect of their daily lives engaged them in parallel activities and immersed them in similar mental worlds.

However, much the same could be said of a fair portion of the female patriot elite in Philadelphia. The characteristics that set these three women and their families apart were their interest in politics and their fulsome participation in the Presbyterian church located on Arch Street in the center of Philadelphia, a congregation led and inspired by the Reverend James Sproat.

From late in 1770, almost from Esther's first months in Philadelphia, she, Margaret, and Elizabeth had met and interacted regularly, not at citywide events for the elite, such as the Philadelphia Dancing Assembly, nor at the tea tables in the great houses of the Quaker and the Anglican rich, but rather at the Arch Street Presbyterian Church. Here, they came to baptize their babies, mourn the deaths of their children, support their pastor and his wife, worship their God, and listen weekly to their spiritual (and possibly their political) advisor as he helped them to understand the meaning and purpose, the pain and the joys, the duties and the obligations, as well as the origins and the ends of their short sojourns on this earth. A New England visitor to Philadelphia in the spring of 1775 had attended service at the Second Presbyterian Church and noted that Esther's minister, Mr. Sproat, had "entertained [them] . . . with a truly American patriotic sermon."[33]

For politically oriented women largely excluded by law or custom from such male public spaces as coffeehouses and taverns, their religious congregation offered an easily accessible, safe, secure, predictable, and respectable physical place to meet beyond their individual households. It constituted a semipublic space inhabited by like-minded people with whom they could join in celebrating, in grieving, in serving, in worshiping, and in considering their collective responsibilities, as well as a space in which they could discuss politics.

Esther and Margaret were particularly close, or at least we have the clearest evidence of their personal ties. They had been friends from the early 1770s, and once the fighting started they had lived overlapping and intersecting lives as each struggled with turmoil, separation, and suffering. In the months after the Declaration of Independence, both women fled from Philadelphia with their families: Esther in a rather orderly way to Burlington, New Jersey, and Margaret in a panic at the last moment into the countryside west of Philadelphia. Margaret's daughter Jane later remembered the house in great turmoil: "boxes piled up in the parlor; furniture packing and . . . confusion and alarm through the house."[34]

From December 1776 to June 1777, while Esther moved from Burlington to Evesham, New Jersey, and then to Norristown, Pennsylvania, Margaret tried one and then another rural refuge, and then settled eighteen miles up the Schuylkill River from Philadelphia near Valley Forge, a place described by Jane as "rendered very agreeable by the near neighborhood of General Reed and family." "[I]intimacy with this family," Jane wrote, "has marked every period of my life." Her father, she knew, thought of Joseph Reed as his closest friend. She also knew that her mother and Esther were friends, and she herself "was much attracted" to Esther's eldest daughter, Patty, one year her senior.[35]

In the terrible winter of 1777–78, these two mothers coped with life largely without their husbands. John Bayard spent much of his time away to the west in Lancaster serving as Speaker of the Assembly. Joseph stuck to the letter of his agreement with Esther with respect to his military involvements but was away more often than home. By the late winter of 1777–78, Esther had come to fear his visits because of enemies lurking to capture and turn him over to the British. Margaret Bayard faced a crisis of her own. Her son, returning from the College of New Jersey at Princeton, was taken by "marauders" and imprisoned in Philadelphia. Margaret had to leave her family, presumably with Esther, while she traveled through no-man's-land and across enemy lines into the British-occupied city to plead for the young man's release.

In March 1778, Esther left Margaret and fled to a remote refuge in New Jersey, and the friends were not reunited until six months later, when Esther returned home with her family. Soon, both women were politically engaged. One of Jane Bayard's favorite memories was of the pains her mother took to prepare her, at the age of eight or nine, to attend a public social-political event at Esther's executive mansion.[36]

Esther's relationship with Elizabeth Bryan is more difficult to document. Elizabeth's husband had worked since the spring of 1777 to bring Joseph into a leadership position in the state government. Shortly after his own 1777 election to the Supreme Executive Council, Bryan tried to convince Joseph to accept the position of chief justice. Despite Joseph's reservations about the state constitution, he had (in partial response to Esther's urging) considered the offer seriously.[37] Bryan, anxious to have him, kept the offer on the table for more than four months. In the end, Joseph turned it down, but Bryan continued his recruitment efforts. The next summer, after the British evacuation of Philadelphia, Bryan again encouraged Joseph to take a more vigorous part in civilian public life and supported his election to the assembly, his appointment as special assistant to the state attorney general to prosecute accused traitors, and finally Joseph's candidacy for election to the Supreme Executive Council and the presidency.

In all of this, Elizabeth Bryan remains largely invisible, at least in part because of the tendency for the men who created so many of our private and public documents to neglect the presence, actions, and thinking of women.[38] We do know, however, that Elizabeth, like Esther and Margaret, identified closely with the Arch Street Presbyterian Church and its charismatic pastor, the Reverend James Sproat. We also know that by 1778, she, Esther, and Margaret had become the three most prominent partisan political women in their congregation.[39]

It seems reasonable to assume that these three women talked about private and public affairs on a casual basis and met together with their husbands over a meal in one or another's home to discuss political men, political issues, and political strategies. Such social-political gatherings had long been common events in Esther's life as well as among the patriot leadership families in Revolutionary Philadelphia. In London, politics had dominated the DeBerdt Sunday dinners, and Esther and her mother had been regular participants. In Philadelphia, while the First Continental Congress was meeting in 1774 and 1775, Esther entertained prominent figures from Virginia and New England over meals in her home, and she and her mother engaged these guests in political and military discussions. At the same time, just down the street from the home of the Reeds, the wife of one of the radical leaders of resistance to the British, Mrs. Christopher Marshall, hosted dinners for political and military discussions that included such luminaries as John Hancock and his wife, and other pairs of married patriots. Nor was this unique to Philadelphia. In 1775–76, in faraway Massachusetts, Abigail Adams, the wife of one of Esther's dinner guests in Philadelphia, dined with officers of the Continental Army and their wives.[40]

In her first few months back in the city, Esther had, by necessity, focused on her family: reassembling their possessions, settling their new home, and preparing for the long-delayed baptism of the young Dennis. By January, she had acquired a new title, the Lady of His Excellency Joseph Reed, and, as she wrote to her brother in the early fall of 1779, "every part of our life is intertwined in politics."[41]

She joined Joseph in mobilizing those they saw as the true patriots against a diverse and informal coalition of the timid, the trimmers, the religiously concerned, the honest neutrals, the persistent Tories, the principled opponents of war, and, among the patriots, those who were overly forgiving or overly self-seeking. The Reeds, in collaboration with Vice President George Bryan and Esther's old friend John Bayard, Speaker of the Assembly, soon emerged as the most visible representation of a nascent political party as they defined the core issues that would structure partisan politics in the state for the following decade: the state constitution, the Test Acts, and the College of Philadelphia.[42]

The divisions over the new state constitution, at least on one level, revolved around the question of how best to preserve liberty. Many Americans still regarded the British constitution as the ideal model and saw its great advantage as its ability to limit the probability of hurried, unwise, arbitrary, or tyrannical government by distributing power among three independent units: the king, the House of Lords, and the House of Commons. In sharp contrast, the Pennsylvania constitution of 1776 rested on the assumption that simple, direct, popular government best preserved liberty. It lodged all real power in an annually elected unicameral legislature. The executive could neither introduce nor reject legislation, and the courts remained open to the influence of the legislature that controlled judicial salaries. Some patriots in Pennsylvania preferred the British model; others preferred the Pennsylvania one. This disagreement and other disputes over the new frame of government had emerged in September 1776, and over the next two years, the intensity of that debate rose and fell as the fortunes of war impinged on the lives of the people and their elected officials. After the British evacuation of the city in June 1778, however, the issue flared up again, and then continued to divide patriots in Pennsylvania.

Joseph had initially sided with those who preferred the British model, and that preference played some part in his reluctance in the spring of 1777 to accept appointment to the office of chief justice. Esther had no such reservations and pushed Joseph hard to take that job. A year later, in the fall of 1778, she also expressed no qualms about Joseph's willingness to accept appointment and ultimately election to office in the government operating under that constitution. Once elected, Joseph tried to broker a compromise, but when that failed early in 1779, he moved on to other issues that he saw as more pressing and closer to his heart. The party he was now joining, however, remained adamant in its support of the state constitution of 1776, and the defense of that document became its defining issue for the next decade.

For Joseph, however, the question of loyalty was more important and more pressing. The earlier Test Acts (loyalty oaths) required residents of the state to abjure allegiance to the king and swear loyalty to Pennsylvania. Punishments for failure to comply appeared more persuasive than punitive. However, after the British left Philadelphia, Joseph, driven into action by his own military and family experience, especially in the previous year, emerged as one of the principal proponents of new legislation. He wanted to identify and punish the explicit enemies of the American cause as well as those who now sought to enjoy the benefits won by the suffering of the true patriots without themselves paying the price. The legislature, guided by Speaker Bayard, enacted far more rigorous and punitive Test Acts in 1778 and 1779. On this question, Esther remained more pragmatic. In the spring of 1778, she had felt more pity than anger at those who had drawn the wrath of the angry patriots, but by the winter of 1778–79 she seemed to have acquiesced in Joseph's determination to separate the sheep from the goats. Bayard pushed in the assembly for legislation that would compel all residents of Pennsylvania to become citizens or be punished. These new and more rigorous Tests Acts became a defining plank in the emerging partisan agenda.

The dispute over the future of the College of Philadelphia began a little more than a month into Joseph's presidency in a personal exchange with the Reverend William Smith, the Anglican provost of the college. Smith raised questions about Joseph's treatment of Mrs. Elizabeth Graeme Fergusson, an Anglican whose husband had been accused of treason and whose property the state was confiscating.[43] Joseph responded to Smith, and the exchange continued in one venue or another until September 1779. By that time, Joseph and his colleagues in the assembly, again ably led by Speaker Bayard, had come to see Smith and his college as a center of antipatriot sentiment in the city. They unleashed a full-scale attack, and within months legislation voided the college's charter, transferred its resources to the new University of Pennsylvania, and installed the Presbyterian minister, John Ewing, as the university's provost. George Bryan, who had published his fears about a growing Anglican threat in Pennsylvania before the war, would have concurred easily.

Esther has left us with no record of her feelings on this question, but of the three issues defining the emerging partisan rivalry, she was undoubtedly most sympathetic to the position taken by Joseph, the Bayards, and the Bryans on the question of the college. She was an avid "dissenter" from the Anglican Church, as was her mother. They worshiped regularly at the Second Presbyterian Church, and, at least on the surface, Esther identified more strongly with it than did Joseph. Moreover, Esther's father had been an ardent religious dissenter in London and had championed the efforts of colonial dissenting churches to resist what he saw as Anglican aggression toward them in the decade or more before he died. Thus, Esther's personal theological orientation, her congregational identification, and her family history left her with little residual sympathy for an Anglican woman and her chief supporter: an Anglican minister and provost of the Anglican-oriented College of Philadelphia. Indeed, it remains at least possible, if not probable, that Esther felt more strongly on this issue than did Joseph. Joseph's mother had come from a strong Anglican family in New Jersey and even now, he maintained close contacts with his Anglican aunts, his mother's sisters.

It had been a momentous year for the Reeds and for party politics in Revolutionary Pennsylvania. Between the fall of 1778 and December 1779, Esther had succeeded in channeling Joseph's anger and energy into political leadership. He had become president of the Supreme Executive Council, and in cooperation with the Bayards and the Bryans the Reeds defined the issues that would structure partisan politics for the next decade, in the legislature as well as in the electorate. In the spring of 1779, their political opponents, those who opposed the state constitution, the rigorous Test Acts, and the destruction of the College of Philadelphia, announced their formation of the Republican Party. The next month, the Constitutionalists responded by announcing the formation of their own party.[44]

In this new public and political life, Esther and Joseph complemented each other. Joseph had little experience in electoral politics and hated what he saw as an unending argument among ignorant or self-interested men. More immediately and more importantly, he was infuriated with those in Philadelphia who had frolicked while the Continental Army paid a high price at Valley Forge, his wife and children suffered in the wilderness, and his youngest daughter died. He also found himself increasingly at odds with those of his fellow patriots whom he saw as too quick to forgive and forget, as well as those patriots who transposed their pecuniary ambitions wholesale into the realm of public policy, putting private gain above public need and thus advancing policies that agitated popular emotions, provoked violence, and frustrated the state's ability to mobilize its people and its resources to defeat the enemy.

Joseph's natural inclinations, those characteristics that had contributed so much to his success in law, in international trade, and in the military, seemed ill-suited for his present situation. Washington described him as a man of "discipline, ability, activity, and bravery." We might add that he was also confident, ambitious, and determined. In addition, he had a penchant for assigning tasks to subordinates and a habit of criticizing poor decisions by his peers. He had little taste for diplomacy and regarded compromise as settling for second best. He wanted to do things, he wanted to do things properly, and he had little patience for inaction and even less for incompetence. In the past, these traits had not served him well in the political realm. In the fall 1776 campaign, he had criticized Washington's inaction as well as the leveling behavior of the New England militia officers. Washington later forgave him and recommended that Congress appoint him brigadier general of the Continental Cavalry. Congress, however, had refused. Quite possibly, New England representatives in that august body remembered the aspersions Joseph had cast on their leveling militia. Joseph brought energy, focus, talent, and determination to any task he undertook, but in the new dynamic and democratic political life of Revolutionary Pennsylvania, these assets, while necessary, were not sufficient.[45]

Pennsylvania had a long history of popular political participation and organized competition for elected office.[46] The Revolutionary agitation, especially after the Tea Act in 1773 and the Coercive Acts of 1774, intensified this popular political culture. The new state constitution of 1776 institutionalized that culture. A near-universal adult male taxpaying suffrage annually elected representatives to the all-powerful unicameral legislature. Thus, political success in Pennsylvania depended on the nearly continuous mobilization of a statewide constituency to gain or hold a majority in the Assembly. And, by 1779, a growing proportion of that electorate was alienated by what it saw as the efforts by the few to advance their private economic concerns at the expense of the many who had sacrificed their time, their comfort, their resources, and even the lives of their loved ones for the common cause. Joseph shared these popular concerns about the efforts of some of his social peers to expropriate the fruits of the Revolution while delegating its costs to others.[47]

Esther was much more comfortable in this new political context and was more politically skilled than Joseph. She had learned one kind of politics at her father's knee: the politics of ingratiation and the cultivation of great men. In London, her family's religion had put them at a political disadvantage. Despite this impediment, however, her father had succeeded rather well in using the byzantine system of British patronage politics to advance the family's interests. For most of the last three years of his life, Esther had been at his side serving as his amanuensis. That kind of politics was in Esther's blood.

In Philadelphia, as in the older world of patron and client, Esther continued to seek éclat for her family, but America was a different place.[48] To some degree, power continued to depend on the close cultivation of men and interests. Now, however, it rested increasingly on one's ability to mobilize a popular majority and, in this case, to tap into the growing resentment against assertions of privilege and exclusivity and the exploitation of public office to further personal profits while avoiding military duty.

Neither the Reeds nor any of the other leaders of the Constitutionalists defined this division in terms of what we would think of as a socioeconomic class. They and their fellow leaders of the Constitutionalists in Philadelphia, like those who led the Republicans, were members of the elite. In the city, as in the eastern agricultural counties and across the state to Pennsylvania's far western outposts, both parties drew their leadership from the top ranks of the local electorate.[49]

Moreover, Joseph and Esther were not levelers. Although they led a party that was particularly sensitive to popular concerns over the maldistribution of the benefits and burdens of the war, they did not identify with or aspire to be part of the middling and laboring classes. Joseph had been trained to lead and had criticized what he saw as far too much leveling in the ranks of the Continental Army. Esther came from a society characterized far more than Revolutionary America by rigid social hierarchies, and she expected professional and business families to play key political parts.

Joseph, probably more than Esther at this point, felt the responsibilities of elite leaders toward those who had elected them: to inspire them by heroic action; to succor them with wise public policies; and to avoid insulting and aggravating them by flaunting wealth, by pretentions to privilege, and by conspicuous indifference to all needs of those they led. Esther, from her early years in London and throughout her time in Philadelphia, tended to see politics in utilitarian terms: using influence of one kind or another to advance her family's aspirations. Joseph had also proven himself fairly adept at this game of patronage before the Revolution, but after his military experience, especially with Washington, he more readily criticized his peers for exploiting public opportunity to advance their private interests. One might say that his close attachment to Washington, especially in the fall of 1775 and after, had heightened his sensitivity to a military ethic of honor and sacrifice. Esther here, as later, continued to understand politics in her Old World patron/client frame of reference, in which politics was giving and gaining those benefits necessary to advance the family. Not until later in the summer of 1780 do we begin to see hints that she too was coming to see politics as a duty that entailed responsibilities for the advancement of broader collective goals.

But in 1778–79, Joseph was already there. He saw himself as the leader of the "popular" party in contrast to the "commercial" or the "merchants" party.[50] His feelings resonated well with those of the angry militiamen who in 1779 had demonstrated in the streets of Philadelphia against runaway inflation, against those who sought to monopolize scarce goods, and against stay-at-home profiteers who stole customers from those who were off fighting the enemy. He had given eloquent expression to the same resentments in 1778, and these feelings continued to shape his political decisions.[51]

That led him to defend a policy agenda that reflected the interests, possibly the ideology, and certainly the concerns of a significant constituency in Revolutionary Pennsylvania: those who believed that the state constitution best served the needs of the people, those who wanted to convert the Anglican-dominated College of Philadelphia with its arrogant Anglican minister into the nonsectarian University of Pennsylvania, and those who wanted to exclude from voting and public office any and all who had refused to support the Revolution and the new government of Pennsylvania in its hour of most pressing need. On these issues and the coalition that supported these measures, the Reeds' ascent depended. Their ability annually to mobilize an electoral majority on these issues would also determine their future.[52]

Electoral politics was not entirely new to Esther. In London, she and her mother had followed politics closely in the newspapers, and they were among the first women ever to attend a meeting of the House of Commons. In the buildup to the war between the colonies and the mother country, Esther had hoped that the London merchants would pressure Parliament for reconciliation with the colonies, and she had done what little she could to influence the parliamentary election. Nevertheless, participating in Pennsylvania's new popular democracy, and especially in supporting the agenda of the Constitutionalist Party, brought her into a new realm.

Her first political task, largely a private one, was to channel Joseph's anger and energy into effective action in a realm where he had little experience and even less patience. Here, she added subtlety, nuance, and an instinctive feel for the intricacies of popular politics to her skill with words and her personal inclination to charm, persuade, and negotiate. A letter she wrote to Joseph when he was angry with Washington for what he saw as a personal attack illustrates the point. Joseph intended to respond sharply to Washington. Esther urged caution, patience, and understanding. She first calmed him by agreeing with him and by criticizing Washington. "I confess I felt very sensibly his doubting your zeal or exertion in the cause of your country: neither of these, nor your friendship for him, I think, can at this day be called into question." She then cautioned Joseph to remember that Washington was an old friend now surrounded by those who have other schemes in mind and who did not have Joseph's best interests at heart. "His ears have been open to insinuations, perhaps by designing men or at least ignorant men." Move carefully. Suspend judgment. Wait until you see him. And "remember no one is entirely proof against the arts of misrepresentation, or can always act right when those in whom they placed confidence made it a point to deceive . . . or are themselves deceived." Wise counsel in any realm, but especially so in public and political life.[53]

In the summer of 1779, Esther began a more public political role. The Assembly had confiscated the mansion of loyalist Joseph Galloway on Market Street near the State House and converted it into the president's residence. The Reeds' new home soon became the center of politically relevant social events. Invitations were eagerly sought, and those who earned them dressed carefully for the occasion. As we have seen, Jane Bayard, the daughter of Speaker and Mrs. Bayard and a close friend of young Patty Reed, later recalled that "great preparations were made about my dress" as her mother readied her for her first party there.[54] It is probably no accident that years later, Jane Bayard's sister, Mrs. Margaret Bayard Smith, became a famous Washington, D.C., hostess noted for similar events in the early nineteenth century.[55] Dressing up constituted an important but relatively small ingredient in these essential political events. It is difficult to exaggerate the political significance of these ostensibly social gatherings or the power of the hostess and her guests to use them to build alliances, to smooth ruffled feathers, to gather and disseminate political information, to reward and punish political allies, to ease tensions, and not incidentally to demonstrate and reinforce status.[56]

But hosting social-political events at the executive mansion was just the start of Esther's public political roles. Over the next year and a half, she emerged as one of the most prominent and most successful political operatives in Revolutionary Pennsylvania. And by the end of the summer of 1780, the Reeds were poised to play a part on the national stage.

CHAPTER 11

America's Female Politician

The year 1780 should have been good for America's cause and for the Reeds. The French Alliance, signed in the spring of 1778, had promised men, arms, supplies, and tactical support. Victory seemed certain and not too far away. Joseph and Esther, among the leading political families in the state, lived and entertained in the executive mansion at the corner of Sixth and Market Streets, one of the city's great houses formerly owned by loyalist Joseph Galloway. Their political allies, the Constitutionalists, controlled the government. Their four surviving children were safe and in good health, and the memories of the terrible winter of 1777–78 and the searing death of Theodosia were fading. In May, Esther, in the ninth month of her sixth pregnancy, should have been looking forward to a pleasant summer with the children in the new executive summer residence west of the city overlooking the Schuylkill River, recently confiscated from the Tory family the Shoemakers.

But by late spring, both America and the Reeds faced mounting difficulties. The war was far from over, the promise of the French Alliance had produced less tangible fruit than expected, an increasing proportion of patriots were elevating personal interest above the needs of the army, and the British had begun the new campaign by capturing Charleston, South Carolina. Washington's men lacked nearly everything an army needs. The soldiers and their officers were growing resentful of the failure of the civilians they defended to recognize and respond to their difficult situation.[1] General Washington had reached a point of desperation, if not despair. He felt the country's "insensitivity and indifference"; he lamented that "the motives of honor, public good, even self-preservation have lost their influence"; and he pleaded with his old friend, Joseph Reed, now president of Pennsylvania, to mobilize that state for him. "Either Pennsylvania must give us all the aid we ask of her, or we undertake nothing."[2] The Reeds' political opponents at home as well as at camp were maneuvering to shift responsibility for the sad state of the army to the government of Pennsylvania and thus to its current political leaders. Washington seemed to be of a similar mind.

Joseph felt the sting of these criticisms, but in reality, little could be done. Although Pennsylvanians appeared to be prospering, the state lacked money to recruit soldiers or to buy supplies and did not have sufficient popular support to induce its families to give up their men or their goods. Indian raids on the frontier drained vital resources, while in the city and its surroundings the "Tories," "the Royal cause," "the disaffected and mercenary," the "caprice of interested or perverse individuals," and the "rage and discontent of party" impeded every effort. Angry and frustrated, Joseph considered drastic measures, measures that might have solved his immediate problem but would have had questionable long-term consequences. In a comment more typical of his approach than of Esther's, he noted that he was "happy that Major Lee's corps is in the vicinity." Force might be required to execute measures that, though necessary, "are unpalatable."[3] At this point, Esther, seeking to extract her family from this political quagmire, demonstrated again her way with people and with words, her adaptation to the political democracy of Revolutionary Pennsylvania, and her insight into the mental world of patriot women.

Esther's performance in these few months offers us a rare look at female political behavior in Revolutionary America, a view often obstructed by the inherent private nature of much political communication, by the prevalence of verbal rather than written exchanges in rural and in small-sized walking cities, and by the tendency of male participants and male observers of political life to neglect to record the parts played by women in their political exchanges and interactions. In addition, because the laws of coverture denied married women any direct, public, and legal political role, women who acted politically generally did so in ways that would not appear in the public documents on which historians so often rely. In this instance, however, the nature of the crisis, the public attention Esther's political behavior attracted, and the accidents of historical preservation open windows through which we can catch glimpses of her extraordinary political sophistication and efficacy.[4]

On May 26, Esther gave birth to her sixth child, a boy. She turned this event into a political opportunity by naming him George Washington Reed. She then invited the general to be the boy's godfather.[5] The relative power of the father and the mother to determine the name of each new child undoubtedly varied from family to family. In this case, however, the context suggests Esther's initiative. Joseph was upset with Washington and in no mood for conciliation. In naming the baby, it was Esther who was looking for accommodation. She was thinking politically.

The Reeds' past naming pattern suggests the importance of this decision. They had named their first five children after themselves and their blood relatives. By all rights, Joseph's father was next in line, and Esther should have named her baby Andrew in his honor. Instead, she chose "George Washington" and thereby incorporated the general into the Reed family. With this symbolic act, she pledged to continue the respect, friendship, and affection that had begun five years earlier when the handsome soldier from Virginia had charmed the young mother in Philadelphia, and then enticed her husband, the young lawyer, to ride off with him to Boston.[6]

The general acknowledged the gesture and reciprocated, and soon Martha Washington was on her way to Philadelphia to represent her husband at the christening. Martha's protracted stay in Esther's home reestablished the ties of friendship that had first bound these two women together in December 1775, when Martha, on her way to join her husband at Cambridge, visited for a week in Esther's home in Philadelphia. Now, once again, the two friends were united in a common cause and committed to mutual support in protecting and preserving the relationship between their husbands. On one level, this was a political friendship. It also, however, appears to have been a warm and personal connection that enabled both women to be comfortable during a long and complimented visit: a young mother with a house full of children clamoring for her attention, a three-week-old baby at the breast, and a major fund-raising campaign nearing fruition under her direction.

The baptism of George Washington Reed on June 29 provided Esther with a second and more public opportunity to advance her agenda. The guest list made this ceremony the most conspicuous and politically salient event in the city since the British had left two years earlier: La Chevalier de la Luzerne from the French embassy represented America's new French ally; Samuel Huntington, president of the Continental Congress, and his wife represented the new nation itself; Mrs. Martha Washington represented the commander in chief of the military forces of the United States; and the Reverend James Sproat, the family Presbyterian minister, represented the single most numerous constituency in the Constitutionalist Party.[7]

Symbolically, this public christening spoke volumes. In our world, baptism ceremonies and the links they create among the great and mighty appear to have lost much of their political salience. In the world from which Esther came, as well as during the early years of the New Republic, the best politicians understood the power of political theater and appreciated politics as a performance art. Public baptisms, like parades, dinners, toasts, and celebrations of national holidays, carried political weight and conveyed important information. The christening ceremony demonstrated to the world that the Washingtons and the Reeds remained united and mutually supporting political allies. It also reinforced (if it did not affect) the elevation of the Reeds to the apex of social-political status among the popular patriotic forces in Philadelphia, and it demonstrated to the city's elite (friend and foe) that the Reeds remained a power to be reckoned with. At the same time, it proclaimed in unmistakable terms the presence in the city of a pair of contenders for status and influence on the national scene.

But the Reeds' pledge of support for Washington and Washington's reciprocal support of the Reeds did not satisfy the needs of the army. During the first five years of fighting, Congress had financed the war by borrowing in one fashion or another, but that source was drying up. Pennsylvania's own efforts to borrow faced the same growing public skepticism.[8]

Over and above these financial difficulties, however, and to some degree their cause, partisan divisions within the state frustrated effective public action. The Republican Society, created a year earlier by a segment of the city's commercial and professional men, obstructed Joseph's efforts to raise public money. He saw these men as selfish and myopic, seeking personal advantage at public expense, and fatally insensitive to the image they projected and the popular hostility they engendered. These were the same men for whom he had risked his life on October 4, 1779, when, charging into a crowd on horseback, he dispersed a mob of armed men firing on Joseph's political enemies barricaded in the house of James Wilson.[9]

In Philadelphia, Joseph and Esther Reed as well as James and Margaret Bayard, George and Elizabeth Bryan, and the political leadership of the Constitutionalists in the city came from much the same commercial-professional strata as the leaders of the Republican Party.

However, they saw themselves and their party as the popular party making personal sacrifices for the common good and their political enemies as opponents of that good.[10] This partisanship stymied the ability of public authority in Pennsylvania to raise the money Washington needed. Possibly private sources could do what public ones could not.

Esther led the way with her most impressive political "event" of the summer: the door-to-door solicitation by the Ladies Association to raise money for American soldiers, planning for which had begun well before the birth of the new baby. More substantial but no less symbolic and efficacious than the christening, "the first large-scale women's association in American history" made Esther one of America's best-known female patriot leaders.[11] She personified it. She was its focal point, its driving force, its organizational genius, and its public face, first in Philadelphia, then in the countryside, and in time as far north as Massachusetts and as far south as Virginia.[12] In this success, she demonstrated her skill in organizing large-scale public political events, her ability to operate in a democratic and fractured polity, and her insight into the on-the-ground gender ideals against which patriot women measured themselves.

On Saturday, June 10, 1780, an anonymous broadside, "The Sentiments of an American Woman," initiated the campaign of the Ladies Association. A single-page printed sheet of about one thousand words (similar to a piece of modern political campaign literature), "The Sentiments" appealed to the women of the city to join in its effort to raise money for the men in the Continental Army.[13]

The timing of the publication of the broadside is interesting. It appeared in the papers on Saturday. The next day, women throughout the city would gather for Sunday worship. No venue in the city provided a better location for face-to-face exchange among significant numbers of women, and the speed with which the women responded in the first few days of the new week suggests that the Saturday call by "The Sentiments" was much discussed on Sunday.

The popular response among patriot women was instant, electric, and amazing. As one woman described it to her friend: "Those who were in the country returned without delay . . . others put off their departure; those whose state of health was the most delicate, found strength in their patriotism, one lady . . . having an infant too young to leave . . . was soon relieved from her distress by a lady . . . generously offering to nurse it during her absence."[14]

By midweek, a small cadre of women had met, divided the city into canvas districts, and invited forty or so women to join in the actual canvas. Before the week ended, thirty-six volunteers in teams of two to four had spread out across the city and its outlying areas knocking on doors, soliciting contributions, and recording each donor's name and gift. Joseph wrote to Washington on June 20, "The ladies have caught the happy contagion and in a few days, Mrs. Reed will have the honor of writing to you on the subject."[15]

In the last few days of the month, while Martha helped Esther prepare for the christening ceremony, Esther herself wrote to the wives of the executives of the other states, urging them to undertake a similar fund-raising campaign. She included copies of "The Sentiments" and the plan of the Ladies Association. On July 4, 1780, she informed Washington of her results. In the three weeks and three days since the publication of "The Sentiments," Esther's Ladies had walked the streets of a city of approximately thirty thousand people and collected in excess of $300,000 (paper money) from more than sixteen hundred individuals, possibly a majority of the adult female patriot population of Philadelphia. Individual donations ranged from a high of one hundred guineas donated by Lafayette to a low of 7s .6d from "Phyllis the colored lady."[16]

As the movement drew to a close in Philadelphia, women in other parts of the continent took up the crusade. "The Sentiments" appeared in "at least nine other papers in different states," and women in at least three states made an effort to replicate Esther's canvas. We have the best evidence from New Jersey, where the New Jersey Association, "eager to emulate the 'noble example of their Patriotic Sisters of Pennsylvania,'" identified leaders in thirteen counties and involved at least seventy-eight women in the canvas.[17]

Everything about this protracted political event was remarkable. Esther began by adapting to her needs a traditional male political device: the voluntary association. Pioneered by Benjamin Franklin a generation or more earlier, these male associations had proven to be an effective means of mobilizing community resources to advance projects that the government would not or could not undertake. Representing something between a private and a public undertaking, it was an ideal vehicle for Esther, and she adopted it wholesale. She, like her mentor Franklin before her, began with a publicity barrage to focus public attention on the problem, first by publication of "The Sentiments," and then continuing with notices in the press and by letters to friends and neighbors both near at hand and far away. She then, again like Franklin, brought together a cadre of well-intentioned and well-disposed women from among the city's elite, worked with them to make a plan, recruited volunteers, and, finally, completed the project.[18]

Esther's extraordinary success with this form of social-political activity demonstrated its power and its efficacy to American women. It soon became the standard mode whereby women, first in Philadelphia in the late eighteenth century and then in New York City, Boston, and beyond in the early nineteenth century, channeled their energies, religious enthusiasms, and moral concerns into the benevolent and reform organizations that dominated female participation in the public life of the new republic well into the twentieth century and beyond.[19]

Esther's motives, like Franklin's before her, were complex. Most visibly, she intended to raise money for the men at camp. More importantly, she sought to do this by appealing to female patriotism and thereby assuring Washington and his long-neglected and increasingly bitter soldiers that the ladies knew, appreciated, and intended to reward the bravery and the sacrifices of the men protecting them and their families. Esther's least visible but most politically salient motive was what we might call her inclination, again like Franklin before her, to do well by doing good.

The Ladies Association allowed her to transcend the partisanship that had divided the women as well as the men of Philadelphia into two political camps. All of these women in the Ladies Association were members of the city's elite, but these elite women did not constitute a single female network, a self-conscious, cohesive, exclusive female social grouping. Most of them knew each other, or at least knew about each other. They lived in a walking city. They may have passed each other on their way to the market, walked to church on the same streets, and nodded politely to acknowledge each other as they passed, but they attended different churches, visited and dined at different homes (where they engaged in polite and political conversations), and lived in families engaged in a rapidly intensifying and increasingly bitter partisan rivalry.[20] Esther's genius was to temporarily unite these partisan women into teams that solicited money from strangers in the streets of Philadelphia, extraordinary behavior commonly associated with women of abject poverty or compromised morals, and behavior that under other circumstances would elicit accusations of ladylike impropriety and earn enduring social stigma. She thus united Constitutionalist and Republican elite women in the well-publicized and nonpartisan effort to support the American cause and the men who defended it. At the same time, she, like Franklin before her, indirectly but powerfully advanced her own interests, and in this case that meant the interests of her family, her friends such as the Bayards and the Bryans, and her party, the Constitutionalists—a brilliant political performance.

Historians have suggested that "the organization met a mixed reception."[21] And so it did, but not among patriots. The few negative voices we have uncovered originated principally, if not exclusively, from Tories who criticized the canvas as a violation of prescribed female behavior (i.e., unladylike). The most frequently cited example of this came from Anna Rawle, a young unmarried Tory woman left alone in Philadelphia with her sister when the patriots drove their Tory mother, Mrs. Rebecca Shoemaker, and their stepfather into exile in British-occupied New York City. Rawle was lonely, afraid, and angry with the patriots in general and the Reeds in particular. "How often," she wrote to her mother in the summer of 1780, "I regret the disagreeable and painful circumstances of hearing so seldom from my dear Mother, and yet not a hundred miles asunder."[22] Patriot men frightened the young woman when they entered her room and ransacked her trunk looking for guns, and the Revolutionary government of Pennsylvania offended her by severely limiting her ability to correspond with her mother in New York. She associated her suffering most closely and directly with Joseph Reed. In September 1780, at the time she made her most cruel and heartless comments about Esther, she bragged to her mother, "I fancy Joseph would think me a very bold person did he know how often I have transgressed in writing to New York, when he has so positively forbid its being done by anyone without examination." And interestingly enough, she added, "I am as great a predestinarian in regard to his power, as he is in his religion." Although in the context it is not clear how she was using the term, she is here identifying Joseph Reed by the most commonly known characteristic of his Calvinist religion: predestination.[23]

But if Tory voices criticized Esther and her Ladies, patriot criticism was conspicuous by its absence. Far more typical was this paean in the *Pennsylvania Packet* of June 17, 1780: "To the everlasting honor of the ladies of this city be it told, that they . . . have begun a subscription for the noble purpose of their country's good."[24] Benjamin Rush, an ardent Republican, offered fulsome praise for the women who conducted the door-to-door solicitation and noted with pride that his own wife had "distinguished herself by her zeal and address in this business."[25]

The Ladies Association, like Esther's choice of a name for her new son and her orchestration of his public christening, demonstrates Esther's political skills: her sensitivity to others, her inclination to evade rather than confront, her understanding of the power of performance politics, and her ability to organize large-scale public political activity in a fractured electorate.

"The Sentiments," the broadside that mobilized extraordinarily large numbers of women to support the Ladies Association, reflected an additional dimension of Esther's political acumen: her ability to understand and articulate the thinking of patriot women and to use that understanding to mobilize them for dramatic political activity. To appreciate Esther's accomplishment, we need to look closely at her rhetorical strategy, at how she did it, but first a word about Esther's role in the creation of this famous document.

Historians have generally attributed the anonymous broadside to her. She was certainly capable of producing such a document. She was a well-educated young woman blessed with a keen sense of the subtleties of social intercourse, and she had the discipline and the patience to craft her writing to serve her purposes. As she admitted and illustrated in her first letters to Joseph at age eighteen, she chose her words carefully, bending them to her will and weaving them into persuasive prose.[26] She was a wordsmith of the first order. "The Sentiments" was well within her demonstrated capacity to achieve her ends with the written word.

In the same vein, "The Sentiments" was the centerpiece of the fund-raising campaign she had imagined, inaugurated, supervised, and in the end accounted for. The ideas expressed in this broadside comported well with her own wartime experience, with her perception of the nature of the emerging political-military crisis, and with her inclination to conciliate rather than to confront. And, she endorsed it by enclosing it in her letters to the wives of executives of the other states.

It seems probable, however, that she did not draft "The Sentiments" in isolation. Contemporary male political propagandists often shared early drafts with trusted colleagues, and Esther may well have done the same. The text of "The Sentiments" suggests a number of probable influences. Joseph obviously. He and Esther normally collaborated in their written communication with others, and the document's call for sacrifice would resonate well with his often-expressed conviction that selfishness threatened the American cause and only sacrifice for the common good could save this noble enterprise. Thomas Paine may also have played a part. He shared Joseph's feelings about the myopic behavior of rich people. More specifically, "The Sentiments" imitated Paine's *Common Sense*. Like Paine's 1776 publication, "The Sentiments" eschewed the classic Latin and Greek quotations that characterized the political publications of the era. Instead, it relied on well-known historical and biblical examples to illustrate its points, and the biblical names would sound like old friends to Esther, her fellow parishioners at the Arch Street Presbyterian Church, and many patriots whose religious principles made them regular readers of the holy scriptures.

America's new French allies may also have contributed. A letter to Esther dated June 10, 1780, from François Barbé-Marbois, secretary of the French legation, praised her as a most zealous and the most active patriot, apologized for putting this project back in her hands, and hoped that the responsibility would in no way impede her recovery of her health [i.e., after the birth of George Washington Reed in late May]."[27] In addition, some parts of the broadside may reflect French influence. Esther herself would have been uncomfortable penning lines that praised "the Maid of Orleans [Joan of Arc] who drove from the kingdom of France the ancestors of those same British, whose odious yoke we have just shaken off and whom it is necessary that we drive from this continent." She, more than many patriots, remained emotionally attached to her first home and its people. In her correspondence, she speaks of the English more with sorrow and regret than with hatred and bitterness. Nor would she have been comfortable siding with those Catholic forces that had driven her Protestant, Calvinist (Huguenot) grandfather into reluctant exile in England shortly before her own father's birth. But, despite these and possibly other influences, in the final analysis, "The Sentiments," like the Ladies Association, the door-to-door canvas, the record of donors and their donations, and the widespread distribution of the broadside as well as its imitation beyond Pennsylvania, was essentially Esther's work.

"The Sentiments" was first and foremost a political tract intended to produce political action, and it succeeded magnificently. It mobilized patriot women of Philadelphia, and later those in the countryside and up and down the Atlantic coast, to undertake public, political action. It spoke to them in words that resonated with their experience and their aspirations, and it induced an extraordinarily high proportion of them to participate enthusiastically and dramatically in an exciting public celebration of female political agency. It touched them. It moved them. It energized them. It led them to an enthusiasm of patriotism that allowed them to see themselves as true patriots making heroic sacrifices for their families, their community, and their common cause, and thereby asserting and celebrating their own engagement in a world-defining moment: the defense of liberty and the rising glory of America.

As an anonymous woman writing to a friend in Annapolis explained, despite experiencing some condescension, "we have made it a serious business and with great reason: an object so interesting was certainly worth an extraordinary attention.... We *consecrated* every moment we could spare from our domestic concerns to the public good [emphasis added]." The verb *consecrate* has carried powerful historical associations with the Christian consecration of holy places, holy men, and holy rituals. It reflects the seriousness with which these women took their civic responsibility: a profound duty, a sacred covenant. And in this we sense patriot women's understanding of themselves as citizens responsible for making wise political choices to advance the good of the republic in its travail and, at least by implication, an anticipation that that obligation would extend beyond this time of crisis into the more peaceable years once the war had been won. "The Sentiments" hinted at this when it noted that were women more publicly active during times of peace and tranquility, there might be less need for such extreme sacrifices. Female sovereigns such as Queen Elizabeth, "The Sentiments" reminds its readers, established reigns of "sweetness and justice." Not all of Queen Elizabeth's subjects might have agreed with that historical generalization, but the point is that while American women must fight to the death for liberty should the need arise, possibly that need would arise less often if women played a more conspicuous public political role in times of tranquility.

"The Sentiments" mobilized patriot women for public political action by articulating a complex image of women in the American republic that blended their old and new roles, as well as their traditional and Revolutionary responsibilities. Its first concern was the military crisis. The army in the spring of 1780 was in a deplorable state that had more to do with morale than with the actual deprivation, as real and as severe as that was. By the spring of 1780, the men and their officers were having doubts about the civilians they were defending. They had suffered through a terrible winter, more difficult and painful than Valley Forge. The conditions of the families of the soldiers compounded the difficulties of the men in camp. Their wives were urging, even begging, them to come home and care for them and their children, yet at the same time the patriot women for whom these men and their families were suffering ignored the needs of their protectors and indulged themselves in luxury and frivolity.[28]

"The Sentiments" addressed this crisis directly. It acknowledged that the support of patriot women for the men in the army had declined from the heroic days at the beginning of the war. It apologized for women's regression from the "firm resolution" they had "manifested" on the commencement of the actual war, when they were "animated by purest patriotism." It praised the soldiers for their manly defense of the ladies and their families, and it proclaimed the Ladies' intention "to render themselves more really useful" to those who are defending "our lives, our possessions, our liberty."

And if their defenders have come to fear that the ladies have forgotten them, they must be assured. "Forgotten? Never." "I can answer in the name of all my sex. Brave Americans, your disinterestedness, your courage, your constancy will always be dear to America as long as she shall preserve her virtue." Our tranquility, our safety, our families, our husbands in the fields, our children in the home, our babies at the breast, all depend on the shield that you have raised against the "ferocious enemy." So, in thanksgiving, we seek "your benediction" by renouncing our "vain ornaments" as we once again "display the same sentiments which animated us at the beginning of the Revolution" and "offer the homage of our gratitude at the altar of military valour [to] our brave deliverers," who in time will be able to say: "*This is the offering of the Ladies* [emphasis in original]."

The fundamental logic of "The Sentiments" thus rests on a simple proposition: patriot men in the army were doing their duty, and patriot women at home were not. Patriot women admit their guilt and promise to redeem themselves by vigorous action on behalf of the men who were defending and protecting them. Undergirding this proposition was a near-universal assumption about the division of responsibility within the family: men defended the hearth and women tended the hearth and honored and rewarded its protectors.

In addition, however, "The Sentiments" also contained a triumphant statement of female political responsibility in the new republic. It declared that women in America, like men in America, are "born to liberty," and that women, like men, should defend their birthright in this struggle against "tyranny," "disgrace," "humiliation," "slavery," and a life in "irons." It urged women in America, like men in America, to act with "courage, . . . constancy and patriotism." It acknowledged women's weaker physical constitution but distinguished that limitation from the artificial ones placed on women by contemporary prescriptions of genteel behavior. It boldly exhorted patriot women to ignore the conventional "opinion and manners" that consigned them to passivity and "forbid us to march to glory by the same paths as the Men." It praised women in the past who, "forgetting the weakness of their sex," went to war: "building," "digging," "furnishing arms," "darting missiles," and, if necessary, "burying themselves in the ruins" or "throwing themselves into the flames" in order to avoid the "odious yoke" of submission. There were no weak, delicate, vulnerable, timid, or helpless women for the author of "The Sentiments." Rather, in times of need, its heroines shed the artificial mandates of female decorum and joined their men in the dirty, sweaty, messy, bloody, deadly defense of liberty.

This second argument, however, does not obviate or deny the first. It accepts it as a description of women's responsibilities in normal times, but it adds that in the face of extreme danger to the republic, all other considerations become irrelevant: all citizens do what is necessary. In the same vein, although it categorizes the traditional prescriptions for female behavior as social constructions, it does not condemn those prescriptions nor does it preclude the probability that, after this crisis had passed, women will again comply with them. And the historical and scriptural role models "The Sentiments" offers to American women reinforce this by testifying to the honorable nature of this violent, even bloody kind of behavior by women: female warriors who led troops in battle (Batilda and Joan of Arc) and Old Testament heroines (Deborah, Judith, and Esther) who saved their people. (Judith did so by cutting off her husband's head with his own sword.) These women were honored for unladylike acts committed in defense of their people, their communities, and their nations.

Thus, "The Sentiments" defines women as citizens. It declares that women, like men in this new republic, are "born to liberty"; that women, like men, are citizens of the republic; and that female citizens, like male citizens, have a duty, a responsibility to protect the republic and to join with their men in this heroic and glorious march to advance the cause. But it does not challenge the division of labor within the family that women in eighteenth-century America knew and accepted. They expected to marry, to devote the bulk of their adult lives to bearing and nursing babies, and to provide vital economic support to the family in ways consistent with their reproductive responsibilities. For performing these duties well, society conferred considerable respect and honor. Few women in Revolutionary America wanted to change that.

"The Sentiments" accepts that division of labor within the family, but it separates that division from the traditional prescription of male superiority and female exclusion from public political life. Now both wives and husbands, mothers and fathers are citizens; both have public responsibilities, and both must act. Women, advanced the public good in times of peace by means consistent with their traditional reproductive and productive roles. In times of crisis, however, they pursued this end by whatever means necessary, including active participation in war to defend the republic.

The popular response to Esther's broadside suggests the degree to which she articulated a vision of American women that resonated well with their aspirations: decorous and genteel wives, loving and caring mothers, productive partners in a family economy, and citizens responsible for the future of the American republic struggling for life in a largely monarchial world.

Moreover, and of no little significance for the political behavior of American women for the next century and a half, "The Sentiments" offered patriot women a convenient vehicle for meeting their Revolutionary responsibilities in the public political arena: the Ladies Association. Patriot women responded enthusiastically to this female version of the male voluntary association in the summer of 1780, and American women ever since have used voluntary associations to mold the collective lives of their fellow Americans: economically, morally, intellectually, and politically.[29] To many in our modern world, this may seem like half a loaf at best, but it was far more than that in the world of patriot women in the midst of the American Revolution. Indeed, for many, if not most, patriot American women, it was *the* Revolution: equal citizens participating in this glorious and world-transforming event usually in ways consistent with their responsibilities as wives and mothers, but in whatever ways were necessary in times of crisis. That represents a revolution: a fundamental change whose implications we are still working out.

"The Sentiments" eloquently expressed a vision of women in the new republic that resonated well with their support of the resistance before the fighting began, with their suffering and sacrifice during the war, and with their understanding of their role as citizens in the emerging new republic. And in no case is this clearer than in that of Esther herself. Born and bred to be a cosmopolitan urban lady and initially disdainful of American women who shopped and gossiped, during the war she did hot, dirty, and sweaty labor well outside her usual "sphere." She traveled twice in harrowing circumstances: once with three small children without Joseph and once with him, once with a newborn and once in her ninth month of pregnancy, and during both trips she traveled over primitive roads through dangerous territory in horrible weather into exile in remote areas (or, as "The Sentiments" phrases it, "when exiles and fugitives we supported with courage all the evils which are the concomitants of war"). It was she who washed and prepared the body of her dead baby girl for burial in Flemington, New Jersey, in the spring of 1778.

And in this, she was one with Abigail Adams, who during the dysentery epidemic in the vicinity of Washington's military camp at Cambridge, Massachusetts, in the first year of the war, and while sick or recovering herself, cleaned the bodies and washed the linens of those in her family (including her mother) afflicted with the bloody, putrid, and uncontrollable diarrhea of dysentery.[30] And with Judith Sargent Murray of Massachusetts, who claimed that women possessed the courage to take up arms should the need arise, and with Deborah Sampson, who disguised herself as a man and joined the army. And with those women across the land, the guardians of neighborly values and family nourishment, who physically attacked price-gouging male retailers whose greed threatened women's ability to do their duty for their families.[31] These women—Abigail Adams, Judith Sargent Murray, Deborah Sampson, the ladies attacking monopolies, and Esther Reed and her Ladies in the Association—were all doing what needed to be done for their families, their neighbors, their communities, and the broader public good, a sentiment in which "The Sentiments" insisted that women equaled, and probably exceeded, men.

Thus, "The Sentiments" argued explicitly that decorous ladies would gain, not lose, status by acting vigorously in public to advance the good of the republic. And by logic, if not by design, recognizing women's citizenship and their obligation to defend liberty in times of crisis also validated and valorized women's responsible citizenship once victory was achieved and normal times returned.

This vision of heroic, sacrificing, and noble Republican women pleased, flattered, and energized patriot women. Abigail Adams in Massachusetts responded enthusiastically. By the summer of 1780, she had become so disillusioned by the lack of virtue among the people as well as the inefficiencies of popular self-government that she worried she might soon come to be in "favour of Monarchy." However, news of the Ladies Association and its fund-raising campaign revived her confidence. "Yet virtue exists, and publick spirit lives—lives in the Bosoms of the Fair Daughters of America, who blushing for the Languid Spirit, and halting Step, unite their Efforts . . . to alleviate the burden of war, to show that they are not dismayed by defeat or misfortunes. . . . see the Spirit catching from State to State." "America will not wear chains while her daughters are virtuous."[32] Esther, "The Sentiments," and the Ladies Association expressed a view of American women as full and responsible participants in the defense of the American republic. That view made them proud to be American women. Sarah Jay, writing to her husband, declared: "I am prouder than ever of my charming country-women."[33] And in a letter to her friend in Annapolis, a woman from Philadelphia wrote: "I have learned more than ever to respect my countrywomen, and there is no title in which I shall hereafter more glory than in that of an *American woman*."[34]

But if this was a new way for American women to think about themselves, and to see that they had a political part to play and a political responsibility to fulfill as citizens, we should remember that for Esther little of this was essentially new. "The Sentiments," the public fund-raising campaign it inaugurated, as well as the coalition-building and the street-level politics that followed reflected not a new interest in politics, not a new awareness of her relationship to the state, and not a new sense of empowerment but rather a different way for her to imagine her traditional relation to public and political life in a new political context: the popular democracy of Pennsylvania in the emerging new American Republic.

While Esther and her Ladies demonstrated their patriotism and their agency, her political opponents in the city, the commercial men in the Republican Party, had inaugurated their own fund-raising scheme, and the contrast between their effort and that of Esther's highlights her political sense, her instinct for what one might call the politics of image, or the politics of self-presentation. By early June, the city merchants, or at least that segment of it closely associated with the new Republican Party, aware of the military situation and of the rising public dissatisfaction, began a subscription of their own to raise money to hire substitutes for the well-to-do men who preferred not to volunteer to join Washington's underfed and poorly clothed soldiers in defense of the common cause. At a meeting at the Coffee House on June 8, a number of these men pledged to contribute money for bounties to encourage enlistment in the Continental Line.[35]

The origins of this initiative remain unclear. Thomas Paine later claimed credit for it, and the sequence of events makes this claim plausible. On June 4, Paine wrote to Joseph, urging action. Our treasury is empty, our credit is exhausted, something must be done, he wrote. He proposed calling a meeting of the "richer inhabitants of the city" to support the army and to encourage them to do so by reminding them that should Britain win, she would compensate herself for her military expenditures at the expense of those in Philadelphia with property. The logic was clear: those with the most to lose should be the first to fund the army.[36] Paine also urged a comprehensive scheme in which a major financial contribution to the common cause by the rich would serve as an incentive for others to follow suit: "some thousands in this State who had better subscribe thirty, forty, or fifty guineas apiece, than run the risk of having to settle with the enemy."[37] In addition to raising more money, that action would relieve some of the grievances of those from the lower ranks of society who were expected to fight. Within days, the commercial Republicans met at the Coffee House. The chronology thus seems to support Paine's claim to paternity.

However, the final Coffee House proposal differed from Paine's in both substance and purpose. Like Paine's suggestion, the original Coffee House plan focused narrowly on raising money from rich men to hire poor men to defend them from the British, but its authors soon abandoned their initial proposal and offered a much broader and potentially more popular one. In its second iteration, it solicited pledges of loans (not donations) by the rich to be made in ten installments ending in late November and earning interest guaranteed by Congress. The money would be deposited in a bank and the bank, in turn, would issue banknotes that could be used to buy and transport food and drink to the army.[38] Joseph joined in the subscription, as did one or two other Constitutionalists, but he remained skeptical of the motives of its original supporters. By mid-June, he wrote to Washington that the subscriptions to the bank were progressing well and promised "a fruitful supply," but he saw it as closely tied up with party and therefore suspect: "the finger of party is so manifest, that I sometimes have my doubts."[39]

Throughout the month of June, these two fund-raising activities moved in tandem: Esther's canvas for donations to support the Continental Army and the Republican merchants' solicitations of pledges for investment in their bank. Each appeared on the scene in early June, each publicized and pursued its effort through the rest of the month, and each promised to benefit the bedraggled Continental Army and its besieged commander. Esther produced well over $300,000, while the total amount of money raised and spent by the merchants' effort remains unclear.[40] By late August, Joseph believed that that effort was foundering.[41]

The Ladies, in contrast to the supporters of the bank, had constructed for themselves a compelling popular self-image as an altruistic, patriotic, nonpartisan group seeking to unite all ranks and religions, including the disaffected, in raising money for the common soldiers. It solicited gifts, not promises of loans. It recruited its teams from among the leading Republican and Constitutionalist families in the city. It had initially intended to bypass some of the poorer homes in order to avoid embarrassing women who could not contribute, but "the poorest guessed our intent" and insisted on contributing. The organization also courted the Quakers, the largest and most conspicuous neutral group in the city. Its female solicitors visited Quaker homes, praised Quaker religious principles, and complimented Quakers on their benevolent impulses.[42] It also reached out to the disaffected by extending to "our female fellow-citizens an opportunity to relinquish former errors, and of avowing a change of sentiments by their contributions to the general cause of liberty," and thereby of producing "the happy effect of destroying intestine discords, even to the last seed." It then complemented this popular image with a door-to-door canvas that mirrored the street-level political tactics common in popular partisan politics both then in Pennsylvania and nearly everywhere else in America for the next two centuries.[43] The Ladies Association had thus differentiated itself from the merchants' effort by creating an unselfish, nonpartisan, elite-led, popular-based patriotic effort to support the men in uniform. Here, Esther demonstrated convincingly her ability to operate within this new political milieu where building a popular image, mobilizing coalitions of electoral groups, and soliciting support by door-to-door canvases were far more important than the political skills she had learned in the British system of patron and client in London.

The popular response to Esther's campaign suggests the sophistication of its strategy, the breadth of its appeal, and the magnitude of its success. Some sixteen hundred different individuals contributed cash, not promises, with no expectation of personal financial return. In contrast, about ninety individuals pledged to loan money to the merchants' bank in low-risk investment guaranteed by Congress, and on which they could expect to earn 6 percent interest—an effort still tainted by its initial intention to raise money to hire the lower sort of men to take the military risks the better sort of men sought to avoid.[44]

Esther's fund raising scheme provoked no partisan rancor. It drew forth no partisan criticism. It united the patriots: both Constitutionalists and Republicans. Few, if any, patriots in Philadelphia questioned the propriety of the performance of this female-based public fund-raising effort or its tactics of soliciting money door-to-door among strangers of all ranks. The negative comment by Anna Rawle makes the point. She castigated the women who conducted the canvas. She saw their public behavior as inappropriate, especially for genteel women. "Of all the absurdities the ladies going about for money exceeded everything; they were so extremely importunate that people were obliged to give them something to get rid of them," she wrote.[45] But Rawle's criticisms reflect the use of traditional female prescriptions for a particular, personal, political end. She was a loyalist and a royalist, the daughter of a Tory woman living in exile in New York, and the stepdaughter of Samuel Shoemaker, an attainted loyalist whose country estate "Laurel Hill," on the Schuylkill, had been confiscated by the state and converted into a summer home for the president of Pennsylvania. In the summer of 1780, Esther was living in Anna's former country home, Laurel Hill. Rawle reveals the depth of her personal animosity toward Esther, and the personal rather than cultural source of her criticisms, in her later comments on the occasion of Esther's death. "The wife of a certain person [Esther DeBerdt Reed]," she wrote, "can never spend another summer at Laurel Hill. Her pleasures there had a melancholy and short termination. She is dead, and of a disorder that made people whisper about 'that she eat too many of Mr. S . . . 's [Rawle's stepfather] peaches!' her husband fainted at the grave." The insensitivity of the comment is highlighted by Anna's linking Esther's death from the uncontrollable diarrhea of dysentery to the diarrhea usually associated with eating green apples, or too much fruit of any kind. Rawle's animosity would not have surprised Esther or Joseph, both of whom understood and would have gloried in having Royalists and Tories as political enemies.[46]

Nor are the grounds on which Rawle attacked Esther surprising. Esther's behavior did violate widespread and commonly accepted gender prescriptions for ladylike behavior. What is surprising, however, is the willingness of Esther and her elite canvassers to transgress these norms. And, more surprising still, is the near-universal silence of patriot voices on this question. Probably most telling, both female and male patriots lauded the ladies for their zeal in the glorious cause and depicted their efforts as noble sacrifices that reflected the female virtue on which the new republic depended.[47]

Ironically, the Ladies Association, led by the most prominent Constitutionalist woman in the state, united all ranks and all political factions in the city in a nonpartisan demonstration that explicitly castigated fraction while it enhanced the image and the strength of the Reeds and their supporters. Esther, her husband, and her party presented themselves as the popular party, the patriot party, and the antiparty party seeking inclusiveness, tolerance, and reconciliation in their efforts to unite all the people of Pennsylvania in defense of liberty first in the state, and then in the nation.

The significance of this triumph needs to be emphasized. Esther had transcended one of the great dilemmas of popular politics. Americans dislike and distrust political factions. America's common political culture, then as now, condemned factions as selfish efforts to pervert the legitimate ends of government to advance private ends. But only power speaks well to power, and in a democracy numbers and organization are power. That, in turn, creates the problem. An organization seeking to mobilize popular support in opposition to a faction opens itself to charges that it too is a faction. Esther successfully combined patriotic rhetoric with bipartisan canvas teams to depict the Ladies as disinterested patriots making sacrifices for the common good. Her opponents in the bank scheme helped to enhance the public image of the Ladies Association by describing their own campaign first as an effort to raise money to hire poorer men to fight in the place of the rich, and then turning it into a guaranteed loan, possibly a lucrative investment opportunity. Their bank, however useful, could not compare with the selfless efforts of the Ladies. Esther, living in the de facto capital of the new nation, had thus demonstrated an extraordinary level of political sophistication and a keen sensitivity to the subtleties of mass-based politics in a divided polity, skills that could serve well in a future leadership role on the national level.

To the same end, Esther's fund-raising event also extended her reputation and her connections far beyond the Delaware River region. Her letters as the wife of the chief executive of Pennsylvania to the wives of the governors of each of the other states included copies of "The Sentiments of an American Woman" along with suggestions for how to organize a local fund-raising campaign. Some women responded by imitating Esther's Philadelphia fund drive; some did not. But by the end of the summer of 1780, Esther DeBerdt Reed was probably the best-known female public figure in the emerging new republic, second only to her friend Martha Washington.[48]

CHAPTER 12

Triumph and Tragedy

So far, 1780 had turned out well for Esther. The christening of George Washington Reed, the Ladies Association, and "The Sentiments of an American Woman" had demonstrated her extraordinary political talent, solidified her family's leadership position in Pennsylvania, and positioned them for a political role on a broader stage. Then, Esther's protracted but polite disagreement with General Washington during July and August over what to do with the money she had raised again demonstrates her verbal dexterity, her sensitivity to the subtleties of human interaction, her inclination to negotiate rather than to confront, her confidence in herself, and the continuing friendship between the lady and the general. Sadly, however, it was both the peak of her political odyssey and the end of her story.

Once Esther had raised the money, she then faced the question of how best to use it to reward the men in the Continental Army. She had started the campaign with no explicit plan, but she knew what she did not want to do with the cash. Unfortunately, she soon learned that Washington wanted precisely what she had determined not to give him. Over the next two months, they contended. In the end, Esther capitulated, not as a dutiful and subordinate woman deferring to male authority but rather as one of two worthy opponents who, realizing that the other had advanced unanswerable arguments, concedes.

Washington needed money to help solve his immediate military challenges: to augment the number of troops he had, to discipline them into a fighting force, and to feed, clothe, house, and transport them during the emerging campaign. He wanted the Ladies to supply his troops with the necessities of life, especially clothing, in order to compensate for the failure of the states and Congress to meet their obligations.

Esther wanted to do something special for the fighting men, something over and above the ordinary, and something whose symbolic value would exceed its utility, something that would dramatically fulfill the promises of "The Sentiments." She certainly understood that hungry, cold, sick, and ill-clothed men would welcome the necessities of life, but she wanted them to know that she and her Ladies were providing something beyond what society as a whole owed to its defenders. She wanted, as she phrased it, to give them "some public mark of the esteem they [the Ladies] entertained" for them.[1] She understood the symbolic significance of the gift.

She also worried about the political implications of her decision. If the Ladies helped to meet the basic needs of the army, then the civilian authority might shift scarce financial resources to other needs, or worst yet, give up the battle to convince the American people that they must pay the taxes necessary to govern and defend themselves.

Of greater immediate political consequence, the leaders of the Republican Party were publicly criticizing Pennsylvania, and especially its Constitutionalist leadership, for failing to meet its responsibilities to the army. They depicted their own fund-raising effort (their bank) as the response of well-to-do patriots seeking to do the job not being done by an incompetent government and, not incidentally, its incompetent leader, Joseph Reed.

How Esther spent the money thus had partisan political implications. Using her money to buy clothes for the soldiers, an essential item for which the public authority was responsible, would implicitly reinforce the charge of her political opponents, and it would carry greater weight coming from the wife of the chief executive of Pennsylvania: a public admission of her husband's failure. Thus, if Esther followed Washington's suggestions, she would act directly counter to her own original intention, possibly weaken the willingness of Congress and the states to do their duty, and further embarrass her husband, her political friends, and their political base. Hence, her summer debate with Washington.

If Esther and Washington had conflicting views on the question of spending the funds, they sparred in polite and respectful language. Joseph, in his June 20 letter to Washington, defined the terms of the dispute. The Ladies, he announced, soon expected to have completed their task. The funds they raised would be "laid out according to your Excellency's direction" with the exception of "such articles of necessity as clothing which the States are bound to provide" (i.e., no clothes).[2] The *Pennsylvania Gazette* reinforced this point when it reported on June 21 that the Ladies intended to provide an "extraordinary bounty . . . to render the condition of the soldiers more pleasant and not to hold place of the things which they [the soldiers] ought to receive from the Congress or from the States."[3]

Four days later, Washington acknowledged that this posed a problem for him. He admired "the patriotic spirit of the Ladies," but noted, "the terms of the association seem in some measure to preclude the purchasing of any article which the public is bound to find." Nevertheless, he had a compelling need for eight to ten thousand shirts for his men and urged the Ladies to spend their money on these, and only on these. "The Soldiery is exceedingly in want of these and the public has never, for several years past, been able to procure a sufficient quantity to make them comfortable." Then, in closing, he emphasized his advisory role. These are "my Ideas at Present," he wrote, suggesting that with more information from Esther "I shall probably be able to form a more complete opinion."[4] He remained flexible, almost deferential.

Esther, in her draft letter to the wives of the state executives, acknowledged Washington's preference but phrased her statement to keep the door open to alternatives. Washington, she said, has "expressed his opinion that part of the money would be best [appropriated] to purchase Linen for the Army." The telling phrases here are "his opinion" and "part of the money." The first was accurate; the second was less so—Washington wanted all of it spent on shirts.[5]

Esther's July 4 letter to Washington neither challenged him nor capitulated to his proposal. Rather than commenting directly on the underlying issue, she shifted responsibility for the decision back to him. "The Ladies," she wrote, "are anxious for the soldiers to receive the benefits of it [the money] and wait your determination how it can best be disposed of."[6]

Washington, responding quickly, thanked the Ladies profusely, praised their efforts, and then, encouraged by Esther's ambiguity, again urged her to spend the "whole amount" to purchase shirts for the men. He assured her that the shirts would be of "more service" to a soldier and would "do more to preserve his health than any other thing that could be procured." Trying to allay her concerns, he reassured her that this use of the money would not "exclude him [the individual soldier] from the usual supply which he draws from the public" and again reiterated his sensitivity to the Ladies' autonomy and his eagerness to please them by adding, "provided it is approved of by the Ladies."[7]

Joseph, in his July 18 letter to Washington, gave the general reason to think that the Ladies had acquiesced in the principle but were having difficulty obtaining the necessary supplies. He acknowledges that Esther had "received your kind favour a few days ago and is exerting herself to comply with your directions" but offered an excuse for their delay: "there is at present a very great difficulty in procuring the article." In the same letter, he also informed Washington that the state of Pennsylvania "was forwarding 2000 shirts . . . [and] overalls to the state troops" along with a "large supply of refreshments of other kinds."[8]

Washington, acting as if he and the Ladies had reached an agreement, wrote on July 20 about implementation. He suggested that Esther might want to deposit her money in the bank that the Republicans (her political opponents) were organizing. The bank, in turn, would supply her with banknotes in lieu of her cash, and she could use those notes to buy the necessary goods; thus, the two patriotic enterprises would move forward together, each benefiting the other.[9]

Esther, encouraged by recent developments and possibly a bit annoyed by Washington's apparent effort to subordinate her efforts to those of her political enemies, responded with her own counterproposal. She began with her argument: "I have been informed," she wrote, that two thousand shirts have been "sent from this State to their line and . . . that a considerable number is arrived in the French fleet for the use of the Army in general." Therefore, she suggested that "perhaps the necessity of shirts may have ceased" and the Ladies could make the men happy with something other than "an article to which they are entitled from the public." "Those who are of this opinion," she continued, "propose the whole to be changed into hard dollars, and giving each soldier two, to be entirely at his own disposal." But Esther, like Washington, still seeking to avoid a direct confrontation, qualified her point: "this method, she wrote, "I hint only."[10]

Washington responded carefully. He acknowledged the receipt of her letter and said again that he had "no intention to divert" the Ladies' funds. They had asked his opinion. He had given it. Now, as ever, he remained ready to "execute their commands in the manner most agreeable to themselves." At the same time, however, he expressed his apprehension about this specific plan. He pointed out, "a taste of hard money may be productive of much discontent" among his men. Some of them will use it wisely, but "it is equally probable that it will be the means of bringing punishment on a number of others whose propensity to drinking . . . too frequently leads them into irregularities." Then, he would have to correct misconduct by harsh measures.[11]

Washington's letter settled the question for Esther. He had a strong point: cash would do more harm than good. She capitulated. "The Ladies had not the most distant wish that their donation should be bestowed in any manner that did not perfectly accord with your opinion," she responded, and told Joseph, "I shall now endeavour to get the shirts made as soon as possible."[12]

In explaining her decision to Joseph, Esther emphasized that the general "still continues his opinion that the money in my hands should be laid out in linen; he said no supplies he has at present, or has a prospect of, are in any way adequate to the wants of the army." She then added a more personal consideration. "His letter is, I think, a little formal as if he were hurt by our asking his opinion a second time and our not following his directions." In the same conciliatory tone, she devoted much of the rest of her letter to reminding Joseph of their long friendship with Washington and urging him to be patient with the general. Joseph concurred.[13]

Throughout this exchange, the tone of the discussion had remained cordial, respectful, and accommodating on both sides. In writing to Joseph, Esther described Washington's last letter as "very complaisant," and that term seems a fitting way to characterize the tone of the entire interaction.[14] Esther and Washington had conducted a "complaisant" correspondence as they negotiated a fundamental difference in their intentions for the money the Ladies had raised. Washington repeatedly recommended shirts but also repeatedly said that he did not intend to dictate to the Ladies. Esther repeatedly asked for his guidance but resisted the guidance he gave, and then made a specific proposal that ran counter to his stated preferences. He offered a reasoned rebuttal: cash for the soldiers would do more harm than good. She, with no better proposal, acquiesced. But it should be noted that even in this last exchange, Washington was arguing and negotiating, not demanding or dictating. It seems probable that Esther more readily accepted his recommendation because it was a *recommendation* not a command.

Her decision was made easier by the developments within the state. The government of the province was making progress in mobilizing its military forces and was therefore less vulnerable to partisan criticism. At the time she wrote, Joseph was riding off to join Washington at the head of his well-dressed, well-fed, and well-outfitted state militia. At the same time, Joseph and Esther were convinced that the bank scheme of their political opponents was failing.[15]

Possibly the most significant dimension of this polite duel between the lady and the general was that throughout the exchange Esther never doubted and Washington never questioned the legitimacy of her participation in this discussion of important political and military affairs on an equal plane with the commander in chief of the Continental Army. Each saw the other as an opponent worthy of respectful attention.

Esther had conducted most of her negotiations with the general from her summer home in Laurel Hill on the banks of the Schuylkill River. She loved her summer retreats with the children away from heat of the city, but this year her distance from Philadelphia had complicated her communication with Washington, and now she felt restless, isolated, bored, and remote from public life in the nation's working capital, Philadelphia.[16] She complained, "My family is not arranged for two households," and she rationalized that the mild weather would make it safe for her to take the children back to Philadelphia earlier than usual.[17] Her agreement to turn the money into shirts for the men gave her an additional reason for an early return to the city. "I can do little towards it [converting cash to shirts] here," she wrote.[18]

But, as fate would have it, Esther was never to complete that task, and neither she nor Joseph were destined to participate in what Joseph had called the "Rising Glory of this Western World."[19] In mid-August, Joseph, acting as chief executive of the state, left with the Pennsylvania militia to join Washington for the upcoming fall campaign. Esther, looking for a diversion, hinted that she might join him. "I think your situation there, encamped on the banks of the Delaware River, must be very agreeable," she teased him. But, knowing Joseph's feelings about ladies visiting camp, she did not press the issue.[20] Ironically, Joseph was planning a trip to camp for her when Washington canceled the offensive and dismissed the militia. Joseph and the Pennsylvania militia started for home.

Esther, Joseph, and the soldiers arrived back in the city at about the same time, and that set the stage for the Reed family tragedy. The militia brought dysentery with them, and soon the city found itself in the midst of an epidemic.[21] James Madison, representing Virginia in Congress, wrote in mid-September that "the mortality in this place exceeds anything ever remembered." James Lovell of Massachusetts also reported a heavy death toll in Philadelphia but reassured his correspondent that he himself did "not have any of the prevalent maladies of this city fixed upon me—a putrid Fever—a Dysentery."[22]

Shortly after Esther's return to the city and her reunion with Joseph, dysentery struck her down. After a few days of rapid deterioration, she died on September 18, a month short of her thirty-fourth birthday. We have no direct testimony from Joseph or the children about this wrenching event, but her grandson, writing long after the event, wrote, "She breathed her last, her husband, her aged mother, and children, the eldest being eight years of age, watching around her."[23] Jane Bayard, daughter of John Bayard, the Reeds' close friends and herself a close friend of Patty Reed, later recalled the scene of her own mother's death at about the same time. "But the hour was come, when I was taken into her room and kneeled down at the foot of the bed to take my last look at the face now shaded with the paleness of death. A servant of my grandfather took me over to his house, to sob out my sorrow on her lap."[24]

Esther's death destroyed Joseph. His grandson later described it as "a blow from which he never recovered." Joseph himself testified to the truth of this observation. More than a year after Esther's death, he wrote to her brother, Dennis, "I have endeavored to reason myself into a proper submission to the Divine will, but with little success."[25]

Joseph's sister, Polly, came to live with him and to help Mrs. DeBerdt with the children while the momentum of Joseph's daily life carried him through the remainder of his presidency, but without purpose or goal. He traveled west to investigate tax collection in the counties. He involved himself in the controversy over the purported partisan political behavior of the local agents of the quartermaster's office. He engaged in a brutal and wounding fight with his longtime friend and brother-in-law, Charles Pettit. He helped to settle the dispute fueling the mutiny of the Pennsylvania line, and he made a heroic effort to meet Washington's demands for supplies in advance of the Battle of Yorktown, the last major land battle of the Revolution. The breach with Pettit, which Joseph insisted on prolonging despite Pettit's self-effacing efforts at accommodation, suggests the depth of Joseph's underlying agitation, and possibly his growing instability.[26]

In the fall of 1781, Joseph made a half-hearted and unsuccessful effort to win a seat in the Pennsylvania legislature, and then floundered. He optimistically told Nathanael Greene that he "had not the least ambition for public life" and looked forward to being a "private gentlemen, pursuing my profession with activity and industry." However, that was not to be. He accepted a number of short-term public appointments, planned to write a history of the Revolution, practiced law in a limited fashion, made and broke a marriage engagement, and defended himself against partisan attacks on his patriotism. By the fall of 1783, his health was failing, and in December, hoping that a sea voyage would restore him, he sailed to England with his oldest daughter, Patty, and his mother-in-law, Mrs. DeBerdt. His health, however, continued to deteriorate, and he arrived back in Philadelphia in September 1784 a very sick man. By winter 1784–85, he was failing rapidly, losing first the use of his arms and then the power of speech. He died on March 3, 1785, and was buried next to Esther in the graveyard of the Second Presbyterian Church on Arch Street.[27]

Soon after, Joseph's sister, Polly, died, and the orphan children were scattered among relatives. Patty, now in her fourteenth year, remained in London with her grandmother. The Ingersolls raised Joseph, age thirteen, and the Pettits and the Bowes Reeds took responsibility for the three younger children: Esther, Dennis, and George.[28] The American Revolution to which Esther and Joseph had devoted so much, and for which they had sacrificed so much, had extracted a terrible price from them: years of disruption and deprivation, the heartrending loss of Theodosia, the sudden death of Esther, the slow deterioration of Joseph, and five young children set adrift with neither mother nor father.

Coda

Esther's sudden death, Joseph's rapid decline, and the scattering of their children among relatives in England and America all remind us once again of the fragility of life, the devastation of loss, and the limits imposed on love, will, ambition, family, and life itself by what Esther would have called "Providence." However, while acknowledging the sadness of her early death, we should also celebrate the life she lived.

Esther was born into a world that legally and culturally empowered men and relegated women to subordinate status. She, however, marshaled intelligence, determination, charm, and sensitivity to marry the man she had chosen for herself at age seventeen; to build with him a companionate marriage of mutual respect, affection, and economic interdependence; to conceive, bear, nurse, and nurture six babies; and then to achieve a degree of public political engagement, recognition, and admiration in Revolutionary America, second only to that of Martha Washington. We need to recognize and acknowledge these accomplishments.

She was, throughout, a child of the Revolutionary era. The commercial depression at the end of the British war with France (1763) combined with Parliament's new Currency and Sugar Acts (1764) separated her from the young man she loved. The colonial response to the Stamp Act and the Townshend Acts between 1765 and 1770 prolonged and complicated her five-year courtship, destroyed her family's fortune, and then drove her and her new husband to the American colonies. The escalating violence that began with the fighting at Lexington and Concord in April 1775 separated her from Joseph and forced her and her babies first from home in 1776, then into the wilderness in 1777, and finally to tragedy in a remote area of New Jersey in the spring of 1778. It also transformed her from a proud and loyal English subject living reluctantly and temporarily among provincial colonials into an American patriot: a proud member of a new people, a public, political citizen in a new nation, and a participant, at first in partnership with her husband and later in her own right, in the "Rising Glory of this Western World," the new American republic. Then, in 1780, when poised on the cusp of a leadership role among this emerging new people, the war of the American Revolution that had terrorized her days and torn at her heart took her life. The young Esther DeBerdt Reed had paid more than most of her peers for participating in the generation that founded the American republic.[1] We need to honor her for this.

Esther's daily life reveals patterns of behavior that historians increasingly agree constitute the common aspiration, if not the reality, among most of her female contemporaries. Her struggles to marry Joseph and, once married, to negotiate with him their life together illustrates that the impediments to the achievement of these aspirations were many. Moreover, during her courtship she approached, if she did not exceed, the bounds of polite behavior, and certainly Joseph's decision to marry a young woman without a dowry, as both he and she well knew, far exceeded the bounds of prudence prescribed by his society and hers.

Her collaboration with Joseph in building and sustaining the economic foundation of their family autonomy was hardly unique. Most married women did likewise. But her sophisticated understanding of the intricacies of the British Atlantic trading empire, from its internal mechanisms to its cultural norms, set her apart. Her father, frustrated by his son's reluctance to bow to the discipline of commercial trading, had turned to his daughter, and soon she became, for all intents and purposes, an apprentice. By the time she headed her own family, she saw buying and selling wholesale in the import/export sector as a legitimate part of her sphere of activities. In sharp contrast, she regarded buying and selling cattle and bringing in the hay as a farm wife decidedly outside her sphere.

Esther's political engagement set her apart. She was always political, and over time she became increasingly more efficacious in this realm. First in London and then in Philadelphia, she sought to use the British patronage system to bring Joseph back to her, and then to bring the two of them and their children home from America to London.

Esther understood the emerging contest between Great Britain and her North American colonies in political terms: interests at home (in Britain) clashing with interests in America. She thought of herself as a member of the British nation living abroad and bound together with those at home by deep personal and emotional links. She and they were one people. Although a small voice in a distant place, she did what she could to pressure London merchants to mobilize in favor of conciliatory measures. In time, however, she concluded that myopic, possibly ignorant, but certainly powerful, arrogant, and condescending public men in the land that she loved now threatened to destroy in America the English liberties she valued and wanted to pass on to her children. Committing what she regarded as treason, she chose America over England.

During the war, like many women, she gave political significance to her domestic duties and shouldered new responsibilities when Joseph followed Washington first to camp, and then to battle. Like some women, she also engaged in political discussions and calculations in private, and like a few women, she worked with her husband to advance political goals.[2]

But she did more. In 1778–79, Esther joined Joseph and two other families from the Arch Street Presbyterian congregation in nursing into life a new political party in Pennsylvania. The Constitutionals sought first to succor those who had suffered for the cause during the terrible winter of Valley Forge and the British occupation of Philadelphia, then to secure the fruits of the Revolution for those who had paid its price, and finally to exclude from public life those who had done so much to impede the fulfillment of the promises of 1776.

In June 1780, she emerged as a political figure in her own right, acting in public through the Ladies Association to raise money for the men in the Continental Army. Here she displayed a rare aptitude for popular politics in the most democratic, most diverse, and most socially and politically fractured state in the new nation. Between May and September, she demonstrated a mastery of the tactics of popular political mobilization that soon would become the essence of democratic politics in the new American Republic. At the same time, she also taught American women to appropriate to their own use the traditional male voluntary association, a lesson they learned well and used widely and effectively for the next two hundred years and more. Throughout the summer of 1780, she engaged the most powerful man in America, the commander in chief of the Continental Army, in a debate marked by mutual respect over a crucial public political question: how best to spend the $300,000 she and her Ladies had raised for the men in the army. We should marvel at these accomplishments and praise her as one of America's most sophisticated and engaged female political founders.

Although Esther's level of political engagement may seem remarkable to us, for Esther it was largely consistent with her character and her past behavior. She had been political before she came to America, and when first in Philadelphia she had sought to use political means in London to return home. When that failed, she learned how to advance her family's fortunes through the politics of her new home. In both London and America, she respected the gender conventions of her time but recognized no clear line of demarcation between the private and the public, the personal and the political. In her mind, all members of the family acted, as circumstances demanded, to advance its interests.

However, if not radically new for Esther, the Ladies Association and "The Sentiments" took her into a new kind of political engagement. She, a woman, took the lead in one of the largest and most successful popular public fund-raising efforts of the Revolutionary era. For the first time, she appeared in a public political role not as one woman among many but as a public personality, and not as the helpmeet of a husband but as a principal. Moreover, she associated herself and a cadre of women in direct solicitation of money from strangers, door-to-door and woman-to-woman, and, on occasion, in the streets and from men. This mendacity and promiscuous mixing of the sexes in public violated contemporary codes of genteel decorum and involved these women in activities more often associated in the public mind with the most degraded female conditions: poverty and prostitution.

In the same vein, "The Sentiments" itself was not a radically new way for Esther to think about herself in relation to public and political life. Rather, it represented an adaptation of her Old World political instincts, understanding, and skills to a new political context as she used her insight into the revolutionary thinking of patriot women to mobilize them for Revolutionary and Republican America. In this expression of the transformation of the political culture of patriot women, Esther was more cause than effect, more acting than acting upon as she gave eloquent expression to the emerging perception by American women of themselves as citizens with political responsibilities and obligations in the new Republic.

Until this point, Esther had seen political action in instrumental terms: using the levers of power to achieve specific, usually familial, ends. Whether "The Sentiments" reflects a shift in her own self-image, we shall never know. But her commitment to the Ladies Association and her debate with the commander in chief on the question of public policy hint that in this extraordinary summer of political genius she too may have been coming to think in broader terms, that she too might have come to see herself as a citizen with responsibilities for the Republic.

Be that as it may, the most important point here is that Esther effectively employed "The Sentiments" as a tool for political mobilization. A comparison of Esther with Mercy Otis Warren from Massachusetts may help to clarify Esther's intentions and thus highlight her achievement. Both women were gifted political publicists. Warren, a political thinker, wrote to change how people thought about public issues. Reed, a political activist, wrote to use what people thought in order to mobilize them for political action. Warren's success depended on her ability to modify people's thinking. Esther's success depended on her ability to understand what people thought, and then use that knowledge to change their behavior. Her success testifies to her skill.

The popularity of "The Sentiments" demonstrates Esther's insight into the new norms against which patriot American women wished to measure themselves. This new model, like the one it replaced, respected the realities of domestic life and its division of responsibilities. Before 1776, however, this division of domestic labor had also defined a hierarchy: dominant men and subordinate women. But "The Sentiments" insisted that in the new republic, women and men were equally citizens with equal responsibility for advancing the public good. Men and women met their civic responsibilities in normal times in ways that were consistent with their domestic responsibilities. In times of crisis, however, female citizens had to forgo the artificial constraints of social decorum and join male citizens in doing what needed to be done to serve and save the republic, even to the point of shedding blood in violent encounters.

It would take a long time for Americans, both women and men, to work out the implications of this revolution. In the 1790s, a number of women joined in partisan political activity on the state and the national level, but by 1815–20 that kind of female public political activity had declined. At the same time, however, also beginning in the 1790s, an increasing number of American women began to employ Esther's model of the Ladies

Association, first in Philadelphia, then in New York and Boston, and then beyond. Throughout the nineteenth and twentieth centuries, this form of social-political organization provided American women with a powerful vehicle for shaping public policy and thus fulfilling their responsibilities for advancing the public good of the republic.[3]

On a different plane, the patriot support for Esther's fund-raising drive and for its female solicitors as well as the women's enthusiasm for the sentiments expressed in "The Sentiments" did not end the older assumptions that politics was an exclusive male domain into which women entered at their peril. The criticism that Anna Rawle leveled at Esther is particularly relevant here. Rawle, a Royalist and a Tory, and angry at the loss of her family property that had been converted into a summer home for Esther and Joseph, castigated Esther's behavior as inappropriate for genteel women: "the ladies going about for money . . . extremely importunate . . . parading about the streets," she wrote. Patriots used the same rhetoric to punish women with whom they disagreed. In Boston, Elizabeth Murray was reluctant to support the war and separation from Great Britain. The patriot press defined her reluctance as an unladylike political act and condemned her as a "disorderly" person operating outside of her female sphere and committing unnatural and unwomanly acts.[4]

But these same Massachusetts patriots lauded Esther and her Ladies. The governor of Massachusetts urged Samuel Adams to "be so good as to send it [his wife's letter] to Mrs. Reed, and at the same time present my most respectful compliments to that patriotic lady." At the same time, patriot women who challenged men, attacked property, and confronted authorities over unfair prices and immoral marketing tactics remained largely immune from patriot criticism.[5]

Esther's protracted exchange with Washington over the use of the funds that she and her Ladies had raised was her final political act. It demonstrated a firm confidence in her own ability to engage the top levels of American male military leadership in serious discussion of weighty public matters. In this exchange, we find no false modesty, no apologies for stepping out of her proper sphere, no discomfort at breaching prescribed gender constraints, and no sense that she, as a woman, was encroaching on territory that, by custom and law, was lodged exclusively in the male sphere. She was sensitive to the general's feelings and to his frustrations. She did not bedevil him needlessly. She remained firm but polite and considerate. In the midst of her own disagreement with the general, she took time to remind Joseph of the problems that faced the general, and to counsel Joseph to be patient and understanding. And, possibly of greater significance, she remained keenly aware of the provincial, partisan implications of her decisions as well as their long-term consequences for the Reeds in this rising American republic. Here, it might be argued, she blended her understanding of the old British patron/client political system with an intuitive grasp of the essentials of political success in the emerging American democracy.

Moreover, we should never forget that, unlike most of America's female founders, Esther DeBerdt Reed had not been born and raised in the colonies. The contest with Great Britain had compelled American-born English men and women to choose among already-existing political identities. They had always been English, and they had always been American. They had emotional ties to the mother country and took great pride in their Englishness, but London glimmered on the periphery of their consciousness while they lived their daily lives embedded in their own particular communities some three thousand miles away on this side of the Atlantic. In time, these English Americans chose their local identity over their imperial identity. For many of them, the choice was difficult, but the distance they traveled from thinking of themselves as English people living in North America to identifying themselves as part of a new people and a new nation was far shorter and less wrenching than that traversed by Esther. Born and raised in London and proud of her sophisticated and cosmopolitan world, she had been a reluctant immigrant driven into resistance by those at home whose condescending attitude toward the colonies she had once shared. But if Esther traveled further in reconstructing her political identity, the decision she made also illustrates for us how the British political nation, seeking to consolidate and govern its empire, alienated and then lost many of its most ardent supporters in North America.

Esther's lifelong engagement with politics, her growing political efficacy, and her conspicuous part in the political world of Revolutionary America may seem to point toward the future world of independent and autonomous political women. The ends toward which she exercised her political acumen, however, harkened back to an older world, one in which the family outranked the individuals who constituted it, a world in which rights and duties accrued to men and woman more as husbands and wives than as individual persons, and a world in which married couples combined their reciprocal talents and obligations into a reality greater and more important than the simple sum of its parts.[6]

Esther regarded politics not as an end but as a means, first to win and marry Joseph and then to work with him to shape the world in which they lived and the world in which they and those they loved were destined by Providence to work out their earthly and heavenly destiny. In the final years of her life, she saw herself as an American woman acting within the constraints of her time and place to meet her obligations to her husband, her children, her creator, and possibly, in the end, her new people, the emerging new nation of which she too was a citizen.

In sum, in her courtship, her marriage, her childbearing, and her collaboration with her husband in building the economic foundation that supported the family's autonomy, Esther exercised and enjoyed about as much control (or agency, as historians are now wont to say) as is given to most human beings. She saw herself as a free moral agent responsible for her actions doing the best she could in a world that seldom allows any of us to do more. The effort that this required of her, however, and the never-perfect achievement of her goals, testify to the persistence of more traditional ways and to the continued unequal distribution of social and legal power between men and women in her world.

Her political behavior distinguished her. From her early efforts to use the British patronage system to facilitate her marriage to her sensitive and masterly handling of her debate with Washington, Esther acted politically, in private and in public, to create, protect, and advance the family she wanted, the family she and Joseph created, and, possibly in time, the greater family of the new nation that she and he were helping to build. Her lifelong interest in politics and her growing efficacy in the political realm, the range of her political action, and her skill in adapting to the radically different political context emerging in Revolutionary Pennsylvania differentiate her from most, if not all, of her female contemporaries. In time, she emerged as one of the most effective public political woman in Revolutionary America.

But politics constituted only one dimension of the life of this talented, determined woman engaging the world in which her God had placed her. She had been a dutiful but strong-willed and evasive daughter, a passionate lover, and then a proud and affectionate mother, a productive economic partner, and a politically aware and astute young woman living in times of disruption and violence. She valorized but often tested her society's expectation of female decorum while loving and comforting and guiding (sometimes leading) the ambitious, passionate, and talented man whom she, at age seventeen, had seen as "the companion who would make it his endeavor to be both friend and lover to me whom he chose for Life," and with whom she would create "a Religious well-regulated family" while together they sought éclat in the world.[7]

We mourn her early death. In sadness, we empathize with the husband who could not live without her, and with the orphan children they left behind. But we also celebrate her productive life and her loving and fruitful marriage. We remember her as an intense and talented woman who triumphed over all but the last adversity placed in her way by the disruption of the Revolutionary Atlantic world. We marvel at her transformation in the cauldron of war into an American woman. We honor her contribution to the achievement and the protection of the liberty we continue to enjoy more than two centuries after her death. We welcome her into a prominent position in the pantheon of our founders, both female and male.

Notes

Introduction

1. James Madison to Joseph Jones, Philadelphia, September 19, 1780; Paul H. Smith, ed., *Letters of the Delegates to Congress, 1774–1789* (Washington, D.C.: Library of Congress, 1985–98), 16:94.

2. James Madison to Edmund Pendleton, Philadelphia, September 19, 1780, in Smith, *Letters*, 16:94. For a newspaper account of Esther's death, see *Pennsylvania Gazette*, September 23, 1780. The sources do not agree on Esther's date of birth. I have used 1746 throughout this study, but a case could be made for 1747 as well.

3. In this, it should be noted, the Reeds reflected broad historical trends. For a brief, selective review of scholarship on women and business in this era, see the bibliographical essay.

4. The phrase *female politician* is from Zagarri, *Revolutionary Backlash: Women and Politics in the Early American Republic* (Philadelphia: University of Pennsylvania Press, 2007), 5. Here, I use the term as Zagarri does, to mean women interested in politics, not women who had or sought the vote.

5. Quotation from "The Female Advocate" in Linda Kerber, "The Republican Mother: Women and the Enlightenment—An American Perspective," in "An American Enlightenment," special issue, *American Quarterly* 28, no. 2 (Summer 1976): 187–205, quotation on 200. See also Linda Kerber, "The Paradox of Women's Citizenship in the Early Republic: The Case of Martin vs. Massachusetts, 1805," *American Historical Review* 97 (April 1992): 349–78, quotations on 369 and 374. Mary Beth Norton, *Separated by Their Sex: Women in Public and Private in the Colonial Atlantic World* (Ithaca: Cornell University Press, 2011). For a brief, selective review of scholarship on women in public political life in this era, see the bibliographical essay.

6. In this, she appears to have been one with Mercy Otis Warren. Zagarri argues that Warren did not challenge current gender roles and did not share Abigail Adams's views on women's rights. Zagarri, *A Woman's Dilemma: Mercy Otis Warren and the American Revolution* (Wheeling, Ill.: Harlan Davidson, 1995), xvii, 162–65, and 90–92.

7. Esther DeBerdt to Joseph Reed, London, April 13, 1765, December 8, 1765, January 9, 1768, July 20, 1765, September 19, 1765, and November 9, 1765, in BV Reed, Joseph—MS2388, New-York Historical Society (hereafter Reed Papers, N-YHS).

8. Esther remains largely absent from the public iconography in the city of her greatest public accomplishment, Philadelphia.

Chapter 1

1. Esther DeBerdt to Joseph Reed, London, November 15, 1764, in Reed Papers, N-YHS.

2. Ibid. See also Amanda Vickers, *The Gentleman's Daughter: Women's Lives in Georgian England* (New Haven: Yale University Press, 1998), 39–86.

3. David Hancock, *Citizens of the World: London Merchants and the Integration of the British Atlantic Community, 1735–1785* (Cambridge: Cambridge University Press, 1995), 13.

4. Ibid., 87.

5. Ibid., 90–93, 241–42, 288.

6. Ibid., 478, 42.

7. John F. Roche, *Joseph Reed: A Moderate in the American Revolution* (New York: Columbia University Press, 1957), 18; Dennys DeBerdt, *Letters of Dennys DeBerdt, 1757–1770*, ed. Albert Matthews, reprinted from *Publications of the Colonial Society of Massachusetts* 13 (Cambridge, Mass.: John Wilson and Son, University Press, 1911), 294–95, 299–300 n. 2, 307; Michael Kammen, *A Rope of Sand* (Ithaca: Cornell University Press, 1968), 324–25. Martha and Dennys DeBerdt had two children: Esther and Dennis.

8. Esther DeBerdt to Joseph Reed, London, November 15, 1764, in Reed Papers, N-YHS.

9. Bernard Bailyn, *The New England Merchants in the Seventeenth Century*

(Cambridge, Mass.: Harvard University Press, 1955).

10. Esther DeBerdt to Joseph Reed, London, November 15, 1764, in Reed Papers, N-YHS.

11. Vickery, in *The Gentleman's Daughter*, discusses these patterns among the landed elite in eighteenth-century England; see especially chapter 2, "Love and Duty," 39–86.

12. Esther DeBerdt to Joseph Reed, London, November 15, 1764, in Reed Papers, N-YHS. For more on courtship and marriage in Esther's world, see the bibliographical essay.

13. Esther DeBerdt to Joseph Reed, London, various, especially fall 1765, as she remembers.

14. William B. Reed, *The Life of Esther DeBerdt, Afterwards Esther Reed of Pennsylvania* (Philadelphia: Printed privately by C. Sherman, printer, 1854), 25.

15. Ibid., 335–36, lists a number of men from prominent colonial families studying at the Inns of Court in the 1760s and early 1770s, including William Paca of Maryland, Philip Livingston Jr. of New York, Arthur Lee of Virginia, and from Philadelphia, Nicholas Waln, Edward Tilghman, Jared Ingersoll, and William Rawle.

16. William B. Reed, *Life and Correspondence of Joseph Reed* (Philadelphia: Lindsay and Blakiston, 1847), 1:26, 28; Roche, *Reed*, 1–14.

17. William Franklin to Joseph Reed, September 23, 1764, criticizes Joseph for failing to deliver one of the letters he had entrusted to him. Reed Papers, N-YHS.

18. Sam Tucker to Joseph Reed, Trenton, N.J., September 21, 1764, in Reed Papers, N-YHS.

19. Roche, *Reed*, 18. Andrew Reed to Joseph Reed, Trenton, N.J., December 15, 1763; Dan Cox to Joseph Reed, Trenton, N.J., February 2, 1764; Sam Tucker to Joseph Reed, Trenton, N.J., September 21, 1764; Andrew Reed to Joseph Reed, March 14, 1764, all in Reed Papers, N-YHS.

20. DeBerdt, *Letters*, 294; Reed, *Reed*, 1:37, 26, 28; J. Thomas Scharf and Thompson Westcott, *History of Philadelphia 1609–1884* (Philadelphia: L. H. Everts, 1884), 1:278.

21. Dennys DeBerdt to Lord Dartmouth, August 22, 1766; Dennys DeBerdt to William Smith, May 18 and June 14, 1766; Dartmouth fund-raising note, all in DeBerdt, *Letters*, 445, 297 n., 316–17, 324 n. 1, 298–99.

22. Esther DeBerdt to Joseph Reed, London, December 8, 1764, in Reed Papers, N-YHS.

23. Thanks to Professor Lee Ann Caldwell for this observation at the meeting of the Georgia Historical Society, Savannah, Georgia, 1999.

24. See Vickery, *The Gentleman's Daughter*, 307–8 n. 38.

25. Esther DeBerdt to Joseph Reed, London, November 15, 1764, in Reed Papers, N-YHS.

26. Charles Pettit to Joseph Reed, Philadelphia, December 1764, in Reed Papers, N-YHS.

27. Stephen Sayre to Joseph Reed, St. Croix, February 20, 1765, in Reed Papers, N-YHS.

28. Esther DeBerdt to Joseph Reed, London, September 28, 1765, "When you took leave of Enfield this time twelve month." Reed Papers, N-YHS. Esther DeBerdt to Joseph Reed, London, November 9, 1765, in Reed, *Esther*, 65–69; Esther DeBerdt to Joseph Reed, London, December 8, 1764, in Reed, *Esther*, 32–35.

29. Esther DeBerdt to Joseph Reed, London, November 1764, in Reed Papers, N-YHS.

30. See Jan Lewis, "The Republican Wife: Virtue and Seduction in the Early Republic," *William and Mary Quarterly* 44 (1987): 689–721, for a discussion of courtship for young women as a difficult balancing act between the security and safety of patriarchal authority and the twin dangers of freedom: a loveless union contracted for ease, fashion, and luxury or sexual exploitation by a designing man who wins the heart of a naive young woman and leaves her a ruined woman. Lewis depicts the ideal marriage as a union of love and affection, a partnership of equals with reciprocal friendship and mutual respect, esteem and collaboration in shared sacrifice, and disinterested benevolence, indeed, a sort of midpoint between the old patriarchal authority and the newer individualism. For more on this subject, see the bibliographical essay.

31. Abraham Hunt to Joseph Reed, Trenton, N.J., March 22, 1764; Isaac Allen to Joseph Reed, Trenton, N.J., May 9, 1764; Moore Furman to Joseph Reed, Trenton, N.J., June 23, 1763, all in Reed Papers, N-YHS.

32. Bowes Reed to Joseph Reed, Philadelphia, November 11, 1764, in Reed Papers, N-YHS.

33. Daniel Cox to Joseph Reed, Trenton, N.J., February 2, 1764, in Reed Papers, N-YHS. Esther later suggested to Joseph that she thought they could live comfortably in London on £300 a year. John Cox to Joseph Reed, Philadelphia, June 25, 1764, in Reed Papers, N-YHS.

34. Esther Cox to Joseph Reed, Philadelphia, May 11, 1764, in Reed Papers, N-YHS.

35. Sheila Skemp, *William Franklin: Son of a Patriot, Servant of a King* (Oxford: Oxford University Press, 1990).

36. Esther DeBerdt to Joseph Reed, London, March 18, 1766; Stephen Sayre to Joseph Reed, St. Croix, December 5, 1764, both in Reed Papers, N-YHS. *Pennsylvania Evening Post*, April 22, 1775.

37. Esther DeBerdt to Joseph Reed, London, January 30, 1767, in Reed Papers, N-YHS.

38. Esther DeBerdt to Joseph Reed, London, February 28, 1767, in Reed Papers, N-YHS.

39. Esther DeBerdt to Joseph Reed, London, February 7, 1766, in Reed Papers, N-YHS. For a brief discussion of the literature on the legal and social prescriptions regarding courtship and marriage, see the bibliographical essay.

40. Esther DeBerdt to Joseph Reed, London, December 8, 1764, March 16 and November 9, 1765, and March 28, 1766, in Reed Papers, N-YHS. Ruth Bolch, "Changing Conceptions of Sexuality and Romance in Eighteenth-Century America," *William and Mary Quarterly* 60 (January 2003): 13–42.

41. Esther DeBerdt to Joseph Reed, London, December 9, 1765, in Reed Papers, N-YHS.

42. Esther DeBerdt to Joseph Reed, London, April 13, 1765, December 8, 1765, January 9, 1768, July 20, 1765, and November 9, 1765, all in Reed Papers, N-YHS.

43. Esther DeBerdt to Joseph Reed, London, March 17, 1765, in Reed Papers, N-YHS. For an example of a loveless marriage in Revolutionary America, see Susan Klepp and Karin Wulf, eds., *The Diary of Hannah Callender Sansom: Sense and Sensibility in the Age of the American Revolution* (Ithaca: Cornell University Press, 2010).

44. Hancock, *Citizens of the World*, 279–84. Lady John Spencer, raised in the gentry ranks, could read and write Greek as well as French and Italian, and had been trained in feminine deportment, drawing, singing, dancing, geography, and horsemanship. Esther probably matched most of these educational achievements, save for Greek. Amanda Foreman, *Georgiana, Duchess of Devonshire* (New York: The Modern Library, 1998), 8.

45. Reed, *Esther*, 23. Later, living in Philadelphia, she disdained the American education of girls and used that or another reason to return home to London after the birth of her daughter in 1771. Shortly before this time, Joseph's younger sister, Polly [Mary], in her teens, was living in Philadelphia with the Pettit family and studying "dancing, writing, and needle work." Charles Pettit to Joseph Reed, Philadelphia, June 22, September 21, November 11, and December 12, 1764, all in Reed Papers, N-YHS.

46. Esther DeBerdt to Joseph Reed, London, November 19, 1764, in Reed Papers, N-YHS.

Chapter 2

1. For further elaboration on the role of the French and Indian War, which ended with the Treaty of Paris in 1763, and the British legislative efforts to rationalize and centralize the economy of their new empire beginning in the early 1760s, see the discussion of the Reed family's financial problems in chapter 3.

2. Esther DeBerdt to Joseph Reed, London, November 15, 1764, in Reed Papers, N-YHS.

3. Ibid.

4. Ibid.

5. Ibid.

6. Esther DeBerdt to Joseph Reed, London, December 8, 1764, in Reed, *Esther*, 32.

7. Esther DeBerdt to Joseph Reed, London, undated, probably late November 1764, in Reed Papers, N-YHS. Esther here assumes that love had befuddled or confused Joseph.

8. For a discussion of the feeling of falling in love, as well as its valorization and critics in eighteenth-century English literature, see Bloch, "Changing Conceptions of Sexuality and Romance," 13–42, and Lewis, "The Republican Wife," 689–721. For more on this topic, see the bibliographical essay.

9. Esther DeBerdt to Joseph Reed, London, undated, probably late November 1764, in Reed Papers, N-YHS.

10. Ibid.

11. Klepp and Wulf, eds., in *The Diary of Hannah Callender Sansom*, 27–32, indicate that in Philadelphia young men and women often met at social events, such as teas, where the discussions could involve political topics. Christopher Marshall, a political operative in Philadelphia, often mentioned meetings at which husbands, wives, and widows discussed political questions. Christopher Marshall, "Remembrances," June 18–24, 1776, Historical Society of Pennsylvania.

12. Esther DeBerdt to Joseph Reed, London, December 8, 1764, in Reed, *Esther*, 34–35.

13. Ibid.

14. Esther DeBerdt to Joseph Reed, London, undated, probably late November 1764, in Reed Papers, N-YHS.

15. Ibid.

16. DeBerdt, *Letters*, 301 n. 2, 305.
17. Esther DeBerdt to Joseph Reed, London, November 1764, in Reed Papers, N-YHS.
18. John Brewer, *The Pleasures of the Imagination: English Culture in the Eighteenth Century* (London: HarperCollins, 1997), 32, 26, xxiv, xxv, 28, 35, 27, xxvii.
19. Esther DeBerdt to Joseph Reed, London, December 8, 1764, in Reed, *Esther*, 32.
20. Esther DeBerdt to Joseph Reed, London, undated, probably late November 1764, in Reed Papers, N-YHS.
21. Ibid.
22. Ibid.
23. Ibid.
24. Esther DeBerdt to Joseph Reed, London, December 8, 1764, in Reed, *Esther*, 32–35.
25. Ibid.
26. Ibid.
27. Esther DeBerdt to Joseph Reed, London, March 16, 1765, in Reed, *Esther*, 49.
28. Esther DeBerdt to Joseph Reed, London, December 8, 1764, in Reed, *Esther*, 32–35.
29. Ibid.
30. DeBerdt seems to have lost about £50,000 through bad debts among Americans, including the Reed and Pettit debacle. Esther DeBerdt to Joseph Reed, London, June 28, 1765; Joseph Reed to Esther DeBerdt, Amwell, N.J., December 15, 1769, both in Roche, *Reed*, 21.
31. Andrew Reed to Joseph Reed, Philadelphia, December 15, 1763; Charles Pettit to Joseph Reed, Philadelphia, December 17, 1763; Moore Furman to Joseph Reed, Trenton, N.J., December 20, 1763, all in Reed Papers, N-YHS.
32. Charles Pettit to Joseph Reed, Philadelphia, June 22, 1764; Abraham Hunt to Joseph Reed, Trenton, N.J., June 21 and March 22, 1764; John Craven to Joseph Reed, Philadelphia, April 18, 1764; John Cox to Joseph Reed, Philadelphia, June 25, 1764; Charles Pettit to Joseph Reed, Philadelphia, May 2 and June 22, 1764; Daniel Cox to Joseph Reed, Trenton, N.J., April 12 and June 25, 1764; Charles Pettit to Joseph Reed, Philadelphia, June 22, 1764, all in Reed Papers, N-YHS.
33. Abraham Hunt to Joseph Reed, Trenton, N.J., March 22 and June 21, 1764; John Craven to Joseph Reed, Philadelphia, April 28, 1764; Moore Furman to Joseph Reed, Trenton, N.J., June 23, 1764; Abraham Hunt to Joseph Reed, Trenton, N.J., June 21, 1764; Charles Pettit to Joseph Reed, Philadelphia, June 22, 1764; Andrew Reed to Joseph Reed, Trenton, N.J., March 14, 1764; Charles Pettit to Joseph Reed, Philadelphia, March 14, 1764; Abraham Hunt to Joseph Reed, Trenton, N.J., March 22, 1764; Richard Stockton to Joseph Reed, Princeton, N.J., April 4 and 8, 1764; Moore Furman to Joseph Reed, Trenton, N.J., April 11, 1764; Daniel Cox to Joseph Reed, Trenton, N.J., April 12, 1764, all in Reed Papers, N-YHS.
34. Joseph Reed to Charles Pettit, London, June 11, 1764, in Reed Papers, N-YHS.
35. John Craven to Joseph Reed, Philadelphia, April 28, 1764; Charles Pettit to Joseph Reed, Philadelphia, May 2, 1764; Abraham Hunt to Joseph Reed, Trenton, N.J., June 21, 1764; Moore Furman to Joseph Reed, Trenton, N.J., June 23, 1764; John Cox to Joseph Reed, Philadelphia, June 25, 1764; Charles Pettit to Joseph Reed, Philadelphia, June 22, 1764; Bowes Reed to Joseph Reed, Philadelphia, June 22, 1764; Abraham Hunt to Joseph Reed, Trenton, N.J., June 21, 1764; Charles Pettit to Joseph Reed, Philadelphia, June 22 and August 31, 1764, all in Reed Papers, N-YHS.
36. This and the following paragraphs are based on Pettit's letter to Joseph Reed, Philadelphia, December 20, 1764, in Reed Papers, N-YHS.
37. Andrew Reed to Joseph Reed, Trenton, N.J., June 20 or 21, 1764, in Reed Papers, N-YHS.
38. Charles Pettit to Joseph Reed, Philadelphia, December 20, 1764, in Reed Papers, N-YHS.
39. Ibid.
40. Esther DeBerdt to Joseph Reed, London, December 8, 1764, in Reed, *Esther*, 32.
41. Ibid., 34.
42. Esther DeBerdt to Joseph Reed, London, November 15, 1764, in Reed, *Esther*, 31. Esther DeBerdt to Joseph Reed, London, undated, probably late November 1764, in Reed Papers, N-YHS. Esther DeBerdt to Joseph Reed, London, December 8, 1764, in Reed, *Esther*, 32. Esther DeBerdt to Joseph Reed, London, undated, probably late November 1764, in Reed Papers, N-YHS.
43. Esther DeBerdt to Joseph Reed, London, September 19 and November 9, 1765, in Reed, *Esther*, 61–69.
44. Esther DeBerdt to Joseph Reed, London, December 8, 1764, in Reed, *Esther*, 321.
45. Joseph Reed to Esther DeBerdt, Philadelphia, June 17, 1765, in Reed Papers, N-YHS.
46. Esther DeBerdt to Joseph Reed, London, February 8, 1765, in Reed Papers, N-YHS.
47. Ibid.

48. Esther DeBerdt to Joseph Reed, London, February 8, 1765, in Reed Papers, N-YHS. In contrast, Holton, in his biography of Abigail Adams, indicates that she and John took a trip together, "apparently alone," and "caused barely a ripple." Woody Holton, *Abigail Adams* (New York: Free Press, 2009), 19.
49. Esther DeBerdt to Joseph Reed, London, February 22, 1765, in Reed Papers, N-YHS.
50. Ibid.
51. Ibid.
52. Ibid.

Chapter 3

1. Reed, *Esther*, 37, dates Joseph's departure "on or about February 7," but Esther dated a letter to Joseph on February 8 and gave no indication that he had yet left the city. Esther DeBerdt to Joseph Reed, London, February 8, 1775, in Reed Papers, N-YHS.
2. Joseph Reed to Esther DeBerdt, March 4, 1765, in Reed Papers, N-YHS.
3. Moore Furman to Joseph Reed, Trenton, N.J., June 23, 1765; Charles Pettit to Joseph Reed, Philadelphia, June 22, 1765, and December 20, 1764, all in Reed Papers, N-YHS.
4. Charles Pettit to Joseph Reed, Philadelphia, June 22 and September 21, 1764, both in Reed Papers, N-YHS.
5. Charles Pettit to Joseph Reed, London, May 2 and June 12, 1764, both in Reed Papers, N-YHS.
6. Charles Pettit to Joseph Reed, Philadelphia, November 3, 1764, in Reed Papers, N-YHS.
7. Charles Pettit to Joseph Reed, Philadelphia, June 25, August 31, and December 20, 1764, all in Reed Papers, N-YHS.
8. Charles Pettit to Joseph Reed, December 20, 1764, in Reed Papers, N-YHS.
9. Charles Pettit to Joseph Reed, Philadelphia, June 22, September 21, November 11, and December 12, 1764, all in Reed Papers, N-YHS. At the time, Joseph decided to return home; this last sum had not reached him.
10. Charles Pettit to Joseph Reed, December 20, 1764, in Reed Papers, N-YHS.
11. Ibid.
12. Esther DeBerdt to Joseph Reed, London, December 8, 1764, in Reed Papers, N-YHS.
13. Esther DeBerdt to Joseph Reed, London, February 22, 1765, in Reed Papers, N-YHS.
14. Joseph Reed to Esther DeBerdt, March 4, 1765, in Reed Papers, N-YHS.

15. Joseph Reed to Esther DeBerdt, Philadelphia, June 17, 1765, in Reed Papers, N-YHS.
16. Joseph Reed to Esther DeBerdt, aboard *Britannia*, March 4, 1765; Joseph Reed to Esther DeBerdt, Philadelphia, June 17, 1765, both in Reed Papers, N-YHS.
17. Esther DeBerdt to Joseph Reed, London, February 22, 1765, in Reed Papers, N-YHS.
18. Esther DeBerdt to Joseph Reed, London, April 13, 1765, in Reed Papers, N-YHS.
19. Esther DeBerdt to Joseph Reed, London, February 22, 1765, in Reed Papers, N-YHS.
20. Esther DeBerdt to Joseph Reed, London, July 20 and August 8, 1765, both in Reed Papers, N-YHS.
21. Esther DeBerdt to Joseph Reed, London, July 20, 1765, in Reed Papers, N-YHS.
22. Esther DeBerdt to Joseph Reed, London, February 22 and September 19, 1765, both in Reed Papers, N-YHS. For an American example of a mother who risked much to encourage her daughter's marriage aspirations, see Klepp and Wulf, eds., *The Diary of Hannah Callender Sansom*, 271–75.
23. Esther DeBerdt to Joseph Reed, London, February 22, 1765. "As My Father don't know of my writing at all." Esther DeBerdt to Joseph Reed, London, November 9, 1765, in Reed Papers, N-YHS.
24. Esther DeBerdt to Joseph Reed, London, December 8, 1764, February 22 and April 13, 1765, and February 21, 1766, all in Reed Papers, N-YHS.
25. Esther DeBerdt to Joseph Reed, London, February 22, 1765, in Reed Papers, N-YHS.
26. Ibid.
27. Esther DeBerdt to Joseph Reed, London, February 22, 1765; Joseph Reed to Esther DeBerdt, February 26, 1765, both in Reed Papers, N-YHS.
28. Esther DeBerdt to Joseph Reed, London, March 17, 1765, in Reed Papers, N-YHS.
29. T. Wykoff to Joseph Reed, Bath, January 19, 1765, in Reed Papers, N-YHS.
30. Esther DeBerdt to Joseph Reed, London, March 27, 1765, in Reed Papers, N-YHS.
31. Esther DeBerdt to Joseph Reed, London, March 17, 1765, in Reed Papers, N-YHS.
32. Esther DeBerdt to Joseph Reed, London, April 13, 1765, in Reed Papers, N-YHS.
33. Esther DeBerdt to Joseph Reed, London, March 17, 1765, in Reed Papers, N-YHS.
34. Ibid. "Mr. Powel is so kind to carry this to Bristol for me." Esther DeBerdt to Joseph Reed, London, April 13, 1765, Esther DeBerdt to

Joseph Reed, London, March 17, 1765, both in Reed Papers, N-YHS.

35. Esther DeBerdt to Joseph Reed, London, March 17, 1765, in Reed Papers, N-YHS.
36. Esther DeBerdt to Joseph Reed, London, March 27, 1765, in Reed Papers, N-YHS.
37. Ibid.
38. Esther DeBerdt to Joseph Reed, London, March 17, 1765, in Reed Papers, N-YHS. "The Sex" commonly referred to adult females.
39. Esther DeBerdt to Joseph Reed, London, March 27, 1765, in Reed Papers, N-YHS.
40. Esther DeBerdt to Joseph Reed, London, Enfield, May 11, 1765, in Reed Papers, N-YHS.
41. Ibid.
42. Esther DeBerdt to Joseph Reed, London, Enfield, May 11 and June 28, 1765, both in Reed Papers, N-YHS.
43. Esther DeBerdt to Joseph Reed, London, August 8–10, 1765, in Reed Papers, N-YHS.
44. Esther DeBerdt to Joseph Reed, London, September 28 and December 9, 1765, both in Reed Papers, N-YHS.
45. Esther DeBerdt to Joseph Reed, London, November 9, 1765, in Reed Papers, N-YHS.
46. Esther DeBerdt to Joseph Reed, London, November 9, 1764, in Reed Papers, N-YHS.
47. Ibid.
48. Esther DeBerdt to Joseph Reed, London, December 9, 1765, in Reed Papers, N-YHS.
49. Roche, *Reed*, 22.
50. Esther DeBerdt to Joseph Reed, London, July 20 and December 9, 1765, both in Reed Papers, N-YHS.
51. Esther DeBerdt to Joseph Reed, Enfield and London, March 16, August 8, November 9, September 19, August 8, and November 11, 1765, all in Reed Papers, N-YHS.
52. Esther DeBerdt to Joseph Reed, London, September 28, 1765, in Reed Papers, N-YHS.
53. Esther DeBerdt to Joseph Reed, London, December 9, 1765, in Reed Papers, N-YHS.
54. Esther DeBerdt to Joseph Reed, London, September 19 and December 9, 1765, both in Reed Papers, N-YHS.

Chapter 4

1. Esther DeBerdt to Joseph Reed, London, July 20, 1765, in Reed Papers, N-YHS.
2. Esther DeBerdt to Joseph Reed, London, August 8–10, 1765, in Reed Papers, N-YHS.
3. Esther DeBerdt to Joseph Reed, London, August 8–10, 1765, in Reed Papers, N-YHS.
4. Ibid.
5. Esther DeBerdt to Joseph Reed, London, August 8, 1765, in Reed Papers, N-YHS.
6. Carroll Smith-Rosenberg, *The Birth of an American Identity* (Chapel Hill: University of North Carolina Press, 2010), 32–33; Esther DeBerdt to Joseph Reed, London, August 8, 1765, in Reed Papers, N-YHS. The lord chancellor headed the judiciary.
7. Esther DeBerdt to Joseph Reed, London, September 19, 1765, in Reed Papers, N-YHS.
8. Esther DeBerdt to Joseph Reed, London, December 8, 1764, in Reed Papers, N-YHS.
9. Joseph's midwinter letter is not extant, but it must have arrived after December 9, 1765, and before February 7, when Esther responded to it. Her failure to write by the January packet ship suggests that she had received the bad news and was considering her response.
10. For biographical details of Macpherson, see William N. Eyle, "The Federal Constitution, 1787," *Pennsylvania Magazine of History and Biography* 11 (1887): 249–75, and William Macpherson, contributor, "Extracts from the Letters of John Macpherson, Jr., to William Patterson 1766–1773," *Pennsylvania Magazine of History and Biography* 23 (1899): 51–59.
11. Esther DeBerdt to Joseph Reed, London, April 28, 1766, in Reed Papers, N-YHS.
12. Esther DeBerdt to Joseph Reed, London, February 7, 1766, in Reed Papers, N-YHS.
13. Esther DeBerdt to Joseph Reed, London, November 15 and December 8, 1764, and February 7, 1766, all in Reed Papers, N-YHS.
14. Joseph Reed to Esther DeBerdt, May 1, 1766; Esther DeBerdt to Joseph Reed, London, February 7, 1766, both in Reed Papers, N-YHS.
15. Esther DeBerdt to Joseph Reed, London, February 7, 1766, in Reed Papers, N-YHS.
16. Esther DeBerdt to Joseph Reed, London, March 28 and February 7, 1766, both in Reed Papers, N-YHS.
17. Esther DeBerdt to Joseph Reed, London, July 8, May 11, and December 9, 1765, and March 28, 1766, all in Reed Papers, N-YHS.
18. Esther DeBerdt to Joseph Reed, London, February 7, April 28, and May 17, 1766, March 17, 1765, and March 28, 1766, all in Reed Papers, N-YHS.
19. Esther DeBerdt to Joseph Reed, London, April 28 and March 18, 1766, and a letter dated May 1766 without a day but written sometime after her May 17 letter, all in Reed Papers, N-YHS.
20. For example, see Joseph Reed to Dennys DeBerdt, November 5 and December 5, 1765,

NOTES TO PAGES 58–71

and January 13, 1766, all in Reed Papers, N-YHS.

21. Dennys DeBerdt to Joseph Reed, May 2, 1766, in Reed Papers, N-YHS.

22. Dennys DeBerdt to Joseph Reed, March 18, 1766, in Reed Papers, N-YHS.

23. Ibid.

24. Dennys DeBerdt to Joseph Reed, February 13 and March 18, 1766, both in Reed Papers, N-YHS.

25. Esther DeBerdt to Joseph Reed, London, February 7 and March 18, 1766, both in Reed Papers, N-YHS.

26. Esther DeBerdt to Joseph Reed, London, February 7 and May 17, 1766, both in Reed Papers, N-YHS.

27. Esther DeBerdt to Joseph Reed, London, February 7, 1766, in Reed Papers, N-YHS.

28. Esther DeBerdt to Joseph Reed, London, dated May 1766 without a day but written sometime after her May 17 letter, in Reed Papers, N-YHS.

29. Esther DeBerdt to Joseph Reed, London, February 21, February 2, June 11, letter dated May 1766 without a day but written sometime after her May 17 letter, and June 11, 1766, all in Reed Papers, N-YHS.

30. Esther DeBerdt to Joseph Reed, London, March 28, 1766, in Reed Papers, N-YHS.

31. Six letters in ten weeks. Esther DeBerdt to Joseph Reed, London, July 19, August 7, August 15, August 30, September 12, and September 26, 1766, all in Reed Papers, N-YHS.

32. Joseph Reed to Esther DeBerdt, May 1, 1766, in Reed Papers, N-YHS.

33. Ibid. Esther DeBerdt to Joseph Reed, London, July 20, 1765, in Reed Papers, N-YHS.

34. Esther DeBerdt to Joseph Reed, London, July 19 and August 7, 1766, both in Reed Papers, N-YHS.

35. Esther DeBerdt to Joseph Reed, London, August 30, September 26, August 7, August 15, September 12, September 26, June 11, August 15, August 7, August 15, September 12, and September 26, 1766, all in Reed Papers, N-YHS.

36. Esther DeBerdt to Joseph Reed, London, July 19, August 7, and September 12, 1766, all in Reed Papers, N-YHS.

37. Esther DeBerdt to Joseph Reed, London, December 12, 1766, in Reed Papers, N-YHS.

38. Esther DeBerdt to Joseph Reed, London, September 12, July 19, and September 26, 1766, all in Reed Papers, N-YHS.

39. Esther DeBerdt to Joseph Reed, London, November 7, 1766, in Reed Papers, N-YHS.

40. Esther DeBerdt to Joseph Reed, London, March 17, March 27, April 13, and August 8, 1765, and March 18, April 28, July 19, September 26, and November 7, 1766, all in Reed Papers, N-YHS.

41. Esther DeBerdt to Joseph Reed, London, November 16–17, 1766, in Reed Papers, N-YHS.

42. Internal evidence suggests that Esther drafted these notes in late 1766 during and immediately after her father's illness. She dwells heavily on his near death in November and his slow recovery in December. She also mentions her Christmas prayer for Joseph.

43. Esther DeBerdt, undated notes, probably from late 1766, in Reed Papers, N-YHS.

44. Ibid.

45. Ibid.

46. Esther DeBerdt to Joseph Reed, London, December 12, 1766, in Reed Papers, N-YHS.

Chapter 5

1. John Alden, *Stephen Sayre: American Revolutionary Adventurer* (Baton Rouge: Louisiana State University Press, 1983), 18.

2. Ibid., 5–10, 13. Stephen Sayre to Joseph Reed, London, February 20, 1765, in Reed Papers, N-YHS.

3. Esther DeBerdt to Joseph Reed, London, March 28, 1766, in Reed Papers, N-YHS.

4. Alden, *Stephen Sayre*, 12; Stephen Sayre to Joseph Reed, London, March 29, 1768, in Reed Papers, N-YHS; Alden, *Stephen Sayre*, 16.

5. Esther DeBerdt to Joseph Reed, London, August 1, 1766, August 1 and October 22, 1767, and February 21, 1766, all in Reed Papers, N-YHS.

6. Stephen Sayre to Joseph Reed, London, March 29, 1768, in Reed Papers, N-YHS. Miss Nelthorpe had broken her engagement with Sayre while he was in America. Esther DeBerdt to Joseph Reed, London, April 28, August 7, September 12, September 26, and December 12, 1766, all in Reed Papers, N-YHS.

7. Stephen Sayre to Joseph Reed, London, July 3, 1768, in Reed Papers, N-YHS.

8. Stephen Sayre to Joseph Reed, London, July 3 and October 13, 1768, both in Reed Papers, N-YHS.

9. Charles Pettit to Joseph Reed, December 10, 1761, in Reed Papers, N-YHS; Joseph Reed to Esther DeBerdt, April 25, 1765, in Reed, *Esther*, 50. As late as 1767, various members of the DeBerdt family continued to remind Joseph that the firm of Reed and Pettit owed them significant sums of money. Esther DeBerdt

221

to Joseph Reed, London, July 7, 1767; Dennys DeBerdt to Joseph Reed, August 7, 1767; Charles Pettit to Joseph Reed, Halifax, September 10, 1765; Dennis DeBerdt to Joseph Reed, February 13, 1766; Charles Pettit to Joseph Reed, Philadelphia, July 23, 1766, all in Reed Papers, N-YHS.

10. Roche, *Reed*, 22. Moore Furman to Joseph Reed, Trenton, N.J., April 11 and June 23, 1764; Bowes Reed to Joseph Reed, June 22, 1764; A. Hunt to Joseph Reed, Trenton, June 21, 1764; Charles Pettit to Joseph Reed, December 20, 1764, all in Reed Papers, N-YHS. Pettit sailed from Philadelphia on August 26, 1765, and was in Nova Scotia by September 9, 1765. Charles Pettit to Joseph Reed, September 9, 1765; Joseph Reed to Esther DeBerdt, January 13, 1765; Dennis DeBerdt to Joseph Reed, March 18, 1766; Joseph Reed to Esther DeBerdt, January 13, 1766, all in Roche, *Reed*, 71.

11. A. Hunt to Joseph Reed, March 22 and June 21, 1764; Charles Pettit to Joseph Reed, June 22, 1764, all in Reed Papers, N-YHS.

12. Charles Pettit to Joseph Reed, Philadelphia, July 3, 1765; Charles Pettit to Joseph Reed, Philadelphia, July 23, 1766, both in Reed Papers, N-YHS. Pettit apparently gave up his home in Philadelphia when he sailed for Nova Scotia in late August 1765, and then took rooms with a landlady in Philadelphia on his return in 1766. See Joseph Reed to Charles Pettit, December 2, 1767, "My compliments to your Landlady and her Fair Daughters," in Roche, *Reed*, 22. Joseph Reed to Esther DeBerdt, January 13, 1766; Mary Sayre to Joseph Reed, Lancaster, April 11, 1765, and March 28, 1766, all in Reed Papers, N-YHS.

13. Charles Pettit to Joseph Reed, Philadelphia, July 3, 1765; Charles Pettit to Joseph Reed, Halifax, September 9, 1765; Joseph Reed to Esther DeBerdt, January 13, 1766; Joseph Reed to Charles Pettit, September 15, September 29, and December 2, 1767, and August 28, 1768, all in Reed Papers, N-YHS; Joseph Reed to Esther DeBerdt, January 12, 1766, in Reed, *Esther*, 71; Joseph Reed to Esther DeBerdt, January 13, 1766, in Reed Papers, N-YHS.

14. Joseph Reed to Charles Pettit, March 28, July 19, and August 6, 1768, all in Reed Papers, N-YHS.

15. Charles Pettit to Joseph Reed, December 22, 1764; Charles Pettit to Joseph Reed, Burlington, N.J., December 23, 1767, both in Reed Papers, N-YHS. "Mr. Reed has departed for his beloved Iron works before I reached this place on Monday."

16. Roche, *Reed*, 5. The relative power of husbands and wives to determine the name of their new child undoubtedly varied. In this case, either Theodora decided or we have further evidence of Andrew's respect for and desire to cultivate his father-in-law. I am inclined to believe that Theodora decided.

17. Abraham Hunt to Joseph Reed, March 22, May 11, and June 21, 1764; Moore Furman to Joseph Reed, Trenton, N.J., April 11, 1764, Philadelphia, December 20, 1763, and June 23, 1764; Samuel Tucker to Joseph Reed, September 24, 1764; William Franklin to Joseph Reed, Burlington, N.J., September 23, 1764, all in Reed Papers, N-YHS.

18. Charles Pettit to Joseph Reed, July 3, 1765; Joseph Reed to Charles Pettit, Trenton, N.J., June 24, 1765; Charles Pettit to Joseph Reed, Philadelphia, July 23, 1766, all in Reed Papers, N-YHS.

19. Joseph Reed to Esther DeBerdt, Trenton, N.J., June 7, 1765; Esther DeBerdt to Joseph Reed, London, August 8, 1765; Sam Tucker to Joseph Reed, Trenton, N.J., September 24, 1764, all in Reed Papers, N-YHS.

20. Some evidence suggests, however, that local county courts in New Jersey and Pennsylvania remained open. Edmund S. Morgan, *The Stamp Act Crisis: Prologue to Revolution* (Chapel Hill: University of North Carolina Press, 1995), 70, 153, 174, 177 n. 5. Joseph Reed to Esther DeBerdt, January 13, 1766, in Reed, *Esther*, 77.

21. Reed, *Reed*, 1:39. Richard Stockton to Joseph Reed, Princeton, N.J., October 8 and November 21, 1764; Mrs. Mary Sayre to Joseph Reed, Lancaster, Pa., November 9, 1765; "Dear Josie," all in Reed Papers, N-YHS.

22. Enslavement of individuals of African descent was legal in New Jersey.

23. Joseph Reed to Esther DeBerdt, April 24, 1767; Esther DeBerdt to Joseph Reed, London, February 19, 1767; see chapter 7 for more on Joseph's finances in 1774, both in Roche, *Reed*, 30–32, re: "100 acres of land in orange County New York from 1768"; Dennis DeBerdt estimated the annual cost of a full-time servant in London at £25.

24. Joseph Reed to Charles Pettit, September 29, 1767, and July 19 and October 2, 1768; Joseph Reed to Charles Pettit, London, June 25, 1770; Esther DeBerdt to Joseph Reed, London, November 16, 1766; Esther DeBerdt to Joseph Reed, London, February 19, 1767, and

November 9, 1765, all in Reed Papers, N-YHS. "The Bark" refers to quinine.

25. Roche, *Reed*, 26.

26. Ibid. Esther DeBerdt to Joseph Reed, London, August 7, September 12, and November 7, 1766, and March 3, 1767, all in Reed Papers, N-YHS; Roche, *Reed*, 27; Esther DeBerdt to Joseph Reed, London, April 4 and July 7, 1767; Dennys DeBerdt to Joseph Reed, London, October 21, 1767; William Franklin, Esq., "To All to whom these presents shall come Greeting": commissioning Joseph Reed as deputy to Maurice Morgan as secretary of the province of New Jersey. November 19, 1767, all in Reed Papers, N-YHS.

27. Roche, *Reed*, 26–27; Esther DeBerdt to Joseph Reed, London, August 7, 1766, April 4, July 7, and December 10, 1767, all in Reed Papers, N-YHS.

28. Dennys DeBerdt to Lord Dartmouth, February 16, 1768; Dennis DeBerdt to Joseph Reed, February 16, 1768; Esther DeBerdt to Joseph Reed, London, June 13, 1767, all in Reed Papers, N-YHS.

29. Dennis DeBerdt to Joseph Reed, February 13 and March 10–18, 1766, July 4, 1768, and May 4, 1769; Esther DeBerdt to Joseph Reed, London, December 12, 1766, all in Reed Papers, N-YHS.

30. Dennys DeBerdt to William Brattle, London, July 19, 1766, in DeBerdt, *Letters*, 319; Esther DeBerdt to Joseph Reed, London, July 4, 1768, in Reed Papers, N-YHS.

31. Esther DeBerdt to Joseph Reed, London, March 18, 1766; Dennis DeBerdt to Joseph Reed, March 10, 1767; Esther DeBerdt to Joseph Reed, London, April 28, February 7, February 21, March 28, April 28, May 17, June 11, and August 15, 1766, all in Reed Papers, N-YHS.

32. Joseph Reed to Esther DeBerdt, February 10, 1767; Esther DeBerdt to Joseph Reed, London, March 14, 1767; Joseph Reed to Esther DeBerdt, April 5 and April 12, 1767; Esther DeBerdt to Joseph Reed, London, August 4, 1767, all in Reed, *Esther*, 120; Dennis DeBerdt to Edward Sheafe, London, October 21, 1767, in DeBerdt, *Letters*, 327.

33. Esther DeBerdt to Joseph Reed, April 11, 1767, in Reed, *Esther*, 114; Esther DeBerdt to Joseph Reed, London, October 10, 1767, and January 9, 1768, both in Reed Papers, N-YHS.

34. Joseph Reed to Esther DeBerdt, January 14, 1767, in Reed, *Esther*, 107; Esther DeBerdt to Joseph Reed, London, August 7, 1766, and February 19 and September 16, 1767, all in Reed Papers, N-YHS.

35. Esther DeBerdt to Joseph Reed, London, June 13, October 22, and February 15, 1767, and April 1, 1768, all in Reed Papers, N-YHS.

36. Esther DeBerdt to Joseph Reed, London, May 20, June 13, July 7, August 1, and October 22, 1767, all in Reed Papers, N-YHS.

37. Esther DeBerdt to Joseph Reed, London, quoting Joseph, May 13, 1768, in Reed Papers, N-YHS.

38. Esther DeBerdt to Joseph Reed, London, May 13, 1768, in Reed Papers, N-YHS.

39. Esther DeBerdt to Joseph Reed, London, July 4, 1768, in Reed Papers, N-YHS.

40. Esther DeBerdt to Joseph Reed, London, October 12 and July 4, 1768, and August 3, 1769, all in Reed Papers, N-YHS.

41. Esther DeBerdt to Joseph Reed, London, July 4, 1768, in Reed Papers, N-YHS.

42. Esther DeBerdt to Joseph Reed, London, August 19, 1768, in Reed Papers, N-YHS.

43. Esther DeBerdt to Joseph Reed, London, December 8, 1767, and March 12 and May 3, 1768, all in Reed Papers, N-YHS.

44. Esther DeBerdt to Joseph Reed, London, July 8, 1768, in Reed Papers, N-YHS.

45. Esther DeBerdt to Joseph Reed, London, December 7, 1768, in Reed Papers, N-YHS.

46. Esther DeBerdt to Joseph Reed, London, November 2, 1768, in Reed Papers, N-YHS.

47. Franklin had taken two of his slaves with him to London in the late 1750s. Edmund Morgan, *Benjamin Franklin* (New Haven: Yale University Press, 2001), 105–6.

48. Esther DeBerdt to Joseph Reed, London, March 9, 1769, in Reed Papers, N-YHS; William Franklin to Benjamin Franklin, May 11, 1769, in DeBerdt, *Letters*, 305 n. 3; Roche, *Reed*, 22.

49. Esther DeBerdt to Joseph Reed, London, January 28, 1768, in Reed Papers, N-YHS. See Joseph's intense and personal altercation with Colonel Reed of New York in July 1768 for an example of the emotions generated over the collection of these debts from personal acquaintances. Joseph Reed to Colonel Reed of New York, Trenton, N.J., July 28, 1768; Charles Pettit to Joseph Reed, July 3 and September 10, 1765; Esther DeBerdt to Joseph Reed, London, March 9, 1769; see also Esther DeBerdt to Joseph Reed, London, August 3, 1769, all in Reed Papers, N-YHS.

50. Esther DeBerdt to Joseph Reed, London, September 16–18, 1767, in Reed Papers, N-YHS.

51. Esther DeBerdt to Joseph Reed, London, April 1, 1768, and May 19, June 15, and May 14, 1769, all in Reed Papers, N-YHS.
52. Charles Pettit to Joseph Reed, Burlington, N.J., August 15 and August 26, 1769; Joseph Reed to [Morgann], Trenton, N.J., October 1, 1769; Joseph Reed to Esther DeBerdt, Amwell, N.J., December 15, 1769, all in Reed Papers, N-YHS.

Chapter 6

1. Joseph Reed to Charles Pettit, March 16, April 17, and April 19, 1770, all in Reed Papers, N-YHS.
2. Joseph Reed to Charles Pettit, April 19, 1770, in Reed Papers, N-YHS.
3. Ibid.
4. Joseph Reed to Charles Pettit, April 21, 1770, in Reed Papers, N-YHS.
5. Joseph Reed to Charles Pettit, April 25, 1770, in Reed Papers, N-YHS.
6. Joseph Reed to Charles Pettit, June 8, 1770, in Reed Papers, N-YHS.
7. Joseph Reed to Charles Pettit, London, May 7, June 8, June 25, July 3, and July 13, 1770, all in Reed Papers, N-YHS.
8. Joseph Reed to Charles Pettit, June 25, May 7, and June 25, 1770; Charles Pettit to Joseph Reed, July 18, 1770, all in Reed Papers, N-YHS.
9. Joseph Reed to Charles Pettit, May 7, 1770, in Reed Papers, N-YHS.
10. Joseph Reed to Charles Pettit, May 7, June 25, and July 3, 1770, all in Reed Papers, N-YHS.
11. Charles Pettit to Joseph Reed, Burlington, N.J., July 18, 1770, in Reed Papers, N-YHS.
12. Joseph Reed to Charles Pettit, May 7, 1770, in Reed Papers, N-YHS.
13. Joseph Reed to Charles Pettit, June 25, July 3, and June 8, 1770, all in Reed Papers, N-YHS.
14. Joseph Reed to Charles Pettit, London, July 13, 1770, in Reed Papers, N-YHS.
15. Joseph Reed to Charles Pettit, June 25, July 13, and June 8, 1770, all in Reed Papers, N-YHS.
16. Joseph Reed to Charles Pettit, May 7, 1770, in Reed Papers, N-YHS.
17. Joseph Reed to Charles Pettit, June 8, July 3, June 8, and July 3, 1770, all in Reed Papers, N-YHS.
18. Joseph Reed to Charles Pettit, London, May 7, 1770, in Reed Papers, N-YHS.
19. See chapter 1 for a discussion of the relative value of dowries.
20. Joseph Reed to Charles Pettit, June 8, 1770, in Reed Papers, N-YHS.
21. Joseph Reed to Charles Pettit, July 13, 1770, in Reed Papers, N-YHS.
22. Ibid.
23. Joseph Reed to Charles Pettit, May 7 and June 8, 1770, both in Reed Papers, N-YHS.
24. Joseph Reed to Charles Pettit, May 7, 1770, in Reed Papers, N-YHS.
25. Joseph Reed to Charles Pettit, June 25 and June 8, 1770, both in Reed Papers, N-YHS.
26. Joseph Reed to Charles Pettit, July 3, 1770, in Reed Papers, N-YHS.
27. Toby Ditz, "Shipwrecked; or Masculinity Imperiled: Mercantile Representations of Failure and the Gendered Self in Eighteenth-Century Philadelphia," *Journal of American History* 81 (June 1994): 51–80.
28. Joseph Reed to Charles Pettit, June 25, 1770, in Reed Papers, N-YHS.
29. Joseph Reed to Charles Pettit, June 8, 1770, in Reed Papers, N-YHS.
30. Joseph Reed to Charles Pettit, June 3, June 8, and June 25, 1770, all in Reed Papers, N-YHS.
31. Joseph Reed to Charles Pettit, June 25, 1770, in Reed Papers, N-YHS.
32. Joseph Reed to Charles Pettit, May 7, 1770, in Reed Papers, N-YHS.
33. Joseph Reed to Charles Pettit, June 8, June 25, and June 8, 1770, all in Reed Papers, N-YHS.
34. Joseph Reed to Charles Pettit, June 25, 1770, in Reed Papers, N-YHS.
35. Joseph Reed to Charles Pettit, June 8, 1770, in Reed Papers, N-YHS.
36. Joseph Reed to Charles Pettit, London, July 13, 1770, in Reed Papers, N-YHS.
37. Joseph Reed to Charles Pettit, June 25, July 3, June 25, and July 3, 1770, all in Reed Papers, N-YHS.
38. Joseph Reed to Charles Pettit, June 25, 1770, in Reed Papers, N-YHS.
39. Joseph Reed to Charles Pettit, June 8, 1770, in Reed Papers, N-YHS.
40. Joseph Reed to Charles Pettit, June 25, June 8, June 25, and July 13, 1770, all in Reed Papers, N-YHS.
41. Joseph Reed to Charles Pettit, July 13, 1770, in Reed Papers, N-YHS.
42. Esther DeBerdt to Joseph Reed, London, July 20, 1765, in Reed Papers, N-YHS.

Chapter 7

1. Esther DeBerdt Reed to Dennis DeBerdt, Philadelphia, November 14, 1770, in Reed, *Esther*, 158. Thanks to Jack Milko for his calculations of time and distance for this land route travel between Philadelphia and Burlington, New Jersey. See Philip Padelford, ed., *Colonial Panorama: Dr. Robert Honyman's Journal for March and April [1775]* (San Marino, Calif.: Huntington Library, 1939), 22–23, for a description of the stagecoach ride from Philadelphia to New York City and the return in the spring of 1775.

2. Esther DeBerdt Reed to Dennis DeBerdt, Philadelphia, December 12 and November 14, 1770, both in Reed, *Esther*, 160, 158–59.

3. Reed, *Esther*, 158. For similar English perceptions of Philadelphia, see also Padelford, ed., *Colonial Panorama*, 17–21, and Howard B. Gill and George M Curtis III, eds., *A Man Apart. The Journal of Nicholas Cresswell, 1774–1781* (Lanham, Md.: Lexington Books, 2009), 153–56. Esther DeBerdt Reed to Dennis DeBerdt, Philadelphia, November 14 and December 12, 1770, both in Reed, *Esther*, 158–60.

4. Haulman argues that fashion was a "form of female power" and that women "performed for one another" and competed against each other using "taste and style to distinguish themselves from one another both within and among social groups," especially at the assemblies. Kate Haulman, *Problems of Fashion in Eighteenth-Century America* (Chapel Hill: University of North Carolina Press, 2011), 49, 83, 6, 39.

5. Lynn Matluck Brooks, "The Philadelphia Dancing Academy in the Eighteenth Century," *Dance Research Journal* 21 (Spring 1989): 1–6. The European ideal prescribed an erect female stance, often accompanied by the use of stays. Haulman, *Politics of Fashion*, 18. Esther DeBerdt Reed to Dennis DeBerdt, Philadelphia, November 14, 1770, in Reed, *Esther*, 158–59.

6. Esther DeBerdt Reed to Dennis DeBerdt, Philadelphia, January 17, 1771, in Reed, *Esther*, 166.

7. Esther DeBerdt Reed to Dennis DeBerdt, Philadelphia, November 14, 1770, and April 1772, both in Reed, *Esther*, 158–59, 172.

8. Joseph Reed to Charles Pettit, Philadelphia, December 20, 1770; Charles Pettit to Joseph Reed, Burlington, N.J., December 24, 1770, both in Reed Papers, N-YHS.

9. Esther DeBerdt Reed to Dennis DeBerdt, June 15, 1771, in Reed, *Esther*, 168, Arthur Lee to Joseph Reed, Essex Court, London, January 18, 1771, in Reed, *Reed*, 1:43–44; Esther DeBerdt Reed to Dennis DeBerdt, November 2, 1774, in Reed, *Esther*, 202–6.

10. Joseph Reed to Charles Pettit, London, July 13, 1770, in Reed Papers, N-YHS.

11. Brewer, *Pleasures of the Imagination*, 32, 26, xxiv, xxv, 28, 35, 27, xxvii; Clare Walsh, "Shops, Shopping, and the Art of Decision Making in Eighteenth-Century England," in *Gender, Taste, and Material Culture in Britain and North America, 1700–1830*, ed. John Styles and Amanda Vickery (New Haven: Yale University Press, 2006), 151–78, 169; Helen Berry, "Polite Consumption: Shopping in Eighteenth-Century England," *Transactions of the Royal Historical Society* 12 (2002): 377; Walsh, "Shops, Shopping, and the Art of Decision Making," 171.

12. *Pennsylvania Gazette*, February 1, 1775; Silas Deane to Thomas Munford, Philadelphia, October 16, 1774, in Smith, *Letters*, 1:203.

13. Despite the heroics of some importers, including small merchants such as Mary Hamilton in New York, American fashions always lagged behind those in London. Haulman, *Politics of Fashion*, 12–13, 37, 41, 45.

14. Esther DeBerdt Reed to Dennis DeBerdt, December 12, 1770, in Reed, *Esther*, 163.

15. Ibid.

16. Esther DeBerdt Reed to Dennis DeBerdt, October 20, 1772, in Reed, *Esther*, 176, 181.

17. Ibid.

18. Ibid.

19. Esther's London friend, Mrs. Wood, also shopped for Esther, at least during Esther's first few years in Philadelphia. Dennis DeBerdt to Joseph Reed, London, February 21, 1771; Dennis DeBerdt to Esther DeBerdt Reed, London, March 14, 1771; Dennis DeBerdt to Esther DeBerdt Reed, London, July 16, 1771, all in Reed Papers, N-YHS. Esther's use of the word *even* suggests that she relegates shops on Thames Street to a lower status. However, in comparative terms, she was excited to find "here is a street in Philadelphia so very like Thames Street and I rejoice I can go that way." Esther DeBerdt Reed to Dennis DeBerdt, Philadelphia, December 12, 1770, in Reed, *Esther*, 163–64; Arthur Lee to Joseph Reed, London, February 18, 1773, in Reed, *Reed*, 1:48.

20. Esther DeBerdt Reed to Dennis DeBerdt, Philadelphia, May 4, 1771, in Reed, *Esther*, 167; Joseph Reed to Charles Pettit, Philadelphia, May 21, 1771; Charles Pettit to Joseph Reed,

Burlington, N.J., May 22, 1771, both in Reed Papers, N-YHS.

21. Joseph Reed to Charles Pettit, Philadelphia, July 11, 1772, in Reed Papers, N-YHS.

22. Dennys DeBerdt to Lord Dartmouth, August 22, 1766, in DeBerdt, *Letters*, 445. See chapter 1 of the current volume for further references. "Part One: Baptisms," *Records of the Second Presbyterian Church* (Philadelphia), June 1772, Historical Society of Pennsylvania.

23. Esther DeBerdt Reed to Dennis DeBerdt, Philadelphia, June 15, 1771, in Reed, *Esther*, 168.

24. Dennis DeBerdt to Esther DeBerdt Reed, London, July 16, 1771; Joseph Reed to Charles Pettit, Philadelphia, February 18, 1772, both in Reed Papers, N-YHS.

25. Mrs. John Cox, or Esther Bowes Cox, was the younger sister of Joseph's mother, Theodosia Bowes Reed, and less than ten years older than Esther DeBerdt Reed. Joseph Reed to Charles Pettit, November 28, 1772. See Charles Pettit to Joseph Reed, Burlington, N.J., July 18, 1770, for news that Mrs. Cox is pregnant. Joseph Reed to Charles Pettit, January 4, July 23, and August 8, 1773; Joseph Reed to Dennis DeBerdt, July 23, August 8, August 16, and August 23, 1773; Esther DeBerdt Reed to Dennis DeBerdt, Philadelphia, May 14 and October 28, 1774, September 8 and October 28, 1775, and February 25, 1776, all in Reed, *Esther*, 193, 235, 227, 232, 246; John Cox to Joseph Reed, Philadelphia, September 22, 1775, in Reed Papers, N-YHS.

26. Joseph Reed to Dennis DeBerdt, Philadelphia, July 23, 1772; Dennis DeBerdt to Esther DeBerdt Reed, London, November 7, 1772, both in Reed Papers, N-YHS; Esther DeBerdt Reed to Dennis DeBerdt, Philadelphia, October 12, 1772, in Reed, *Esther*, 172.

27. Esther DeBerdt Reed to Dennis DeBerdt, Philadelphia, October 20, 1772, in Reed, *Esther*, 181.

28. Joseph Reed to Charles Pettit, July 2, 1774, in Reed Papers, N-YHS.

29. Esther DeBerdt Reed to Dennis DeBerdt, Philadelphia, October 12, 1772, and May 14 and November 2, 1774, all in Reed, *Esther*, 172–73, 189, 202.

30. For Mrs. DeBerdt's use of snuff, see Joseph Reed to Dennis DeBerdt, undated letter, probably drafted between March 31 and April 3, 1774. Dennis DeBerdt to Esther DeBerdt Reed, February 27, 1774; Joseph Reed to Dennis DeBerdt, May 14, 1774, and August 8 and October 30, 1773, all in Reed Papers, N-YHS.

31. Joseph Reed to Charles Pettit, May 7, 1770, in Reed Papers, N-YHS.

32. Dennis DeBerdt to Joseph Reed, London, April 20, 1771, and November 17, 1772, both in Reed Papers, N-YHS; Esther DeBerdt Reed to Dennis DeBerdt, Philadelphia, October 28, 1773, in Reed, *Esther*, 184.

33. Esther DeBerdt Reed to Dennis DeBerdt, Philadelphia, January, 17, 1771, in Reed, *Esther*, 165.

34. Joseph Reed to Dennis DeBerdt, Philadelphia, October 30, 1773, in Reed Papers, N-YHS; Esther DeBerdt Reed to Dennis DeBerdt, Philadelphia, January 17, 1771, October 20, 1772, and October 28, 1773, all in Reed, *Esther*, 165, 179, 186.

35. See earlier chapters of the present volume. Esther DeBerdt Reed to Dennis DeBerdt, Philadelphia, November 14, 1770, in Reed, *Esther*, 157.

36. Esther DeBerdt Reed to Dennis DeBerdt, Philadelphia, November 14 and December 12, 1770, both in Reed, *Esther*, 157, 160–62. For additional references on the question of women in business, see the bibliographical essay.

37. Joseph Reed to Charles Pettit, June 25, 1770, in Reed Papers, N-YHS.

38. Dennis DeBerdt to Joseph Reed, London, January 26, 1771; Dennis DeBerdt to Esther DeBerdt Reed, London, March 14 and July 16, 1771; Arthur Lee to Joseph Reed, London, January 18, 1771; Dennis DeBerdt to Esther DeBerdt Reed, London, September 4 and December 1, 1771, all in Reed Papers, N-YHS.

39. Esther DeBerdt Reed to Dennis DeBerdt, Philadelphia, December 12, 1770, and October 20 and October 22, 1772, all in Reed, *Esther*, 160–63, 177–82; Dennis DeBerdt to Esther DeBerdt Reed, London, November 7, 1772; Dennis DeBerdt to Joseph Reed, London, November 14, 1772, and February 17 and October 1, 1773, all in Reed Papers, N-YHS.

40. Esther DeBerdt Reed to Dennis DeBerdt, Philadelphia, October 12, 1772, in Reed, *Esther*, 174–76.

41. Esther DeBerdt Reed to Dennis DeBerdt, Philadelphia, June 24, 1775, in Reed, *Esther*, 217; Joseph Reed to Dennis DeBerdt, December 5, 1774, in Reed Papers, N-YHS.

42. Branson illustrated the operation of a family economy of mutual interdependence in "Women and the Family Economy in the Early Republic," 47–71. For an example of a married woman who conducted business on her own, see Bodle, "Jane Bartram's 'Application,'" 185–220. See also Hartigan-O'Connor, *The Ties*

That Buy; Wilson, "A Marriage 'Well-Ordered,'" 78–87; Miller, *The Needle's Eye*; Cleary, *Elizabeth Murray*; and Wulf, *Not All Wives*. For more references on the question of women and business, see the bibliographical essay.

43. Dennis DeBerdt to Joseph Reed, London, February 17 and March 18, 1773, July 24, 1774, and September 4, 1771; Esther DeBerdt Reed to Dennis DeBerdt, Philadelphia, October 28, 1772, all in Reed, *Esther*, 187; Dennis DeBerdt to Esther DeBerdt Reed or Joseph Reed, London, December 2, 1772, February 17, March 4, July 24, October 1, and November 12, 1773; Dennis DeBerdt to Joseph Reed, London, August 5 and August 25, 1772, all in Reed Papers, N-YHS.

44. See, for example, Joseph Reed to Charles Pettit, December 6, December 7, and December 20, 1770, January 13, February 15, July 25, and August 24, 1772, and December 12, 1774; Charles Pettit to Joseph Reed, May 22 and June 6, 1771; Joseph Reed to Charles Pettit, Philadelphia, March 27 and March 9, 1771; Charles Pettit to Joseph Reed, Burlington, N.J., January 18, 1774, all in Reed Papers, N-YHS.

45. Esther DeBerdt Reed to Dennis DeBerdt, Philadelphia, April 1772, in Reed, *Esther*, 171; Joseph Reed to Charles Pettit, February 28, 1772, in Reed Papers, N-YHS.

46. Esther DeBerdt Reed to Dennis DeBerdt, Philadelphia, February 29 and October 20, 1772, both in Reed, *Esther*, 170–71, 179. "I have a cause to try every day except Sunday till the 29." Joseph Reed to unknown, Philadelphia, October 7, 1773; Joseph Reed to Dennis DeBerdt, Philadelphia, October 30, 1773, both in Reed Papers, N-YHS.

47. Joseph Reed to Charles Pettit, Philadelphia, December 8, 1773, and November 28, 1772; Charles Pettit to Joseph Reed, August 31, 1773; Jared Ingersoll to Joseph Reed, London, February 16, 1774; Joseph Reed to Dennis DeBerdt, April 1, 1774, all in Reed Papers, N-YHS.

48. Joseph Reed to the Trustees of the DeBerdt Estate, January 4, 1773; Joseph Reed to Joseph Jacobs of South Hampton, Long Island, August 10, 1772; Joseph Reed to the Trustees of the DeBerdt Estate, November 13, 1772, and January 4, 1773; Joseph Reed to John Smith in New York, January 6, 1773. Joseph continued to collect debts owed to trustees and submit the money to London throughout 1773 and well into 1774. See Joseph Reed to R. Morris, March 31, 1774; Dennis DeBerdt to Joseph Reed, January 4, 1775; Joseph Reed to Joseph Jacobs of South Hampton, Long Island, August 11, 1772; Joseph Reed to Trustees of the DeBerdt Estate, November 13, 1772, regarding two trips to New York City, all in Reed Papers, N-YHS.

49. Dennis DeBerdt to Joseph Reed, May 6, November 7, and November 14, 1772, in Roche, *Reed*, 30–32; Charles Pettit to Joseph Reed, December 24, 1770; Joseph Reed to Dennis DeBerdt, December 24, 1773; Joseph Reed to Charles Pettit, January 31, 1775, and December 24, 1770; Joseph Reed to Dennis DeBerdt, December 24, 1773, in Reed Papers, N-YHS.

50. Roche, *Reed*, 36. Joseph Reed to Dennis DeBerdt, October 19, 1772; Richard Cary to Joseph Reed, March 3, 1775, both in Reed Papers, N-YHS.

51. Joseph Reed, "Estimate of My Estate," July 7, 1774, in Roche, *Reed*, 30–31. A note on slavery: Joseph, like a significant number of patriots, owned slaves. Indeed, in Bucks County, the ownership of slaves tended to differentiate those who became patriots from those who resisted the patriots. The Quakers, who only recently had taken formal action to rid themselves of this institution, stand out in their opposition. There were few, if any, voices among the patriots raised against the institution at the time of the Declaration of Independence, but by 1779–80, the party headed by Joseph Reed, John Bayard, and George Bryan, and especially by Bryan (all Constitutionalists), legislated the gradual abolition of the institution in the state. With this act, Pennsylvania became the first state in the new nation to put this institution on the road to oblivion. See Owen S. Ireland, "Bucks County," in *Beyond Philadelphia: The American Revolution in the Pennsylvania Hinterland*, ed. John B. Frantz and William Pencak (University Park: Penn State University Press, 1998), 23–46, and Owen S. Ireland, "Germans Against Abolition: A Minority's View of Slavery in Revolutionary Pennsylvania," *Journal of Interdisciplinary History* 3 (1973): 687.

52. Craftsmen earned five shillings per day, laborers three shillings per day. Gary Nash, "Artisans and Politics in Eighteenth-Century Philadelphia," in *The Origins of Anglo-American Radicalism*, ed. James R. Jacobs and Margaret C. Jacobs (London: Institute for Research in History, 1984), 162–84, 164.

53. Joseph Reed to Dennis DeBerdt, November 16, 1772, in Reed Papers, N-YHS; Joseph Reed to Dennis DeBerdt, August 3, 1772; Esther DeBerdt Reed to Dennis DeBerdt, Philadelphia, May 14, 1774, in Reed, *Esther*, 195; Joseph Reed to Dennis DeBerdt, Philadelphia,

January 5 and December 24, 1773, December 2, 1772, and October 30, 1773, all in Reed Papers, N-YHS; Esther DeBerdt Reed to Dennis DeBerdt, October 12, 1772, in Reed, *Esther*, 176.

54. For a brief description of how one family arranged this, see Wulf, *Not All Wives*, 85.

55. Esther DeBerdt Reed to Dennis DeBerdt, Philadelphia, December 12, 1770, in Reed, *Esther*, 164; Dennis DeBerdt to Joseph Reed, London, January 26 and February 12, 1771, both in Reed Papers, N-YHS; Esther DeBerdt Reed to Dennis DeBerdt, Philadelphia, December 12, 1770, in Reed, *Esther*, 164; Dennis DeBerdt to Joseph Reed, London, August 23, 1773; Joseph Reed to [Moore Foreman], Bucks County, February 5, 1774, in Reed Papers, N-YHS.

56. Joseph Reed to Charles Pettit, Philadelphia, November 20, 1773, and February 11, February 17, and March 9, 1774, all in Reed Papers, N-YHS.

57. Joseph Reed to Dennis DeBerdt, Philadelphia, November 16 and December 3, 1772, and December 24, 1773, all in Reed Papers, N-YHS.

58. For reference to Sansom's estate, see Klepp and Wulf, eds., *The Diary of Hannah Callender Sansom*, 20.

59. George B. Tatum, *A Philadelphia Georgian: The City House of Samuel Powel* (Middletown: Wesleyan University Press, 1976), 11–12; John Adams, "Diary," September 1, 1774, in Smith, *Letters*, 1:6.

60. John Adams, "Diary," September 8, 7, 11, 22, and 3, 1774, all in Smith, *Letters*, 1:45, 33–34, 64, 90, 9.

61. Esther DeBerdt Reed to Dennis DeBerdt, Philadelphia, October 28, 1773, in Reed, *Esther*, 183; Joseph Reed to Dennis DeBerdt, February 14, 1776, in Reed Papers, N-YHS.

62. Esther DeBerdt Reed to Dennis DeBerdt, Philadelphia, February 13 and June 24, 1775, both in Reed, *Esther*, 208, 216.

63. Joseph Reed to Esther DeBerdt, Philadelphia, December 15, 1769, in Reed, *Reed*, 1:42; Dennis DeBerdt to Esther DeBerdt Reed, London, December 6, 1771, and November 7, 1772, both in Reed Papers, N-YHS.

Chapter 8

1. Roche, *Reed*, chapter 4, "The Patriot Who Would Be Peacemaker."

2. Joseph Reed to Charles Pettit, Philadelphia, August 20, 1775, in Roche, *Reed*, 57.

3. Esther DeBerdt Reed to Dennis DeBerdt, Philadelphia, October 28, 1773, in Reed, *Esther*, 185–86. At about the same time, Abigail Adams in Massachusetts wrote to tell her husband "she could not join 'in the petition of our worthy parson [Reverend Wibird] for a reconciliation between our, no longer parent State, but truant State, and their Colonies.' 'Let us Separate.'" Holton, *Abigail Adams*, 95.

4. Esther DeBerdt Reed to Dennis DeBerdt, Philadelphia, October 28, 1773, in Reed, *Esther*, 185–86.

5. Esther DeBerdt Reed to Dennis DeBerdt, Philadelphia, May 17, 1774, in Reed, *Esther*, 193. See Bodle, "Jane Bartram's 'Application,'" 184–200.

6. Esther DeBerdt Reed to Dennis DeBerdt, Philadelphia, November 2, 1774, in Reed, *Esther*, 204.

7. For similar political dinners bringing males and females together for food and discussion, see Christopher Marshall, "Remembrances," between June 18 and June 24, 1776, Historical Society of Pennsylvania.

8. Esther DeBerdt Reed to Dennis DeBerdt, Philadelphia, November 2, 1774, in Reed, *Esther*, 204. For her participation in her father's Sunday dinners, see Esther DeBerdt to Joseph Reed, London, November 9, 1765, in Reed Papers, N-YHS. The meaning of this variation in Adams's reporting, however, remains less clear than it might at first appear. In Philadelphia, as in Esther's home in London, political dinners often brought together men and women, husbands and wives, and, on occasion, widows and widowers. Contemporary reports tended to neglect the mixed nature of these social-political events, and modern historians tend to neglect those contemporary reports that detail the presence of females. In contrast, Klepp and Wulf, eds., in *The Diary of Hannah Callender Sansom*, 27–32, indicate that young men and women often met at social events, such as teas, where the discussions could involve political topics.

9. For a sampling of John Adams's descriptions of the various dinners he attended in private homes in the fall of 1774, see John Adams, "Diary," August 30, September 7, September 8, September 11, and September 14, 1774, in Smith, *Letters*, 1:4, 33–34, 45, 64, 69. For Esther's participation in the discussions at her own dinners in Philadelphia, see Silas Deane to E. Dean, Philadelphia, September 23, 1774, in Smith, *Letters*, 1:92. See also Klepp and Wulf,

eds., *The Diary of Hannah Callender Sansom*, 27–30.

10. Esther DeBerdt Reed to Dennis DeBerdt, Philadelphia, November 2, 1774, in Reed, *Esther*, 203–4.

11. Esther DeBerdt Reed to Dennis DeBerdt, Philadelphia, February 13, 1775, in Reed, *Esther*, 206.

12. Ibid., 207.

13. Esther DeBerdt Reed to Dennis DeBerdt, Philadelphia, March 14, 1775, in Reed, *Esther*, 209–10.

14. Esther DeBerdt Reed to Dennis DeBerdt, Philadelphia, February, 13, 1775, in Reed, *Esther*, 207–8.

15. Esther DeBerdt Reed to Dennis DeBerdt, Philadelphia, November 2, 1774, and March 14 and February 13, 1775, all in Reed, *Esther*, 203, 209–10, 207–8.

16. Esther DeBerdt Reed to Dennis DeBerdt, Philadelphia, November 2, 1774, and March 14, 1775, both in Reed, *Esther*, 203, 209–10. See also Caesar Rodney, *Letters to and from Caesar Rodney, 1756–1784*, ed. George Herbert Ryden (Philadelphia: University of Pennsylvania Press for the Historical Society of Delaware, 1933), 57–58.

17. May 9, 1774. Samuel Curwen, *The Journal and Letters of Samuel Curwen, 1775–1783*, ed. George Atkinson Ward (Boston: Little, Brown, 1864), 28.

18. Esther DeBerdt Reed to Dennis DeBerdt, Philadelphia, April 1772, in Reed, *Esther*, 171; Dennis DeBerdt to Esther DeBerdt Reed, London, January 26 and June 1, 1775, both in Reed Papers, N-YHS.

19. Esther DeBerdt Reed to Dennis DeBerdt, Philadelphia, October 28, 1773, in Reed, *Esther*, 185–86.

20. Joseph Reed to Dennis DeBerdt, Philadelphia, September 26, 1774, in Reed Papers, N-YHS; Esther DeBerdt Reed to Dennis DeBerdt, Philadelphia, June 24, 1775, in Reed, *Esther*, 216–18.

21. Joseph Reed to Esther DeBerdt Reed, Cambridge, Mass., July 26, 1775; Andrew Hodge to Joseph Reed, Philadelphia, August 28, 1775, both in Reed Papers, N-YHS; Esther DeBerdt Reed to Dennis DeBerdt, Philadelphia, July 22, 1775, in Roche, *Reed*, 64; Reed, *Esther*, 218–19.

22. Dennis DeBerdt to Esther DeBerdt Reed, London, October 6, 1775, in Reed Papers, N-YHS.

23. Esther DeBerdt Reed to Dennis DeBerdt, Philadelphia, June 24, 1775, in Reed, *Esther*, 218.

24. He invited not all of them but "as many of your family as you think proper." Charles Pettit to Esther DeBerdt Reed, Perth Amboy, N.J., July 24, 1775; John Cox to Joseph Reed, Philadelphia, July 26, 1775; John Cox to Joseph Reed, Philadelphia, September 9, 1775, all in Reed Papers, N-YHS.

25. Joseph Reed to Esther DeBerdt Reed, Cambridge, Mass., July 26, 1775, in Reed Papers, N-YHS; Esther DeBerdt Reed to Dennis DeBerdt, Perth Amboy, N.J., September 8, 1775, in Reed, *Esther*, 227.

26. Esther DeBerdt Reed to Dennis DeBerdt, Philadelphia, October 28, 1775, in Reed, *Esther*, 234. For more on the political roles of women in this era, see the bibliographical essay.

27. Esther DeBerdt Reed to Dennis DeBerdt, Philadelphia, May 13, 1775, and November 2, 1774, both in Reed, *Esther*, 214–15, 203, 207; Esther DeBerdt to Joseph Reed, London, November 11, 1764, and July 7, 1767, both in Reed Papers, N-YHS; Esther DeBerdt Reed to Dennis DeBerdt, Philadelphia, November 2, 1774, in Reed, *Esther*, 204–5.

28. See earlier in the current volume and DeBerdt, *Letters*, 294, 297, 298–99, 316–17, 445. The Reeds belonged to the Second Presbyterian Church at Arch and Third Streets. Roche, *Reed*, 32.

29. Fragments of Esther's early writings, in Reed Papers, N-YHS.

30. For a discussion of Presbyterian theology and revolution, see Joseph Tiedemann, "Presbyterianism and the American Revolution in the Middle Colonies," *Church History* 74 (June 2003): 306–44, especially 322–26, and Rosemary Keller, *Patriotism and the Female Sex: Abigail Adams and the American Revolution* (Brooklyn, N.Y.: Carlson Publishing, 1994), 67–69. Curwen, *Journal*, Sunday, May 7, 1775, 28.

31. Joseph Reed to Dennis DeBerdt, Philadelphia, February 13, 1775, in Reed Papers, N-YHS.

32. See chapter 7 of the current volume for details.

33. Joseph Reed to Samuel Spraggs, Philadelphia, May 30, 1775; Joseph Reed to John Antill(e), Philadelphia, June 5, 1775, both in Reed Papers, N-YHS.

34. Joseph Reed to Dennis DeBerdt, Philadelphia, December 5, 1775, in Reed Papers, N-YHS. Alison G. Olson, "The London Mercantile Lobby and the Coming of the American Revolution," *Journal of American History* 69 (June 1982): 26, identifies Dennis as

part of the small cadre of well-to-do and politically connected London merchants trading to America. Roche, *Reed*, 34. Dennis DeBerdt to Esther DeBerdt Reed, London, June 1, 1775, in Reed Papers, N-YHS.

35. Dr. Robert Honyman, "Journal," in *The Colonial Panorama 1775: Dr. Robert Honyman's Journal for March and April*, ed. Philip Padel Ford (San Marino, Calif.: Huntington Library, 1939), 71–72.

36. Joseph Reed reported that the court, sitting when news arrived, "immediately closed." Joseph Reed to Samuel Spraggs, Philadelphia, May 20, 1775, in Reed Papers, N-YHS; Curwen, *Journal*, Philadelphia, May 5 and May 6, 1775, 27–28; Margaret Wheeler Willard, ed., *Letters on the American Revolution, 1774–1776* (Boston: Houghton Mifflin, 1925), 102, 103; Curwen, *Journal*, May 10, 1775, 28–29; Caesar Rodney to Thomas Rodney, Philadelphia, May 11, 1775, in Smith, *Letters*, 1:58; Curwen, *Journal*, May 9, 1774, 28.

37. Joseph Reed to Charles Pettit, Philadelphia, September 4, 1774, in Reed Papers, N-YHS; Gary Wills, *Inventing America: Jefferson's Declaration of Independence* (Garden City, N.Y.: Doubleday, 1978), 3–4, 10–12.

38. "Extract from a Letter from Philadelphia, PA in the Morning Post and Daily Advertiser [London] January 16, 1776," in Willard, *Letters*, 228; Abigail Adams to John Adams, Braintree, Mass., July 16, 1775, in Charles Francis Adams, ed., *Familiar Letters of John Adams and His Wife Abigail Adams During the Revolution* (Boston: Houghton, Mifflin and Company, 1875), 79.

39. For Washington's attachment to Joseph Reed, see his letters to Joseph in the winter of 1775–76, after Joseph had returned home to Philadelphia. Washington to Reed, Cambridge, Mass., January 23, January 31, February 10, and February 26–March 9, 1776, all in George Washington, *The Papers of George Washington, Revolutionary Series*, vol. 3, January–March 1776, ed. William Abbot (Charlottesville: University Press of Virginia, 1988), 172–73, 225, 286–91, 369–79.

40. Joseph Reed to Dennis DeBerdt, Philadelphia, May 4 and December 24, 1774, and February 13, 1775; Joseph Reed to Josiah Quincy, Philadelphia, October 25, 1774, all in Reed Papers, N-YHS.

41. Charles Pettit to Joseph Reed, Burlington, N.J., January 18, 1774, in Reed Papers, N-YHS; Esther DeBerdt Reed to Dennis DeBerdt, Philadelphia, October 28, 1773, and November 2, 1774, both in Reed, *Esther*, 185–86, 206.

42. Reed to Dennis DeBerdt, Philadelphia, February 13, 1775, in Reed Papers, N-YHS; Esther DeBerdt Reed to Dennis DeBerdt, Philadelphia, March 14, 1775, in Reed, *Esther*, 209; Joseph Reed to Dennis DeBerdt, Philadelphia, February 13, 1775, in Reed Papers, N-YHS. Reed undoubtedly expected his proposals to find their way to the ministry. He knew that DeBerdt was in close contact with Dartmouth, and he suspected that the government was breaking into and reading his mail.

43. Unsigned letter dated July 11, 1774, in Reed Papers, N-YHS. Internal evidence suggests it came from Dartmouth.

44. Dennis DeBerdt to Joseph Reed, London, October 8 and January 4, 1775, both in Reed Papers, N-YHS.

45. Josiah Quincy to Joseph Reed, London, December 17, 1774, in Reed Papers, N-YHS. Then strong ministerial hostility to them as a group left them in disarray. Olson, "The London Merchants," 39. Esther's brother, Dennis, was a part of this group and undoubtedly conveyed news of its division and disintegration to Esther in the late spring or early summer of 1775. Joseph Reed to Dennis DeBerdt, Philadelphia, February 13, 1775, in Reed Papers, N-YHS.

46. Esther DeBerdt Reed to Dennis DeBerdt, Philadelphia, June 24, 1775, in Reed Papers, N-YHS.

47. Esther DeBerdt Reed to Dennis DeBerdt, Philadelphia, June 24, 1775, in Reed, *Esther*, 216.

48. Esther DeBerdt Reed to Dennis DeBerdt, Philadelphia, June 24, 1775, in Reed, *Esther*, 218.

49. Esther DeBerdt Reed to Dennis DeBerdt, Philadelphia, July 22, 1775, in Reed, *Esther*, 219.

50. John Cox to Joseph Reed, Philadelphia, September 9, 1775, in Reed Papers, N-YHS.

51. Esther DeBerdt Reed to Dennis DeBerdt, Perth Amboy, N.J., September 8, 1775; Joseph Reed to Charles Pettit, camp, September 11, 1775, both in Reed Papers, N-YHS.

52. Esther DeBerdt Reed to Dennis DeBerdt, Perth Amboy, N.J., September 8, 1775, in Reed, *Esther*, 228.

53. Ibid.

54. Ibid.

55. Her use of the term *country* here remains confusing but probably applies to the English-speaking nation threatened by ministerial tyranny. Esther DeBerdt Reed to Dennis DeBerdt, Perth Amboy, N.J., September 8, 1775, in Reed, *Esther*, 228–29.

For an extended discussion of whether, under late eighteenth-century coverture and English common law, a married woman could be charged with treason for failing to separate herself from her husband's treasonable acts, see Linda Kerber, *No Constitutional Right to Be Ladies: Women and the Obligations of Citizenship* (New York: Hill and Wang, 1998), 3–46.

56. Esther DeBerdt Reed to Dennis DeBerdt, Philadelphia, October 28, 1775, in Reed, *Esther*, 232; Joseph Reed to Charles Pettit, camp, October 8, 1775, in Reed Papers, N-YHS.

57. Esther DeBerdt Reed to Dennis DeBerdt, Philadelphia, October 28, 1775, in Reed, *Esther*, 233; Joseph Reed to Charles Pettit, camp, October 8, 1775, in Reed Papers, N-YHS; Esther DeBerdt Reed to Dennis DeBerdt, Philadelphia, October 28, 1775, in Reed, *Esther*, 234.

58. Esther DeBerdt Reed to Dennis DeBerdt, Perth Amboy, N.J., September 8, 1775, in Reed, *Esther*, 228.

Chapter 9

1. Roche, *Reed*, 76.
2. Dennis DeBerdt to Joseph Reed, October 4, 1775, in Reed, *Esther*, 240.
3. Joseph Reed to Dennis DeBerdt, February 24, 1776, in Reed, *Esther*, 242–43.
4. Esther DeBerdt Reed to Dennis DeBerdt, February 25, 1776, in Reed, *Esther*, 247–48.
5. Joseph Reed to Dennis DeBerdt, February 14, 1776, in Reed, *Esther*, 241; John T. Faris, *The Romance of Old Philadelphia* (Philadelphia: J. B. Lippincott, 1918), 256.
6. Joseph Reed to Charles Pettit, March 30, 1776, in Reed, *Reed*, 1:182.
7. Sarah Eve, "Extracts from the Journal of Miss Sarah Eve," in Eva Eve Jones, ed., *Pennsylvania Magazine of History and Biography* 5 (1887): 19–35, 191–201.
8. Joseph Reed to Charles Pettit, March 30, 1776, in Reed, *Reed*, 1:182–84.
9. Joseph Reed to Charles Pettit, March 30 and 31, 1776, both in Reed, *Reed*, 1:182–84.
10. For studies of women, either as independent traders or as the widows of traders, see Hartigan-O'Connor, *The Ties That Buy*; Holton, *Abigail Adams*; and Cleary, *Elizabeth Murray*.
11. Joseph Reed, "Sketch of My Affairs and Last Will and Testament," signed June 11, 1776, in Reed Papers, N-YHS.
12. Joseph Reed to Esther DeBerdt Reed, November 6, 1776, in Reed Papers, N-YHS.

13. Joseph Reed to Charles Pettit, December 30, 1775, in Reed Papers, N-YHS.
14. Joseph Reed to Charles Pettit, March 30, 1776, in Reed, *Reed*, 1:181.
15. Joseph Reed to Charles Pettit, no date, probably December 1775 or January 1776, in Reed Papers, N-YHS.
16. Joseph Reed to Esther DeBerdt Reed, June 5, 1776, in Reed, *Reed*, 1:190.
17. Joseph Reed to Esther DeBerdt Reed, June 5, June 26, and June 4, 1776, all in Reed, *Reed*, 1:190, 192, 194.
18. Mary Silliman to her husband, April 2, 1776, in Joy Day Buel and Richard Buel Jr., *The Way of Duty: A Woman and Her Family in Revolutionary America* (New York: W. W. Norton, 1984), 109, 129; Zagarri, *A Woman's Dilemma*, 105.
19. Buel and Buel, *Way of Duty*, 129.
20. Joseph Reed to Esther DeBerdt Reed, June 16, 1776, in Reed Papers, N-YHS; Roche, *Reed*, 83.
21. Joseph Reed to Esther DeBerdt Reed, August 13, 1776, in Reed, *Reed*, 1:216.
22. Joseph Reed to Esther DeBerdt Reed, June 22 and June 16, 1776, both in Reed, *Reed*, 1:193, 190; Joseph Reed to Esther DeBerdt Reed, July 3, 1776, in Reed Papers, N-YHS.
23. Reed, "Last Will."
24. Joseph Reed to Charles Pettit, June 26, 1776; Joseph Reed to Esther DeBerdt Reed, August 9, 1776, both in Reed Papers, N-YHS.
25. See, for example, Joseph Reed to Esther DeBerdt Reed, August 29 and September 2, 1776, both in Reed, *Reed*, 1:225, 230.
26. Joseph Reed to Esther DeBerdt Reed, September 14, 1776, in Reed, *Reed*, 1:235.
27. Joseph Reed to Esther DeBerdt Reed, September 6, September 17, and September 22, 1776, all in Reed, *Reed*, 1:231, 236–39.
28. Joseph Reed to Esther DeBerdt Reed, September 22, 1776, in Reed, *Reed*, 1:237.
29. Joseph Reed to Esther DeBerdt Reed, June 21 and 26, 1776, both in Reed, *Reed*, 1:191, 193; Joseph Reed to Esther DeBerdt Reed, June 27, June 28, June 30, and August 18, 1776, all in Reed Papers, N-YHS; Joseph Reed to Esther DeBerdt Reed, October 11, 1776, in Reed, *Reed*, 1:243.
30. Joseph Reed to Esther DeBerdt Reed, June 21, 1776, in Reed Papers, N-YHS; Joseph Reed to Esther DeBerdt Reed, August 7 and October 11, 1776, both in Reed, *Reed*, 1:214, 242.
31. Roche, *Reed*, 117.

32. Joseph Reed to Esther DeBerdt Reed, June 16, July 16, and July 22, 1776, all in Reed, *Reed*, 1:190, 203, 208.

33. Joseph Reed to Esther DeBerdt Reed, July 22, 1776, in Reed, *Reed*, 1:208.

34. Joseph Reed to Esther DeBerdt Reed, August 7, 1776, in Reed, *Reed*, 1:214.

35. Joseph Reed to Esther DeBerdt Reed, August 17, August 18, and August 23, 1776, all in Reed Papers, N-YHS.

36. Joseph Reed to Esther DeBerdt Reed, August 7, 1776, in Reed Papers, N-YHS; Joseph Reed to Esther DeBerdt Reed, August 9, 1776, in Reed, *Reed*, 1:215; Joseph Reed to Esther DeBerdt Reed, August 23, 1776, in Reed Papers, N-YHS; Joseph Reed to Esther DeBerdt Reed, September 15, 1776, in Reed, *Reed*, 1:236.

37. Esther DeBerdt Reed to Dennis DeBerdt, March 1777, in Reed, *Esther*, 259–60; Joseph Reed to Esther DeBerdt Reed, September 15 and October 11, 1776, both in Reed, *Reed*, 1:236, 242.

38. Joseph Reed to Esther DeBerdt Reed, August 17, 1776, in Reed Papers, N-YHS.

39. For the valorization of female fertility in late eighteenth-century America, see Susan Klepp, "Revolutionary Bodies: Women and the Fertility Transition in the Middle-Atlantic Region, 1760–1820," *Journal of American History* 85 (December 1998): 910–45. For the emergence of the mind-set of limits and its impact on the fertility of married women in the same period, see Susan Klepp, *Revolutionary Conceptions: Women, Fertility, and Family Limitation in America, 1760–1820* (Chapel Hill: University of North Carolina Press for the Omohundro Institute of Early American History and Culture, 2009).

40. Joseph Reed to Esther DeBerdt Reed, August 17, August 23, September 6, and October 11, 1776, all in Reed, *Reed*, 1:216, 219, 230, 242.

41. Joseph Reed to Esther DeBerdt Reed, November 6, 1776, in Reed, *Reed*, 1:251.

42. Ibid., 251–52.

43. Ibid., 253.

44. Joseph had sent Jack home to Burlington on October 14. Roche, *Reed*, 100, and 241 n. 51. For the weather, see Gerald J. Mulvey and Elliot Abrams, "A Forensic Meteorological Perspective on the American Revolutionary War Battles of Trenton and Princeton," January 23, 2008, viewed at accuweather.com, January 21, 2008. Joseph Reed to Dennis DeBerdt, February 23, 1777, in Reed, *Esther*, 262; Esther DeBerdt Reed to Dennis DeBerdt, March 1777, in Reed, *Esther*, 258.

45. Joseph Reed to George Washington, December 22, 1776, in Reed, *Reed*, 1:272; Roche, *Reed*, 102–10.

46. Esther DeBerdt Reed to Dennis DeBerdt, March 1777, in Reed, *Esther*, 259–60.

47. Roche, *Reed*, 116. Joseph Reed to Timothy Matlack, April 3, 1777, in Reed Papers, N-YHS; Reed, *Esther*, 266; Roche, *Reed*, 118.

48. Esther DeBerdt Reed to Joseph Reed, June 21, 1777; Joseph Reed to Charles Pettit, August 26, 1777, both in Reed Papers, N-YHS.

49. Esther DeBerdt Reed to Joseph Reed, June 21, 1777, in Reed, *Esther*, 267–70; James Grant, *Memorial of Andrew Kirkpatrick and His Wife Jane Bayard* (New York: Printed privately for Mrs. and Dr. How, 1870), 56–68; Esther DeBerdt Reed to Joseph Reed, June 21, 1777, in Reed, *Esther*, 267–70.

50. Roche, *Reed*, 117, 120–21; Reed, *Reed*, 1:295–96.

51. Joseph Reed to Dennis DeBerdt, February 23, 1777, in Reed, *Esther*, 264–65.

52. Joseph Reed to [unknown], [undated], in Reed Papers, N-YHS.

53. Cox was being considered for appointment as one of two assistants to the new quartermaster general, Nathanael Greene. Esther DeBerdt Reed to Mrs. Cox, February 23, 1777, misdated, in Reed, *Esther*, 282.

54. Barbara C. Smith, "Food Rioters and the American Revolution," *William and Mary Quarterly* 51 (1994): 3–38.

55. Joseph Reed to Esther DeBerdt Reed, November 6, 1776, in Reed, *Reed*, 1:248.

56. Esther DeBerdt Reed to Joseph Reed, June 21, 1777, in Reed, *Reed*, 2:254, 295–96, 290–99; Roche, *Reed*, 119–20.

57. Joseph Reed to George Washington, June 12, 1777, in Reed Papers, N-YHS; Roche, *Reed*, 119–20.

58. Esther DeBerdt Reed to Joseph Reed, June 21, 1777, in Reed, *Esther*, 267–70.

59. Esther DeBerdt Reed to Joseph Reed, June 21, 1777; Joseph Reed to Timothy Matlack, Burlington, N.J., June 21, 1777, both in Reed Papers, N-YHS; Reed, *Reed*, 1:276; Roche, *Reed*, 120. Esther conceived her fifth child in the first weeks of August.

60. Reed, *Reed*, 1:265–304.

61. Ibid., 304, 313–11, 317, 320–21, 334, 345–50; Roche, *Reed*, 124. The datelines of Joseph's letters suggest both his mobility and his relative proximity to Esther. See, for example, "Headquarters, 20 miles from Philadelphia," October 18, 1777; "Merion Meeting House," October 23, 1777; "Blue Bell on Chester Road,"

October 24, 1777; "Near Derby," October 24, 1777, all in Reed, *Reed*, 1:325, 326, 327.

62. Joseph Reed to George Washington, Norristown, Pa., September 21, 1777, in Reed, *Reed*, 1:313; Esther DeBerdt Reed to Mrs. Cox, February 23, 1778, in Reed, *Esther*, 282; Roche, *Reed*, 124–25 n. 42; Elias Boudenot to Wharton, December 9, 1777; General Armstrong to Wharton, December 9, 1777, both in Reed Papers, N-YHS.

63. Joseph Reed to George Washington, Norristown, Pa., December 2, 1777, in Reed, *Reed*, 1:344.

64. Joseph Reed to Wharton, December 13, 1777. See also February 1, 1778, both in Reed, *Reed*, 1:355, 358.

65. Esther DeBerdt Reed to Mrs. Cox, February 23, 1778, in Reed, *Esther*, 281.

66. Roche, *Reed*, 127. For details of these irregular forces harassing civilians in this region, see Wayne Bodle, *The Valley Forge Winter: Civilians and Soldiers in War* (University Park: Penn State University Press, 2000), especially 177–88. Esther DeBerdt Reed to Mrs. Cox, March 1778, in Reed, *Esther*, 283–84.

67. Roche, *Reed*, 128. Joseph Reed to Charles Pettit, March 5 and May 13, 1778; Joseph Reed to Dennis DeBerdt, May 24, 1778, all in Reed Papers, N-YHS.

68. Esther DeBerdt Reed to Mrs. Cox, June 16 (continued on July 6), 1778, in Reed, *Esther*, 290–94. For another example of the devastating impact of a child's death on the mother, see Buel and Buel, *Way of Duty*, 61–64, quotation on 64; Martha Ballard of Hallowell, Maine, lost three very young daughters in ten days. She never forgot. Twenty years later, she was still regularly noting the anniversaries of their deaths in her diary. Ulrich, *A Midwife's Tale*, 12.

Chapter 10

1. For a brief discussion of the literature on women and politics in this era, see the bibliographical essay.
2. Joseph Reed to Esther DeBerdt Reed, June 15, 1778, in Smith, *Letters*, 16:103.
3. Joseph Reed to Dennis DeBerdt, May 24, 1778, in Reed, *Esther*, 286.
4. Esther DeBerdt Reed to Dennis DeBerdt, September 16, 1779, in Reed, *Esther*, 296–98.
5. Esther DeBerdt Reed to Mrs. Cox, Flemington, N.J., June 16, 1778, in Reed, *Esther*, 91.

6. Joseph Reed to Esther DeBerdt Reed, August 16, June 15, and August 16, 1778, all in Smith, *Letters*, 10:459.

7. Esther DeBerdt Reed to Mrs. Cox, July 6, 1778, in Reed, *Esther*, 293–94.

8. Earl of Carlisle to George Selwyn, Philadelphia, June 10, 1778, in Reed, *Reed*, 1:380; Joseph Reed to Esther DeBerdt Reed, June 15, 1778, in Smith, *Letters*, 10:103.

9. Joseph Reed to Esther DeBerdt Reed, July 16, 1776, in Reed, *Esther*, 203. See also Joseph Reed to Esther DeBerdt Reed, July 22, July 26, and July 28, 1778, all in Reed, *Esther*, passim.

10. Joseph Reed to Dennis DeBerdt, February 23, 1777, in Reed, *Esther*, 264–65.

11. Joseph Reed to Dennis DeBerdt, May 24, 1778, in Reed, *Esther*, 288.

12. Roche, *Reed*, 248 n. 14.

13. Ibid., 248–49 n. 17. See instructions to the Carlisle Commission in Reed, *Reed*, 1:430–36. Joseph Reed to Dennis DeBerdt, July 9, 1779, in Roche, *Reed*, 148 n. 12.

14. Meredith Lair, "Redcoat Theater: Negotiating Identity in Occupied Philadelphia, 1777–1778," in *Philadelphia's Revolution*, ed. William Pencak (University Park: Penn State University Press, 2010), 193.

15. Ibid., 195, 192.

16. Ibid., 192–210, especially 193, 195. Lair suggests the "permeable boundaries" between those in and those outside the city during the British occupation of Philadelphia (210).

17. Elizabeth Ellet, *The Eminent and Heroic Women of America* (New York: Arno Press, 1974), 125–29; Elizabeth Drinker, *Diary of Elizabeth Drinker*, vol. 1, ed. Elaine Forman Crane (Boston: Northeastern University Press, 1991), 306. For a more detailed description of this Meschianza and the behavior of some residents of Philadelphia during the occupation, see Benjamin H. Irvin, "The Streets of Philadelphia: Crowds, Congress, and the Political Culture of Revolution, 1774–1783," *Pennsylvania Magazine of History and Biography* 129 (January 2005): 7–44.

18. Lair, "Redcoat Theater," 198.

19. Joseph Reed to Nathanael Greene, November 5, 1778, in Reed, *Reed*, 2:38–39.

20. Ellet, *Women*, 271, 272.

21. Joseph Reed to Dennis DeBerdt, May 24, 1779, in Reed, *Esther*, 286–88.

22. Esther DeBerdt Reed to Mrs. Cox, July 16, 1778; Joseph Reed to Dennis DeBerdt, May 24, 1778, both in Reed, *Esther*, 294, 286–88.

23. Joseph Reed to Esther DeBerdt Reed, August 10, 1778, in Smith, *Letters*, 10:458; Esther DeBerdt Reed to Mrs. Cox, June 16, 1778, in Reed, *Esther*, 292.

24. Joseph Reed to Dennis DeBerdt, July 19, 1778, in Smith, *Letters*, 10:312.

25. Alan Taylor, *Liberty Men and Great Proprietors: The Revolutionary Settlement on the Maine Frontier, 1760–1820* (Chapel Hill: University of North Carolina Press for the IEAHC, 1990); Alan Taylor, *William Cooper's Town: Power and Persuasion on the Frontier of the Early American Republic* (New York: Vintage Books, 1995).

26. Roche, *Reed*, 149.

27. Joseph Reed to Esther DeBerdt Reed, August 16, 1778, in Smith, *Letters*, 10:457.

28. Ibid.

29. Joseph Reed to Esther DeBerdt Reed, August 26, 1778, in Smith, *Letters*, 10:504; George Bryan, vice president, Supreme Executive Council, to Joseph Reed, August 21, 1778, in Reed, *Reed*, 2:29.

30. Joseph Reed to General Greene, November 5, 1778, in Reed, *Reed*, 2:38; Joseph Reed to Esther DeBerdt Reed, September 6, 1778, in Smith, *Letters*, 10:592.

31. Joseph Foster, *In Pursuit of Equal Liberty: George Bryan and the Revolution in Pennsylvania* (University Park: Penn State University Press, 1994), 76.

32. Reed and Bayard from 1774 on, and Bryan principally in the 1760s, first as a Pennsylvania delegate to the Stamp Act Congress, and then as a participant in the merchant-led boycott of British imports. However, for reasons that his biographer calls "mysterious," Bryan had largely disappeared from public life in the years immediately before the Declaration of Independence in 1776. Foster, *Bryan*, 74. The three men also differed to some degree in their choice of public activities. John Bayard had served with Joseph as an officer in the Philadelphia Second Battalion of volunteers in 1775 and, like Joseph, had fought at the Battles of Trenton and Princeton as well as at Germantown. But while Joseph had gone off to full-time war with Washington, Bayard had remained in the city, leading the opposition to the new state constitution, winning election to the assembly in November 1776, and then leading the legislature as its speaker in 1777 and 1778. Bryan, after a period of political quiet, remerged early in 1777, won election to the Supreme Executive Council, and then became its vice president.

33. Curwen, *Journal*, Sunday, May 7, 1775, 28.

34. James Grant Wilson, *Memorial of Andrew Kirkpatrick and His Wife Jane Bayard* (New York: Printed privately for Mrs. and Dr. How, 1870), 58.

35. Ibid., 62, 66, 62.

36. Ibid., 62–63.

37. Foster, *Bryan*, 88; see also chapter 9 (June 1777).

38. Bodle, "Jane Bartram's 'Application,'" 185–220. The more we look, however, the more we find women in the "interstices" of public political life in Revolutionary America. Linda Kerber used this apt word when she urged historians to rethink the narrative of the Revolution in such a way as to reveal the "women who live in the interstices of institutions that we once understood as wholly segregated by gender." Kerber, *Toward an Intellectual History of Women: Essays by Linda K. Kerber* (Chapel Hill: University of North Carolina Press, 1997), 98. In general, women in political families, both patriot and Tory, like men in these families, were interested in public political affairs and casually incorporated into their lives ways and means to gather, discuss, and even argue about and share news. For example, see Christopher Marshall, "Remembrances," between June 18 and 24, 1776, Historical Society of Pennsylvania. In addition to face-to-face social meetings, patriot Sarah Alexander mailed this kind of information to Loyalist family members in British-occupied New York. Tory Rebecca Shoemaker in British-occupied New York City did the same with her daughters in Philadelphia. Loyalist men, in some circumstances, relied on "female family, friends, acquaintances, 'Negros Wenches', [and] tenant wives" for their information. See Judith Van Buskirk, *Generous Enemies: Patriots and Loyalists in Revolutionary New York* (Philadelphia: University of Pennsylvania Press, 2002), 54, 62.

39. Elizabeth's father, a prominent Philadelphia Presbyterian, had been active in the Arch Street Church for years, and his family, including Elizabeth, had long identified with both the congregation and its minister. At least one of Elizabeth's brothers belonged to the Arch Street congregation. From 1768 to 1772, Elizabeth and George were officially affiliated with this church, but in 1772 George reestablished his own original links with the First Presbyterian Church on Market Street and assumed lay leadership responsibilities there. The evidence, however, suggests that he and

Elizabeth and their children continued to worship at the Arch Street Church. Both Elizabeth and George were particularly attracted to the Reverend James Sproat. Elizabeth's father had championed Sproat's cause, and a dispute over Sproat had precipitated George's abrupt departure from the First Presbyterian Church in 1768. Moreover, after he reestablished his own link with the First Presbyterian Church, the family continued to pay pew rents to both congregations. When George died in 1791, Elizabeth buried him in the Arch Street cemetery, and when she died in 1798 she was also buried there.

40. Holton, *Abigail Adams*, 101.

41. Esther DeBerdt Reed to Dennis DeBerdt, September 16, 1779, in Reed, *Esther*, 297.

42. Foster, *George Bryan*. For more on the emergence of the Constitutionalist Party in 1778–79 as a persistent voting bloc in the legislature with a well-defined policy agenda and a reliable electoral constituency, see Owen S. Ireland and Wayne L. Bockelman, "The Internal Revolution in Pennsylvania: An Ethnic-Religious Interpretation," *Pennsylvania History* 41 (April 1974): 124–59; Owen S. Ireland, "The Ethnic-Religious Dimension of Pennsylvania Politics, 1778–1779," *William and Mary Quarterly* 30 (July 1973): 423–48; Ireland, "The Crux of Politics: Religion and Party in Pennsylvania, 1778–1788," *William and Mary Quarterly* 42 (October 1985): 453–75; and Ireland, "The Ratification of the Federal Constitution in Pennsylvania" (PhD dissertation, University of Pittsburgh, 1966).

43. For more on the dispute involving Fergusson, Smith, and Reed, see Anne M. Ousterhout, *The Most Learned Woman in America: A Life of Elizabeth Graeme Fergusson* (University Park: Penn State University Press, 2004).

44. See *Pennsylvania Gazette*, March 24, 1779, for the Republican announcement and the *Pennsylvania Packet*, April 1, 1779, for that of the Constitutionalists.

45. George Washington to Joseph Reed, October 2, 1779, in Roche, *Reed*, 157.

46. Alan Tully, *Forming American Politics: Ideals, Interests, and Institutions in Colonial New York and Pennsylvania* (Baltimore: Johns Hopkins University Press, 1994).

47. See Steven Rosswurm, *Arms, Country, and Class: The Philadelphia Militia and the "Lower Sort" During the American Revolution, 1775–1783* (New Brunswick: Rutgers University Press, 1987), passim, for an extended exposition of the grievances of the middling and lower sorts in Philadelphia against those they saw as men with pretentions to superiority who avoided the costs of the war while imposing those costs on others. See also Michael McDonnell, *The Politics of War: Race, Class, and Conflict in Revolutionary Virginia* (Chapel Hill, N.C.: Omohundro Institute of Early American History and Culture, 2007), passim, for similar resentments on these issues in Virginia.

48. For a brief but useful depiction of this British system in the early twentieth century, see Barbara Tuchman, *The Proud Tower* (New York: Macmillan, 1962), 3–63, and especially 3–6, 13–16, 26–27. For a fuller treatment of the fundamental differences between America and the mother country in the late eighteenth century, see Gordon Wood, *The Radicalism of the American Revolution* (New York: Vintage Books, 1993).

49. Ireland, "The Crux of Politics," 453–75. Arendt's evidence supports the contention that in Philadelphia both parties drew their leadership from approximately the same social strata. Emily J. Arendt, "'Ladies Going About for Money': Female Voluntary Associations and Civic Consciousness in the American Revolution," *Journal of the Early Republic* 34 (Summer 2014): 157–86.

50. "Mr. Clymer, who is full in opposition here [i.e., in Pennsylvania] and of the party with the commercial gentlemen of Congress." Joseph Reed to George Washington, Philadelphia, no date, in Reed, *Reed*, 2:80.

51. See Rosswurm, *Arms, Country, and Class*, 172–81, for a detailed exposition of the grievances of the militia and of Joseph's sympathy for expressing these grievances.

52. Ireland, "The Crux of Politics," 453–75.

53. Esther DeBerdt Reed to Joseph Reed, London, August 22, 1780, in Reed, *Reed*, 2:268.

54. Roche, *Reed*, 171; Wilson, *Memorials of Andrew Kirkpatrick*, 62–63.

55. See Zagarri, *Backlash*, 133.

56. Cynthia Kierner argues that women of Virginia participated in a range of hospitality and social rituals that provided them with vehicles for access to the public world beyond the household and served as the first step in the pre-Revolutionary politicization of elite women. Cynthia Kierner, "Hospitality, Sociability, and Gender in the Southern Colonies," *Journal of Southern History* 62 (August 1996): 449–80. See also Susan Branson, *Those Fiery Frenchified Dames: Women and Political Culture in Early National Philadelphia* (Philadelphia: University of Pennsylvania Press, 2001); Rosemarie

Zagarri, "Female Politicians," in *Revolutionary Backlash*; and Zagarri, "Women and Party Conflict in the Early Republic," in *Beyond the Founders*, ed. Jeffrey Pasley et al. (Chapel Hill: University of North Carolina Press, 2004). This female hospitality as a vehicle for political interaction and advancement seems to have been less conspicuous in New England. See Zagarri, *A Woman's Dilemma*, and Catherine Allgor, *Dolley Madison: The Problem of National Unity* (Boulder, Colo.: Westview Press, 2013).

Chapter 11

1. General William Irving to Joseph Reed, camp near Morristown, N.J., May 26, 1780, in Reed, *Reed*, 2:201-2.

2. George Washington to Joseph Reed, Morristown, N.J., May 28, 1780, in Reed, *Reed*, 2:202-6.

3. Joseph Reed to George Bryan, Philadelphia, May 18, 1780, in Reed, *Reed*, 2:199; Joseph Reed to George Washington, Philadelphia, June 5, 1780, in Reed, *Reed*, 2:209-13.

4. Bodle, "Bartram"; Van Buskirk, *Generous Enemies*, especially 54, 62. For more on women and politics in this era, see the bibliographical essay.

5. Reed, *Reed*, 2:232, gives May 26, 1780, as the baby's birthdate, but the records of the Second Presbyterian Church in Philadelphia give the date as May 22, 1780. See *Records of the Second Presbyterian Church*, "Part One: Baptisms," Historical Society of Pennsylvania.

6. George Washington to Joseph Reed, June 4, 1780, in Reed, *Reed*, 2:222.

7. Roche, *Reed*, 172, 258 n. 30.

8. Joseph Reed to George Bryan, Philadelphia, May 18, 1780, in Reed, *Reed*, 2:199-201.

9. For a well-balanced study of that incident, see John K. Alexander, "The Fort Wilson Incident of 1779: A Case Study of the Revolutionary Crowd," *William and Mary Quarterly* 31 (October 1974): 589-612.

10. Joseph Reed to George Washington, Philadelphia, June 4, 1780, in Reed, *Reed*, 2:201.

11. Mary Beth Norton, *Liberty's Daughters: The Revolutionary Experience of American Women, 1750-1800* (Boston: Little, Brown, 1980), 178. For more on the history of voluntary associations in Philadelphia, see Jessica Choppin Roney, "'Effective Men' and Early Voluntary Associations in Philadelphia, 1725-1775," in *New Men: Manliness in Early America*, ed. Thomas A. Foster (New York: New York University Press, 2011), 155-71.

12. Arendt, "'Ladies Going About for Money,'" 157-86.

13. For the broadside, see *The Sentiments of an American Woman* (Philadelphia: John Dunlop, 1780); Clifford K. Shipton, ed., *Early American Imprints, 1639-1800* (Worcester, Mass.: Readex Microprint Corporation and American Antiquarian Society, 1953-63); and Charles Evans, *American Bibliography: A Chronological Dictionary of All Books, Pamphlets and Periodical Publications Printed in the United States of America from the Genesis of Printing in 1639 Down to and Including the Year [1800]*, 13 vols. (Chicago: The Blakely Press for the Author, 1943-55). Also printed in *Pennsylvania Magazine of History and Biography* 18 (1894): 361-66. Mary Beth Norton, "The Philadelphia Ladies Association," *American Heritage* 31 (Summer 1980): 102-7; Norton, *Liberty's Daughters*, 178-86; Kathryn Sklar and Gregory Duffy, eds., "How Did the Ladies Association of Philadelphia Shape New Forms of Women's Activism During the American Revolution, 1780-1781?," in *Women and Social Movements in the United States, 1600-2000* (Alexandria, Va.: Alexander Street Press, 2001), available by subscription at http://womhist.alexanderstreet.com. See Reed, *Reed*, 2:216, for a description of these activities.

14. "A Letter from a Lady in Philadelphia to her Friend in this Place, 20 June 1780," *Maryland Gazette*, July 21, 1780. Document 12 in Sklar and Duffy, eds., "Ladies Association of Philadelphia."

15. Joseph Reed to George Washington, Philadelphia, June 20, 1780, in Reed, *Esther*, 315-16.

16. Guineas: English coins containing approximately a quarter of an ounce of gold. Esther DeBerdt Reed to George Washington, Philadelphia, July 4, 1780, in Reed, *Esther*, 318-19.

17. For an extensive treatment of the results of Esther's efforts beyond Pennsylvania, see Arendt, "'Ladies Going About for Money,'" 157-86. George Washington to Mary Dagworthy, headquarters, August 16, 1780, in Fitzgerald, *Writings*, 19:333-34.

18. For Franklin and voluntary associations, see Edmund S. Morgan, *Benjamin Franklin* (New Haven: Yale University Press, 2002), 47-70.

19. For a sample of the literature on women and voluntary associations from the 1790s through the early twentieth century, see the bibliographical essay.

20. Arendt has identified twenty of the thirty-six canvassers as coming from partisan families: eleven Republicans and nine Constitutionalists. Arendt, "'Ladies Going About for Money,'" 157–86.

21. Ibid., 159.

22. Anna Rawle to Mrs. Rebecca Shoemaker, Philadelphia, July 29, 1780, in "Letters and Diaries of Rebecca Shoemaker," Rebecca Shoemaker Papers, Historical Society of Pennsylvania.

23. Anna Rawle to Mrs. Rebecca Shoemaker, Philadelphia, September 22, 1780, in Rebecca Shoemaker Papers, Historical Society of Pennsylvania. For more on her cruel comment on Esther at the time of Esther's death, see following discussion in text.

24. Arendt, "'Ladies Going About for Money,'" 165.

25. Benjamin Rush to John Adams, Philadelphia, July 13, 1780, in Benjamin Rush, *Letters*, ed. L. H. Butterfield (Princeton: Princeton University Press for the American Philosophical Society, 1951), 1:253.

26. Esther DeBerdt to Joseph Reed, London, November 19, 1764, in Reed Papers, N-YHS.

27. Reed, *Reed*, 2:260. Congressman John Walker, writing to Thomas Jefferson on June 13, 1780, attributes the entire plan to De Marbois. John Walker to Thomas Jefferson, Philadelphia, June 13, 1780, in Smith, *Letters*, 15:316.

28. Charles Royster, *A Revolutionary People at War* (New York: W. W. Norton, 1979), 295–96.

29. For examples of how women used voluntary associations from the 1790s until well into the twentieth century, see the bibliographical essay.

30. Abigail Adams to John Adams, September and October 1775, in Adams, ed., *Familiar Letters*, 94–106.

31. Barbara Clark Smith, "Food Rioters and the American Revolution," *William and Mary Quarterly* 51 (January 1994): 2–18. Sheila Skemp notes that Judith Sargent Murray "pointed out that women were physically and emotionally capable of donning a suit of armor and slaying the enemy in a righteous cause. 'Courage is by no means exclusively a masculine virtue.'" Sheila Skemp, *Judith Sargent Murray: A Brief Biography with Documents* (Boston: Bedford Books, 1998), 39. Alfred Young, *Masquerade: The Life and Times of Deborah Sampson, a Continental Soldier* (New York: Knopf, 2004).

32. L. H. Butterfield, ed., *Adams Family Correspondence* (Cambridge, Mass.: Harvard University Press, 1973), 3:377–78.

33. Sarah Jay to John Jay, quoted in Norton, "The Philadelphia Ladies Association," 107.

34. "A Letter from a Lady in Philadelphia to her Friend in this Place, 6 July 1780," *Maryland Gazette*, July 28, 1780. Document 18 in Sklar and Duffy, eds., "Ladies Association of Philadelphia."

35. Robert L. Brunhouse, *The Counter-Revolution in Pennsylvania, 1776–1790* (Harrisburg: Pennsylvania Historical Commission, 1942), 86.

36. Thomas Paine to Joseph Reed, Philadelphia, June 4, 1780, in Reed, *Reed*, 2:218–20.

37. Ibid., 219.

38. Robert R. Livingston claimed, in a letter dated June 16, that he had first suggested the idea to a few Philadelphia merchants "at table" "a few days" earlier and that they had responded favorably, creating a committee and opening negotiations with Congress. In time, Congress agreed to "indemnify the subscribers" and to repay them in six months at 6 percent interest. Robert R. Livingston to Philip Schuyler, Philadelphia, June 16, 1780; Ezekiel Cornell to the governor of Rhode Island, Philadelphia, June 27, 1780, in Edmund C. Burnett, ed., *Letters of Members of the Continental Congress* (Washington, D.C.: Carnegie Institution of Washington, 1931), 5:220, 239–40. For an explanation of how the bank worked, see George Washington to Esther DeBerdt Reed, July 20, 1780, in Fitzpatrick, ed., *Writings*, 19:216.

39. Joseph Reed to George Washington, Philadelphia, June 20, 1789, in Reed, *Reed*, 2:214; Joseph Reed to George Washington, Philadelphia, June 22, 1780, in Reed, *Reed*, 2:215–16; Brunhouse, *Counter-Revolution*, 86–87; Bray Hammond, *Banks and Politics in America from the Revolution to the Civil War* (Princeton: Princeton University Press, 1957), describes these contributions as loans or pledges that Congress promised to guarantee against loss, and that by 1784 the loans had been repaid and the bank liquidated.

40. William B. Reed states, "The fund . . . subscribed by the merchants and others for the creation of a bank amounted to . . . about four hundred specie dollars more than was contributed for mere charity by the ladies of the city." Reed, *Esther*, 317. For a different calculation of

the total amount of the money raised by Esther and the merchants, see Hammond, who quotes Robert Morris as describing the merchants' contributions as a "subscription of continental money" and therefore approximately equal to the amount raised by the Ladies. Hammond, *Banks and Politics*, 43–45.

41. "[T]hat bubble [the bank] is now sinking to nothing." Joseph Reed to Nathanael Greene, Bloomsbury, September 2, 1780, in Reed, *Esther*, 330.

42. For the response of a young Quaker woman to these female patriot canvassers, see Anna Rawle to her mother, Philadelphia, June 30, 1780, in "Letters and Diaries of Rebecca Shoemaker," transcript, in Rebecca Shoemaker Papers, 1780–1786, vol. 4, Historical Society of Pennsylvania.

43. "A Letter from a Lady in Philadelphia to her Friend in this Place," Philadelphia, June 20, 1780, in *Maryland Gazette*, July 21, 1780. Document 12 in Sklar and Duffy, eds., "Ladies Association of Philadelphia." This apparent circular letter was one of two such letters appearing in the *Maryland Gazette*. The second was dated "Philadelphia, July 7" and appeared in the *Gazette* on July 28. Although the author remains unknown, the letters themselves use much of the same language as Esther used in her letter to the wives of the chief executives of the states on June 30. They also make direct and indirect reference to "[a]n American Woman." All three letters thus seem to have emerged from the same source—probably Esther, directly or indirectly. The list of canvassers included Mrs. Robert Morris, wife of the most conspicuous and powerful organizer of the Republican society and of the new bank; Mrs. Tench Francis, sister of Mrs. Samuel Powel and daughter of Thomas Willing, head of the house of Willing and Morris; and Mrs. Julia Rush, daughter of Richard Stockton, Joseph's old mentor and erstwhile competitor in New Jersey and wife of Dr. Benjamin Rush, one of Joseph's most caustic critics. See Reed, *Reed*, 2:429–49 for a listing.

44. Brunhouse, *Counter-Revolution*, 86–87.

45. Anna Rawle to Mrs. Shoemaker (her mother), Philadelphia, June 30, 1789, in "Letters and Diaries of Rebecca Shoemaker," Rebecca Shoemaker Papers, Historical Society of Pennsylvania. See also William Brook Rawle, "Laurel Hill and Some Colonial Dames Who Once Lived There," *Pennsylvania Magazine of History and Biography* 35 (1911): 398, and Norton, *Liberty's Daughters*, 180–81.

46. Anna Rawle to Mrs. Shoemaker, September 20, 1780, in "Letters and Diaries of Rebecca Shoemaker," Rebecca Shoemaker Papers, Historical Society of Pennsylvania.

47. See, for example, Abigail Adams to John Thaxter, Massachusetts, July 21, 1780, in Butterfield, ed., *Adams Family Correspondence*, 3:377, and Benjamin Rush to John Adams, Philadelphia, July 13, 1780, in Butterfield, ed., *Rush Letters*, 1:253.

48. But Esther's letters to the chief executives were not the only, or possibly not the principal, popular source of information on her and her campaign. Abigail Adams, writing in Massachusetts, admonished her correspondent to "read the Pennsylvania papers." Abigail Adams to John Thaxter, Massachusetts, July 21, 1780, in Butterfield, ed., *Adams Family Correspondence*, 3:377. For a suggestion about a future national political role for the Reeds, see General Greene to Joseph Reed, Ramapaugh, N.J., June 29, 1780, in Reed, *Reed*, 2:217. Martha Washington was no mean competitor, as she built and protected her husband's image and influence with the political skills she learned as mistress of a Virginia plantation. For an exploration of the role of southern women, especially plantation wives, in what might be called social-political entertaining, see Kierner, "Hospitality, Sociability, and Gender," 449–80.

Chapter 12

1. Esther DeBerdt Reed to "Madam," June 30, 1780, in Reed Papers, N-YHS.

2. Joseph Reed to George Washington, Philadelphia, June 20, 1780, in Reed, *Esther*, 316.

3. *Pennsylvania Gazette*, June 21, 1780. Quoted in Norton, *Liberty's Daughters*, 179.

4. George Washington to Esther DeBerdt Reed, Whippany, near Morristown, N.J., June 25, 1780, in Fitzpatrick, ed., *The Writings of Washington*, 19:70–71.

5. Esther DeBerdt Reed to "Madam," June 30, 1780, in Reed Papers, N-YHS.

6. Esther DeBerdt Reed to George Washington, July 4, 1780, in Reed, *Esther*, 318.

7. George Washington to Esther DeBerdt Reed, July 4, 1780, in Fitzpatrick, *Writings*, 19:167.

8. Joseph Reed to George Washington, Philadelphia, July 15, 1780, in Reed, *Reed*, 2:229–30.

9. George Washington to Esther DeBerdt Reed, headquarters, July 20, 1780, in Fitzpatrick, *Writings*, 19:216.

10. Esther DeBerdt Reed to George Washington, Banks of the Schuylkill, July 31, 1780, in Reed, *Esther*, 322–24. Although Washington opposed providing hard money to the troops, others disagreed. On July 8, 1780, Chevalier de Luzerne wrote to Lafayette that he was frustrated by his inability to find a way to give the soldiers in the Continental Army "one solid dollar a month." Chevalier de Luzerne to Lafayette, July 8, 1780, in Stanley J. Idzerda, ed., *Lafayette in the Age of the Revolution: Selected Letters and Papers* (Ithaca: Cornell University Press, 1980), 67 n. 6.

11. George Washington to Esther DeBerdt Reed, headquarters, Tappan, August 8, 1780, in Fitzpatrick, *Writings*, 19:350–51.

12. Esther DeBerdt Reed to George Washington, Banks of the Schuylkill, August 16, 1780, in Fitzpatrick, *Writings*, 19:351 n.

13. Joseph Reed to Esther DeBerdt Reed, August 26, 1780, in Reed, *Reed*, 2:246.

14. *Complaisant*, as Esther used the word, meant agreeable, accommodating, and willing to please others and to accept what they do or say without protest. See her earlier use of the term in Esther DeBerdt to Joseph Reed, London, 1764, in Reed Papers, N-YHS.

15. "[T]hat bubble [the bank] is now sinking to nothing." Joseph Reed to Nathanael Greene, Bloomsbury, N.J., September 2, 1780, in Reed, *Esther*, 330.

16. Joseph Reed to Dennis DeBerdt, July 9, 1779, in Roche, *Reed*, 148 n. 12.

17. Esther DeBerdt Reed to George Washington, July 4, 1780, establishes that Esther was still in the city at this time. Esther DeBerdt Reed to Joseph Reed, August 22, 1780, in Reed, *Esther*, 318, 325, 308, 311.

18. Esther DeBerdt Reed to Joseph Reed, August 22, 1780, in Reed, *Esther*, 318, 322, 311.

19. Roche, *Reed*, 248–49 n. 17. See instructions to the Carlisle Commission in Reed, *Reed*, 1:430–36. Joseph Reed to Dennis DeBerdt, July 9, 1779, in Roche, *Reed*, 148 n. 12.

20. Roche, *Reed*, 177–79. Esther DeBerdt Reed to Joseph Reed, August 22, 1780, in Reed, *Esther*, 310.

21. Dysentery often accompanied the army and threatened the civilian population. Late in the summer of 1775, for example, a similar epidemic had struck Braintree, Massachusetts, the home of Abigail Adams. It devastated her family and pushed her to the edge of despair. On August 11, 1775, John Adams's brother, returning from camp, died of dysentery. That began a scourge that ravaged Abigail's community until mid-October. Eighteen were buried in two weeks and eight more the third. Abigail and her three-year-old son came down with the affliction, and her mother came to help until she too fell ill and died. "How can I tell you (o my bursting Heart) that my dear Mother had left me this day about 5 o'clock.... Blessed Spirit," she cried out, "where art thou?" Abigail Adams to John Adams, August 11, October 21, September 10, September 16, and October 1, 1775, in Adams, ed., *Familiar Letters*, 93, 111, 96, 96, 102.

22. James Madison to Edmund Pendleton, Philadelphia, September 19, 1780; James Lovell to Samuel Holton, both in Smith, *Letters*, 16:96, 94. Oscar Reiss, *Medicine and the American Revolution: How Diseased and Their Treatments Affected the Colonial Army* (Jefferson, N.C.: McFarland and Company, 1998), 14, 25, 154, 178, 181.

23. Reed, *Esther*, 331.

24. Ibid.; Roche, *Reed*, 179; Wilson, *Memorials*, 67.

25. Reed, *Esther*, 331, Joseph Reed to Dennis DeBerdt, November 28, 1781, in Reed, *Esther*, 332.

26. Roche, *Reed*, 180–81, 185–87, 188–98.

27. Joseph Reed to Nathanael Greene, November 1, 1781, in Roche, *Reed*, 193, 198, 195, 191, 201–13, 213–14, 218–19.

28. Roche, *Reed*, 269 n. 112.

Coda

1. In many ways, the Reed family success in the "creole" world of Philadelphia (the commercial and communications center of British North America), Joseph's ambition to join the "metropolitan" world of London in the 1760s, his and Esther's alienation from that world in the 1770s, and their rapid rise to political prominence in the new "imagined community" of the American republic approximate Anderson's description of a "creole," professional, mercantile elite sharing a language and a common descent with those in the metropolitan population but excluded from its most promising opportunities by the accident of overseas birth. See Benedict Anderson, *Imagined Communities* (London: Verso, 1991), especially 50–58.

2. Edmund Morgan, *Benjamin Franklin* (New Haven: Yale University Press, 2002)

argues that the ignorance, arrogance, and condescension of the British political nation defeated Franklin in his efforts to nourish a British empire based on the mutual respect and affection of English-speaking peoples at home and abroad, all of whom were equal. The work of Jack Greene has generally informed my thinking on the causes of the American Revolution, and the choices made by Joseph and Esther are largely consistent with my understanding of Greene's view. British policy and policymakers alienated them and drove them into resistance, rebellion, revolution, and the commitment to the creation of a new people. For a fuller elaboration of this way of seeing the American Revolution, see Jack Greene, "The American Revolution," *American Historical Review* 105 (February 2000): 93–102; Jack Greene, "Interpretative Frameworks: The Quest for Intellectual Order in Early American History," *William and Mary Quarterly* 48 (October 1991): 515–30; Jack Greene, *Peripheries and Center: Constitutional Development in the Extended Polities of the British Empire and the United States, 1607–1788* (Athens: University of Georgia Press, 1986); and Jack Greene, *Pursuits of Happiness: The Social Development of Early Modern British Colonies and the Formation of American Culture* (Chapel Hill: University of North Carolina Press, 1988).

3. For a sampling of the literature on women and voluntary associations from the 1790s through the twentieth century, see the bibliographical essay.

4. Cleary, *Elizabeth Murray*, 181–202.

5. James Bowdoin to Samuel Adams, Boston, July 31, 1780, in *Proceedings of the Massachusetts Historical Society*, 1st ser. 12 (1871–73): 229; Smith, "Food Rioters," 3–38, quotation on 29.

6. For example, see Joseph's strenuous and persistent attention to the needs of his extended family and to Esther's brother and her mother once he and Esther had married. Consistent with this view, Ellen Hartigan-O'Connor makes the point that for economic analysis in late eighteenth-century America, the family, not the individual, was the smallest unit of economic action. Hartigan-O'Connor, "Gender's Value in the History of Capitalism," *Journal of the Early Republic* 36 (Winter 2016): 618.

7. Esther DeBerdt to Joseph Reed, London, July 20, 1765, in Reed Papers, N-YHS.

Bibliographical Essay

Principal Sources

This biography of Esther DeBerdt Reed relies first and foremost on her letters and those of her husband, Joseph. Both of these are located in the BV Reed, Joseph—MS 2388, New-York Historical Society. The library has made most of this collection available on microfilm. Esther's grandson included excerpts from many of Esther's letters in his biography, and in some cases the letters he had in his possession are not available in the N-YHS collection. See William B. Reed, *The Life of Esther DeBerdt, Afterwards Esther Reed of Pennsylvania* (Philadelphia: Printed privately by C. Sherman, printer, 1854), 15–20. W. B. Reed's two-volume collection of Joseph Reed's papers is invaluable but contains few of Esther's letters: *Life and Correspondence of Joseph Reed* (Philadelphia: Lindsay and Blakiston, 1847). A collection of the letters of Esther's father is also useful: Dennys DeBerdt, *Letters of Dennys DeBerdt, 1757-1770*, ed. Albert Matthews, reprinted from *The Publications of the Colonial Society of Massachusetts* 13 (Cambridge, Mass.: John Wilson and Son, University Press, 1911), 294–95, 299–300. The standard work on Joseph—John F. Roche, *Joseph Reed: A Moderate in the American Revolution* (New York: Columbia University Press, 1957)—is excellent on Joseph but says relatively little about Esther. For select bibliographies of secondary sources on courtship and marriage, women and business, women in public and political life, and women and voluntary associations, see the following sections.

Courtship and Marriage

Historian Nancy Cott describes marriage in this era as consensual and contractual, involving reciprocal rights and responsibilities, companionate, as least in ideal. See Cott, *Public Vows: A History of Marriage and the Nation* (Cambridge, Mass.: Harvard University Press, 2000), chapter 1 and especially 10, 11, 15, 19, and 16. Esther usually describes herself and Joseph as friends. Jan Lewis, "The Republican Wife: Virtue and Seduction in the Early Republic," *William and Mary Quarterly* 44 (1987): 689–721. Judith Ridner agrees that both partners in a marriage sought affection and companionship, but she cautions that "each relationship, like all relationships, was unique," and she provides us with a vivid example of a man systematically and persistently abused by his wife. Ridner, "'What an Addition to My Happiness Has My Wife and Children Been to Me'?: Three Eighteenth Century Pennsylvania Husbands 'Talk' to and About Their Wives," *Pennsylvania History* 70 (Autumn 2003): 305–30, quotation on 310. John R. Gillis argues that this conjugal model of marriage has "always been more an illusive dream than an attainable reality": Gillis, *For Better, for Worse: British Marriages, 1600 to the Present* (New York: Oxford University Press, 1985), 5. Anya Jabour makes the point that even in a marriage uniting two individuals committed to the principle of equality, the disparity of resources privileged the husband and subordinated the wife: Jabour, *Marriage in the Early Republic: Elizabeth and William Wirt and Companionate Marriage* (Baltimore: Johns Hopkins University Press, 1998). Andrew Cayton concurs, reminding us that "companionate relationships formed in defiance of patriarchy almost always founder over time on the disparity of power": Cayton, "The 'Rights of Women' and the Problem of Power," *Journal of the Early Republic* 35 (Summer 2015): 295–301, quotation on 300.

Women and Business

Wayne Bodle demonstrated that although the law generally denied a married woman the right to act on her own behalf to buy, own, or sell property; to enter into legally binding contracts; or to sue or be sued, Jane Bartram, a contemporary of Esther's in Philadelphia, managed to do most of these things. See Bodle, "Jane Bartram's 'Application': Her Struggle for Survival, Stability, and Self-Determination in Revolutionary Pennsylvania," *Pennsylvania Magazine of History and Biography* 115 (April 1991): 185–220. Ellen Hartigan-O'Connor agrees with Bodle. Focusing on women in business, she argues that they evaded coverture and were ubiquitous in commercial transactions: Hartigan-O'Connor, *The Ties That Buy: Women and Commerce in Revolutionary America* (Philadelphia: University of Pennsylvania Press, 2009). Susan Branson illustrated the operation of a family economy of mutual interdependence in "Women and the Family Economy in the Early Republic: The Case of Elizabeth Meredith," *Journal of the Early Republic* 16 (Spring 1996): 47–71. See also Marla Miller, *The Needle's Eye: Women and Work in the Age of Revolution* (Amherst: University of Massachusetts Press, 2006); Patricia Cleary, *Elizabeth Murray: A Woman's Pursuit of Independence in Eighteenth-Century America* (Amherst: University of Massachusetts Press, 2000); Karin Wulf, *Not All Wives: Women of Colonial Philadelphia* (Ithaca: Cornell University Press, 2000); and Lisa Wilson, "A Marriage 'Well-Ordered': Love, Power, and Partnership in Colonial New England," in *A Shared Experience: Men, Women, and the History of Gender*, ed. Laura McCall (New York: New York University Press, 1998), 78–87. For a different view, see Deborah Rosen, "Women and Property Across Colonial America: A Comparison of Legal Systems in New Mexico and New York," *William and Mary Quarterly* 55 (March 2003): 354–81. Rosen argues that coverture defined women as subordinate, dependent, domestic, and private, and thereby limited in their economic opportunities, frustrating their accumulation of property, enforcing their dependence, reducing their stature, and compromising their autonomy. Kate Haulman emphasizes both the power of the law and male "control of economic resources, social capital, and political and legal power": Haulman, "The Return of Patriarchy," *Reviews in American History* 35 (2007): 483–89. However, an ever-increasing number of studies find significant differences between the legal and social strictures imposed on all women and the actual lives of particular women. Lisa Wilson suggests that historians who focus on the law see subordination, while those who focus on individual women more often see agency: Wilson, review of *Within Her Power: Propertied Women in Colonial Virginia* by Linda L. Sturtz, *American Historical Review* 108 (October 2003): 1139–40.

Women in Public and Political Life

For extended discussion of the extraordinary range of female political participation in late eighteenth-century America, from conscientious rejection to the emergence of what historian Rosemarie Zagarri calls "female politicians," see the following works: Laurel Thatcher Ulrich, *A Midwife's Tale: The Life of Martha Ballard, Based on Her Diary* (New York: Knopf, 1990), 76, 32; Ulrich, "'Daughters of Liberty'. Religious Women in Revolutionary New England," in *Women in the Age of the American Revolution*, ed. Ronald Hoffman and Peter Albert (Charlottesville: University Press of Virginia for the United States Capitol Historical Society, 1989), 211–43; Cleary, *Elizabeth Murray*; Wulf, *Not All Wives*; Joy Buel and Richard Buel, *The Way of Duty: A Woman and Her Family in Revolutionary America* (New York: W. W. Norton, 1985); Anne M. Ousterhout, *The Most Learned Woman in America: A Life of Elizabeth Graeme Fergusson* (University Park: Penn State University Press, 2004); Cynthia A. Kierner, "Patrician Womanhood in the Early Republic: The 'Reminiscences' of Janet Livingston Montgomery," *New York History* 73, no. 4 (1992): 389–407; Kierner, "Hospitality, Sociability, and Gender in the Southern Colonies," *Journal of Southern History* 62 (August 1996): 449–80; Alfred Young, "The Women of Boston: Persons of Consequence in the Making of the American Revolution, 1765–1776," in *Women in the Age of the Democratic Revolution*, ed. Harriet B. Applewhite (Ann Arbor: University of Michigan Press, 1990), 181–226; Barbara Smith, "Food Rioters and the American Revolution," *William and Mary Quarterly* 51 (January 1994): 3–38; Rosemarie Zagarri, *A Woman's Dilemma: Mercy Otis Warren and the American Revolution* (Wheeling, Ill.: Harlan Davidson, 1995), xvii, 162–65, and 90–92; Zagarri, *Revolutionary Backlash: Women and Politics in the Early American Republic* (Philadelphia: University of Pennsylvania Press, 2007), 5.

Women and Voluntary Associations

For examples of women using voluntary associations from the 1790s well into the twentieth century, see Margaret Morris Haviland, "'Beyond Women's Sphere': Young Quaker Women and the Veil of Charity in Philadelphia, 1790–1810," *William and Mary Quarterly* 51 (July 1994): 419–46; Anne Boylan, *The Origins of Women's Activism: New York and Boston, 1797–1840* (Chapel Hill: University of North Carolina Press, 2002); Carroll Smith Rosenberg, "Beauty, the Beast, and the Militant Woman: A Case Study in Sex Roles and Social Stress in Jacksonian America," *American Quarterly* 23 (October 1971): 562–84; and Alison M. Parker, *Purifying America: Women, Cultural Reform, and Pro-censorship Activism, 1873–1933* (Urbana: University of Illinois Press, 1997).

Index

Adams, Abigail
   business affairs, 108
   description of George Washington, 127
   epidemic of dysentery in home of, 239n21
   John Adams and, 219n48
   patriotism of, 192
   political views of, 228n3
   social and political gatherings, 170
Adams, John, 113, 119
Adams, Samuel, 211
Alexander, Sarah, 234n38
Alexander, William, 69
Allen, Isaac, 13
American colonies
   birth control in, 148, 232n39
   British constitution as model for, 171
   courtship for young women, 216n30
   economic crisis, 26–27
   family economies, 72, 240n6
   political developments, 120
   relations with Britain, 66–67, 116, 129–30
   slavery, 227n51
   voluntary associations, 183
   women in public politics, 179–80, 234n38
   women's commercial activities, 108
American war of independence
   alliance with France, 178
   Battle of Brandywine, 153
   Battle of Long Island, 143–44, 145
   Battle of Monmouth, 163
   Battles of Trenton and Princeton, 150
   bloodshed at Lexington and Concord, 120
   British capture of Charleston, 178
   British occupation of New Jersey, 149–50
   British occupation of Philadelphia, 138, 153
   causes of, 3, 240n2
   civilian population during, 122–23, 154, 188
   Esther's view of, 137–38
   evacuation of Boston, 135
   fundraising campaigns, 181–82
   Joseph's role in, 121–22, 125, 139, 140, 141, 148, 151–52
   Joseph's view of, 136–37
   military preparations, 126–27, 130
   obstacles to reconciliation, 130
   preparations for battle for New York, 143
   separation of Esther and Joseph, 137, 141–42, 145
   threat to New Jersey, 149
   Virginia planters, 127, 128
   Washington as commander in chief, 121
   women during, 141–42, 152, 237n31
   See also Continental army; First Continental Congress
Arch Street Presbyterian Church in Philadelphia, 100, 124, 170
Arnold, Benedict, 162

Bache, Sarah, 162
Ballard, Martha, 233n68
Bank, Merchants', 193–196
Barbé-Marbois, François, 187
Bath, city of
   social life in, 44–45
Bayard, Jane, 177
Bayard, John, 167, 169, 170, 172, 227n51, 234n32
Bayard, Margaret Hodge, 167, 168
Bernard, Francis, 74

INDEX

Boston
    British evacuation of, 135
    political situation in, 63
    Reed's connections in, 110–11, 119
Boston Tea Party, 118
Bowes, Francis, 73, 140
Bryan, Elizabeth, 167, 168, 169, 170, 234–35n39
Bryan, George
    political career, 167, 169, 170, 227n51, 234n32
    relations with Joseph Reed, 150, 166
    religious views, 172, 234–35n39
Burkitt, Wright, 39, 40–41, 49, 85
Burlington, NJ
    British threat to, 149
    description of, 138
    Esther's refuge in, 138–39, 142
    Pettit's home in, 75, 98–99

Carter, Robert "King," 127
Cary, Richard, 109, 111, 119
College of Philadelphia, 172, 173, 176
Common Sense (Paine), 186
Constitutionalists, 172, 173, 178, 184, 208
Continental Army
    in Brooklyn, defeat of, 135
    camp at Cambridge, 136
    conditions in, 188
    controversy over funds allocation for, 198–202
    debates over provision of hard money for, 239n10
    diseases in, 143, 239n21
    fundraising campaigns for, 198, 199
    improvement of procurement system, 164
    need for clothing, 200
    recruitment efforts, 141, 167, 169
Cooper, William, 165
courtship of Esther and Joseph
    beginning of, 5, 7, 8
    colonial affairs and, 33–34, 206–7
    Esther's affection, 15–16, 18
    financial problems, 27–28
    Joseph's departure to America, 25, 30, 32, 33, 35–36
    Joseph's view of, 13–14
    lack of privacy, 31
    marriage proposal, 12, 17, 29
    Martha DeBerdt and, 31
    meetings at social gatherings, 21–22
    Mr. and Mrs. Woods and, 32–33
    plan to settle in London, 24–25, 64
    prospect of moving to America, 23–24, 31
    secret letter exchange, 18, 19–21, 29–30, 32–34, 45
    separation period, 33–34
Cox, Dan, 27
Cox, Esther, 103, 109, 123, 139, 142, 146, 150, 152, 155, 159, 163, 226n25 (why list only this footnote when Mrs. Cox appears in a number of footnotes?
Cox, John, 14, 27, 88, 108, 123, 132, 150, 152, 164, 232n53 (why list only this footnote when John Cox appears in a number of fotnotes?)
Craven, John, 27
Currency Act (1764), 19, 206

Dartmouth, William Legge, Earl of
    as DeBerdt's patron, 54, 57, 58, 107
    Joseph's correspondence with, 126, 129–30
    political career, 63, 75, 105
Davies, Samuel, 10
Deane, Silas, 101, 119
DeBerdt, Burkitt, and Sayre See DeBerdt firm
DeBerdt, Dennis (Esther's brother)
    appointment as London agent for New Jersey, 126
    business affairs, 84, 106–8, 109, 230n45
    income of, 106–7, 126
    marriage prospects, 107
    partnership with Joseph Reed, 96, 107–9
    personality of, 87
    relations with Joseph, 12, 53, 54–55, 112
    report on British preparations for war, 136
    social status of, 229–30n34
DeBerdt, Dennys (Esther's father)
    appointment as agent in Massachusetts, 60, 82

INDEX

attitude to Esther's romance, 2, 10–11, 43, 54, 60
business affairs with Joseph Reed, 9, 58–59, 60
death of, 84, 87
family of, 7
health problems of, 64–66, 80
impact on Esther's education, 2
loss of money and influence, 86–87
love letters to his wife, 16
opinion about Joseph Reed, 10, 22, 43, 76
personality of, 6
rejection of Joseph's marriage proposal, 8, 9, 12, 13, 28–29
religious values of, 10, 124
social events in house of, 21–22
social status and reputation of, 6, 7, 11
sympathy to Stephen Sayre, 76
DeBerdt, Martha
Esther's courtship and, 22, 42–43
financial settlements after husband's death, 84–85, 88, 96
involvement in family business, 7, 49
life in America, 100, 104–5, 226n30
plans for Esther's marriage, 78
relative youth of, 42
social status of, 87–88
support of Esther, 31, 53–54, 104
widowhood of, 87, 88
DeBerdt firm
American debtors, 81, 218n30
business affairs with Reed and Pettit, 9–10, 26–27, 28, 71
collapse of, 83, 86
decision of trustees on affairs of, 94–95
financial difficulties, 49–50, 77, 81, 85, 86, 218n30
DeBerdt Reed, Esther
admirers of, 46–47, 57, 63, 64
children of, 99, 102–4, 146, 147, 155, 159, 180, 205
in collective memory, 3
comparison of England and America, 99
death of, 1, 4, 196, 204, 206
departure to America, 96–97
depression of, 104
early life of, 2

education of, 18, 217n44–45
family of, 2
feelings towards Joseph, 5, 16, 47, 49–50, 77–79, 97, 139–40, 142
financial situation after death of father, 88–89, 93
health problems of, 33, 45, 48, 64
identity of, 212
interest in commerce, 53–54, 82, 106–7
interest in politics, 57–58
involvement in family business, 2, 7, 48, 49–50, 52–53
knowledge of international trade, 40, 41, 108, 207
life experience of, 191–92
life in Bath, 41, 44–45, 46
life in London, 23–24, 57–58
marriage of, 92, 207
maturity of, 79, 81–82
mother's support of, 53–54
on occupation of lawyer and merchant, 53
outburst against Captain Macpherson, 56, 57
personality of, 2–3, 18, 99, 123, 202, 206, 210, 213–14
prospect of marriage, 78, 89–90
relations with brother Dennis, 12, 106, 107, 131, 132–33
relations with father, 11, 33
religious beliefs of, 65–66, 100, 124, 172–73
reluctance to move to America, 56
social status of, 18, 170, 175
Stephen Sayer and, 15, 17, 69, 70, 71
summer at Enfield estate, 47
views of marriage and love, 15–17
See also Esther's life in America
Dickenson, John, 109
Drinker, Elizabeth, 162

East India Company, 117, 118
Edmunds, Miss, 41
Esther's life in America
alienation from English people, 128, 130–31, 132–33, 134, 158–59

247

INDEX

Esther's life in America (*continued*)
   American Revolution and, 2, 117, 123–24, 133–34, 137, 206–7
   arrival to America, 98
   assistance in Joseph's legal affairs, 99, 109, 121
   birth of daughter Martha, 102–3
   comments on the Quakers, 120
   complaints about weather, 100
   coping with Joseph's absence, 122, 132
   desire to return to London, 103, 104, 105, 106, 114, 125–26
   difficulty of adaptation, 98, 99
   dinners for Congress delegates, 118–19, 121
   domestic duties, 208
   fears of war, 122–23
   home in Philadelphia, 96, 99–101
   Joseph's military service and, 146, 153, 154
   lifestyle, 96, 112, 113–14, 125
   membership in church congregation, 100
   nostalgia for England, 101–2
   opinion about American women, 100
   overview of, 2–4
   Philadelphia society, 99–100
   political news from Britain, 120
   refuge in Burlington, 138–39, 142
   refuge in Evesham, 149–150
   relationship with Elizabeth Bryan, 169
   relocation to Flemington, 155, 164
   reputation as public figure, 197
   shopping habits, 102, 225n19
   social connections of, 110–11, 168, 169, 170
   social status of, 111–12
   summer retreat in Laurel Hill, 203
   Virginia planters and, 128
   See also Reed family; wartime suffering
Esther's political engagement
   ability to mobilize popular majority, 174–75
   attitude to George Washington, 176–77, 211–12
   authorship of "The Sentiments," 1, 186
   comments on the Quakers, 120
   community projects, 183–84
   criticism of Benjamin Franklin, 120
   disagreement with Washington over fund spending, 198, 199–202, 211
   fund-raising campaign, 182, 183, 198, 199
   political skills, 1–2, 185–86, 212–13
   public baptism of George Washington Reed, 180–81, 184–85
   social and political gatherings, 119, 177
   support of American Revolution, 2–3, 207, 208
Ewing, John, 172

fashion
   as form of female power, 225n4
Fergusson, Elizabeth Graeme, 172
First Continental Congress, 118–19, 120–21, 126
Foxcraft, Mrs., 99
Franklin, Benjamin, 14, 105, 120, 183, 240n2
Franklin, William, 9, 14, 73, 75, 99
Furman, Moore, 13, 27, 38

Galloway, Joseph, 109, 177, 178
Great Britain
   colonial tax policies, 86
   conflict with American colonies, 66–67, 116, 130
   economic and political situation in, 19, 33–34, 67, 68
   financial crisis, 5, 71–72
   foreign policy of, 19, 23, 36
Greene, Catherine, 146
Greene, Jack, 240n2
Greene, Nathanael, 164, 204

Hancock, John, 170
Harrison, Benjamin, 127
Hartigan-O'Connor, Ellen, 240n6
Haulman, Kate, 225n4
Honyman, Robert, 126
Howe, William, 161, 162
Hunt, Abraham, 13, 27
Huntington, Samuel, 180

Ingersoll, Jared, 164–65

INDEX

Jackson (agent in Massachusetts), 60, 63
Jay, Sarah, 193

Kierner, Cynthia, 235n56
Klepp, Susan, 148
Knox, Henry, 165

Ladies Association of Philadelphia
    canvassers, 237n20, 238n43
    circular letters, 238n43
    criticism of, 185, 195–96
    fund-raising campaign, 182–83, 192–93, 195, 200, 208–9
    as nonpartisan organization, 184, 196
    political role of, 191
    public image of, 194, 195, 197
    recruitment of members, 194–95
La Luzerne, Anne-César, Chevalier de, 180, 239n10
Lee, Arthur, 101, 102, 106
Lee, Richard Henry, 127
Lewis, Jan, 216n30
Livingston, Robert R., 237n38
London
    annual cost of full-time servant in, 222n23
    business community in, 6
    cultural attractions, 23
    income for comfortable life in, 216n33
Lovell, James, 204

Macpherson (Captain), 25, 40, 55
Madison, James, 1, 203
marriage
    considerations of wealth and social status, 13–15
    in early American Republic, 216n30
    power of parents over, 8
    principles of, 93
    right of parents to choose name of child, 222n16
Marshall, Christopher, 170
Maryland Gazette, 238n43
military values, 166
Morgann, Maurice, 75, 86
Morris, Robert, Mrs., 238n43
Murray, Elizabeth, 108, 211

Murray, Judith Sargent, 192, 237n31

Nelthorpe, Charlotte, 15, 69, 221n6
New Jersey Association, 183
Noel, William, 15

Paine, Thomas, 186, 193–94
Paris, Treaty of (1763), 23
Pennsylvania
    abolition of slavery in, 227n51
    during American war of independence, 179
    financial difficulties, 179, 181
    Indian raids, 179
    political culture of, 174, 181–82, 235n49
    Test Acts (loyalty oaths), 171–72
Pennsylvania constitution (1776), 171, 176
Pennsylvania Gazette, 200
Pettit, Charles
    arrangements for Joseph's arrival, 95
    on arrogance of Englishmen, 128
    business affairs of, 36–38, 71–72, 110
    complaint about DeBerdt, 26
    correspondence with Joseph, 11, 28–29, 94
    financial situation of, 27, 36, 39, 140
    health problems, 27, 38
    home in Burlington, 75, 98–99
    invitation to Esther to live in his house, 123
    Joseph's courtship and, 29, 30
    rent of property in Philadelphia, 222n12
Pettit, Sally, 72, 74, 164
Philadelphia, PA
    Arch Street Presbyterian Church, 100, 124, 170
    average income of craftsman in, 227n52
    British collaborators in, 161–62
    British occupation of, 135, 153, 157, 162–63
    comparison to London, 99
    "creole" world of, 239n1
    description of, 101–2, 112
    escape of civilians from, 138
    Esther's view of, 101
    fund-raising campaigns, 182, 183, 185, 193, 194, 237n38–40

Philadelphia, PA (*continued*)
　loyalists, 196
　military preparations, 126–27
　outbreak of dysentery, 203–4
　political life in, 167, 170, 171
　population of, 112
　retirement of top lawyers, 109
　social life in, 99–100, 113, 168, 217n11, 228n8–9
　Southwark Theatre, 162
　wartime experience of women of, 168–69
Philadelphia Dancing Assembly, 100
Powel, Samuel, 21, 39, 46–47, 100, 113, 160

Quakers, 195, 227n51
Quincy, Josiah, 110, 111, 130

Rawle, Anna, 185, 195–96, 211
Reed, Andrew
　bankruptcy of, 49
　business affairs of, 9–10, 26, 27, 36
　illness and death of, 36, 82
　marriages of, 73
　personality of, 71
Reed, Bowes (Joseph's brother), 13, 27, 38, 72, 123, 139
Reed, Bowes, Mrs., 142
Reed, Dennis (Esther's son), 205
Reed, Esther (Hetty) (Esther's daughter), 104, 205
Reed, George Washington (Esther's son), 180–81, 205
Reed, Joseph
　ambitions of, 22
　attitude towards military profession, 148
　on British model of governance, 171
　business affairs, 52, 58–59, 64, 71, 73–74, 75, 76, 77
　children of, 102–4
　concern of Esther's frequent pregnancies, 147–48
　death of, 4, 205, 206
　demand of punishment for collaborators, 162
　departure to America, 32, 35–36
　description of Battle of Long Island, 143–44
　dispute over ship Britannia, 58
　education of, 9, 11–12, 22, 30
　Esther's death and, 204
　family responsibilities, 39, 72–73, 75, 89, 93, 240n6
　feelings towards Esther, 29, 30–31, 56, 93, 146–47
　financial situation of, 11, 28, 30–31, 74, 75, 111
　George Washington and, 166, 176, 201
　health problems of, 74
　home town of, 23, 72
　introduction into DeBerdt circle, 7, 12–13, 15
　investment in land, 110
　last will of, 143
　legal practice of, 106, 109–10, 111, 114, 128, 150–51, 164–65, 166, 169
　letters to Charles Pettit, 90–91, 91–92, 94, 95
　letters to Dennis DeBerdt, 161
　life in London, 9
　London connections, 14
　marriage of, 92–93
　military service of, 139, 144–45, 151, 152–53, 163, 203, 234n32
　opposition to the Tea Act, 116
　partnership with Dennis DeBerdt, 107–8
　perception of politics, 165
　personality of, 14, 62, 90–91, 158, 173–74
　plans to bring Esther to America, 61, 62
　plans to settle in London, 40
　political activities of, 121, 173, 181, 204–5
　proposal of marriage, 9, 12–13, 14, 17, 29
　prospect of engagement, 76
　public service of, 75, 77, 114, 119, 140, 163, 167
　reaction to Theodosia's death, 157–58
　religious beliefs of, 10, 125
　reputation of, 74–75, 91, 92
　resignation from the army, 145
　service in Pennsylvania militia, 153–54
　settlement of the DeBerdt estate, 85–87, 90, 95–96, 223n49, 227n48
　as slave owner, 227n51
　social connections of, 73, 110–11

250

support of American resistance, 117, 136–37, 160, 161
travels across America, 12, 109
trip from Philadelphia to London, 83–84
visits to Burlington, 142, 149
See also courtship of Esther and Joseph; separation of Esther and Joseph
Reed, Joseph (Esther's son), 103–4, 205
Reed, Martha (Patty), 102–3, 123, 131, 132, 159, 169, 177, 204, 205
Reed, Mary (Polly), 38, 72, 75, 80, 89, 142, 149, 204, 205, 217n45
Reed, Theodosia (Esther's daughter), 146, 147, 155, 158, 205
Reed, Theodosia Bowes (Joseph's mother), 73, 226n25
Reed and Pettit firm
 business operations, 37–38
 collapse of, 39, 71–73
 distilleries in Philadelphia, 37
 financial problems, 26, 27–28, 36–38, 218n30, 221n9
 investment in land speculation, 37
 prospects of recovery, 38–39
Reed family
 control of the West Jersey Society, 165
 income of, 142, 165
 period of prosperity, 98–99, 113–14
 period of separation, 141–42
 political gatherings and, 177, 178
 purchase of horses, 112
 social connections, 127, 136, 181
Republican Society, 181, 193, 194, 199
Rhea, John, 109
Rush, Benjamin, 185

Sampson, Deborah, 192
Sansom, Samuel, 113
Sayre, Mary, 72
Sayre, Stephen
 broken engagement, 221n6
 business affairs of, 59, 69–70
 DeBerdt's opinion about, 76
 education of, 69
 Esther's relations with, 57, 64, 69, 71
 as intermediary in Esther and Joseph's courtship, 60, 66

Joseph's relation with, 68–69, 70–71
marriage plans, 15, 69–70
opinion on Joseph's marriage proposal, 11
prediction of DeBerdt's appointment in Massachusetts, 60, 64
"Sentiments of an American Woman, The" (anonymous pamphlet)
 fund-raising campaign and, 186, 187
 on patriotism of women, 189
 political influence of, 187, 188–89, 192
 popularity of, 183, 210
 publication of, 182
 question of authorship, 186–87
 reference to female warriors, 190
 as tool for political mobilization, 209–10
 vision of role of women in American republic, 1, 189–90, 191
separation of Esther and Joseph
 DeBerdt's life in Bath, 41, 45–46
 discussion of future, 48–49, 52–54, 55–56, 60, 61–63
 Esther's admirers, 46–47, 57, 63
 Esther's anxiety, 57–58, 63–65
 Esther's emotional collapse, 39–40, 43, 44–45
 Esther's feelings towards Joseph, 48–50
 exchange of social news, 57–58
 illness and death of Dennys DeBerdt, 64–66, 84
 Joseph's neglect of Esther, 41–42
 plans to move to America, 55–57
 prospects of marriage, 76, 77–81
 schemes to settle in London, 40, 55–56, 58–59, 60–63, 64, 66–67, 79–80
 secret correspondence during, 40–42, 43–44, 45–46, 47–49, 220n9
 support of Esther's mother during, 42–43, 54
 uncertainty about future, 80–81
Shippen, R. W., 37
Shoemaker, Rebecca, 185
Shoemaker, Samuel, 196
Silliman, Mary, 141, 155
Smith, Jonathan, 13
Smith, Margaret Bayard, 177
Smith, William, 10, 172
Spencer, Lady Margaret Georgiana, 217n44

251

INDEX

Sproat, James, 103, 168, 170, 181, 235n39
Stamp Act (1765)
    colonial reaction to, 33, 51, 58–59, 60, 86
    controversy over, 59, 63
    debates about, 57, 67
    economic impact of, 48, 49, 52, 58–59, 73, 77
    repeal of, 51
Stockton, Richard, 9, 27, 63, 71, 73, 74
Sugar Act (1764), 19, 37, 206

Tea Act (1773), 115, 116, 117
Townshend Acts (1767)
    colonial response to, 33, 68, 86, 206
    economic impact of, 77
    introduction of, 33
    repeal of, 84, 98
transatlantic travel, 41
Trenton, NJ
    description of, 23
Tucker, Samuel, 73

University of Pennsylvania, 172, 176

Virginia planters, 127, 128

Waln, Nicholas, 109
Warren, Mercy Otis, 141, 210, 215n6 (Intr.)
wartime suffering
    escape to Evesham, 150
    farming in Norristown, 151
    loneliness of Esther, 155
    loss of child, 155–56
    periods of separation, 163–64
    refuge in Flemington, 155, 162, 164
    winter of 1777–78, 169
    of women of Philadelphia, 168–69
Washington, George
    appearance of, 127
    disagreements with Esther over funds spending, 198–202
    as godfather for Esther's child, 180
    Joseph's military appointments by, 140–41, 145
    personality of, 127
    retreat from Philadelphia, 149
    visits to the Reeds' house, 121, 122
Washington, Martha, 136, 146, 180, 181, 238n48
Willing, Elizabeth, 113
Willing, Thomas, 100
Wilson, James, 110
women
    in American Revolution, 141–42, 152, 191–93, 210–11, 237n31
    commercial activities of, 108
    courtship for young, 216n30
    effect of childbirth on, 233n68
    fertility control, 148
    general standards of education for, 217n44–45
    political engagement of, 179–80, 188, 210–11, 234n38, 235n56
    wartime experience of, 168–69
Wood, Mrs., 57
Wykoff, Mr., 47

Yorktown, Battle of, 204